A Tax Cut Pays for itself
when you have 10% Inflation
mr Lafer - but not
with O Inflation .

THE
TRIUMPH
OF
POLITICS

———

DAVID A.
STOCKMAN

THE BODLEY HEAD

LONDON

For Jennifer and Rachel

Photo credits:
All but the following photos
are from UPI/Bettmann Newsphotos:
1, 28, 35, 36, 47 — Wide World
29, 34 — White House
33 — Lisa Leavitt
41 — *Wall Street Journal*

British Library Cataloguing
in Publication Data
Stockman, David A.
The triumph of politics: the crisis in
American government and how it affects the world.
1. United States — Politics and government — 1981 —
I. Title
320.973   JK261
ISBN 0-370-30752-6

Published by arrangement with Harper & Row,
Publishers, Inc., New York
Printed in Great Britain for
The Bodley Head Ltd
30 Bedford Square, London WC1B 3RP
by Redwood Burn Ltd, Trowbridge

Acknowledgments

This book is a story about politics, so many people contributed to it in ways large and small. Because its conclusions are not equivocal, there are doubtless many who would just as soon be spared the honor of a mention.

But some are as deeply implicated as I. My colleagues at OMB and before that on Capitol Hill—David Gerson and Don Moran—lived nearly every moment of the story and offered invaluable suggestions for the improvement of its telling. Ed Dale and Mike Horowitz joined me when the Reagan Revolution began and insisted that an earlier manuscript did not do justice to what actually transpired. This version may not either, but I am grateful for their critical reviews.

Dick Darman was a key participant in much of the history herein chronicled. I learned much from him as the story originally unfolded and again as I sought to recapture it in these pages.

There are many among my former colleagues in Washington who did not read the manuscript but who nevertheless decisively shaped its content. Foremost among these I count Bob Dole and Pete Domenici. I do not especially like the idea that the supply-side ideology I began with found no place in the nation's politics. But the knowledge that a more conventional approach to economic governance is ably advocated by statesmen such as these is more than enough consolation.

Writing a book about budgets and numbers is enough to test the literary skills of even an accomplished writer. Chris Buckley, who knew something about the White House and even more about writing, gave me invaluable advice. Such readability as these pages may now have is in good part due to his guidance, red pencil, and the

ACKNOWLEDGMENTS

reworking of some sections that originally defied comprehension.

My editors at Harper & Row—Harriet Rubin and Ed Burlingame—merit more than just gratitude. They are also due an award for patience. By normal standards this book was written quickly—a characteristic more than amply evidenced by the original manuscript. Much of it found its deserved demise on the cutting-room floor, but not until they had heard me expound at length in the process of discovering that they were right. My amateur's disdain for editors has now been at least partially cured, and their efforts have made the book immeasurably better.

I would be remiss if I did not mention that Senator Daniel Patrick Moynihan also was kind enough to read the entire manuscript. He did not agree with many of my original solutions, but my conclusions he did not find nearly so stray of the mark. I have been tapping his wisdom for a long time, and the final manuscript is no exception.

Bill Greider had a lot to do with this book, including a critical and helpful review of the original draft. He was also kind enough to let me quote extensively from the transcripts of our 1981 conversations that made a big splash at the time, but had since been stacked away in his basement. I didn't like some of the things I found in them, but they were one source with which I didn't even try to argue.

Through it all, my wife, Jennifer, suffered above and beyond the call of duty. She heard every episode as it happened, and then its rendition draft after draft. She caught as many inconsistencies as anyone else involved in the project, and more fits of bad temper and frustration on my part than everyone combined. But she was unwavering in her support during all those years and through months of hectic writing. In the end that was more important than anything else.

List of Plates

Political Figures in the Book

Baker, Howard	Senate Majority (Republican) Leader
Baker, Jim	White House Chief of Staff
Bell, Ted	Secretary of Education
Brock, Bill	United States Trade Representative
Carlucci, Frank	Deputy Secretary of Defense
Clark, William 'Judge'	Director of the National Security Council
Conable, Barber	Chairman of the House Ways and Means Committee
Darman, Dick	Assistant to the President
Dole, Bob	Chairman of the Senate Finance Committee
Dole, Elizabeth	Chief of the White House's Office of Public Affairs
Domenici, Pete	Chairman of the House Budget Committee
Donovan, Raymond	Secretary of Labor
Edwards, Jim	Secretary of Energy
Friedersdorf, Max	Congressional Liaison
Fuller, Craig	Deputy Assistant to the President for Cabinet Affairs
Gergen, Dave	Press Secretary
Haig, Al	Secretary of State
James, Penn	White House Chief of Personnel
Jones, Jim	Chairman of the House Budget Committee
Lewis, Drew	Secretary of Transportation
Lott, Trent	House Minority (Republican) Whip
Meese, Ed	Counsellor to the President
Michel, Bob	House Minority (Republican) Leader
Nofzinger, Lyn	Assistant to the President for Political Affairs
O'Neill, Tip	Speaker of the House
Regan, Don	Secretary of the Treasury
Rostenkowski, Dan	Chairman of the House Ways and Means Committee
Schweiker, Dick	Secretary of the Department of Health and Human Services
Stevens, Ted	House Majority (Democratic) Whip
Tower, John	Chairman of the Senate Armed Services Committee
Volcker, Paul	Chairman of the Federal Reserve Bank
Watt, Jim	Secretary of the Interior
Weidenbaum, Marty	Chairman of the Council of Economic Advisors
Weinberger, Caspar	Secretary of Defense
Wright, Jim	House Majority (Democratic) Leader

Contents

Prologue

The President's eyes were moist. It was unmistakable—they glistened. But while he made no effort to hide it, I had barely even noticed. My own eyes had hardly wavered from the center of my plate, from the olive atop the scoop of tuna salad. I had been trying to explain my involvement in the article in the *Atlantic* magazine and had rambled on nonstop for fifteen minutes. It seemed like forever.

The press had made it into a roaring overnight scandal. The story line made for a red-hot melodrama: The President had been cynically betrayed. I was the Judas who had disavowed the President's economic program and undercut his presidency . . . His mettle was being tested . . . I was hanging by a thread . . . He was angry. That's what the newshounds in the White House press room were braying. And they were building it up by the hour.

The reality inside the Oval Office was quite different. We were sitting at a small luncheon table in front of a crackling fire. Aside from the popping sound of the wood sap, it was quiet and serene. It was the only time I had ever been alone with him.

After the White House stewards had served soup and tuna salad, the President turned to the business at hand. 'Dave, how do you explain this?' he said softly. 'You have hurt me. Why?'

My explanation soon meandered off into a total digression. It amounted to a capsule of my life story . . .

I had grown up in a small midwestern town as he had. My grandfather had taught me the truths of Christianity and Republicanism. I'd been thrilled by Ronald Reagan's clarion call to conservatives at the 1964 Republican Convention.

But then I had gone off to college and fallen into the clutches of campus radicalism. Like many in my generation, I took up Marxism and America-hating. Liberal professors and anti-war agitators shattered everything I believed in.

When the radicals turned violent, however, I finally saw the light. Just as he had stood up to them as governor of California, I had, too. Slowly I discovered that the left was inherently totalitarian.

Step by step I then worked my way back to where I had started. I rediscovered the virtues of unfettered capitalism, the dangers of Soviet communism, and the promise and ideals of American democracy.

For ten years I labored in the vineyards of Capitol Hill—first as a staff member, then as a congressman. I worked hard and long to learn everything there was to know about the behemoth called the federal government. In digging into the details of its vast expanse of programs, regulations, and bureaucracy, I discovered that it was riddled with waste, excess, and injustice. I came to believe that Ronald Reagan had been right all along.

The politicians were wrecking American capitalism. They were turning democratic government into a lavish giveaway auction. They were saddling workers and entrepreneurs with punitive taxation and demoralizing and wasteful regulation.

I had become a supply sider, dedicated to his cause of shrinking Big Government.

The President's speech to the 1980 Republican Convention had been even more overwhelming than the one sixteen years earlier. This time I was there. I had now reclaimed my conservative birthright. And I had helped write his bold platform calling for sweeping economic policy change.

His unexpected call to serve in the administration would always rank as the greatest privilege of my life. It showed that the promise of America was real. Only in America could a farm boy from Scottdale, Michigan, be called upon by a President to help him rescue the nation's failed economy.

Ever since then I had worked day and night on the tax cuts and budget cuts. There was no greater challenge or higher calling than the matter of translating his vision for the nation's future into the policy of the land. And we had made progress.

That was what the *Atlantic* article was all about. Conservative idealism. It reflected my experience of the struggle between the Reagan Revolution and the conventional politicians who had thwarted and sabotaged it.

We were engaged in a battle of ideas. The Reagan Revolution could never be won unless the establishment politicians and opinion makers gave our ideas a fair hearing. They had to be convinced that sound money, lower tax rates, and a vast curtailment of federal spending, welfare, and subsidies was the only recipe for sustained economic growth and social progress.

Which was why I had been talking to Bill Greider, the author of the *Atlantic* article. He was a friend and committed liberal, but he had an open mind. Since January 1981, I had used him as a sounding board week in and week out in order to test 'our' arguments and learn 'their' objections. It had helped. *The Washington Post*, where he worked as an editor, had given us a fair shake—at least sometimes.

But we had become so absorbed in the argument between our side and theirs that we hadn't clarified the ground rules about quotations. That's how the 'trojan horse' slipped out . . .

So I'd rambled on, turning the *Atlantic* crisis into my story.

Then I looked up and saw the President's eyes. I realized it was time to stop. I had been speaking from the heart, but I had said enough.

So I concluded with, 'Sir, none of that matters now. One slip and I've ruined it all.'

The President responded by putting his hand on mine. He said, 'No, Dave, that isn't what I want. I read the whole article. It's not what they are saying. I know the quotes and all make it look different. I wish you hadn't said them. But you're a victim of sabotage by the press. They're trying to bring you down because of what you have helped us accomplish.'

The President stood up and reached out his right hand. I grabbed it and noticed for the first time how fine, delicate, and well, old it was. For a second it seemed like my grandfather's—the same hand which had started me on my way to Ronald Reagan's.

After a moment the President said, 'Dave, I want you to stay on. I need your help.'

He turned and began walking toward his desk, then stopped suddenly as if he had just remembered something. 'Oh,' he continued, 'the fellas think this is getting out of control. They want you to write up a statement explaining all this and go before the press this afternoon. Would you do that?'

I agreed. My only lunch with the President was over.

*   *   *

The woodshed story* happened later. It was the metaphorical
pound of flesh demanded by the 'fellas'—Mike Deaver (Deputy
Chief of Staff), Ed Meese (Counsellor to the President), Jim Baker
(Chief of Staff), Lyn Nofzinger (the President's Assistant for
Political Affairs), and the President's confidential secretary, Helene
von Damm. All except Jim Baker had wanted me fired on the spot
and had browbeat the President all morning. But having read the
article, he had been reluctant.

So they went around and around. Mike Deaver was the most
insistent. 'He's highhanded. He's arrogant. He's never been on the
team in the first place. How can we let him get away with this?' That
was the bill of indictment he and others laid out.

Finally, Baker had said to the group, 'Mike's right, but it ain't
going to be easy to run this government without him. Mr President,
why don't you have him in for lunch and see if he's learned anything?
You've got to make your own judgment and give us a decision
today.'

Shortly after 11.00 am that morning I had been abruptly
summoned to Baker's office. When I arrived, he stiffly motioned me
to sit down at the long table in his West Wing corner office. Without
really thinking I pulled out the same chair I always sat in at the end
of the table, diagonal from him at the head.

For eleven months I had sat there almost daily, dominating the
conversations of the inner circle of White House aides who gathered
to plot strategy and policy. We called this group the 'LSG'; these
were the initials for the Legislative Strategy Group. It was a
prosaic-sounding entity that wasn't even on the White House
organization chart.

But the LSG was, in fact, the very top of the heap in the whole of
Washington—at least in those days. From Baker's table, it had
plotted victory after victory on Capitol Hill. It had managed the
enactment of what the press labelled the most sweeping revolution in
national economic policy since the New Deal.

Only today was different. A different Jim Baker was now sitting
two feet away. He had just plunked himself down in his chair without saying a word. His whole patented opening ritual had been

* In American folklore, the woodshed is the place where a bad child is taken to be
beaten.

completely dispensed with. No off-color joke. No casual waltz around his big office before he sat down. No jump shot that resulted in the arched flight of a paperwad across the room and without fail into the wastebasket.

This time it was all business, and his eyes were steely cold.

'My friend,' he started, 'I want you to listen up good. Your ass is in a sling. All of the rest of them want you shit-canned right now. Immediately. This afternoon.

'If it weren't for me,' he continued, 'you'd be a goner already. But I got you one last chance to save yourself. So you're going to do it precisely and exactly like I tell you. Otherwise you're finished around here.'

Baker continued his verbal thrashing without blinking an eye. 'You're going to have lunch with the President. The menu is humble pie. You're going to eat every last mother f'ing spoonful of it. You're going to be the most contrite sonofabitch this world has ever seen.'

Baker then asked me if I understood the script. I mumbled that I did and got up to leave. As I walked across the room and reached for the door to his office, Baker turned and said, 'Let me repeat something, just in case you didn't get the point. When you go through the Oval Office door, I want to see that sorry ass of yours dragging on the carpet.'

As I tripped down the White House stairway and out onto the west executive parking lot I was in a daze. My legs were wobbly. My head was exploding with both fear and anger. Never in my life had I been treated to such a rude, unsparing humiliation.

Somehow I got back to my office in the Old Executive Office Building next door and slumped into my chair.

But by then I had figured out what was happening. Baker wasn't behind it. The hangmen were the others—especially Deaver. They had gone into another one of their overnight panics. Jim had just been trying to shock me into a realization that the shark feed was on.

That was how they operated. Reality happened once a day on the evening news. They were now going to kill last night's 'bad story'. The decks would be cleared for something more favorable.

Baker knew I needed warning. The White House temperature had gone into sudden and feverish convulsions in the seventeen hours since CBS correspondent Leslie Stahl had gone with the *Atlantic* story 'two nights in a row'.

Only a day earlier it had been different. I had attended an LSG meeting in Baker's office and the *Atlantic* article had been the object of considerable merriment. The group had even presented me with a framed plaque for the 'best cover story in the December 1981 issue of the *Atlantic* magazine.' They had all signed the framed cover—Ed Meese, Jim Baker, Don Regan, Secretary of the Treasury, Dick Darman, Assistant to the President, Craig Fuller, Deputy Assistant to the President for Cabinet Affairs.

I had been furious at Greider for using the quotes so carelessly, especially the one describing the Kemp-Roth as a trojan horse. I hadn't worked around the clock for seven months to enact the Reagan Revolution because I thought the supply-side tax cut was a scam.

But now the White House press room was littered with copies of a one-page 'quote sheet'. The loose quotations were turning the fifty pages of heavy intellectual lifting encompassed in Greider's article into a cynically manufactured scam. The press was twisting these half dozen quotes into an entire thesis, utterly unsupported by even the text of the *Atlantic* article.

To say nothing of reality. Where had the White House press corps been for eleven months? Weren't there hundreds of politicans on Capitol Hill hopping mad about how I had strong-armed them into voting for the administration's tax and spending cut program? Hadn't the press itself written feature stories a few months back about how I had practically single-handedly put the whole massive package together in February? Wasn't everybody accusing me of too much revolutionary zeal and dogmatism, of being some kind of supply-side Robespierre? Did they really think I could have been a double agent through all those battles and not have been detected? The whole notion was Kafkaesque.

So I had thought the *Atlantic* story would quickly fade. I was obviously naïve on that score. Still, I had asked two of my most intelligent, trusted, and world-wise friends to read it and render a verdict.

'Delicious,' said my columnist friend George Will. 'It's too bad this whole thing will quickly blow over. Some of your colleagues could profit from reading it.'

Dick Darman had taken a different angle, perhaps reflecting his own view of the world. 'Thank God for those stray quotes!' he exclaimed. 'Nobody in this town would believe you were as idealistic and naïve as the story actually reveals.'

True, Greider's story had conveyed doubts and worries. But that wasn't news inside the White House. I had nagged them for months with reminders about how tough it would be to keep the whole sweeping plan on track. 'It adds up—but not easily,' I had been saying all along.

Greider's story had been about a radical ideologue who had dramatically burst upon the scene of national governance eleven months earlier. He had fairly and sympathetically portrayed my idealism and principled approach to national policy.

'We are going to attack weak claims, not weak clients,' he had accurately quoted me as saying. That principle meant cutting subsidies to big corporations as well as to undeserving food stamp recipients. There was unaffordable excess in both categories.

My whole thesis had been that the social goals of the liberal establishment could only be achieved through a revival of non-inflationary economic growth. You needed a rising tide to lift all boats. That had been the basic objective of the Reagan Revolution.

By midsummer I had become somewhat disillusioned. Greider had captured that, too. But my worry was not about the President's basic program. The problem was just the opposite. The congressional politicians were threatening to split his program at the seams by intransigently blocking the deep spending reductions that had to be matched up with the big tax cut. This resistance was now incubating a deficit that could soar out of control and hobble the economy.

I had feared that from the beginning. But I hadn't reckoned that there would be so much opposition on our side of the aisle. I was shocked to find that the Democrats were getting so much Republican help in their efforts to keep the pork barrel* flowing and the welfare state intact. I had been worried because the votes didn't add up, not the economic plan.

I had also come to realize that in my haste to get the Reagan Revolution launched in February, we had moved too fast. There were numerous loose ends. The spending reductions needed to pay for the tax cuts had turned out to be even bigger and tougher than I had originally thought.

* A government project or appropriation that benefits a political district and its representative.

But the loose ends could be fixed, I had told Greider. The program could be got back on track. It would take a long, unrelieved struggle, but I thought it could be done. It was all right there in 400,000 copies of the magazine.

I seriously doubted the Deaver crowd had read it. They lived off the tube. They understood nothing about the serious ideas underlying the Reagan Revolution. They were above the rough, exhausting, demanding business of the daily struggle down in the machinery of government against the overwhelming forces of the status quo.

In a way, I had felt good after absorbing Baker's flogging. I knew without question that I had made a critical difference. Now the White House staff was going to lynch me on account of a metaphor. I had seen them go into action before. Deaver and the others had done it to Secretary of State Alexander Haig, and other members of the Cabinet.

I had a clear-eyed grasp of their power. I therefore thought I knew what I had to do. If they didn't know the difference between reality and a metaphor, I would have to give them what they wanted. A counter-metaphor. A woodshed story. A self-inflicted public humiliation.

If I didn't decisively shut down the *Atlantic* story with a new one, the White House shark feed would continue.

So, that afternoon I played out the script that the White House public relations men had designed. And the *Atlantic* scandal soon faded away.

But the real *Atlantic* story was just getting started. Much later on I would realize that the *Atlantic* affair's hours of white heat on 12 November 1981, had brought into bold relief the ultimate flaw of the Reagan presidency. The episode underscored all the essential reasons why what started out as an idea-based Reagan Revolution ended up as an unintended exercise in free lunch economics. Even then the massive fiscal policy error that had been unleashed on the national and world economy was beyond recall. It should have been evident to me in the circumstances of those bitter hours. But it wasn't because I did not yet know that I was as much the problem as my would-be executioners.

The fact was, metaphor and reality had been at odds from the very beginning. The Reagan Revolution had never been any more real than the Judas thesis or the woodshed story.

Revolutions have to do with drastic, wrenching changes in an established regime. Causing such changes to happen was not Ronald Reagan's real agenda in the first place. It was mine, and that of a small cadre of supply-side intellectuals.

The Reagan Revolution, as I had defined it, required a frontal assault on the American welfare state. That was the only way to pay for the massive Kemp-Roth tax cut.

Accordingly, forty years worth of promises, subventions, entitlements, and safety nets issued by the federal government to every component and stratum of American society would have to be scrapped or drastically modified. A true economic policy revolution meant risky and mortal political combat with all the mass constituencies of Washington's largesse: Social Security recipients, veterans, farmers, educators, state and local officials, the housing industry, and many more.

Behind the hoopla of the Kemp-Roth tax cut and my thick black books of budget cuts was the central idea of the Reagan Revolution. It was minimalist government, a spare and stingy creature, which offered even-handed public justice, but no more. Its vision of the good society rested on the strength and productive potential of free men in free markets. It sought to encourage the unfettered production of capitalist wealth and the expansion of private welfare that automatically attends it. It envisioned a land the opposite to the coast-to-coast patchwork of dependencies, shelters, protections, and redistributions that the nation's politicians had brokered over the decades.

The true Reagan Revolution never had a chance. It defied all of the overwhelming forces, interests, and impulses of American democracy. Our Madisonian government of checks and balances, three branches, two legislative houses, and infinitely splintered power is conservative, not radical. It hugs powerfully to the history behind it. It shuffles into the future one step at a time. It cannot leap into revolutions without falling flat on its face.

That was the truth of the *Atlantic* article. Bill Greider had caught me in the first, conscious acts of finding out. The wound to the Reagan presidency resulted not from my newfound doubts about whether the Reagan Revolution could be made to succeed. Instead, it flowed inexorably from my original insistence that it be tried at all.

So I was the real issue in the *Atlantic* affair . . . but for reasons far more profound than the public relations men in the White House thought or the gaggle of reporters in the press room understood.

The fact was, due to the efforts of myself and my supply-side compatriots, Ronald Reagan had been made to stumble into the wrong camp on the eve of his final, successful quest for the presidency. He was a consensus politician, not an ideologue. He had no business trying to make a revolution because it wasn't in his bones.

He leaned to the right, there was no doubt about that. Yet his conservative vision was only a vision. He had a sense of ultimate values and a feel for long-term directions, but he had had no blueprint for radical governance. He had no concrete program to dislocate and traumatize the here-and-now of American society.

I supplied the latter. Only the further tragedy was that he grasped just half of this revolutionary equation—owing to a fluke of experience. He embraced Kemp-Roth because it seemed to be validated by an anecdote from his own personal history. But the anecdote was not applicable to his task of governance and he understood little of the blueprint's bone-jarring remainder.

Like all revolutionaries, we wanted to get our program out of the fringe cell group where it had been hatched and into the mainstream. The brave new world it promised was too good and urgent for its radiant light to be left under a bushel of ideological scribblings.

So we pitched it in tones that were music to every politician's ears. We highlighted the easy part—the giant tax cut. The side of the doctrine that had to do with giving to the electorate, not taking from it.

In January 1980, Governor Reagan's campaign managers had sent him to school for a few days to get brushed up on the national issues. There, Jack Kemp, Art Laffer, and Jude Wanniski thoroughly hosed him down with supply-side doctrine.

They told him about the 'Laffer curve'. It set off a symphony in his ears. He knew instantly that it was true and would never doubt it a moment thereafter.

He had once been on the Laffer curve himself. 'I came into the Big Money making pictures during World War II,' he would always say.

At that time the wartime income surtax hit ninety percent.

'You could only make four pictures and then you were in the top bracket,' he would continue. 'So we all quit working after four pictures and went off to the country.'

High tax rates caused less work. Low tax rates caused more. His experience proved it. And stated that way, he was right.

But the Laffer curve was about government revenues, not making movies or widgets. It was an academic paradigm. Its translation into the real economic world of 1981 was complicated and slippery.

A tax cut will increase revenues only if you start in a zero inflation economy. Then, if more movies and widgets are made, you will get more GNP and more revenues. That is common sense.

But Ronald Reagan inherited an inflation-swollen economy. Prices were racing upward at twelve percent. There had been just one imperative: Stop the inflation. The American electorate, his older traditional conservatism, and the new supply-side doctrine (it was based on a zero-inflation gold standard) all demanded it.

Yet when you pump the inflation out of the economy, something funny happens. The government's finances end up in the same boat with farmers, oil drillers, and commodity speculators. All previous revenue projections collapse. The relationship between income and outgo suddenly goes haywire.

Stopping inflation means that you stop tax bracket creep, too. Compared to a high inflation economy, which automatically raises taxes by pushing people into higher brackets, a low inflation economy itself provides a huge 'tax cut'. It dramatically depletes the Treasury's inflation windfall. In fact, the latter was the only thing keeping the federal government even half solvent when Ronald Reagan took the oath of office.

His new radical economic program, therefore, embraced *two tax cuts*: an end to inflationary bracket creep and a thirty percent rate cut on top. The Laffer curve couldn't pay for both. Not even close. To keep the budget solvent required draconian reductions on the expenditure side—a substantial and politically painful shrinkage of the American welfare state.

My blueprint for sweeping, wrenching change in national economic governance would have hurt millions of people in the short run. It required abruptly severing the umbilical cords of dependency that ran from Washington to every nook and cranny of the nation. It required the ruthless dispensation of short-run pain in the name of long-run gain.

To make a revolution required defining fairness in terms of exacting, abstract principles—not human hard-luck stories. It meant complete elimination of subsidies to farmers and businesses. It required an immediate end to welfare for the able-bodied poor. It meant no right to draw more from the Social Security fund than retirees had actually contributed, which was a lot less than most were currently getting.

These principles everywhere clashed with the political reality. Over the decades, the politicians had lured tens of millions of citizens into milking . . . cows, food stamps, Social Security, the Veterans Hospitals, and much more. They were getting more than they deserved, needed, or were owed. For the Reagan Revolution to add up, they had to be cut off. The blueprint was thus riddled with the hardship and unfairness of unexpected change. Only an iron chancellor would have tried to make it stick. Ronald Reagan wasn't that by a long shot.

Even my private exoneration at lunch in the Oval Office by a fatherly Ronald Reagan showed why a Reagan Revolution couldn't happen. He should have been roaring mad like the others—either about the bad publicity or my admission of a flawed economic plan.

But Ronald Reagan proved to be too kind, gentle, and sentimental for that. He always went for hard-luck stories. He sees the plight of real people before anything else. Despite his right-wing image, his ideology and philosophy always take a back seat when he learns that some individual human being might be hurt.

That's also why he couldn't lead a real revolution in American economic policy.

The President's non-revolutionary instincts and sentimentality were vastly compounded by the inveterate tube watching of the 'fellas'. That was apparent in the *Atlantic* episode, too.

Our revolutionary blueprint required the relentless hot pursuit of the politicians, interest groups, and organized constituencies which resolutely defended all of the unaffordable largesse. It required taking huge political risks. The White House had to be transformed into a roaring bully pulpit.

For the unorganized taxpayers, workers, and producers of the nation to get and keep their tax cut, the White House had to become the dragon slayer of the organized spenders. It could give no quarter to the constituencieswhich had to lose their benefits. It had to name names.

But the 'fellas' would have none of that. It would have meant worse than an *Atlantic* story. It would have meant a bad time at reality time—every night at 7.00 pm. They couldn't have stopped it by flogging the messenger who brought the bad news, either.

The problem was they knew nothing about the true substance of domestic governance. The California crowd—Mike Deaver, Ed Meese, Lyn Nofzinger—were competent enough at their trades. But they were illiterate when it came to the essential equation of policy.

Even Jim Baker was not immune from the unreality. He was a decent student of policy, but he was an awesome student of politics. He was therefore always caught in the crossfire.

The latter was dramatized by a recurrent, symbolic incident at the LSG meetings in his office. They were often held late in the afternoon. There was always a hand calculator next to my place at the table and a TV remote control switch next to his. From a distance they're hard to tell apart—electronic marvels both.

But at 6.30 pm the early edition of the network news came on. At that point, the remote control switch always won. The meeting shifted from the policy problem in the numbers to the political problem on the screen.

What the group didn't understand was that in opting for a giant tax cut, we had made our own bed of political misery. We were obligated to lie in the latter or let go of the former.

That's why the public relations men missed the target when they went for my scalp during the *Atlantic* affair. They meant well enough. They thought loyalty to Ronald Reagan required drastic action to nip a bad story in the bud. But it was petty loyalty that amounted to profound disloyalty in the larger scheme of things.

By 12 November 1981, I could have performed a useful public service. I knew almost enough to tell the whole bloody tale, a far more alarming story than anything hinted at in the *Atlantic* article. My last two sessions with Bill Greider had been in July and early September. Between the latter date and November, the veil of illusions had parted almost completely.

I had been flooded with new evidence about the course of the economy and the resourceful intransigence of the congressional politicians. I knew we were on the precipice of triple-digit deficits, a national debt in the trillions, and destructive and profound dislocations throughout the entire warp and woof of the American economy. By then all the major errors which would eventually shatter the nation's fiscal stability were apparent. I had most of the diagnosis down already. It was only the full and final magnitude of the numbers that would materialize later.

But I kept quiet and tried to work inside. It proved to be of no avail. After November 1981, the administration locked the door on its own disastrous fiscal policy jail cell and threw away the key. The President would not let go of his tax cut. Cap Weinberger hung on for dear life to the $1.46 trillion defense budget. Jim Baker carried around a bazooka, firing first and asking questions later of anyone who mentioned the words 'Social Security'. Deaver, Meese, and the others ceaselessly endeavored to keep all the bad news out of the Oval Office and off the tube. The nation's huge fiscal imbalance was never addressed or corrected; it just festered and grew.

By 1982, I knew the Reagan Revolution was impossible: it was a metaphor with no anchor in political and economic reality. I never gave up the supply-side ideology, however. I just put it in my safe, along with other intellectual valuables. It was simply not oper-ationally relevant in the world of democratic fact where the politicians have the last and final say.

So I changed jerseys and joined their side. We succeeded in reducing the size of the nation's fiscal disaster modestly, despite the White House. In four different tax bills, we replenished the revenue coffers by about $80 billion per year. We whittled down defense. I got them to make a few more domestic spending cuts, too. In all, we got the deficit down to $200 billion.

I didn't like joining forces with the congressional politicians at all. I couldn't stand the idea of making all those deals to preserve their booty and waste. I disliked the idea of raising new tax revenues in order to pay farmers not to milk their cows or developers to build a luxury hotel in the ghetto.

But the congressional politicians had one redeeming virtue. They were willing to face economic and democratic reality. The dreamers and public relations men in the White House were not.

In the final analysis, there has been no Reagan Revolution in national economic governance. All the umbilical cords of dependency still exist because the public elects politicians who want to preserve them. So they have to be paid for. That is the unyielding bottom line. Economic and financial disaster is the only alternative.

I joined the Reagan Revolution as a radical ideologue. I learned the traumatic lesson that no such revolution was possible. I end up giving two cheers for the politicians. But only that.

The fact is, politicians can be a menace. They never stop inventing illicit enterprises of government that bleed the national economy. Their social uplift and pork barrel is wasteful; it reduces our collective welfare and wealth. The politicians rarely look ahead or around. Two years and one Congressional District is the scope of their horizon.

There is only one thing worse, and that is ideological *hubris*. It is the assumption that the world can be made better by being remade overnight. It is the false belief that in a capitalist democracy we can peer deep into the veil of the future and chain the ship of state to an exacting blueprint. It can't be done. It shouldn't have been tried.

This is the story of the lessons which taught me why.

PART ONE

1

The Odyssey of an Ideologue

'*David!*'

'Yes, sir.'

'You're a mess. Everything is a mess.'

'I didn't intend it, sir.'

'This is going to hurt me more than you, but one of these days you will learn that what counts around here is what you do, not what you intend.'

Late August, summer of 1958. It was the end of the day, and we had been picking the ripe red tomatoes since early that morning. My hands were stained with the juice. So were my face and shirt, arms and back; that was the reason for my father's wrath.

He had raised his five children according to his stern German Protestant ethic, but even the well-visited woodshed in the barn was not enough to prevent us from becoming rambunctious at the end of the day. Boys are boys. My brothers and I had started throwing tomatoes at each other, more and more until they were flying in a red hail. The stains all over did not escape my father, and as the eldest of four boys and one sister it fell to me to set the example, which is why from time to time the strap fell across my rear end.

My family had been working those one hundred acres near Scottdale, Michigan, since the 1870s, when my grandfather's father got off the boat from Germany. Except for the odd cousin who helped at harvest time, we worked it ourselves. There were harvests about every two weeks: asparagus in the spring, strawberries in early June, followed by red raspberries. The black ones came soon after; then the tomatoes in August, along with the peaches. Grapes in September, corn in October, soybeans in November. Our life was lived according to those rhythms. It was cyclically frantic work. Either we got out the crop or it perished, and it was that that determined my father's no-nonsense view of the world he inhabited. Hard work was what he knew, and what we learned.

I learned quickly, and by the time I was ten—in 1956—I could outpick all the adults. I won all the races and got all the praise. My brothers didn't think that was so great, and they devised a scheme to outdo me. Each day one of them was secretly designated my challenger. He would work like a dog, and when I wasn't looking the others would sneak him their harvested tomatoes or berries. Although I knew exactly what they were up to, I had too much pride to use that as an excuse. I was going to beat them all, and I did. Every time.

Growing up on a farm instills you with ambition. The results of your work are so visible—a field of ripening tomatoes, a vineyard carefully, painstakingly cultivated and maintained. Those are tangible things, evidence that you can impose your will and ideas and have them come out according to your plan. I grew up wanting to be a farmer, because I imagined I could be a better one than my father.

Behind his back, my brothers and I used to call my father 'Al the Stick', as in stick-in-the-mud. He was a good man, but he was practical and cautious and was always taking things one step at a time. He didn't believe in leaping before he looked. We boys imagined ourselves to be the big thinkers on the Stockman farm. We would sit out in the field and talk up our grand plans for the place. You couldn't get a decent-sized strawberry crop off five acres; you needed twenty times that. When we grew up, we would rent the extra acres, dig a pond, put in irrigation equipment. Our ten dairy cows would never allow you to make a profit; you needed two hundred. We were forever plotting how we'd do it when it came to our turn. From a very early age I had the idea that my elders needed a lot more imagination.

My grandfather was an exception to all this. His name was William H. Bartz. He had farmed those same hundred acres, but had gone on to a career in politics. He had become County Treasurer, known and respected throughout the state. He was a striking, handsome man; only his rough hands betrayed he had been a farmer.

I remember visiting him in his office from a very early age. He had one of those gigantic (so it seemed to me) rolltop desks with lots of pigeonhole drawers that I used to explore with endless fascination. The desk was always cluttered with copies of *Human Events*, the *Liberty Lobby* newsletter, the *Christian Messenger*, and other such right-wing fare.

He had been to the Moody Bible Institute in Chicago, and when he was not occupied with the virtuous labor of keeping sound ledgers he was preaching about the Word of God. Grampa Bartz took the Bible literally. God had created the world in six days, the atheistic assertions of the scientists notwithstanding. And God voted Republican. Capitalism was the way of free men; the New Deal was a socialist way to perdition. The countryside cultivated morals and character; the big cities, vice. Smoking, drinking, gambling, and violating the sabbath were the way of fallen sinners; temperate living and churchgoing the mark of the saved.

Despite his fundamentalist Christianity, he would read to us from the Old Testament sometimes. The book of Amos was always my favorite. I remember his voice, rising to symphonic heights of righteousness as the prophet Amos delivered the wrath of Yahweh upon the corrupt Israelites. Maybe I learned a little too much from old Amos.

In my senior year of high school I won an essay contest sponsored by the local branch of the Council of Churches on the theme 'What Non-Violence Means to Me'. My entry was an ode to Martin Luther King, Jr., and Mahatma Gandhi. By political standards, both of these men were clearly left-wing. But what I saw in them was the distilled essence of my grandfather's Christian teachings. All men were God's children and deserved better than poverty, racism, and indignity. I was gripped by a vision of a better world even then.

While Grampa Bartz may not have approved of my heterodoxical leanings, he was confident that I would be in good hands when I went off to the faraway cities of New York and Washington for the seven-day seminar that was the prize. What he did not know was that the trip was sponsored by the American Friends Service Committee. His eldest grandson, whom he wanted to watch grow to become a good Christian and a good Republican, was being escorted to two sin cities by a bunch of left-wing peace freaks.

The seminar was a nonstop immersion course in all the liberal verities—nuclear disarmament, racial integration, the works. But

Grampa had a strong hold on my heart and mind, and I remember my sheer terror standing in the lobby of the United Nations Building, bastion of the One-Worlders, Communists, and left-wing heretics. I trembled—literally—thinking of God's wrath at my presence in this plaza of iniquity, the fate of Lot's wife heavy in my mind.

Later that week I found myself standing in another marble echo chamber, but this one triggered a vision of another sort. It was in the rotunda of the Capitol Building, at the head of the stairs that lead to the House of Representatives chamber. Seventeen-year-olds are full of ridiculous, grandiose thoughts, and I was no exception. Staring at the busts of Washington, Jefferson and others enveloped in the stony womb of the nation's government, I promised myself that someday . . . I would return.

'Rubbish!'

Professor Saltzman had scrawled his rather concise opinion of the paper I had submitted during the fall of 1964, my first semester at Michigan State University (MSU). My essay established an unbroken line of continuity between Thomas Paine's *The Rights of Man* and Senator Barry Goldwater's *Conscience of a Conservative*, and Professor Saltzman was not amused.

On the first day of class, he had announced in his deep Brooklyn accent that he was Jewish by culture, an atheist by conviction, and a socialist 'by virtue of being educated'. The MSU computer had randomly put me in the hands of a witty, acerbic, exceedingly fluent blasphemer of everything Grampa Bartz had taught me. Professor Saltzman did not seem especially happy with his lot at this cow college out in the sticks. When he looked down from his podium, he saw all these kids like me with hayseeds sticking out their ears. He seemed to have the attitude that by God—or Jean-Paul Sartre—he was going to get a rise out of them.

I was determined not to betray Grampa. I often read from the handsome present he had sent me off to college with, a leather bound Bible with my name embossed in gold on the front. I would come back from Professor Saltzman's peppery diatribes against religion and read a chapter of scripture. But despite my repairings to the onion-skin world of prophets, kings, and the Savior, the disturbing evidence began to mount. My paper on the Scopes Trial came back scrawled with humanist graffiti: 'Visit the Geology Department!' 'Which day did God create the dinosaur fossils?'

My political certainties were under attack, too. One night the parents of a girlfriend arrived to take us out to dinner in East Lansing. They lived in an affluent Chicago suburb, belonged to the country club, drove a new Lincoln Continental, dressed expensively. They took us to the ritziest restaurant in town, unfamiliar turf to me, where meals cost five dollars and they served snails.

The '64 presidential election was imminent, and I started chattering about how great Goldwater was and how he was going to save us from that socialist, Johnson.

They were stunned. Goldwater was an extremist, a dangerous radical. And decent, educated people—like my hosts—were scared of him. Grampa had convinced me Goldwater was going to save the nation; yet here these affluent Republicans were telling me the man was irresponsible. The dinner left me completely bewildered.

After a while I had some new answers. The New Deal and Great Society didn't look so bad when my MSU professors were done with them. Poverty, racism and capitalism looked a lot worse. And anti-communism didn't cut it at all; it actually was an excuse for US exploitation of the Third World's impoverished masses. My idealism and desire to figure how to make the world better thus led me to the left and the utopian promises of Marxism.

'Comrades,' the letter to my brothers began,

> Things are moving like hell up here. We are going to Detroit Saturday to join with a number of other groups who will be carrying money across the Windsor bridge [into Canada] to give to the Canadian Friends Service Committee who will channel it to North Vietnam. . .

Perhaps what is most revealing about this yellowing piece of paper is its closing salutation: 'Peace, damn it!'

By now I was a full-fledged (if half-baked) neo-Marxist. My hair was long, my nose was deep into *The Village Voice*, *Ramparts*, and Thomas Altizer's *God Is Dead*, as well as the mandatory classics of Camus, Ginsberg, and the other oracles of existentialist ennui. It was my coffee house period. We hung out at the Methodist Church

Student Fellowship, but we weren't talking a lot of scripture in those days.

That Thanksgiving, I tried to convince Grampa Bartz that Genesis wasn't literal. Boy, was that a mistake. His face took a grim turn at my observation that there were five historical strands in the Old Testament and that one of them had been lifted from the Sumerian *Epic of Gilgamesh*.

'Well,' he said gravely, 'I don't care what they tell you. I know what I believe. The Bible is the revealed Word of God. Pass the cranberry sauce.'

I had been hectoring him for some time now with my new views, and I wasn't getting anywhere. Finally, I decided it wasn't any use, he wasn't going to let me enlighten him, so I resolved to keep it to myself. Fifteen years later, in the White House, it would be almost exactly the same.

By 1966 our Methodist student group had cross-pollinated extensively with other radical campus groups, including the Students for a Democratic Society. This interjected a harder, more militant edge to our radicalism—as the political issue of the Vietnam War and the need to mobilize against it took on increasing urgency. As we now had it, Vietnam wasn't an accident; it was the natural result of a corrupt, materialistic, violent capitalist system. Radical change was the only cure.

But all this ideological militancy was somewhat deceptive. In the end our goal was not political revolution but social and personal redemption. It was Peter, Paul and Mary who told us where we were ultimately going. Our destiny was a land of peace, community, brotherhood, altruism, and classless, raceless harmony. Unburdened by the opium of mass consumption, everyone would be free to progress all the way to Maslow's* highest level of self-actualization. With power abolished, wealth redistributed, and true spirituality reestablished, heaven would come to earth; the perfection of man would be at hand. The innocence of this soft-core Marxism knew no limits. Indeed, it might have been said that the last stage of the dialectic of history had finally been revealed as Puff the Magic Dragon's Kingdom by the Sea.

Still I hadn't completely turned my back on Grampa; if anything

* The psychologist-philosopher, Abraham Maslow.

his long arm still held me in its grasp, even if I was already deep into my first revolution. I worked feverishly on its behalf, canvassing neighborhoods and dorms, having beer cans thrown at me. *This Bud's for you!* In our Vietnam Summer Project headquarters were maps of all the voting precincts. We were going to educate the masses into voting for the correct candidates in '68, who would stop the madness. But the real radicals in the movement—as opposed to the 'peace liberals'—thought all that was a waste of time, or 'Bullshit!' as they put it. Electoral politics was bourgeois, a rigged process of the ruling class. The only way to stop the war was to shut down the machine.

I couldn't accept that. I had grown up in my grandfather's office amid the accoutrements of democracy, his campaign fliers, brochures, the matchbooks that said

VOTE FOR
WILLIAM H. BARTZ
COUNTY TREASURER

I was discovering that for all my soft-core Marxism, there was a deep, conservative wellspring within me that kept me from storming the barricades. Perhaps I was not a revolutionary at all, only a democrat with a small 'd'. These people who wanted to bring about change with the barrel of a gun made me nervous. Looking back, they reminded me of the reason Gary Cooper had given the House Committee on Un-American Activities for being opposed to communism: 'From what I hear about it, I don't like it because it isn't on the level.'

Later that year I watched as mobs of my peaceloving 'comrades' threw rocks, bags of human excrement, and whatever they could lay their hands on at the police ringing the Pentagon, taunting them with screams of 'Fascist!' and 'Pig!' until finally the provocations worked and they got cracked over the head with a billy stick.* The whole point was to get bloodied. The ones who did ran back into the crowd, gleeful over their wounds, displaying them like stigmata. I'd spent the night driving a busful of these admirers of Gandhi and King and Ho Chi Minh all the way from Michigan so we could lay

* Truncheon.

siege to the warmongers, and all of a sudden I was no longer sure our side was on the level.

Not long afterwards one of our comrades either committed suicide or died of diabetes. No one was sure, but at a candlelit memorial ceremony everyone stood up and said that he had not died in vain, that his work in the Movement would live on in glory. On and on. When it came to my turn, I said that he had died, no more, no less. It didn't mean much either way. My comrades were shocked and incensed, but by then I knew that my revolutionary fires had gone out in the night.

'What do we do now?' I wrote to my brother Steve. He was spending a semester at Tuskegee Institute in Alabama, a predominantly black university, and had recently found himself the only white in a large audience as Stokeley Carmichael delivered a red-hot tirade against the 'white devils'. He had the crowd so worked up that one word and Steve would have been an ex-white devil. It had left him pretty shaken, and now neither of us knew where to turn.

> Where do we take hold? On what do we center ourselves? God is dead; causes are vacuous, transient, and often ulterior. Who or what can capture our allegiance? Call forth our potential moral and intellectual powers? Do you have any answers?

I signed it: 'Carry on and keep the Faith (I should say *find* the faith) baby!!!'

I found a kind of faith in the library of the man who became my second mentor: the Reverend Truman Morrison who was pastor of a liberal church near MSU. He was a man of vast learning and awesome intellect. He spoke eloquently about the tragedy of Vietnam, but he opposed unilateral US withdrawal; supported the peace movement, but warned of the dangers of storm trooperism. He had extraordinary physical presence, standing over six feet, with full dark hair and eyes that held you and wouldn't let go until he was ready to let go. He was the sort of charismatic man to whom it was natural to turn at a time when I needed answers. He became my intellectual father.

While Grampa Bartz's office had been full of right-wing magazines, some of them pretty kooky, the Reverend Morrison's library was packed, carpet to ceiling, with all the literature of Western civilization: political science, psychology, sociology, history, theology, philosophy. From Sumeria to the latest issue of *Dissent*, it was all there, and I fed greedily.

The Reverend Morrison was a disciple of the great social philosopher Reinhold Niebuhr. Niebuhr had been a quasi-Marxist in the 1930s, but had emerged after the war as the most powerful and eloquent voice urging the left to decide once and for all between democracy and totalitarianism. On that issue, there was no middle ground. He and the other founders of Americans for Democratic Action had led most of the left-wing intellectuals back from the Stalinist steppes into the mainstream of American politics. It was in the Reverend Morrison's library, where I read Niebuhr's classic *The Children of Light and the Children of Darkness*, that I learned that up until then I had been reading the tracts of those non-democrats on the left who had remained behind.

The scales fell from my eyes as I turned those pages. Niebuhr was a withering critic of utopianism in every form. Man is incapable of perfection, he argued, because his estate as a free agent permits— indeed, ensures—both good and evil. The institutions of society cannot perfect him; the defects of any particular social and economic order did not corrupt him. This condition of original sin is given. It cannot be removed from the temporal world, and no scheme of man, revolutionary or otherwise, will bring heaven to earthly life.

Through Niebuhr I dimly glimpsed the ultimate triumph of politics. Fallen men, hobbled by their darker possibilities but impelled by their brighter potentialities, would forever struggle over the task of making an imperfect but improvable world better, if never perfect. There was no doctrine that could ever settle the question. Democracy edged man away from the abyss in increments; doctrine caused him to lurch back toward it, and sometimes down into it.

All this sobered me, and enabled me to understand the mob outside the Pentagon. But how, I wonder, was it possible I could have forgotten it by the time I arrived at the White House?

In the spring of my senior year I'd applied to Harvard Divinity School. I had looked at two other theology schools, Chicago and Columbia. I took Harvard for no better reason than that it was Harvard. No one in my family had ever completed college, let alone graduate school, and so I thought I might as well attend the best.

My decision to enroll in Harvard Divinity continued my exemption from the draft. I felt no shame about it at the time. In the spring of 1968, several months after the Tet Offensive, everyone had made up his mind about the war, Walter Cronkite included. Even the anti-totalitarian Niebuhrian foreign policy experts with whom I was now familiar—George Kennan, Hans Morganthau—were saying the war was a misguided tragedy that did not serve the national interest, and did not warrant the spilling of American blood, mine included.

So I summoned all my intellectual powers of rationalization to convince myself that a retreat into the quasi-monastic womb of an Ivy League theological school was exactly the right thing. I would pursue my study of anti-totalitarianism, far from the guns of those who were seeking to impose that kind of world on the people of Southeast Asia. The war changed everyone's lives, even those who did not fight it. In my case it brought me to the gateway which would lead to my career in Washington.

Harvard was Shangri-la. It was the Reverend Morrison's library on a vast scale, but it wasn't so monastic as all that. The streets and classrooms were crowded with people who had just got off the Washington–Boston Shuttle. Many had been a part of President Kennedy's 'Camelot' entourage: Richard Neustadt, John Kenneth Galbraith. To an awestruck provincial far more sophisticated about books than the real world, breathing the same air as these famous men was exhilarating beyond belief. It did not take long before I was thoroughly infected with the desire to find a place in the world at the other end of the shuttle.

Up to then, all the intellectuals I had been exposed to were men of the left. I had no use for the right; it was inhabited by anti-intellectuals and Bible-thumpers. At Harvard, I discovered Walter Lippmann. Lippmann had turned atheist as an undergraduate at Harvard and had been briefly seduced by the allure of socialism. At twenty-three he had founded *The New Republic*. President Wilson had drafted him, while still in his late twenties, to go to Europe with him and write Wilson's 'Fourteen Points'. Before he was thirty, he was a high practitioner of statecraft. And then, in the depths of the 1930s, when the order of the day was expedience and experiment, he had had the wisdom and maturity to grasp that the requisite of a free society was a free economy. What a role model I began to think.

His devastating critique of the New Deal, *The Good Society*, made the case for a free economy and limited, constitutional government. A free society and central planning were antithetical; the latter inexorably led to totalitarianism. Socialism and economic statism were incompatible with true democracy. I soon embraced his conservative realism as a far more coherent doctrine than anything I could find on the left. It gave me renewed impetus in the search for my own 'Grand Doctrine', for an answer to how the world should work.

Exciting as these intellectual discoveries were, I was still reading secondary sources, far removed from the actual arena of governance. One day, however, while preparing a paper that required original research, I stumbled across a trove of documents and memos from the Office of Price Administration, the War Production Board, and other wartime economic agencies. The papers had been dumped in an obscure corner of the basement of Littauer Library by the returning Harvard dons, and had been yellowing and gathering dust for decades, undisturbed, when I came on them.

I doubt Howard Carter, discoverer of King Tut's tomb, was any more excited than I was. The boxes were filled with treasures: memos to Presidents Roosevelt and Truman from all the big names of that era. They were the first primary documents I had ever seen, and as I pored over the onion-skin carbon copies, nearly as fragile themselves as the papyrus scrolls of ancient Egypt, I wanted more than ever to go to Washington as soon as I could.

But how? I was living a pretty rootless, penniless, cerebral existence, feasting on tuna and macaroni most nights, and I did not know a single human being in all of Washington, not even in the lowest branches of government. I needed a new mentor, a rabbi who could show me the way.

About this time I struck up an acquaintance with a divinity student who was a live-in babysitter at the home of Daniel Patrick Moynihan. Moynihan, an erstwhile Harvard professor, was then chief domestic adviser in the Nixon White House. Nixon had stunned everyone by appointing this Kennedy Democrat to his Cabinet, and Moynihan was a big name on campus. My friend told stories that made me sigh, of Moynihan coming home every Friday, of late night conversations over brandy about the latest goings-on at the White House. I would have given my eye-teeth to trade my dingy, other-side-of-the-tracks apartment for his room on the third floor of the Moynihans'.

One afternoon after a long spell in the Littauer basement, the great opportunity presented itself. My acquaintance was leaving the Moynihan household to become a pastor, and the Moynihans needed a new babysitter. I entombed myself in the library, reading every single book, every article, every monograph, pamphlet, letter, memo and laundry list that Pat Moynihan had written. I read the footnotes and looked up the references and read those. By the time I got the call to come by one Sunday afternoon, I was more familiar with Pat Moynihan's oeuvre than he was. In my earnestness, it had not crossed my mind that he might actually need a babysitter rather than a research assistant.

It didn't matter. When I arrived at the appointed hour, my head stuffed full of the master's quotations and insights, Professor Daniel Patrick Moynihan had something altogether different in mind. First he ushered me into the kitchen for instruction in the proper mixing of Bloody Marys; then into the library for a briefing on the management of the fireplace and brandy cabinet. And that was that—I had a new job, and the Washington-connected rabbi I was looking for.

He was away five days a week, but late at night on Saturday nights, after the guests had gone and the children were in bed, he'd invite me down from my third-floor abode to sit by the fire and have a brandy or two or three. The talks went on late into the night. He was a natural, florid, Irish storyteller, and he would alternate between his stories of growing up poor in Hell's Kitchen and the latest power struggle in the West Wing of the White House. By now I had read almost cover to cover ten years of *The Congressional Quarterly*, to ensure that I'd be familiar with whatever issue came up.

These late night sessions were a treat, but a few months into the arrangement something happened that allowed me to get an even more graphic—and lurid—glimpse into the inner workings of Washington. Moynihan's famous 'Benign Neglect'* memorandum was leaked to the press.

---

* In which he suggested that the best government policy towards American blacks for a while might be 'benign neglect'.

In the public furor that resulted from the leak, he became convinced someone had been rifling through his papers. So he shipped them all home to Cambridge. And there they were in the library, hundreds of documents on the inner workings of the White House! He never told me not to read them, but he never told me to help myself. It was more than I could resist. Late at night, or when no one was around, I read them greedily. They made the boxes in the basement of Littauer seem medieval. Here were memos to a *sitting* President. The more I read, the faster my heart pumped. I *had* to get down there.

At about that time I read that David Broder was coming to teach a seminar at Harvard. I'd been following his political reportage in *The Washington Post* avidly, and I raced to sign up for the course. It was filled, but Liz Moynihan took pity on my panic and phoned Broder that same evening to tell her old friend that he had one more slot available after all. I was profoundly grateful to Liz for that, and amazed at how smoothly the networks of Washington actually worked.

I worked hard to impress Broder. The paper I did for the course was a not-bad piece of work based on the ideas of James MacGregor Burns and E. E. Sachschneider, who argued that American democracy did not function well because the political parties were weak and it therefore tended to be dominated by special interests. It was a grand interpretation of the conflict between Madisonian democracy and parliamentary government, between a system of strong parties and one that was fragmented by myriad groups of narrow concern. Broder pronounced it a 'remarkable' paper and took the unusual step of asking me to elaborate on it in front of the class.

Ordinarily, the classes consisted of guest lecturers from the world of Washington politics. One week it was Congressman John Anderson of Illinois, who had just earned himself a laurel by breaking a legislative deadlock on the open housing law.

Not long after Anderson's visit, he told Broder he was looking for a 'bright young idea man' for his staff, and would welcome any suggestions Broder might have. Broder told me about it during one of my office hour visits with him. I couldn't believe my ears. Before I realized what I was doing, I was on my feet sputtering, 'H-how?' Well, Broder knew exactly how. He picked up the phone right away, dialed Anderson. By the time he hung up, I had an interview scheduled for next Wednesday. I made more sputtering noises and flew—*flew*—across Harvard Yard to bring home the incredible news.

Liz sprang into action. She had been stirring a large pot of spaghetti sauce. She handed me the spoon, succinctly instructed me in the art of stirring, and repaired to the phone. She reached Pat in his office in the West Wing of the White House.

'Delightful news!' he boomed. 'There are few men brighter or more high-minded in the whole of Congress.' Incredibly, Moynihan would be meeting with Anderson the next day at the White House. He would take him aside and give me a glowing recommendation. I was so dazed by the day's events I could have stirred that pot of spaghetti with my forearm and not noticed.

The next day I took my one suit to a tailor for such face lifting as he could perform on it, bought a new white shirt, and called my mother to beg for a fifty-dollar loan with which to buy my plane ticket. After what seemed like a hundred years, Wednesday finally came. Slumped in the back of the cab, I watched as the dome of the Capitol hove into sight. It had been six years since I had been there with the Quakers and uttered my ridiculous vow to return, but here I was.

Despite Anderson's need for a 'bright young idea man', his staff soon had me toiling underneath the endless stacks of constituent mail. I couldn't have been happier. This was the real thing; and anyway there was time left over for dipping into the really serious matters of government. My work was pronounced satisfactory, and my salary was soon doubled to $15,000 from $7,000. After so many years as a student pauper, it was an inconceivable amount of money.

As my income flourished, so did my ambitions. I would arrive at the office before everyone else did to look through the mail to see if there was anything interesting. One day I found a letter from John Ehrlichman to Anderson saying the White House needed some congressional support for its revenue-sharing proposal, which was then under attack by Wilbur Mills, chairman of the House Ways and Means Committee.

Though it was probably a form letter, I researched the issue like mad all day. The next morning when Anderson brought it up at the staff meeting and asked for a volunteer to work something up on it, I was ready.

The speech I wrote for him was entitled 'All the Reasons Why Chairman [Wilbur] Mills Is Wrong About Revenue Sharing', and it was a smash hit. An awful lot of hot air is gassed about on the floor of the House on any average day, but even *The New York Times* saw fit to write it up. The White House was profoundly grateful. Ehrlichman called Anderson and asked him to stop by the next day. When Anderson asked if I wanted to accompany him, I didn't have to think twice.

It was my first visit to the White House. I was struck by the peculiar hushed silence of the West Wing. I could never imagine any voices being raised there.

On the way back, Anderson patted me on the back and said, 'We're going to make a great team.' He said he wanted me to work exclusively on the major issues. I had answered my last piece of constituent mail. I was on my way.

In December 1971, Anderson decided on the cockamamie* notion of promoting me to executive director of the Republican Conference, which he, as head of the Republican caucus, could bestow.

It was a high-powered job for a twenty-five-year-old, and I jumped at it, but Anderson was crazy to have given it to me, and it showed how utterly impractical he was as a politician. As recently as the year before, the right wingers and old bulls of the Republican Party had tried to remove him as head of the caucus because he was 'soft' on civil rights, civil liberties, school prayer, abortion, and the other social issues. He should have put a ten-year veteran of the Hill wars in that slot—to protect him.

All of a sudden I went from being as indistinguishable as an elevator operator to Capitol Hill jock. I had a large staff, a salary of $25,000—and it had taken me less than eighteen months.

But now I faced the challenge of figuring out how to keep Anderson out of trouble with his right-wing colleagues. So I set out immediately to look for good Republican deeds. It was a bit of a dilemma. Like Anderson, I had no use for the social issues. I had too much of the East Lansing coffee house still in me to start screaming about abortion and school prayer. I believed in the first and not in

* Zany.

the latter, and Anderson was for tolerance on those and all the social issues. There was only one issue with which he was at peace with his Republican colleagues—economics. I resolved to use that to move him into the spotlight where they would see him fighting the good GOP* fight, giving speeches, introducing bills, leading floor fights.

I plunged into economics with the usual vigor. I read everything in sight, and before long I emerged a disciple of F. A. Hayek, the preeminent Austrian exponent of free market economics.

It wasn't simply a case of Hayek, Milton Friedman, and the other conservative scholars I read being so persuasive. By happenstance, Nixon and his Treasury Secretary, John Connally, had about then launched an experiment in anti-market economics. They had turned traditional Republican economics on its head, imposed wage and price controls, and abolished the gold standard. It was perverse. Everything the free market scholars said would happen—shortages, bottlenecks, investment distortions, waste, irrationality, and more inflation—did happen right before my eyes. I collected dozens of case studies. The experience in John Connally's economics laboratory left me a born-again capitalist.

And these lessons involved more than just the abstract efficiency of the marketplace. Adam Smith's unseen hand did turn out to be a powerful, palpable fact—a stupendous mechanism for calibrating and coordinating more tens of billions of decisions than even the most powerful computer could ever digest. But there was something more. As I studied the Nixon experiment, I could see why Lippmann had been right: Economic controls are the malignant cancer of state power. The wage–price progam clearly demonstrated that the impossibility of controlling markets feeds bureaucratic expansion, coercion, and caprice at a staggering rate, once the erroneous enterprise is launched.

Down in the economic anthill, firms were always being caught with their base period** prices too far up or too far down due to strikes, inventory liquidations, seasonal pricing practices, bad weather, and many other unrepresentative circumstances. Likewise, new or qualitatively improved products always needed an exception to the general control rule, but there were no medieval scholars who

* The Grand Old Party, i.e. the Republican Party.
** A period used as a basis for price controls.

could define the difference between 'restyling' and 'redesigning'. Then, there were total control exemptions for 'essential and critical' goods, the potential supply of which turned out to be limited only by the number of industry lawyers and regulatory bureaucrats that could fit into the office buildings of Washington at any given time.

Finally, as the futile bureaucratic apparatus of control mushroomed, caprice became endemic. The lottery of windfall gains and losses multiplied throughout the economy. Forms and red tape proliferated, got lost in the mail, and lost contact with the English language. The for-hire lobbyists of K Street* became the intermediaries of economic justice, if anyone could define it.

These investigations also demystified the projects of government. Until then, I had tended to take the stated policy objectives and the claims of government to be actually altering the societal status quo with earnest seriousness. I had viewed government as the highly animated actor, society as the largely passive stage.

The Nixon wage and price control program shattered nearly every one of these illusions. In the end, it was simply overpowered and crushed by potent forces emanating from the vast national and global marketplace. Causation in the process of governance, I could see now, was a two-way street.

This led me, too, to a larger discovery of the line that divides right and left. Somewhere in there while trying to keep Anderson out of political trouble, I jumped over the divide and never looked back.

The right starts with history and society as they are, and places the burden of proof on those who would use the policy instruments of the state to bring about artificial change. The left starts with an abstraction—a vision of the good and just society—and places the burden of defense on those who resist the state's attempts to impose it. The second is always the bloody process. Implicit in the conservatism of the right is a profound regard for the complexity and fragility of the social and economic order; and a consequent fear that policy interventions may do more harm and injustice than good. By contrast, the activist impulses of the left derive from the view that a free society is the natural incubator of ills and injustices. The left assumes that society has an infinite capacity to absorb the changes it imposes on it. Now I saw that the good society—the one Lippmann

* A street well-known for its lobbyists' offices.

spoke of—was best served by a smaller, less activist state and by a more dynamic, productive, and fluid marketplace. Social progress was as much a matter of unshackling the powers of the latter as it was of extending the reach of the former.

During the summer of 1972, Senator George McGovern was frantically handing the keys to the Treasury over to every manner of interest group in a desperate but futile effort to revive the old Democratic coalition. I decided to analyze the McGovern budget with a view to showing how he planned to bankrupt the United States.

It wasn't hard, and the study made a predictable splash in the papers. But what was enduringly interesting about it was the disturbing principle it discerned amidst McGovern's wild promises. They were really nothing more than a compilation of the legislative agendas of all the mainline interest groups. Everyone wanted something, from the US Conferences of Mayors to the National Education Association, the Rural Electric Cooperatives, the Wheat Growers Associations, the handicapped lobby, the school lunch administrators, and the mortgage bankers. Something besides McGovern's numbers wasn't adding up. The interest group pluralism I had learned about at Harvard, which had been my answer to Marxism, was getting out of hand.

I decided to go back and reread what in hindsight must be considered one of the more seminal works of modern American political science, *The End of Liberalism*, by Theodore Lowi. His theory was that interest group pluralism had radically transformed American governance. The traditional nineteenth-century notion of constitutional democracy assumed a sharp distinction between the 'state' and the 'society'; established clear delimitations on the proper and valid functions of government and state power; required precise statutory enactments and limited delegating of authority; and assumed that the state was the instrument of the electorate. Lowi called this framework the 'First Republic'; within it the government built canals and lighthouses, and declared wars.

But after the New Deal, the line dividing state and society came tumbling down like the walls of Jericho. Interest groups appropriated its authority, and the uses of state power were defined not by the Constitution, but by whatever claims the organized interest groups could successfully impose on the system. Congress abandoned its role as lawgiver and resorted to Enabling Acts: vast, open-ended delegation of authority to the President, bureaucracies, and regulatory agencies, giving them the power to devise whatever public policies were desired for whatever reason by whatever constituency. Thus, the power to make policy shifted from the institutions of central government to a plethora of mini-govern- ments, made up of the 'iron triangles' of bureaucracy, client and congressional subcommittee.

The sovereign state ended up an open bazaar, its fiscal and legal resources plundered by organized interest groups by means of political muscle, bargaining, and logrolling.* Government was no longer accountable to the people because the instruments of government had been seized, the better to serve the parochial ends of society's modern-day guilds and syndicates: the trade associations, unions, professions, and other organized interests. At the time I reread his book, Lowi called this phenomenon 'interest group liberalism', but within a few years he would rename it the 'Second Republic'.

Thus, Lowi's model the second time through rang out with decisive lucidity. Here indeed was the conceptual formulation that revealed the true scheme of things. Might had become Right. Public policy was not a high-minded nor even an ideological endeavor, but simply a potpourri of parochial claims proffered by private interests parading in governmental dress. Much of the vast enterprise of American government was invalid, suspect, malodorous. Its projects and ministrations were not spawned from higher principles, broad idealism, or even humanitarian sentimentality; they were simply the flotsam and jetsam of a flagrantly promiscuous politics, the booty and spoils of the organized thievery conducted within the desecrated halls of government.

Lowi's model was a welcome find. Being an intellectual of the right continued to strike me as an oxymoron. But if one got to the minimalist government of the right through cynicism—the unmask- ing of the parochial claims behind the alleged good works of government—the trek was more acceptable.

Just as I had discovered that the story of Noah's Ark wasn't all it had been cracked up to be because it had been stolen from primitive Sumerian mythology, now I was finding that progressive govern-

* Doing favors in return for other favors.

ment—rooted as it was in the mundane graspings of clientele politics—did not command belief, either.

My campaign to keep Anderson in the good graces of his Republican colleagues was a success. I became a kind of adopted son to him. When we travelled out to his district, I stayed with him at his house in Rockford, Illinois. I was a frequent guest at his home in Washington for dinner. The family and I would go out for pizza together. If I had had any personal problems at the time, I would have taken them to Anderson rather than my own family.

What I did have was ambition, more and more of it; and one day I told him that some day I wanted to run for Congress myself. He said he was delighted. He had a generally low esteem for most of his colleagues, considering most of them to be either dimwits or pork barrel artists, and told me that he would be glad to see someone like me go into public service. I began to think maybe my dream wasn't so far-fetched after all.

As the Watergate affair gathered momentum, we became even closer. He would return from the Republican leadership meeting at the now crumbling White House in a state of preacherly outrage at whatever latest horror he had just witnessed in the Cabinet Room. Instead of going right back to his office, he'd drop by mine and describe in minute detail what had just transgressed.

One day, after telling me about a particularly disturbing session, he said to me: 'I think Nixon's lying through his teeth.' This was very early in the crisis, back when the mere thought of impeachment was almost unthinkable. Anderson's statement stunned me.

He was a genuinely righteous man, but I had got so caught up in getting ahead that I hadn't even thought about things like the courage it takes to risk your position if you feel the truth warrants it. I ended up learning a lot of things from John Anderson, but the courage he displayed over the Watergate episode was not among them.

The ultimate sin in Congress is for a staffer to run against an incumbent. It is in the order of an ancient tribal taboo. There would be absolute havoc with it; congressmen would be looking over their shoulders every minute. Yet I decided to run for Congress in my home district in 1975. My opponent, a fourteen-year incumbent named Hutchinson, went berserk when he found out. Soon he had a number of the old bulls in the cloakroom* in a fury of indignation. The idea that John Anderson was harboring a threat to one of their own was intolerable. I lost my job as Executive Director of the Republican Conference. Anderson was extremely kind to me and kept me on his personal staff for months. On the day I left for Michigan to start running in earnest I told him, with now characteristic confidence, that I would be back in a year, as his colleague.

I campaigned round-the-clock for a solid year. My encounters with the workaday citizens of Southern Michigan had a profound effect on my quest for the ideological truth. More than anything else, I was struck by the dramatic contrast between how hard and with what care, pride, and discipline the nation's citizens worked to earn our national income and wealth, on the one hand, and the feckless, inconsistent, and muddled manner in which it was shunted around in the halls of Washington, on the other. To be sure, I had long since turned against the pernicious projects of government as an intellectual matter. But now an emotional layer was grafted onto the case.

In particular, as I got to know the drugstore owners, fuel oil distributors, machine shop owners, realtors, life insurance agents, shop foremen, sales executives, grain elevator proprietors, and farmers who formed the nucleus of my campaign organization, I was increasingly drawn to their side of the welfare state issue. I began to see a profound principle that was to prove crucial in the final, impending phase of my own odyssey: before the state can redistribute wealth, the society must first produce it. If incentives and morale among the more enterprising citizens are weakened too much, the resulting economic shortfalls will make the attainment of social justice impossible under any circumstance.

What convinced me more than anything else of these propositions was the plain evidence I had encountered, down in the economic anthills which undergirded each of the district's hamlets, that meritocracy was indeed a real, palpable fact of life. The most successful farmers, realtors, industrialists, and lawyers got more

---

* The place for Congressional gossip and informal talk, like the House of Commons tea room.

income and rewards out of the system than their less successful peers because they put more in—in the form of competence, discipline, imagination, elbow grease, and sheer dedication.

Indeed, every hamlet had its self-made millionaires, or nearly so, and their unpublished Horatio Alger* stories required no literary embellishment. In one instance, the original small, old wooden barn still stood beside the rows and rows of computer-managed, metallic sheds where a multi-million-dollar scientific hog-farming operation had now sprung up. In another case, a giant furniture factory betrayed the fact that the tiny block building at its center where the owner had started had been added to time and time again as his enterprise expanded. At still another factory, nestled in row after row of corn fields, the family business's trucks loaded precision steam valves for installation in every oil refinery complex on the globe.

These vignettes were omnipresent, and the message for my Grand Doctrine was clear. Satisfying the entrepreneur's requirement for incentives and rewards was as important to the good society as satisfying the claims of the poor for justice. The one couldn't be had without—indeed, was dependent upon—the satisfaction of the other.

Fortunately enough, however, the solid entrepreneurs of Southern Michigan's hamlets did not exhibit the same hypocrisy toward the projects of government as was endemic in their trade organizations in Washington. The good farmers—the ones who attended Farm Bureau meetings and voted—knew the federal subsidy programs were wrong and demanded only an end to federal red tape and inspections, not higher, or even any, subsidy payments at all. Among the doctors some were agitated by moves afoot to permit advertising and price competition, but most of them were willing to overlook my support for that development because they were attracted to my resolute opposition to Big Government overall.

And so it went. Absolute fidelity to a free market, the anti-statist position was accepted and rewarded by the voters because I had come to them with a doctrine to sell, not a menu of existing or new state indulgences to promise. In subsequent years, as one electoral success followed another, I formulated a rule derived from my campaign experiences that would have serious consequences later

* Poor young man who makes good through hard work and honesty.

down the road. It was weak-kneed, weak-minded politicians, not overwhelming electoral power, that was responsible for the squeaky wheels getting so much undeserved grease in the halls of government.

It turned out that no one had especially high regard for Hutchinson. He had been in office fifteen years, but to most he was simply a name on the ballot, a face at the banquets.

In early February 1976 I had officially launched my campaign. The next day I began a blitzkrieg at 5 am. By 10.30 am I had appeared at half a dozen events. I had just entered the Branch County Courthouse for a round of handshaking when I heard a noisy commotion in the hallway. When I heard the word 'Hutchinson' I rushed to see what was happening.

Hutchinson had quit. It was over.

He said he was leaving because 'it wasn't fun anymore'. Now my fun was about to begin.

I have a picture from the day I officially won the election. It's from the front page of the *Herald Palladium* and shows me and Grampa Bartz clasping our arms together in a victory sign. The banner headline overhead shouts:

STOCKMAN NEW REPUBLICAN POWERHOUSE IN
SOUTHERN MICHIGAN

As I look at the photo, I see how frail and emaciated his eighty-three-year-old hands were.

He did not have long to live. He was now in the hospital with his last illness. He wanted to come to Washington for my swearing in, but the doctors forbade him from coming. He was too weak by then.

On the day I was sworn in, I called him. He told me he was proud, because I was embarking on a career that had been his dream all along.

In December 1976, I tried to secure a seat on the House Appropriations Committee and, not surprisingly, failed. The old bulls in the GOP hierarchy take a dim view of awarding seats on such powerful committees to mere freshmen.

If I had got a seat on the Appropriations Committee, I might have developed a more realistic attitude toward politics. The Appropriations Committee is the cash register of the Second Republic. Sitting there, day by day, as the politicians greased every squeaking wheel, might have shown me that my anti-political, anti-welfare state ideology would never succeed.

Instead, I landed on the Commerce Committee, and it reinforced my whole critique of Big Government and economic statism. In those early years of the Carter presidency, the Commerce Committee was the front line in the war between the statists and the anti-statists, between those who wanted government to dominate every aspect of American life and those who didn't.

In the spring of 1977, Carter unveiled his 'moral equivalent of war' with great gravity and piousness: the National Energy Plan. It was a plan to regulate every BTU that flowed through the US economy, and by marvelous coincidence its acronym, NEP, exactly matched Lenin's 1921 plan to rescue the Russian economy from the anarchy wrought by 'workers Soviets'.

Other plans followed: environmental regulations whereby every by-product of technological progress was to be declared carcinogenic; air bags, windfall profit taxes—innumerable ways to regulate the way Americans lived and worked. Invariably these statist initiatives had been concocted by some arrogant, self-important appointee possessed of a degree in English and contempt for free enterprise. One day I listened, incredulous, as an obnoxious troll of this genre pounded the witness table and demanded that Congress delegate to him absolute, open-ended power to establish energy efficiency standards for *all* American-made appliances.

The 'moral equivalent of war' and its attendant issues was really a front for state control of resources and the economy. It was a neo-Malthusian ideology that held that we were running out of everything and that only the state could be trusted to hoard our diminishing supplies. We were exhausting our resources, and by using what resources we had, we were making the world unlivable. Capitalism was poisoning the earth with chemical time bombs.

Neo-Malthusianism was our term, of course; the Carter Administration preferred to speak of the 'era of limits'. The current glut of oil on the world market is eloquent refutation of how idiotic their position was, but at the time they were prosecuting their views with a determination befitting the smallness of their minds. The New Deal had given birth to the statist impulse; during the Great Society it had gathered momentum; with the 'Era of Limits' it had become an imperative.

In the trenches of the Commerce Committee, I did battle with this monster every day, hacking away at it with a sword forged in the free market smithy of F. A. Hayek. I became a militant anti-neo-Malthusian.

As such I was one of the very few in the chamber of the politicians. To most of them, depletion and environmental degradation was a boon. It kept them busy passing laws, meddling everywhere, and throwing their weight around from coast to coast.

But there was one other of my kind. I had met Congressman Jack Kemp of New York while working for John Anderson. Now he was looking for allies on behalf of a new theory of economics that meshed perfectly with my own still emerging views. It was called 'supply-side' economics, in stark contrast to the 'demand side' that Congress so steadfastly defended. We lived in an era not of limits but of limitless possibilities. Capitalism was endlessly resourceful. If people had enough incentives, prosperity was inevitable.

I liked Kemp. He was an unusual politician—he read books and talked about them. His head, like mine, was stuffed full of sweeping theories, historical knowledge, and insights about the patterns of things, not merely the particulars. One day we fell to discussing Ludwig Erhart's brilliant memoir on how sound money reform, low tax rates, and deregulation of commerce had brought about the postwar German economic miracle. Kemp had a seriousness of mind and intellectuality of approach that made him stand out like a lighthouse in a sea of fog. As I had been, he was searching for his own Grand Doctrine.

Kemp had formed a cadre of brilliant and iconoclastic theoreticians. They possessed intellectual powers and ambitions as limitless as the economic growth they espoused. One day he handed me the manuscript of a book that would soon burst on the world in a blaze of illumination: Jude Wanniski's *The Way the World Works*. Wanniski was a former editor of *The Wall Street Journal* and a peripatetic polemicist, and his book hit me with the force of revelation. It reordered everything I had previously known or thought about economics.

Wanniski was a frequent visitor to Kemp's office. It was there too that I met Professor Arthur Laffer, the father of supply-side economics and a dazzling thinker. A number of talented congressional staffers would drop by as well: Craig Roberts, Steve Entin, John Mueller, and others. All of them would play significant roles in the wrenching debates of the Reagan era. In the meantime, Kemp's office became a kind of postgraduate seminar in supply-side economics. Kemp was our political guru, Wanniski and Laffer our chief theoreticians. Ceaselessly and happily we hammered out counter positions to every statist proposal or initiative Carter or Congress came up with. It was exciting. Our ideas could change history. For the first time since my shaggy-haired days in the East Lansing coffee house, I began to feel as if I were part of a movement. My revolutionary fires had been rekindled once again.

In some basic sense, however, the new supply-side doctrine was but a reincarnation of my old social idealism in the form of a new and, I was inclined to think, more mature ideological garb. The world could indeed be started anew. Its current, accumulating economic and social breakdowns could be repaired and its older, inherited ills of racism and poverty vanquished by sweeping changes in the policies which caused or prolonged them.

Above all else, the supply-side doctrine offered a plausible premise for idealism amidst the prevailing cynical and pessimistic ethos of the time. The latter had been perfectly captured in Carter's politically fatal 'malaise' formulation. It was an epigrammatic, if unwitting, expression of all the muddled and destructive notions of scarcities, catastrophes, closing frontiers, economic limits, incurably embedded inflations, and unavoidable financial breakdowns that had by then come to enthral his administration and most of official Washington.

The new supply-side gospel seemed at the time to be a fair bet for the monumental task of reversing this trend. As we had formulated it, the supply-side synthesis encompassed vastly more than a single nostrum—the Kemp-Roth thirty percent personal income tax cut. Only much later did it become reduced to a single piece of legislation by the glib simplifiers among the press, its opponents, and, regrettably, some of its own advocates.

In those days of the movable Kemp seminar, however, we viewed the supply-side doctrine as all-encompassing. It implied not merely a tax cut but a whole catalogue of policy changes, ranging from natural gas deregulation, to abolition of the minimum wage, to repeal of milk marketing orders, to elimination of federal certificates of 'need' for truckers, hospitals, airlines, and anyone else desiring to commit an act of economic production. It even encompassed reform of the World Bank, and countless more.

Indeed, the whole catalogue of policy reforms was designed to remedy the central global economic failure of the late 1970s. That failure was popularly described as 'stagflation'—the simultaneous occurrence of roaring inflation and vanishing output growth. But conventional economists had utterly failed to comprehend either its causes or its cures.

They generally attributed it to a mysterious new *delirium economens*: an outbreak of public irrationality, fevered psychology, and animal spirits that caused wage-price spirals, energy gluttony, weak investment spending, selfish speculation in unproductive enterprises, and numerous other malefactions. The truth of the matter, however, was that the reigning Keynesian economic model of the era was being so massively invalidated by empirical events that its practitioners—especially the Carter Administration economists— had been reduced to offering blatherings and gibberish in lieu of analysis.

Amid this background of double-talk and illogic, the supply-side synthesis offered two powerful, classic economic truths.

The first truth explained why real economic growth was falling toward zero, or was even signalling an outright shrinkage in living standards. In essence, our capitalist economy's natural capacity to expand and generate new wealth and societal welfare was being badly hobbled by the sweeping anti-supply and incentive-destroying policies of the modern state. The marketplace had become riddled with sumps of waste in the form of subsidies and protectionism. Its economic arteries had become sclerotic with tax and regulatory barriers to commerce and production. The supply-side solution thus required the radical dismantling of state-erected barriers to economic activity—punitive tax rates, as well as all of the other misbegotten enterprises of the Second Republic.

On the price and financial side of the economy's ledger, all the indicators were feverishly and destructively rising. A turbulent monetary disorder of double-digit commodity inflation, massive flight from financial assets, rampant speculation in land, baubles, and other tangible assets, prodigious expansion of dangerously leveraged pyramids of credit, and swirling volatility in global exchange and capital markets had been unleashed on the entire world economy.

The second classic economic truth explained this destructive hyperinflation loose in both the US and global economy. It was anchored in the failure of the US government to maintain a stable purchasing power and reliable value for the dollar—the world economy's overwhelmingly dominant money for transactions, reserves, and storing wealth. Inflation was no less mysterious than it was destructive. As the deliberate policy of the world's leading economy, it had touched off a revolt against Uncle Sam's age-old trick of clipping the coins that now reverberated through world markets from Cleveland to Calcutta. In place of all the silly and futile anti-inflation projects of the Carter Administration—wage and price guidelines, excess wage and price taxes, hospital cost controls, energy import antidotes, tripartite compacts in basic industries— but one step was required. The dollar had to be made stable again by fixing its value to a constant quantity of real economic goods.

As thus formulated, the supply-side synthesis closed the final loop in my quest for the Grand Doctrine.

As an intellectual and moral matter, this comprehensive supply-side doctrine had a powerful appeal. It offered a rigorous standard of justice and fairness and provided a recipe for economic growth and prosperity—the only viable way to truly eliminate poverty and social deprivation. But its elegant idealism was hostile to all the messy, expedient compromises of daily governance.

This was made dramatically evident when toward the end of my second term, the Chrysler Corporation demanded that the Federal government rescue it from its own mismanagement. The action was justified by an army of lobbyists who represented every imaginable local interest group and no discernible policy principle.

The notion that the Federal government should, on demand, re-finance inefficient, bankrupt private enterprises was so loath-some to me that I resolved not only to vote against it, but to take the lead in trying to stop it. So I took the Floor of the House to speak out against this abomination that was about to pass. I preached to the politicians my most fevered anti-statist sermon. Both the fevers and the sermon were still with me when I moved into the White House a year later:

> We have to be pragmatic. Fix it up now and worry about the consequences later. Don't bother yourself with elegant theories about whether it is sound public policy.
>
> Don't trouble yourself with the economic effects of catapulting Chrysler from the back of the credit line to the front. Somebody else is going to be squeezed out of the credit market—small manufacturers, construction firms, auto dealers, farmers—with reduced production and employment elsewhere in the economy as a result.
>
> These latter firms and workers are not speculative. They are just politically invisible.
>
> No one on the globe with real money to invest is willing to come forward to Chrysler's rescue: not the banks, insurance companies, or the bond markets ... unless Uncle Sam promises to underwrite the risk.
>
> Well, P. T. Barnum once said, 'There's one born every day—you can count on it.' Apparently the US Congress is the only one left.

Despite its disdainful tone and righteous indignation, my speech was applauded even by some of those who had declared they would vote for the bail out (while holding their noses). For my opposition I was oxymoronically hailed by many as an 'intelligent' politician.

Looking back on that, I am not at all sure I deserve the praise. I spoke of economic doctrine but did not manage to see a stark, dramatic truth. The Chrysler bail-out passed by a margin of over one hundred votes because the affected voters wanted it. And if the House of Representatives would go for the raw, unprincipled expediency of that measure, why should I have assumed, only a year later, that the institution, and the electorates it represented, would accept the kind of sweeping austere ideological blueprint the Reagan Revolution called for? I finally had my Grand Doctrine, but it completely overwhelmed my grasp of what the politics of American governance was all about.

2

The Coming of the New Order

In September 1980, a curious thing happened. I was asked by the Reagan campaign to help prepare Ronald Reagan for the presidential debates, but these sessions turned into an audition that soon would give me an opportunity to implement my own Grand Doctrine. This unexpected yet rather welcome opportunity came by way of a phone call from David Gergen, who was on the Reagan debate team.

'We'd like you to play the part of your old boss,' he told me. He said they wanted someone who knew how John Anderson would come at Reagan. It was a great opportunity to see the candidate close up and to meet the inner circle people I knew only from reading the papers.

Though I didn't hesitate to say yes, I was a bit uneasy about playing the role of my former rabbi. Anderson would obviously find out about it. Just as obviously, he would feel betrayed. I didn't like that prospect because I valued Anderson's friendship and all that he had taught me; but what could I do? His candidacy was hopeless, and the cause of sinking a blow against the Carter Democrats and their disastrous policies seemed more important than anything else.

Getting myself prepared for the rehearsal was a crash, round-the-clock exercise.

I holed up for several days and studied Anderson's campaign propaganda. It seemed he was changing some of his earlier positions, making them more palatable to the brie-and-Chablis* set. I drew up my outlines; soon I was ready.

I was nervous, pulling up to the gate of the estate in Wexford,

* Intellectuals who feast on brie and Chablis, a sign of their effeteness.

Virginia, where the rehearsals were to be held. It was the country home of Senator John Warner and Elizabeth Taylor. The Warners had offered it to the Reagans to use as their east coast retreat.

The place was nicely remote, with one of those two-mile-long driveways. 'Here we go,' I thought, as the car went through the gate, leaving the clutch of security men and reporters behind. By the time we'd reached the end of that interminable driveway, I was even more nervous. I was about to meet the big-time players who, if their candidate won, would be running the country.

This always happened—every time I took a step up the ladder. You always thought the people up on the next rung were going to be supermen. Few of them actually were.

This group appeared, on first inspection, a pretty regular lot. Everyone seemed to have a clipboard. William Casey, the campaign director, mumbled much of the time. But I figured he had to be smart. You didn't get where he'd been—SEC* chairman, Wall Street tycoon—simply on bad elocution.

Jim Baker seemed like an efficient production foreman, with a pencil behind his ear. He cussed a blue streak and told off-color jokes. He was tall, trim, and self-confident. He had a way of moving things along, of pointing to the ceiling and spinning his arm around in a 350-degree circle, saying, 'Let's go, let's move it.' He struck me as the one who really knew what he was doing.

Ed Meese came across as almost the opposite of Baker. He was heavyset, rumpled, and jowled; he always appeared relaxed and had a kind of twinkle in his eyes. But he was clearly the closest to Reagan, the one who understood his mind best. He had worked alongside him for a decade and Reagan trusted him. Meese seemed to have two or three short points on every topic. Some of them didn't make much sense, but I figured that was due to the wear and tear of the campaign.

Mike Deaver was on the sidelines, saying very little. I think he spent most of the time inside the house with Mrs Reagan.

As for the object of this gathering, Ronald Reagan, he was very affable, dressed in plaid shirt and cowboy boots. He seemed somewhat distracted.

* Securities and Exchange Commission, the agency that regulates stock market trading.

They wanted everything to be as realistic as possible, so they had converted the garage into a kind of mock TV studio. Four, sometimes five expert 'panelists' were involved: John Tower (defense), Marty Anderson (domestic policy), Alan Greenspan (economics), Howard Baker (politics), and Jeane Kirkpatrick (foreign policy).

There were about twenty people milling around, but finally Ed Meese called the session to order. I didn't have an especially easy task, taking a completely alien viewpoint and fitting into the tight time frame the debate format called for.

Reagan's performance was, well, miserable. I was shocked. He couldn't fill up the time. His answers just weren't long enough. And what time he could fill, he filled with woolly platitudes.

There was one question about the upcoming MBFR (Mutual and Balanced Force Reductions) conference. After a few lines he broke off, smiled, and said, 'You guys will have to forgive me now . . . I've just lost that one completely.'

You felt kind of sorry for the guy, but his lack of agility was disquieting.

But by then it was too late for second thoughts. I'd already converted—since Reagan had been converted to supply side—so for better or worse, Reagan now *was* the voice of the revolution. It was just a matter of getting him up to speed for the debates.

The trouble was that John Anderson, self-righteous as he may have been, was smart. His brain was an encyclopedia, and he was about as fluent as they came. At the end of the first session I thought, 'Anderson's going to *kill* him. The whole campaign will be upended, and Jimmy Carter will be the beneficiary.'

I was there as an actor, so it wasn't for me to take the lead in the follow-up critique. But nobody seemed to want that role. The campaign staff handled him with kid gloves. No one would tell him, 'That was a lousy answer.'

It was all on-the-one-hand . . . on-the-other-hand. Reagan doesn't even have thin skin. He would sometimes rise to his own defense, but very lightly. They could have told him where he was slipping up.

I should probably have stopped in the midst of all this for some serious rumination, because by now two things were clear. One, that the candidate had only the foggiest idea of what supply side was all about; and two, that no one close to him had any more idea.

THE COMING OF THE NEW ORDER

When it came to specific policy issues, the whole group tended to back and fill,* searching for the woolliest generalization possible. Agriculture, environmental regulation, the Chrysler bailout, textile protectionism—these issues raised the basic agenda of supply side. Their answers: We're concerned and going to carefully look into it.

You couldn't take a stand at the Alamo on everything. I knew there was an election to win. But you couldn't get a mandate if you kept your agenda buried in oatmeal answers, either. Yet on every domestic issue the staff kept leading him back to a pat answer. Chrysler? It's a symptom of Carter's failed economy. Farm subsidies? More Carter failure. Aid to the cities? Still more Carter failure.

There was a tone to all this that really bothered me: their notion of policy ideas stopped at name-calling and partisanship. Perhaps I should have questioned whether the Reaganites were really revolutionaries, after all. This sure sounded like scape-goating politicians.

But when the siren of ambition is wailing, you end up hearing the most favorable case. Governor Reagan was firmly committed to our program—Jack Kemp said so himself. And his advisers had the right slogans.

At the time I thought that what they needed was some help in articulating why radical economic policy change was necessary and in formulating a detailed action plan to carry it out. So I decided to stay on the campaign bus.

My doubts at Wexford were actually bearing witness to a huge accident. By September 1980, a revolutionary chain reaction had already penetrated deep into the mainstream of American politics. It had begun only a few short months before.

'Jack should run for President,' Jude Wanniski unhesitatingly proclaimed; 'the future of Western civilization depends on it.'

When Wanniski had said that back in 1979, it was hard to know which part of his declaration was more unlikely: Jack Kemp's candidacy or the predicted consequences.

Still, as Wanniski uttered it that day it didn't surprise me. Jack

---

* Extemporize, create makeshift solution.

Kemp and our supply-siders group had gathered at the Washington Circle Hotel to consider precisely what Wanniski was recommending.

But I was deeply sceptical, and not just about my friend Jack Kemp running for President. I simply didn't believe the world of Washington politicians was ready for the radical doctrines of the supply side.

I had been burned once before by the eschatological fevers of revolution—back in the brave new world of the campus coffee house. Now I had to see the evidence. The New Order of capitalist prosperity and shrinking government was a shining ideal. But I doubted it would come to pass—at least at any time soon.

Wanniski was no help here. He thought we could change things. And it wasn't merely the IRS code he had in mind. It was the course of history itself.

I had to wonder to myself, 'How could a guy this smart actually believe that a few people could change the course of history?' I put it down to hyperbole. I figured he was just trying to jack up our morale.

Yet over and over again he kept repeating it. It was his mantra: 'Overturning an existing order starts with one person and an idea. An idea persuades a second person, then a third, then a fourth . . .' I'd studied Lenin's trip from Zurich to Russia in the sealed carriage, so I knew that Wanniski wasn't talking historical rot. Chain reactions occur in politics; the Soviet precedent, of course, was not exactly inspiring.

In any case, the vast, shuffling hulk of the American Second Republic was different. Even the so-called Roosevelt Revolution hadn't been based on a single radical doctrine. It amounted to a desperate burst of activism orchestrated by an astute politician who had been willing to grab any idea that was handy. For Wanniski and we supply siders, there were no relevant precedents. Change in American democracy was glacially slow.

That's what I thought, anyway, until Wanniski's chain reaction started to unfold right before my very eyes. Before long I was caught up in it; then I started to believe it and ended up a link in it.

The process started when I arrived at the hotel. I was quite surprised to find there three men of considerable rank: Irving Kristol, Frank Shakespeare, and Larry Silberman. Shakespeare I knew slightly. He was an old, old hand, head of RKO and head of the

USIA* in Nixon's administration. Larry Silberman I had known from when I'd been a kid laboring in John Anderson's vineyard. He was a big name as a cabinet officer in the Nixon-Ford era. But the real star guest as far as I was concerned was Kristol. To me, Kristol was a secular incarnation of the Lord Himself.

Kristol was a genuine intellectual who had been shaped to the left-wing culture and politics of New York City's postwar intelligentsia. But beginning in the 1960s, he had become a powerful advocate of a contrarian viewpoint that rejected the Old World socialism and internationalism of the American left in favor of a new premise, centered on the values of unfettered capitalism at home and a strong, nationalist US policy abroad.

Kristol was also a prodigious writer and publisher. A short, genial man, professorial in his bearing and rarely seen not puffing on his pipe, he was an indefatigable organizer of intellectual projects— seminars, think tanks, and publications like *The Public Interest*, an influential and iconoclastic journal which he founded in the mid-1960s.

By 1979 *Esquire* magazine was getting around to discovering him and putting him on its cover as the godfather of neo-conservatism. I'd been following Kristol's intellectual map along much of my journey back from the left. I knew his presence—together with that of the other two ideological elders—at this meeting meant we had embarked on something more than just a whim.

When Wanniski made his declaration, I watched Kristol closely. His reaction rendered his view self-evident. He accepted the suggestion as a plausible idea. I was struck. I thought, 'My God, maybe we are moving along the curve. This thing might be getting serious.'

Despite our ideological enthusiasm, we were mostly realistic about Jack's chances. They were 'not wonderful', as the cliché then went. But a Kemp campaign would give us a pulpit from which to broadcast the supply-side religion. That was the important thing.

I was thus completely unprepared when the first link in the chain came together. One day, a few months after the Washington Circle Hotel meeting, Kemp called me to say he wasn't running.

* US Information Agency.

'You sure we shouldn't look at it again?' I replied.

'No. I've worked out a little treaty with the Reagan camp,' he said. 'I won't run, but in return we're going to be in on the ground floor on policy.'

'The policy role sounds good,' I said, trying to disguise my shock. 'But, Jack! I can't believe you're hooking up with Reagan.'

That was putting it mildly. After I hung up the phone, I didn't know whether to giggle or kick the side of my desk.

Ronald Reagan?

The man was more ancient ideologically than he was in years. I considered him a cranky obscurantist whose political base was barnacled with every kook and fringe group that inhabited the vast deep of American politics.

My viewpoint was that of the intellectual conservative. How do you get a prosperous economy and hold off the Russians at the same time? I didn't give two hoots for the Moral Majority, the threat of unisex toilets, the school prayer amendment, and the rest of the New Right litany. I was still basically an unreconstructed sceptic on the so-called social issues; I'd never got rid of that part of the coffee house. My soft-core Marxism had annealed into libertarianism. I didn't believe in economic regulation and I didn't believe in moral regulation.

But now my close friend had just told me he was going with Reagan. In the process, he was aligning himself with Jerry Falwell, the anti-gun control nuts, the Bible-thumping creationists, the anti-Communist witch-hunters and small-minded Hollywood millionaires to whom 'supply side' meant one more Mercedes.

So there I was, thinking, 'How is this antediluvian going to help us? He's *exactly* what the establishment needs to discredit our ideas.'

It was the establishment opinion makers who had to be persuaded that our synthesis of hard money, lower taxes and smaller government was an intellectually credible, pedigreed idea. The establishment had to be taught that you couldn't stop inflation with wage and price controls; you had to stop printing money. It had to be taught that you couldn't create economic growth by expanding the welfare state; you needed to start dismantling it and cutting taxes. And I was afraid that message, in the California governor's hands, was going to get lost during the discussions about 'why Johnny can't pray'.

Thus, having no use for Reagan, all I could do was to wish Jack well and get back to the business of fighting the daily battle against statist error in the House of Representatives.

Kemp kept me posted on his new role as chief policy theoretician in the Reagan camp. Then, early in 1980, he gave me an excited report. Reagan had been successfully 'converted'. There had been a powwow out in California on the eve of the day-to-day primary campaigning. Ed Meese decided the governor should be drilled on supply side—so he'd get the basic message down.

Kemp arrived brimming with enthusiasm and zeal, bringing Jude Wanniski and Art Laffer with him. According to Jack, they'd spent days out there with Reagan, discussing the gold standard, the tax cut, supply-side theory, economic growth, the whole enchilada. And Governor Reagan had responded enthusiastically, Kemp said he had an intuitive 'feel' for the Laffer curve. He didn't say why, but I figured I'd stay tuned.

In any event, Kemp considered the sessions 'historic'. The governor's campaign would be on the 'cutting edge' of the revolution.

'He's ninety percent with us,' Kemp enthused.

My scepticism was losing a bit of its edge. But the pervasive scepticism of the House Republican politicians was still a real barrier. They just weren't wholeheartedly buying Kemp-Roth or the supply-side agenda.

Yet without them, there wouldn't be a supply-side revolution—at least not in the near future as Jack Kemp had in mind. If we couldn't refute to their satisfaction John Anderson's silly charge that the only way to cut taxes, raise defense and balance the budget was with 'smoke and mirrors', the supply-side agenda wasn't going anywhere.

The GOP rank and file's reservation about the Kemp-Roth tax cut really bothered me. That was the political gravy—the easiest part of the revolution. The average voter out there, informed that his congressman wants to give him a thirty percent tax cut, isn't about to pick up the phone and give his representative a chewing out.

So if we couldn't get them to cut taxes, how on earth were we going to get them to do all the rest? My Grand Doctrine required the politicians to swallow some real political horse pills. You had to strip the borders clean of protectionist barriers. You had to get rid of overkill in environmental regulation. You had to dismantle the energy boondoggles.*

In fact, the supply side had a solution to everything. How do you regulate toxic substances? You enact a prudent risk law. What do you do about farmers? You tell them they're now running a business like everyone else; you let them sink or swim in the marketplace. What do you do about steel? You don't worry about steel, because capital will migrate to more productive uses in Silicon Valley.

Those were the right answers, but politically they were 'dynamite'. It's not easy taking away farm subsidies, cutting the Merchant Marine off at the waterline, getting the pork barrel out of so-called water resource projects.

Beyond that there was radical monetary reform. Yet hard money cut across every one of the inflationist illusions you constantly heard in the GOP cloakroom. A fair portion of the allegedly conservative stalwarts would line up at the drop of a hat for the folly of a national interest rate ceiling. That was the very antithesis of hard money.

Here we were, meanwhile, trying to persuade our own that they should give the voters a gift of a thirty percent income tax cut. If they couldn't do that, how were they going to stand up and take on all the tough items on the supply-side agenda?

Consolidation of GOP support for the Kemp-Roth tax cut became the critical next step in the chain reaction. Here is where Congressman Phil Gramm got involved.

Gramm was a thirty-eight-year-old former economics professor who'd run as a Democrat from Texas's conservative Sixth District in 1978 and won. He was assigned to the Interstate and Foreign Commerce Committee, where he occupied a seat right at the bottom of the heap, with me. Within weeks I was praising the gods for this unexpected, easygoing, brilliant and sympatico new ally.

Gramm knew the entire supply-side catechism backwards and forwards. He understood instinctively the fundamental conflict between the foolish and wasteful enterprises of the Second Republic and the laws of capitalist prosperity and freedom.

Unlike many in my supply-side seminar, he was also steeped in detailed knowledge of basic federal programs. To win the battle you

* Schemes that waste money and time.

had to be adept at more than just big picture formulations and articulating the first principles of the anti-statist case.

Gramm understood fully that high marginal tax rates were but one manifestation of the welfare state problem. Down in the briar patch of the budget and regulatory agencies, hundreds of similar policy errors demanded correction. He could rip through the alleged facts and mythical rationalizations which support little sinkholes of waste such as physicians' training subsidies or big ones like open-ended Medicaid reimbursement and synfuels demonstration plants.

Deep down in his soul, Phil Gramm was a hard-core anti-spender. In his mind, as in mine, the first principles of the anti-statist revolution were complementary. They required an enormous shrinkage of the vast expenditures that the Congress pumped into illicit and inappropriate functions of the state. That permitted lower taxes. Capitalist dynamism also required lower taxes. That necessitated far less spending.

So, Phil and I thought of ourselves as the compleat supply siders. We wanted to shrink both sides of the budget equation. The economic and political circumstances of early 1980 suddenly gave us a chance to try just that.

In that overheated last year of the Carter Administration, the sky was falling—inflation was at thirteen percent and interest rates were heading toward twenty-one percent. All the Republican pols* started clamoring for a balanced budget. It wasn't a bad idea, but only if you *balanced down*, and didn't leave the spending levels built in.

The latter point was the crucial distinction between supply siders and the welfare state politicians. The Carter Administration had got the balanced budget religion, too. But it was proposing to *balance up*. You had only to look once at the Carter Administration 'born-again' concept of fiscal restraint to see the point. The balanced budget they had in mind had spending at twenty-two or twenty-three percent of GNP. That amounted to a twenty percent bigger government than we'd ever had before 1970.

At the time I thought there was a hairline fracture of difference between Gramm and myself and the other supply siders on the question of fiscal policy and balanced budgets. Eventually it would prove to be some kind of hairline!

* Politicians.

Laffer and Wanniski, the two high priests of supply side, sometimes argued that the tax cuts would pay for themselves. They implied the Treasury would take in *more* after the tax cuts than before. I never bought that literally and didn't think they did, either. I put it down to salesmanship.

To be sure, they had an important point in their disparagement of the old-time GOP religion. The GOP had to get off its mindless and abstract preoccupation with a balanced-budget-above-all-else-and-at-any-price. The 'Hooverite' balanced budget commandment was a trap, both economically and politically.

If you insisted on a balanced budget but accepted all the illicit welfare state spending commitments that had been accumulated over the years, you ended up with a miserable job. You became the tax collector for the welfare state. Even on the basis of pure politics, conservatives needed a more noble mission than that.

None of the old guard ever acknowledged their plight quite that way. But it was what caution and incrementalism led you to just the same. You needed a radical anti-welfare state premise to break out of the trap. That's what I conceived the supply side to be all about.

But Laffer and Wanniski had now become rather glib rhetorically, as well as disingenuous intellectually, about deficits. Wanniski especially was a clever phrasemaker and an inveterate amateur politician. He had dubbed the GOP's orthodox budget cutting approach as 'the root canal theory of politics'. The obvious idea was that budget cutting included sacrifice and pain.

Yes, budget cutting carried an unwelcome political message. Only I was not at all comfortable with Wanniski's spending's-not-the-issue patter. You couldn't keep what we had to do under a bushel. The gifts of government that the electorate wasn't properly entitled to receive had to be taken back. My Grand Doctrine implied dismantling vast segments of the Second Republic's budget, slashing all the expenditures that reflected its statist enterprises.

We therefore had to find a way to make this politically viable and palatable. The liberation of American agriculture from the whole rot of USDA* subsidies and price supports, for example, was a glorious task. It would free the labor and capital trapped in inefficient, surplus farm output for redeployment to productive, profitable uses

* US Department of Agriculture.

elsewhere in the national economy. We had to go out and sell that gospel. Make it sound good—because it was good. I thus didn't appreciate at all Wanniski's careless branding of this and dozens of other necessary and principled budget surgeries as an exercise in political 'root canal'.

In the final analysis, the federal deficit represented the ultimate putrefied fruit of the established governmental regime. The rhetorical task, therefore, was to strengthen it as a symbol of what had to be radically changed, not weaken it as I feared Laffer and Wanniski were doing.

But Jack Kemp liked the sound of their music on this issue. They were leading him, too, into a shriller and shriller anti-balanced budget, the-tax-cut-will-pay-for-itself and deficits-don't-matter-that-much position. Kemp was now making ebullient, anti-Hooverite, rhetorical flourishes on the House floor and in the Republican caucus meetings.

The GOP old guard was beginning to resent it. They were also becoming alarmed by the Carter White House's success in labelling the 'Republican Tax Plan', as Kemp-Roth was now being called, as a disastrous prescription for huge deficits and runaway inflation.

Most of the mainstream GOP didn't buy this bit of Democratic hypocrisy, but they were demanding assurances that these supply-side wildmen weren't about to lead them into a trap. They wanted to know that we took spending control and deficit reduction seriously. They wanted to know that the numbers would add up.

Here is where the story of Kemp-Roth should have ended. The GOP politicians would almost surely have ditched it in the spring of 1980 in favor of a balanced budget once Carter and the Democrats came up with their own plan.

But the two anti-spending supply siders stepped into the breach. Gramm and I decided we had to find some way to bridge the growing split between supply siders and the orthodox conservatives in both GOP and southern Democratic ranks. So we launched into the nitty-gritty of the budget and eventually did come up with what appeared to be a balanced budget and a big tax cut, too.

The irony was that the supply-side idea was properly suspect by the GOP politicians from the very beginning: they knew in their bones they couldn't live with massive tax and spending reductions. Given the breadth of their scepticism, supply side by rights should never have been the centerpiece of the 1980 GOP platform, the 1980 presidential campaign, or the new Reagan Administration's economic policy. But Wanniski's unlikely chain reaction had started. Kemp had made his connection. Now we would get the GOP politicians hooked on Kemp-Roth.

What kept the chain going in the incipient days was the efforts of two of the stoutest anti-free lunch politicians ever elected to Congress. We had our faults, a shortage of humility being one of them. But we had no idea where our intentions would eventually lead when we started doing the supply-side fiscal math in early 1980.

Gramm and I worked more or less around the clock putting together a new budget and building a political coalition to support it. Eventually, we got our balanced budget cobbled together and called a press conference for 12 March 1980. We would unveil our 'Bipartisan Coalition for Fiscal Responsibility', and it would, we imagined, be nothing less than a sensation.

That morning the two of us walked into the conference room with our fifty-page budget document in hand. We took our places at the podiums. Behind us were enormous colored charts. In front of us were . . . well, nobody. That's not quite accurate; our interns had shown up. But no one else had, other than maybe one or two yawning reporters whose noses were deep in the sports sections.

'This is awful,' I whispered to Gramm, who did not disagree.

'They're probably late,' he said.

'No,' I said, 'I don't think so.'

We went out into the corridors and shuffled around while our press secretaries dashed about practically bribing people to come to our press conference.

Finally we persuaded some reporters they were about to miss out on a major event and our conference got covered—by the stringer for a local Texas paper and the *Detroit News*.

But we kept at it. Over the next few weeks we worked the corridors like Fuller Brush men.* It was sheer door-to-door. We told them, 'Look, the conservatives have *got* to have an alternative. Carter's trying to steal the balanced budget issue, and you know what a fraud *that*'s going to turn out to be. Here's our plan. It'll work.'

After an exhaustive round of salesmanship, we had raised fifty

* The archetypal door-to-door salesmen.

names in support of our budget plan. Those fifty formed the nucleus of what would become the Reagan coalition in the House of Representatives. They represented all the key blocs.

The old guard House Republican leadership was represented by Bob Michel and then Minority Leader John Rhodes. The 'young turk' Republican backbenchers in our group included Newt Gingrich and Trent Lott. Our plan also had the endorsement of a broad array of what were coming to be labelled Boll Weevil* Democrats, including Charlie Stenholm and Kent Hance from Gramm's own Texas delegation. Once in tow, the fifty elements became the mainstay of our coalition as the fiscal drama of the early 1980s got under way.

The content of our 1980 bipartisan budget was as similar to the first Reagan budget as were the players in our coalition. Both included several big ticket, multi-billion-dollar savings proposals: elimination of the CETA** public jobs boondoggle and reform of the out-of-control food stamp program were on the top of the list. Capping open-ended Medicaid reimbursement to the states and eliminating twice per year cost of living adjustments for federal retirees were also major savings items. Reform of the federal unemployment benefits and elimination of school lunch subsidies for upper-income families were part of the savings plan, too.

Our plan included a lot of smaller sized cutbacks as well. Legal Services, health grants, compensatory education, subsidized housing, low-income energy assistance and the community action agencies were on the chopping block for solid reasons. All these cuts would touch off raging hot controversies down the road in 1981.

By March 1980, almost a full year before he became President, the cuts that would be such a crucial part of Ronald Reagan's budget had been 'market-tested' among the coalition that would seize control of the House.

In the process of fashioning our sweeping new budget, Gramm and I discovered something important. Even the appearance of being an expert is self-validating. I didn't know much about budgets, but I knew more than the rest of them. It was a new market,

* The conservative Southern Democrats. The boll weevil is an insect native to the American South, which attacks the cotton plant from the inside.
** Comprehensive Employment and Training Act.

a new era—the era of budget *subtraction*. For the first time since the New Deal, everyone was talking about cutting the budget instead of adding to it.

It's hard to overemphasize how new this all was. We'd reached the demarkation point. Up to this point the legislative culture had only produced experts on how to add. They knew how to build up one program at a time. No one knew budget subtraction, the shrinking of everything at once.

But now the panic over the deteriorating economy was on. The stampede toward trying to get a balanced budget produced Congress's first plenary exercise in budget making in modern times —perhaps ever. Suddenly the entire budget was on the operating table, and for the first time the rank and file was demanding precise protocols for surgery.

So when our carefully organized script on how to balance the budget had begun to circulate through conservative and GOP ranks, our phones started ringing off the hook. Because we had the answers.

One of the old guard who was particularly impressed by our approach was then Minority Whip Bob Michel. He had spent years on the Appropriations Committee, nibbling away where he could. But no one had given him a big plan for real budget reduction before, because none had been demanded.

I overheard him one day reassuring a cold-footed colleague that the 'Bipartisan Plan' was OK to support. 'Stockman and Gramm have all the poop* you'll need to explain it back home, and it's packaged up right where you can get your hands on it,' he said.

The second phase of our project—incorporating the Kemp-Roth tax cuts into the plan—proved to be much harder. Our problems here foreshadowed the tensions and disagreements that would plague the Reagan coalition in 1981.

Once Carter and the Democrats announced their own balanced budget plan, to the accompaniment of much born-again chest-thumping about 'fiscal responsibility', the tension between Republican budget balances and tax cutters became acute. This was the case because it turned out that Kemp-Roth wasn't the only Republican tax-cutting idea designed to jump-start the economy. Barber Conable, who was the senior Republican on the tax committee and a

* Information.

genuine expert on the IRS* code, now had his tax plan ready to go, too.

Conable and his Ways and Means Committee Republicans had by now consolidated their own coalition. It was an awesome assembly of business lobbies and trade associations representing everything from autos to real estate, steel and zinc smelters. Their business interest groups were all united behind a proposal for a drastic liberalization of corporate depreciation allowances called '10–5–3'.

Essentially, 10–5–3 allowed companies to write off their buildings, machinery and vehicles, respectively, in a much shorter period of time. It thus greatly reduced their corporate taxes.

The old guard was much more comfortable with this approach than with the supply-side marginal tax rate reduction plan. Their idea of economic revival was to create loopholes and let the IRS take care of the micro-management. They'd been pushing these kind of threadbare palliatives for years. They were supposed to stimulate investment, jobs and economic growth. But what they mainly did was build up governmental power and economic inefficiency—the very things they professed to abhor.

The Republicans had thus come up with two tax cuts: Conable's interest group cut and the supply-side rate cut. The one was Washington politics; the other would liberate the private economy and entrepreneurs. They clashed philosophically, and it would be hell trying to get their two different kinds of math to add up.

In April 1980, Republican House members began meeting in an attempt to try to get our vastly different numbers to add up. These sessions were mind-numbing, wrenching, table-pounding, and abrasive. They were also endless.

In fact, they're still going on today, defying every effort to reach a consensus. But the outcome of the April 1980 meetings was that the old guard, confronted with something completely different, found it necessary—alas—to call on the services of their new 'expert' at budget subtraction to try to mediate.

So I dug in, trying, somehow, to reconcile $30 billion in tax cuts with the defense spending increases that were also being demanded by the more hawkish elements. The bottom line was that the whole

---

* Internal Revenue Service, the tax-collecting agency.

thing had to balance. We couldn't have a deficit—not in those days. The stakes were high. If I couldn't get the figures to come out right, supply side might abort right there and then.

By the end of March we'd revised the Gramm–Stockman plan in order to get everyone to agree to it. It now had both GOP tax cuts. We pumped up the spending cuts to $38 billion, instead of the original $26 billion. We got the entire package to come out at a balanced budget of $591 billion in spending and revenue.

Such miracles were possible in those pioneering times for two reasons. First, in those days the institution worked exclusively on a one-year budget time frame. The problem of massive, long-run fiscal imbalance had not yet materialized.

Under the circumstances, this approach wasn't unreasonable. Double-digit inflation was fueling nominal income growth at a prodigious rate and the tax code was not yet indexed. Consequently, out-year* estimates of current law revenue grew like Topsy—being pushed up by both inflation and bracket creep.

In fact, it was nearly impossible to produce a budget plan that caused a deficit in the out-years. The Carter Administration's 1980 mid-year budget was a representative projection of the time: it projected more than a $100 billion budget surplus by the fifth year. Even the big spending Democrats couldn't keep us out of the black!

This should have been a cause for suspicion. Something didn't parse there. If the horrendous inflation then under way were to be actually, abruptly stopped, as we were demanding, what would happen to all these happy budget numbers? We never got around to understanding the answer. But it was at the heart of the ruin we were driving toward.

Thus we were happy and dangerous innocents. We were able to embrace two big tax reduction plans and keep our numbers balanced. We concluded that a veritable gusher of revenue loss amounted to but a trickle.

The cost of the thirty percent Kemp-Roth rate cut and the 10–5–3 depreciation plan, after the economy's entire asset stock became eligible, was staggering. It would have reduced federal revenue by at least *one quarter of a trillion dollars* annually after four or five years. But you didn't get that far working on just the 1981 budget

---

* The period after a particular budget year.

numbers. By going only one year into the future, you got just the startup cost. In fact, we were able to reduce the revenue loss to only $16 billion, or six percent of its true long-run cost!

Shortly after all this giddy pencil work was completed, Minority Leader John Rhodes called a meeting of the House Republican Policy Committee. The time had come to settle on a Republican alternative to the Carter budget. It was incredibly noisy and contentious. Rhodes kept banging away at his podium like a besieged auctioneer trying desperately to maintain some vestige of decorum.

Having finally hammered the roomful of amok politicians to something resembling silence, he cleared his throat and in his natural soothing tones said, 'Fellas, I don't know whether everything you want in our budget can be reconciled or not. But I'm gonna call Dave Stockman up here to the podium, because he's got the closest thing to an answer that I've seen.'

Then, turning to me, he said: 'Dave, you're our expert. Come on up here and tell us how it all adds up.'

Thus I was officially anointed 'expert', a radical drafted into service by a nervous herd of pols who couldn't do it themselves but had no other choice.

Politicians, like baby ducklings, go through an 'imprinting' in the infancy of every major new issue. They learn where they stand and what side they're on. The Bipartisan Coalition Budget that Gramm and I launched in early 1980 constituted one of these experiences. It became the decisive 'imprinting' of our coalition on the economic and fiscal issues that would confront the Reagan Revolution in its early days.

The numbers and details would change a hundred times. Most of the rank and file never did keep up. But a basic lesson had now been learned.

'It might be possible to cut taxes, raise defense, and balance the budget,' they began to think. Gramm and Stockman have got it all penciled out.

And so I learned a lesson, too: it might be possible. Maybe you could harness a gutless herd of self-proclaimed conservative politicians to a sweeping fiscal policy revolution. Maybe the combination of supply-side tax cuts and at least the first installment of my anti-statist agenda for dramatically shrinking the federal budget was doable in the political world.

And so my scepticism about the prospects for a big change in national economic policy after the 1980 election further abated. The House opposition had now consolidated behind Kemp-Roth. It was time for the next phase in the chain reaction.

That took place two months later at the Republican Convention. I'd never been to a convention before I arrived in Detroit on a hot day in July. That admission should quickly dispose of the question of my expertise at pulling off platform coups. But that's why I'd come.

By now the Reagan camp had opened its doors and, to my mind, let in every crazy who'd knocked. There was no percentage to these groups and it looked like our scintillating supply-side platform was going to be trod all over by the ERA*-denouncing sour matrons of Phyllis Schaffley in their high-heeled shoes. That made the horror of a Carter reelection all the more plausible. There was work to do.

Conventions work on the principle of feigned democracy: lots of shouting and hollering and bargaining about the platform, as if it's all happening at the moment. Really, ninety-eight percent of it has all been decided by the time everyone gets there. The Republican 1980 Convention established a new record in the field of oligarchical writ. The head of the platform committee was the savvy GOP warhorse, John Tower of Texas.

Tower was possessed of a very powerful intellect and a rather domineering personality. He was something of a Napoleonic figure, standing as he did five foot four in his cowboy boots, and anyone who crossed him did so at great peril.

Tower was, at any rate, not only learned and brilliant, but extremely articulate. He was a big picture man; he had the larger view of things, especially where defense and foreign policy were concerned.

The last thing he wanted in Detroit was a squealing match about what the Republican Party stood for, and he had no patience whatsoever with amateurs from the political hinterlands—which is to say, almost all of the one hundred delegates on the committee—who wanted to meddle. Zero.

His co-chairman was Trent Lott, a fast-rising Republican star

---

* Equal Rights Amendment, a projected women's rights equality measure, attacked by many conservatives, among whom Phyllis Schaffley is prominent.

from Mississippi, a very smooth operator, the epitome of the new southern pol, and an ambitious one. Trent wanted to be the House Minority Whip and he became Minority Whip, in no small part due to his having put as many House Republicans as he could into leadership slots at the convention. I got one of these plums—the chairmanship of the Energy subcommittee. Even better, Lott had bent over backward to appoint supply siders. Senator Roth got the (crucial) Economic Policy subcommittee, and Brother Kemp was given the Defense and Foreign Policy chair. It was a coup, and another link in Wanniski's chain. Jude Wanniski was starting to look like a seer . . . and starting to act like one.

The draft platform we arrived in Detroit with—the same one that was supposedly to have been hammered out at the convention—was as near perfect as could be. I was ecstatic. The Republican Party was finally abandoning its muddled, 'me-too' statism. Our document wasn't a laundry list of Democratic ideas that we could do on the cheap; there were no fatuous pledges of 'government-industry cooperation' to 'help' i.e., override the market. It was a statement of principles and it was splendid.

I had written the Energy plank pretty much entirely myself. It was the plank that most clearly manifested an anti-statist breakthrough. The Carter energy 'Gosplan'* was then reaching its final absurdity. Nonsense had been springing up all over Washington's bureaucratic corridors: the windfall profits tax, the Synfuels Corporation**, deep tax credits for every kind of alternative energy, mandatory efficiency standards for cars and refrigerators and power plants, fuel allocation schemes of every manner. These had all been enacted, and more mischief lay waiting in the wings.

While much of the Republican herd had gone for this nonsense— especially western senators like Pete Domenici of New Mexico and Jim McClure of Idaho—they were now about to get new marching orders: *Dismantle it, all of it.*

The platform draft we pounded out in John Tower's Washington office had but one flaw. The whole seventy-five-page document contained only one, fairly anemic paragraph on the fundamental global menace of the hour: inflation. It just lay there on the page, standard jargon about 'too much money chasing too few goods'.

* The Soviet economic plan.
** A government agency set up to fund synthetic fuel research.

That was accurate enough. But it fell a long way short of expressing the gravity of the problem. Hyperinflation was the ultimate statist evil: *the deliberate debauching of the nation's money in a futile effort by politicians to compensate for the shortfalls of capitalist growth that their own misbegotten bureaucratic enterprises had caused.*

At a luncheon gathering of what amounted to the supply-side central committee, Kemp, Wanniski, Jeff Bell, others, and I decided that the monetary policy statement needed a little brain transfusion. It needed some intellectual content and grandeur.

With his eye toward history, Kemp immediately grabbed a napkin and started taking notes on it. (When scholars peer into the supply-side archive, all they're going to find is napkins.)

But as we sat around that table, we started to argue about our differences about the gold standard. They seemed to be superficial. I would have characterized them as 'nuancal'—except Al Haig hadn't invented the term yet. What I didn't realize at the time was that that argument foreshadowed a very deep split among supply siders on monetary policy too.

Jeff Bell had campaigned on the gold standard. He believed it had helped him politically. To Wanniski, gold was like the True Cross. They both wanted a 'strong statement' in there for the immediate restoration of the gold standard.

I was reluctant for both tactical and conceptual reasons. By then my worst fears about the press coverage of the convention had been realized. All the press was paying any attention to was the deletion of the Equal Rights Amendment from the GOP platform.

So now the entire supply-side gospel was being obscured by the anti-feminists and moral majoritarians. In this kleiglit atmosphere, gold was a potential four-letter word; it had a far-out ring to it. If we were going to say anything about restoring the gold standard, we had to be extremely careful.

We all agreed that the proximate cause of inflation was the excessive creation of money by the central bank. But the essence of whether you needed to get serious about restoring to a real live gold standard went deeper. Why did the Fed or any central bank persist in behavior that was economically destructive? Did it deliberately bring about a phenomenon that had no socially redeeming value whatsoever?

There were two ways to look at it. One emphasized intellectual error and a failure of technique by the central bank managers. If that was right you could solve the problem by shackling Federal Reserve Chairman Paul Volcker and his colleagues to the gold window. They would speed or slow money supply growth by buying or selling gold at a fixed price established in statute. Since no brainwork would be required, they wouldn't make any mistakes. Wanniski held to that view.

My own view was that the gold standard was really a metaphor for hard money and political discipline. Inflation traced back to the financial excesses and free lunch illusions of the politicians. The central bank managers didn't want inflation. They got pressured into it by the politicians' demands for the destructive antidote of easy money.

A clarion call on restoring the gold standard would thus cause more political problems than it was worth. So I argued for a statement directing the central bank to stand firm against the politicians. Wanniski agreed to it, but only after some language was put in strongly implying a return to the gold standard.

Wanniski and I argued over every word. But finally a compromise was made and inserted into the platform:

> Until the decade of the 1970s, monetary policy was automatically linked to the overriding objective of maintaining a stable dollar value. The severing of the dollar link with real commodities in the 1960s and 1970s, *in order to pursue economic goals other than dollar stability, has unleashed hyperinflationary forces at home and monetary disorder abroad, without bringing any of the desired economic benefits.* One of the most urgent tasks in the period ahead will be restoration of a dependable monetary standard— that is, an end to inflation.

As with most compromises, it didn't, in the end, stick. Eventually Wanniski would blame all the economic problems of the Reagan era on our failure to follow through on our platform's wan pledge of going back to gold. Yet as I learned, in the years ahead, about the realities of governance, the impulses I had had in Detroit grew into firm convictions. It was the indiscipline of the politicians, not the wilful and avoidable errors of the central bank, that threatened the integrity of the nation's money; in 1980, and always.

But for the time being this was just another small crack in our unity. The platform embodied our *Weltanschauung*. Supply side was the talk of the town, and our little circle was shaping the upcoming Reagan campaign against Carter. Kemp had hit prime-time TV—as a result of indefatigable backstage manoeuvering—and had delivered a pretty stirring call to the New Order.

And just five years after stumbling into politics, I'd left my mark on the national party and taken a turn at the podium myself (during non-prime time) to explain my piece of the platform to the faithful.

By the end of the convention I also had a new view of our nominee. The old Reagan had been transformed. He'd got the supply-side religion. He was a visionary national leader. His time had come. This was *our* Reagan.

I was not an emotional type, but it was impossible not to get caught up in the fervor that swept Cobo Hall. I finally understood why they called him the Great Communicator.

In a single rhetorical flourish he swept aside all the conventional Washington wisdom. His anti-statist tones were modern, progressive, and big-hearted. While it was Jack Kemp and Jeff Bell who put in the line 'No one shall be left behind', that completed his transformation from a sectarian champion of the privileged. His grand vision now contained all the supply-side code words: sound money, capitalist prosperity, social mobility, entrepreneurial dynamism, individual incentives. And they were coming in loud and clear.

After the speech, I was quite charged up. When I saw Wanniski, who looked like he'd been torched by the Burning Bush, I said: 'You're right. The Revolution is at hand.'

So now another link had snapped into place. We had a candidate and a platform; and the Republican Party was moving toward the supply side. That's what it looked like then, anyway.

When I got back from the convention, I was exhausted. Things were happening, and fast.

I saw my first task as turning the supply-side platform into a blueprint for governance. In hindsight, no one commissioned me to hold forth on exactly how to run the United States government. But there was substantial justification for my new endeavors.

The GOP had an economically radical platform, only the regular politicians didn't know what to do with it. What could Howard Baker do with the gold standard, for example? Probably he'd trade it in for another Clinch River breeder reactor or two.

Nevertheless, Reagan was ahead in the polls. It looked like he might pull it off in November. I kept pouring coffee into my body and churning.

By now the great ideological polarities of my mind had reached a zenith of definition. The supply-side celebration of growth was directly opposed to the neo-Malthusian dirge of scarcity. The capitalist idea of wealth creation stood at odds with the welfare state notion of redistribution. The requirements of market efficiency contradicted every work of political governance.

But though these ideas had reached prominence, their empirical content had still to be quantified. While I knew I had more than half the facts, I needed all of them. So I devoted much of the months of August and September to producing new material to defend the comprehensive supply-side economic program.

Here the chain reaction should have been disrupted. In doing my supply-side penal work I discovered that our two napkins* added up to a much more radical economic program than I had previously understood. If you implemented the Gold Standard Napkin and stopped inflation, Professor Laffer's Tax Cut Napkin didn't work. You would get more real economic growth but no gain in federal revenues. Consequently, only sweeping domestic spending cuts could balance the budget—an action that I believed was desirable but which the other supply siders had denied would be necessary.

I discovered this one napkin at a time, starting my homework by writing a defense of the gold standard. It was being regularly pounced on by economists and journalists as evidence of the 'far out' nature of supply-side economics. But these attacks were based on a Keynesian view of inflation—the refutation of which led me straight into the conflict between supply-side and federal deficits.

Supply-side doctrine held that inflation is a *monetary* phenomenon caused by the policies of the central bank, not an economic disorder caused by workers, businesses, investors or even speculators. The Keynesian revisionism of the prior two decades had stood this classic monetary view of inflation on its head.

* Laffer is popularly supposed to have drawn the first Laffer curve on a table napkin.

Consequently, rising real energy costs, protectionist trade barriers, mandated pollution control investments, agricultural price supports and much else had been erroneously identified as inflationary 'external shocks'. But these were actually impediments to growth of output and living standards. The only effective cure was cutting tax rates, subsidies and regulation.

This confusion about the cause of inflation was due to the fundamental Keynesian notion of 'monetary accommodation'. The latter had originally been used to justify deficit spending as a stimulant to national economic expansion. But if budget deficits are financed honestly—that is by borrowing in the capital markets, they don't stimulate the economy—they weaken it. Honest deficit financing merely shifts the economy's savings supply from productive private investment to wasteful public sector expenditures.

It was only the false Keynesian economic alchemy of dishonest deficit financing that made budget red ink look stimulative. If you financed fiscal deficits with printing press money—'monetary accommodation'—you could pump up the economy for at least a while.

The trouble was the whole easy money scheme was inherently unworkable for any sustained period of time. You couldn't make everyone wealthier by printing more money. It always and everywhere lead to inflation, speculation and cheap, unsustainable debt creation.

It was this 'accommodationist' imperative of Keynesian fiscal policy that had also destroyed the Bretton Woods hard money regime. By providing the politicians and policy makers with a fancy academic excuse for running chronic budget deficits, the 'new economists' had generated the proximate cause of Nixon's 1971 closure of the gold window. After that, paper money was no longer disciplined. All of the anti-growth influences of the 1970s had then been used to justify an orgy of central bank money creation both here and abroad. The result of this drastic policy error had brought the world to the brink of a dollar led hyperinflation by 1980.

The supply-side growth program would now remove any excuse for pressuring the central bank. The Fed had to be given a complete free hand to focus exclusively on the task of defeating inflation.

The crucial step toward restoring hard money was, therefore, the political insulation of the Federal Reserve. 'Chairman Volcker—the nearest proxy for gold on the horizon—needs time to reconstruct the dollar's integrity,' I wrote, 'by putting the economy on a leaner diet of new money and credit.'

Next I went to work on the budget math. It was no longer possible to rely on the contrived one-year balanced budget we had fashioned during the spring budget resolution battle. The economy had deteriorated badly in the interim. The optimistic economic assumptions that both sides had used were already out the window. The fiscal year 1981 budget—both ours and theirs—was now deeply in deficit.

The Democrats had also issued long-range budget projections purportedly showing that the Republican fiscal program would generate an endless flood of red ink. This brought a further urgency to the task.

So I began a stint of round-the-clock efforts. By early August I had produced a systematic estimate of the 1982–85 Republican fiscal plan. These numbers amply backed my contention that the Democrats' deficit predictions were 'built on a house of cards'.

This was the first effort ever made by our side to carefully price out the multi-year impact of deep tax cuts and a major defense build-up. It showed a $60 billion surplus by 1985!

In arriving at this miraculous conclusion the new House Republican budget 'expert' did not come close to measuring up to what he was being cracked up to be. The new estimates were neither logical, careful or accurate within a country mile.

The fatal error was embodied in the starting point that I had simply taken for granted. To calculate the impact of the Republican budget plan, I'd used the baseline economic assumptions of the Carter Administration's mid-session budget.

The latter assumed continued double digit inflation for several years *and* strong real GNP and employment growth, too. *That is, it embodied an economic scenario that I'd just proven to be impossible in the gold standard piece.*

The Carter revenue estimates assumed the greatest, sustained period of income tax bracket creep in US history. But when you started with an inflation and bracket creep swollen revenue level and trotted it out four or five years into the future, fiscal miracles were easy. You could have a whopping big tax cut and not create a deficit. Essentially, high inflation was raising projected taxes as fast as you were cutting them.

Thus stood unrecognized for the moment what would become the Achilles heel of supply-side budget math. A thirty percent rate reduction spread over three years in a ten percent inflation per annum economy amounts to a zero reduction in real tax rates. Such a tax cut wouldn't help the economy much and wouldn't hurt the budget much.

The same thirty percent tax reduction plan in an inflationless, gold standard economy was a horse of another color. It would amount to a thirty percent reduction in real tax rates. You would therefore need whopping big expenditure cuts to make the budget balance.

While continuing my supply-side pencil work in September I discovered the essence of this fundamental matter in an ironic way. It happened while I was playing tit for tat with the Democrats.

I had set my staff to work digging through the 1980 Democratic platform and Carter campaign statements in order to comprehensively document the other side's budget-busting promises. Then we would pin the 'disastrous deficit' charge back on the donkey where it belonged.

The budget impact of the Democrats' numerous spending promises such as national health insurance and more aid to education would have been staggering: they amounted to $100 billion per year in added spending by 1985 alone.

Then something screwy occurred. When you added the enormous cost of these new spending initiatives to the Carter budget under current policy, your hand calculator went tilt. It said the bottom line still came out in surplus by 1985!

'This can't be!' I declaimed, while storming around my office like some dervish.

So I went back to the drawing board. This time I discovered the illusionary revenue windfalls owing to continued double-digit inflation. When I substituted a rapid decline in inflation, the Democrats' spending promises resulted in plenty of red ink. But there was no $60 billion budget surplus at the end of the supply-side rainbow either.

Instead, I discovered that to balance the budget we would need huge spending cuts too—more than $100 billion per year. The fabled revenue feedback of the Laffer curve had thus slid into the grave of fiscal mythology forty days after the supply-side banner had been hoisted up at the GOP convention.

These dramatic changes in both my comprehension of budget estimating and the true fiscal math of the supply-side program occurred almost overnight. That should have been cause for second thoughts and reassessment of the whole proposition.

But it didn't happen that way.

At the time, the prospect of needing well over $100 billion in domestic spending cuts to keep the Republican budget in equilibrium appeared more as an opportunity than as a roadblock. Once Governor Reagan got an electoral mandate for Kemp-Roth and 10–5–3, then we would have the Second Republic's craven politicians pinned to the wall. They would have to dismantle its bloated, wasteful, and unjust spending enterprises—or risk national ruin.

The idea of a real fiscal revolution, a frontal attack on the welfare state, was beginning to seem more and more plausible. Now, the fiscal element had been linked into the chain reaction, too.

My election night headquarters were in a bankrupt car dealership in Buchanan, Michigan, a heartland town that took its unfailing Republicanism more seriously than anything except basketball. After forty years in the political wilderness, the local stalwarts were about to see their philosophy triumph. I thought it was kind of an ironic place in which to celebrate a Republican victory, but at least it wasn't a Chrysler dealership.

I put a lot of stock in the victory being celebrated that night—too much, as it turned out. Carter's concession was gratifying, but the other results were more instructive.

As the evening wore on, my eyes remained fixed on the House and Senate races across the nation. We needed a substantial transfusion of fresh conservative blood. Otherwise, the world's greatest parliamentary institution would grind the revolution to a halt, presidential mandate or not.

The news that the rogues gallery of midwestern liberal senators and congressmen were being chucked out provided all the answer I needed. Birch Bayh of Indiana, Frank Church of Idaho, Dick Clark of Iowa, House Minority Whip John Brademas, George McGovern—all went down and out.

Kemp and I kept calling one another in a delirium of excitement, pausing amid the reports only to remind each other that unless we got to work immediately, the landslide would end in a heap of rubble. But there was so much good news that night.

There had been a string of unmistakably conservative victories: Alfonse D'Amato in New York, Paula Hawkins in Florida, Don Nichols in Oklahoma, Mack Mattingly in Georgia, Jim East in North Carolina. The Republicans had gained control of the Senate for the first time since 1954. At 2.00 am I left the Buick dealership and went home to catch four hours of sleep at my parents' farmhouse in Scottdale. Tomorrow, the revolution would begin.

Now it was time for the year's unlikely chain of events to reach its apotheosis. As soon as I got back to Washington, Kemp and I launched a campaign to secure me a position in the new Cabinet. The odds were long. I was young and relatively inexperienced.

We had lunch with columnist Bob Novak. He's a brooding, brilliant reporter who is known around Washington as the 'Prince of Darkness'. Novak has a steeltrap mind and he knew our catechism cold. He wasn't like many of the other self-righteous reporters who pretended that they were objective but were really liberals.

Novak's typewriter didn't even work in the objective mode. Everything which came out was pure bias—in behalf of the supply side. Naturally I considered that first-class reporting. He was dealing in truth, not just news.

Novak wrote a column saying there was a movement growing to put Stockman in at the Office of Management and Budget. At the time he wrote it, it was a movement of three or four, if you included the minority of my staff that favored the idea. But after his column appeared, it did become a movement of sorts.

Dick Whalen, the economics writer and a good friend of mine, spoke to Senator Paul Laxalt, Reagan's closest Washington adviser. Whalen then personally escorted me to Laxalt's office for a close-up inspection.

We continued to plot. 'We're going to have to make an Inchon landing,' Kemp said. Jack would be the MacArthur of this daring operation. He was heavily influenced by Wanniski's facility for putting everything in terms of changing the course of Western civilization. But, essentially, he was right that we had to mount some operation to make sure the revolution wouldn't be stillborn.

We decided that we needed a statement, a bell-ringer that would focus the economic discussions on the supply-side model and agenda. It would put the details and numbers on the whole sweeping economic plan.

The only paper on hand that contained any hard, multiple year budget numbers was a quick and dirty estimate Marty Anderson and Alan Greenspan had put together to accompany a speech made by Reagan on September 9 in Chicago. But in their understandable haste to make the numbers add up, they had taken too many shortcuts. They had reduced the prospective Republican defense build up from seven percent real growth to five percent, and had used a far less costly business tax cut than 10–5–3.

They had also used a high inflation revenue baseline which was more mucked up than the one I had earlier got myself impaled upon. To achieve its fifteen percent annual growth rate for nominal GNP would have required the biggest explosion of printing press money in US history. Hence, the 'Chicago statement', as it was known, added up to budget balance without draconian domestic spending cuts. The trouble was, the numbers were worthless.

I volunteered to write the needed, accurate blueprint. I wanted to get the true, sweeping magnitude of the budget retrenchment we needed out on the table. People needed to know what we were biting off. Jack agreed, and said he should have the paper with him when he flew out to California to meet with the Reagan economic high command several days hence.

I knew that if my paper were good enough it would improve my chances. So I embarked on the usual round-the-clock stint, getting home after midnight, getting up at five.

I went Kemp's Inchon one better and titled it: 'On the Danger of a GOP Economic Dunkirk.' Its tone was admittedly alarmist.

By then I had had exposure to all of the players in the emerging new Republican regime. I began to realize that a rather awesome responsibility rested on my shoulders. It seemed unaccountable but I knew it was true. I was the only one who had done even a minimal degree of careful, serious homework on the fundamental fiscal math of the whole economic policy revolution that was about to be launched. It was a pretty frightening thought.

By now I was also sweating about the budget numbers for another reason. Not only had every current and prospective short-term economic indicator taken a turn for the worse during the course of the campaign, but Congress had not even enacted the modest budget cuts it had endorsed the previous spring. The Reagan Administration would inherit a budget deeply in deficit. It would also face a grim long-term fiscal outlook.

There was a clear danger that if this deterioration went too far, the political cohesion of the new conservative congressional coalition would be strained to the breaking point. Draconian domestic spending cuts would then be needed to maintain a reasonably balanced budget while the tax cuts were being phased in. If the spending cuts couldn't be achieved, we might fail to enact Kemp-Roth. The revolution would be over before it started.

This foreboding sense of being overtaken by events and economic conditions motivated the alarmist tone of my GOP economic Dunkirk memo. The split between tax cutters and budget balancers was already gaining new intensity within the recently victorious conservative governing coalition. A Dunkirk-scale economic setback might be the final outcome by November 1982. But it would have originated in a self-administered political breakdown among the conservative forces early in 1981.

The somber economic outlook of late 1980 had raised yet another profound new issue in my mind regarding supply side. The possibility now loomed that the tight money cure for inflation might bring the economy down before the tax cut and other supply-side cures took hold.

Doctrinaire monetarists and true gold bugs probably anticipated a recession all along. But in the supply-side circle, we viewed the idea of putting the economy through a recessionary wringer as a politically costly and economically futile form of Hooverism.

The heart of the supply-side synthesis rested on the notion of a 'push-pull' economic dynamic. Hard money policies would 'pull-down' the rate of inflation and nominal GNP growth. The tax cut and whole range of supply-side economic policy changes would 'push-up' the rate of real output and employment expansion. Both effects would occur in a simultaneous time frame.

You could argue the theoretical merits of this hypothesis a long time. But you started to believe in push-pull once you understood that a recession would bring a deficit horror show.

Still, by November it was getting pretty hard not to worry about the push-pull scenario. Money supply growth from mid-summer onward had nearly gone into orbit, necessitating an abrupt, compensating slow down that risked tilting the economy into recession during 1981.

But I had acquired some amateur's knowledge of rational expectations theory and the mechanics of financial markets. This permitted me to sidestep the precipice of recession with a *fiscal expectations* theory of rapid and dramatic financial market recuperation resulting from the new Administration's policies.

The markets would soon see that we were not fiscal con men or practitioners of 'voodoo economics', waiting for economic magic to balance the budget as the opposition had charged. The real Reagan supply-side program would embody a solid and sweeping anti-free lunch plan based on unprecedented retrenchment of Federal entitlement, subsidy and cheap credit programs.

The assurance would permit the capital markets—stocks and bonds—to revive and thrive. The nation's business balance sheets, now bulging with short-term loans, could then be refinanced with long-term capital. This would alleviate money market pressures sufficiently to grant the Fed* a narrow margin in which to sharply curtail money growth without triggering a recession.

These worries and brave answers were stuffed into the Dunkirk memo. It's strange that it became known as the blueprint for the Reagan-Revolution. It was actually a treatise on the risks of a fiscal shipwreck.

Bleary-eyed, I eventually handed Jack the document and he flew off to Los Angeles to meet with the glitterati of the economic world. Arthur Burns, former chairman of the Fed, would be at the meeting. So would Herb Stein and Paul MacCraken, both former chairmen of the Council of Economic Advisors. 'Dunkirk' was more than a thirty-five page operational blueprint for reviving the economy. It was my résumé.

Apparently, it made a good impression in those economic salons. A few days later the phone rang. It was Cap Weinberger, wondering if I would be interested in being the President's Secretary of Energy.

I surprised myself by telling him no. My decision wasn't based on

* Federal Reserve Bank.

the fact Reagan had campaigned on a pledge to abolish the Department of Energy. Actually, I wanted the OMB, the Office of Management and Budget. I told Weinberger that if he wasn't interested in his old job again, I was.

Throughout November, the winds from California bore whispers that my prospects were good. What I would have rated a virtual impossibility a month earlier now looked increasingly possible.

One day in early December, Jack Kemp, who had been laboring mightily on my behalf, said to me, 'They've made a decision. You're going to get a call.'

Not long afterwards, the transition office* called mine and asked where I would be the evening of December 3.

My friend Dick Fairbanks, a lawyer and itinerant policy activist who'd been in the Nixon and Ford administrations and was now involved in the Reagan transition, was having a dinner party at his house near the Washington Cathedral. I told him beforehand that the call would be coming. (And of course Dick told everyone who was coming. They were kind enough to pretend they didn't know it.)

He had a beautiful library, and had quietly made arrangements for me to take the call there when it came. We were in the middle of cocktails when it did.

Since I knew the call was coming, it was somewhat anticlimactic. Still, my mouth went dry and my pulse started to pound.

I'd worked out a little script with some clever lines. But during the interminable two minutes I spent pacing in Dick's library waiting for the operator to call back the lines just . . . vanished from my mind. When the phone finally rang, my hands were trembling. It was the first time I had ever spoken to a President.

All that came out was a flat midwestern 'Haallo?'

It didn't matter. As I would learn again and again, Ronald Reagan had the gift of setting you utterly at ease.

'Dave, I've been thinking,' he said in a relaxed, melodious voice, 'about how to get even with you for that thrashing you gave me in the debate rehearsals. So I'm going to send you to OMB.'

I forget exactly what came out of my mouth in response, but I think it was something along the lines of, 'This is the opportunity of a lifetime, and I'm ready to give it everything I've got.'

* An office set up by an incoming president to organize the change of administration and of office holders.

When I got back to the dinner party, I said, 'I've got a new job.'
Everyone pretended to be surprised, and Dick made a toast. Jennifer
Blei, who would become my wife two years later, knew that she was
about to become a widow, losing me to the twenty-four hour days at
the White House. But she too smiled and congratulated me. And so
the adventure began. Another link in the chain had been snapped
into place.

But soon trouble on the supply-side also began. By mid-December
that same year the financial markets were in a total rout. On
December 18, I travelled to New York to make a whirlwind
it's-gonna-be-OK trip of the major financial houses. I took along a
flying hit squad: Wanniski, the tax-cutter, and Dick Whalen, a more
orthodox, hard money, anti-deficit Republican.

I went straight to the premier anti-supply-side bear on Wall
Street, Dr Henry Kaufman of Salomon Brothers. He was, to put it
mildly, deeply sceptical of supply side. Try as I did to persuade him,
I left him as unconvinced as I had found him. He did, however, say
that he was relieved—even amazed—that I had a massive, detailed
plan to cut spending, and that I wasn't a complete creature of
Laffer's contention that tax cuts would be self-financing.

'The tax cut has to be *earned*,' I told him, 'through the sweat of the
politicians.'

I repeated this message at a half-dozen sceptical finance houses.

I went from my no-free lunch to a free dinner at the Century Club
hosted by Lew Lehrman. Jack Kemp was there, as well as Alan
Greenspan.

No sooner had dinner begun than Wanniski turned from digging
into his food to digging into me.

'The street's delirious!' he said. 'Stockman spent the whole day
selling root canal and threatening to heave widows and orphans into
the snow.' Great, I thought.

There ensued one of those discussions of the kind that are usually
described in the press as 'frank and businesslike'. It was heated, but
it was also scintillating.

Together, Jude Wanniski and Lew Lehrman were the Odd
Couple of supply side. Wanniski was very easygoing and a bit
unkempt. Lehrman was very formal, rigid, austere. He wore
suspenders and never had a hair out of place. What they had in

common was their revolutionary temperament. Their type was much in evidence in St Petersburg in 1917.

Thus the Wanniski faction insisted—more strongly than ever before, now that we were no longer just talking theory—that a sweeping budget reduction blitzkrieg would be a serious strategic mistake.

'If the administration wastes its political capital on budget cutting and imposing a lot of societal pain and sacrifice,' insisted Wanniski, 'the battle for marginal tax rate reduction, the gold dollar, and supply-side prosperity will be lost. We'll end up with Republican austerity as usual.'

Wanniski and his allies were, empirically speaking, wrong. The 'coast-to-coast soupline' that I had warned about in my Dunkirk memo could only be prevented by two things, according to Wanniski: growth and gold. I'd sensed from the beginning of my supply-side indoctrination that that proposition was theoretically upside down. Taming the welfare state was the real problem. And failure to tackle it head on would only ultimately discredit the growth and gold approaches. As I left the Century Club that night, I knew that the central committee had arrived at a moment of truth, but I would cling for a while longer to the hope that our differences were more a matter of tactics than doctrine.

Now came the final link. I soon discovered that it would be up to me to design the Reagan Revolution. December brought hints, suggestions and circumstantial evidence that the Californians— including the most crucial Californian—were neither equipped nor inclined to launch the kind of sweeping anti-statist revolution implied in the supply-side platform.

Ed Meese, Counsellor to the President, was clearly in charge, and was doggedly pursuing a dawn-to-dusk schedule of meetings, events and endless 'planning' sessions. Meese had a massive network of worker bees churning out voluminous reports on every single federal agency. The daily plenary staff sessions started at 7.00 am sharp, with Meese ploughing through a list of 'agenda items' that got longer with each day. On one occasion he briefed me on his grand design for cabinet government by proudly displaying an organization chart that looked like a plan for the invasion of Normandy, so mind-boggling was its detail.

THE COMING OF THE NEW ORDER

But by Christmas I had realized that all the frantic motion and organization was just a screen. The Californians had no strategic plan for launching their government, to say nothing of a 'Reagan Revolution'. You couldn't fault Meese for energy and earnestness, but really he was just playing pick-up sticks on a table that was groaning beneath the weight of minutiae. Everything was getting attention; nothing was getting priority.

Meanwhile, the economic indicators were worsening by the day, making the new administration's essential job—restoring non-inflationary prosperity—a nearly insuperable challenge. Yet the economic team wasn't being assembled with any more urgency than anything else.

It was evident that Meese was the acting President. But it was also obvious that the Lilliputians already had him tied down on the mat. They had him thrashing around with everything.

There was one other troubling sign.

We had had a few informal sessions with the President-elect, during which he simply listened, nodded, and smiled. 'We have a great task ahead of us,' he would presently say, but he never finished the sentence. He gave no orders, no commands; asked for no information; expressed no urgency. This was startling to me. All my mentors and rabbis had been intellectual powerhouses: Morrison, Moynihan, Anderson, Kemp. Even Grampa Bartz. They had all burned with ideas, curiosity.

Now my greatest rabbi of all, the President-elect of the United States, seemed so serene and passive. He conveyed the impression that since we all knew what needed to be done, we should simply get on with the job. Since I *did* know what to do, I took his quiet message of confidence to be a mandate. If the others weren't going to get his administration's act together, I would.

On December 19, I wrote a memo to Meese and Jim Baker. It began: 'Our enemy is time.' I sketched out an action plan for launching the entire Reagan Revolution for economic recovery within three weeks of the inauguration. To my surprise, they both agreed with it.

Now I had the ball. I began a backbreaking day and night stint that would be as frantic and exhausting as baling the hay before the rain in the years of my youth. But with the revolution at hand, I could do no less.

PART TWO

3

Blitzkrieg

Two months later, on 18 February 1981, the new President went before a joint session of the Congress to announce a sweeping, revolutionary economic program—his 'Program for Economic Recovery'. It was a prosaic name for a plan that was, in fact, an astounding aberration in the rhythms of American democratic government.

Most great national policy enterprises are nurtured, shaped, screened, debated, refined—and virtually resolved—in the clamorous and multiple chambers of our Madisonian democracy. Only later are they given final articulation and blessing in a message of state.

Major presidential initiatives are almost always incrementalist; that is, they reflect a consensus that has already congealed. If they are 'bold' or 'new' or 'visionary', those qualities are usually to be found in the accompanying rhetorical flourishes and trumpet blasts.

Ronald Reagan's plan was different. It had not been around very long at all. It had travelled the more abbreviated and singular path postulated by Jude Wanniski's relay chain of revolutionary advance.

Wanniski's chain reaction had, incredibly, reached the fifth and final link that night of 18 February 1981. It proved him at once prescient and lucky—the odds of its happening were in the one thousand-to-one range.

The mere fact of the President's proclamation did not, of course, mean that supply side had become national policy. But Ronald Reagan was the Great Communicator, the most impressive and compelling head of state since Roosevelt.

On the night of February 18, he was speaking to an assembly of desperate politicians who had come into the chamber clutching the bloodied remains of their Keynesian and statist solutions. They knew they had lost their way—and now they were looking to him for a new way. They applauded him again and again that night, leaving no doubt that they were predisposed to grant him extraordinary latitude in finding a new remedy for the nation's economic ills. They were disposed to gamble, not because they understood the plan or even accepted it, but because they had lost all faith in the remedies tried before.

Ronald Reagan's radical economic program, therefore, was already well advanced toward becoming policy the night it was proclaimed. Peer review would, of course, occur in the legislative chambers. But the plan already had momentum, and few were standing in its way.

Soon it would affect the national and global economy with a gale force that would not blow itself out until the end of the decade, possibly even the century. American governance would also be profoundly transformed. For the moment, at least, the President's speech represented the astonishing triumph of the ideology of a few over the political necessities of the many.

That night I crossed the exact spot on the stairway to the House Chamber where I had stood as an impetuous seventeen-year-old vowing, like MacArthur, to return. A funny thing happened: I got goosebumps again. This time they weren't caused by youthful illusions of grandeur but by profound satisfaction. It had been a rough forty days.

Rough—and exceedingly presumptuous, as I reflect back on it. Designing a comprehensive plan to bring about a sweeping change in national economic governance in forty days is a preposterous, wantonly reckless notion. At the time I had thought it was merely an exhausting but exhilarating ordeal. Somewhere deep in my mind, though, lurked a patina of doubt.

I did have a secret sounding board off which I was able to bounce these embryonic, confused thoughts: William Greider of *The Washington Post*.

Greider was a tall, thin man in his mid-forties with a weather-beaten face. He looked like a reporter who'd been through the wringer.

I'd called him on occasion to ask him to publish one of my articles in the *Post*'s 'Outlook' section. He was a very able articulator of the liberal point of view, and a good arguer. Like me, he was anti-political. He felt that policy ought to be built on ideas, not power. We'd established a good rapport and he had gradually become my intellectual sparring partner. Recently, he'd been promoted to assistant managing editor for national news.

Back in December 1980, he had called me with a proposition. The supply-side experiment was going to be a fascinating time, although he didn't believe that the political system would ultimately buy it. So, he said, let's hold regular meetings and discuss the progress of the experiment. He'd keep a record of how it went and someday write the story.

I had a lot of trust in, as well as respect for, Greider. The reason I accepted had, in large measure, to do with my background. I would never be comfortable with what I viewed as the primitive, right-wing conservatism of my grandfather or Goldwater—or Reagan.

My intellectual impulse was to try to penetrate the citadel of establishment opinion makers—and those opinion makers hung out, so to speak, in the pages of *The Washington Post*. They were the modern secularists I was trying to convert.

We agree that Greider wouldn't publish anything on our meetings until after the season's political battles were over and our program had become legislation. We didn't talk over any of the precise details of the arrangement; I assumed there would be time for that down the road. I did not realize what exactly lay awaiting me at the end of that road.

So, oddly enough, it was to a member of the liberal press that I found myself inadvertently confessing the haste with which I was turning my Grand Doctrine into a national economic policy blueprint. Not long before the President's February 18 announcement, Greider cut short one of my Gatling-gun bursts of fact and detail about the plan. He asked me to step back and reflect: 'Where are you physically and spiritually?'

I ducked the question, but the answer I gave revealed something of how the most sweeping change in twentieth-century national economic policy was coming about.

'I'm sort of into a permanent mobilization,' I told him. 'I just go home and sleep for a few hours and come back and start pushing. I'll philosophize about it afterwards. I can't do it now. I've just got to keep moving.'

The feverish work of January and early February 1981 was not policymaking, at least in the normal sense. No basic policy options were appraised, discussed, or debated.

There was no final compromise, reflecting an ultimate balance between the policymaker's claims as to what should be done and the politician's sense of what *can* be done. Yet this is the very equation which ordinarily keeps the system hitched. It is what bends every aspiration to make things better toward the powerful inertia which keeps everything the same.

The fundamentals of the Reagan fiscal program—the big tax cut, the defense buildup, an anti-inflation monetary policy, and a balanced budget—had been given *a priori*. The tumultuous work prior to February 18 was purely ministerial. It amounted to the translation of doctrine into the customary details, numbers, and formats of workaday policy.

The broad policy architecture of the plan was riddled with potential contradictions. It cried out for a good afternoon and evening's debate.

The main reason there was no debate was that the remaining variable in the policy equation was domestic spending cuts, and in the mind of the plan's architect—me—that remained almost infinitely elastic. The domestic spending cut could be sized modestly or massively, depending upon what was required to make everything else add up.

There was only one heavy task to perform prior to the February 18 launching of the revolution. In forty days the budget-cutting assembly line would have to be geared up to run at breakneck speed.

Ordinarily, the White House politicians would have had their eyes glued on this aspect of the operation especially. The size of the spending-cut number was where ideological doctrine and political possibility should have had their showdown.

But the showdown never happened. The pace was so hectic that the White House never really knew what the domestic spending-cut number was. The lynchpin of the plan was shrouded in a haze of rapidly changing figures.

There was another problem, too. None of the key White House

advisers—Meese, Deaver, Baker—knew enough about American fiscal politics to assess the number, even if they had had it. The President had no idea of its political implications at all.

Nevertheless, I began cranking up the budget-cutting machinery on a frantic schedule in late December. The President's two most senior advisers, Chief of Staff Jim Baker and Counselor Ed Meese, had both given me the go-ahead—for different reasons.

Baker was clearly the most competent of the inner circle, but for the time being he was staying away from all economic policy. His appointment as Chief of Staff had come as an utter shock to the true blue Reaganauts. To them, Baker was tainted goods. He'd been Gerald Ford's campaign manager and George Bush's campaign manager. And where economic policy was concerned, Jim Baker was a bright neon light that blinked: 'VOODOO ECONOMICS!'

On matters of policy and substance, Baker was a 'leaner'; that is, given the choice between more central government and bureaucracy versus greater emphasis on private markets and local government, he inclined strongly toward the latter. But Baker was, deep down, neither very versed on matters of policy nor intensely interested in them. As long as it was directionally sound, he was satisfied.

In late December, Jim Baker recognized one fact above all else: with the prime rate* at an incredible 21.5 percent and with another recession threatening, the economy would dominate the national agenda during the first year of his boss's administration.

He also knew he wouldn't get any policy ideas from others in the inner circle. Meese had by now entombed himself beneath a pyramid of paper and disorganization. He never met a committee he didn't like.

Mike Deaver had never even feigned an interest in policy. But then he was busy stage-managing the upcoming inaugural—hiring elephants and Frank Sinatra. So when Baker saw that his new colleague from the congressional back benches was eager and organized and had a script almost ready to go, he was relieved.

Meese's reason for giving me the mandate had to do with a failure to comprehend what I would be doing. Feeling the way he did about committees, he readily agreed when I proposed that we form another one, an Economic Policy Steering Committee.

* The rate of interest set by banks to their prime customers, which then becomes a standard rate by which other commercial interest rates are set.

He was the world's greatest compartmentalizer. He believed that broad policy would be made in the Cabinet and its departments with presidential review and approval. The government's technical 'budget and auditing' work, as he called it, would go on in OMB. What he didn't fathom was that policy and the budget are inextricable. He granted me a much greater charter than he realized.

I had urged a monstrously ambitious schedule for launching the administration's first—and most critical—initiative. It would have to be done, I warned, *within ten to fifteen days of [the] inauguration.*

My motivation for such an inhuman schedule was grandiose. I reckoned that the 'window' for successfully launching sweeping change in national economic policy would be exceedingly brief. The deteriorating economy and resurgent political forces of the status quo would quickly overtake the new administration. In combination, the two could blow apart the tenuous budget equation that held the supply-side program intact.

If the plan were launched nearly instantly after inauguration, maybe these forces could be preempted. The administration's plan might take the Congress by storm and achieve enactment by late spring. Successful enactment would jolt the economy onto a new, healthier path. We would get ahead of the political curve before the politicians reverted to the customary destructive business of the Second Republic.

Neither Meese nor Baker probably ever appreciated the tenuousness of the opening that I saw or the risks of racing for it. Certainly, they did not understand the reason for doing so.

Nevertheless, Meese made only a single change in the action plan I proposed. The word 'Coordinating' was substituted for 'Steering' in my committee's title: the Economic Policy Coordinating Committee. Undoubtedly, he fancied himself doing the steering. The breakneck enterprise of remaking the fiscal world in forty days was on its way.

Neither Meese nor Baker attended the Committee's first meeting, but Don Regan* did. It was during this period that I got my first chance to size him up.

To the world I inhabited, Regan was an ideological neuter. He'd

---

* Secretary of the Treasury.

1

My family worked a hundred-acre farm near Scottdale, Michigan, since the 1870s, when my grandfather's father got off the boat from Germany. Growing up on a farm instills ambition in you. The results of your work are so visible.

2

3

4

(*Left*) In my senior year of high school, I won an essay contest with a prize that took me to Washington, D.C. I promised myself that someday I would return. (*Above*) In college I fell into the clutches of campus radicalism. Like many in my generation, I took up Marxism and America-hating.

6

Congressman John Anderson of Illinois needed a "bright young idea man" for his staff in Washington. This was the real thing. I was on my way.

5

At Harvard Divinity School, I got a job working for Daniel Moynihan (*right*), Harvard prof and chief domestic adviser to the intrigue-laden White House. In him I found my Washington-connected rabbi. Soon Nixon's anti-market economics left me a born-again capitalist.

Carter's futile anti-inflation projects closed the loop in my quest for the Grand Doctrine. Ronald Reagan saw Tip O'Neill *(right)* as the embodiment of what had gone wrong with government over the past forty years.

7

ELECT
DAVE STOCKMAN
U.S. CONGRESS

8

At the victory party with me were my parents *(right)* and my grandfather, William H. Bartz, who had farmed those same hundred acres but had gone on to an inspiring career in politics.

9

10

At the 1980 convention, I had helped write the President's bold platform calling for sweeping economic policy change. "The revolution is at hand," I thought. My attitude was that revolutionaries don't cut deals, they cut heads.

11

(Above) Designated as director of the Office of Management and Budget by President-elect Reagan, I didn't know much about budgets, but I knew more than most of them.

(Right) Richard Darman was more patient than I was. He believed you had to inch the political process along. You couldn't expect to get there tomorrow. I learned the hard way that he was right.

12

13

At a breakfast meeting with Jesse Helms *(center)* and my political guru Jack Kemp *(right)*, who was at the center of the supply side movement. Helms's beloved tobacco subsidy was the worst symbol of the old order we intended to overthrow.

Jim Baker was a decent student of policy but an awesome student of politics. He struck me as the one who really knew what he was doing.

14

15

Gramm-Latta was our own "bipartisan substitute" budget plan. It was this document that the House would approve on the day of the vote. Del Latta *(left)* was one of the few stalwart anti-spenders among the House GOP. Phil Gramm *(right)* was an ally of mine from Congress days. Democrats don't lightly vote Republican. They needed one last shove and he provided it.

Don Regan (*left*) was determined that his view should prevail at the policy review sessions. (*Second from left*) Ed Meese's kind of consensus is the sort that makes everybody happy, which is no way to make a revolution; it was evident that he was the acting President. (*Right*) William Clark's sole qualification was a desire to serve his country.

John Block (*left*) professed to be a stout free marketer and I believed him; once he got his "running room," he never stopped running—backward. Richard Schweiker (*center*) didn't want to get skinned by his committees; he knew exactly where *not* to cut. Sam Pierce (*right*) launched a successful campaign to spare the Urban Development Action Grant program, called UDAG, when PORK would have been more accurate.

18

For Mike Deaver and the others, reality happened once a day, on the evening news. They lived off the tube.

19

G. V. "Sonny" Montgomery, shown here, and Charlie Stenholm were the pivotal Democratic "Boll Weevils."

I got rolled by Al Haig. He never doubted who was in charge.

20

Ed Koch (*left*), the mayor of New York City, received a gift from the mayor of the nation. I intended to scrap local transit and transportation subsidies. The Secretary of Transportation, Drew Lewis, turned completely white when I first laid out my plans.

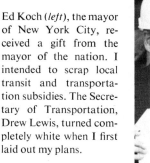

21

The irony was extreme: Caspar Weinberger, the Secretary of Defense of the most tight-fisted and anti-bureaucratic administration of this century, had produced a trillion-dollar budget. Cap the Knife had become Cap the Shovel.

22

We were engaged in a battle of ideas. The Reagan Revolution could never be won unless the establishment politicians and opinion makers gave our ideas a fair hearing. *(Left to right)* Senator Russell Long: No one passed a tax bill without him in twenty years; his pet projects were cut out of the budget but reinstated. Senator Bob Dole: Never before was the game of fiscal governance played so seriously and brilliantly as it was in his office. Senator Harry Byrd: A true fiscal conservative who quit early in the game.

23

been all over the lot. On the one hand, he'd been in favor of wage and price controls; on the other, he'd been an innovator of deregulation in the securities industry. He told me he was working hard to 'get up to speed' on the plan, but didn't suggest a more deliberate pace. My blitzkrieg schedule was OK by him because he didn't know any better, either.

Late in the evening of December 30, I called Ed Meese in California to tell him our plan and to urge him to reserve a slot in the President-elect's schedule the following week. He agreed. Things were moving rapidly forward.

Since the economic forecast was crucial to the architecture of the whole economic plan, we had placed high priority on it at the December 30 meeting. Ordinarily there would have been numerous heavy oars in the water. But it ended up being the work of ideologues and technicians. That, too, was another mishap of the blitzkrieg now under way.

The professional economist who heads the CEA* is usually the one in charge of such forecasts. But by early January, no one had been appointed head of the Council.

The Secretary of the Treasury also usually plays a major role in economic forecasting. However, Don Regan somehow got the idea that it was only technical formality—something the OMB director needed in order to come up with his budget numbers. 'It looks to me like I'm going to have a month to catch up while you work your tail off on budget cuts,' he said. 'I didn't come to make tax policy. My job is to execute and sell what the President has already decided. So there's not much left to do except tie the ribbon on Kemp-Roth and 10–5–3.'

I was relieved to know that there would be no debate about supply-side tax doctrine with the Secretary of the Treasury. But with the first big presidential review only a week off, we faced a serious dilemma. The interim forecasters group could not agree on a five-year economic scenario. I immediately realized it was going to take a lot more time than we had allotted to produce any kind of consensus forecast.

This meant that we would be flying blind for a while as to the precise size of the spending cut needed to balance the equation. We'd

* Council of Economic Advisors.

be scrambling to assemble the budget cut package while working against a moving target.

While this was an inherently dangerous strategy, I did not perceive its political implications at all. My anti-spending ideology meant that the tax cuts could be paid for under any economic forecast.

The January 7 meeting at Blair House, across the street from the White House, was the new administration's first serious look at the economic horizon and the choices it would have to make.

The President-elect's attendance drew all his senior officers— Bush, Meese, Baker, me, Anderson—into the same room for the first time. I was seated next to the President-elect. I hadn't spoken with him, except for one or two brief encounters, since the night he called me to offer me my job.

I was in charge of this briefing, and I was nervous as a wet hen. As an anointed, President Reagan had acquired considerable aura. It was also my first experience of the pomp and circumstance of official White Housedom: nameplates, White House note pads, and sharpened pencils at every place setting, heavy water pitchers, stewards quietly circling the table. More importantly, it was my first inkling of how short two hours are at a table surrounded by the heaviest hitters in the nation's government.

I knew how little time there was. The calendar was already winning the race against my ambitious schedule. But now another schedule, that of the inaugural activities, was also emerging. That meant even less time. Whole days would be disappearing.

So I tried to make up for all of this disappearing time by stuffing the January 7 briefing book with the whole enchilada. The paper covered the deteriorating near-term economic outlook and the dramatic, recent rise in the current year deficit projections. It sketched out the huge size of the necessary domestic spending cut.

It also outlined a strategy to move the whole program swiftly through the Congress. I'd added a long list of the 'big ticket' items we'd need to close the deficit gap. With all the information in a neatly tabbed black book at each place setting, the meeting began.

Within an hour I had fresh insight into how difficult it would be to get the Reagan White House to concentrate on the complex, confusing, vexing, numbers-ridden business of formulating national economic and fiscal policy.

First came the obligatory speeches.

The President led off with some remarks about how the time had now come to begin the work we had been sent here to do, and with some stories to illustrate his point. He then turned to the Vice President-elect and said, 'George, do you have anything to add by way of overview?'

Bush replied with a firm negative, noting that the President had said it all. Then he proceeded to rephrase every single one of the generalizations the President had just made.

Next came Ed Meese. He said he was going to take advantage of the opportunity to bring everyone up to date on the 'splendid' progress of his transition teams. They would have us ready to 'hit the ground running' on January 20. Finally Meese concluded.

'Jim,' he said, turning to Baker, 'do you have anything to add?'

Well, yes, he did, as did Don Regan, Marty Anderson, and most of the others.

In due course Alan Greenspan gave a quick assessment of the near-term economic outlook. I had drafted Alan Greenspan into the group; as head of the Council of Economic Advisors under Ford, Greenspan was no supply sider by a long shot. But I'd struck up a solid friendship with him then and he was someone I wanted close at hand as the situation gathered critical mass.

I felt in him a kindred philosophical spirit. Upon his arrival in Washington years ago, Greenspan had been accused of being a disciple of Ayn Rand, the epitome—or *reductio ad absurdum*, depending on your view—of the anti-statist, intellectual conservative.

Another aspect of Greenspan drew me to him as well: he loved facts, numbers, and empirical data as much as I did. It was something I found lacking among the more theoretically inclined supply siders of Kemp's central committee.

Greenspan's presentation was given in his customary trenchant and succinct manner. It was the questions that followed that were neither trenchant nor succinct. One question was on how the Federal Reserve Board set the prime interest rate charged by the banks. Greenspan patiently explained that the prime rate was set by market forces, not the Fed. That point, in turn, led to a discussion about the new Volcker monetary policy based on controlling monetary aggregates rather than interest rates.

This was puzzling new information to most of those gathered around the table. I was surprised. My inclination to explain less and do more was further reinforced.

Nearly an hour had gone by already, but at last we got to my presentation on the budget outlook.

In order to dramatize the problem and convince them that the campaign's earlier budget projections were no longer valid due to the deteriorating economy, I had come with a chart showing what had happened to Carter's Fiscal Year (FY) 1981 'balanced budget'. It was quite vivid: by September, the FY 1981 budget was already $20 billion in deficit. By November, it had been revised to $38 billion in deficit. Now, in January, it stood at a staggering $58 billion.

'Damn it!' exclaimed the President, 'I knew they were going to do this to us. It just proves what we've been saying all along.'

There followed a vigorous round of Carter-bashing and complaining about his 'fraudulent' 1981 budget.

I was dismayed. They were acting as if the main point of my briefing was that we had been sabotaged by the outgoing administration. They thought I was scoring a political point when I had simply been trying to sensitize them to the magnitude and difficulty of the real-world policy problems facing us. But what the group wanted to talk about was 'them'.

I finally managed to get them off the irrelevant FY 1981 budget, but it wasn't easy. I pointed out it was already 'baked into the cake', and that we had to focus on FY 1982 and beyond.

Near the end of my allotted time, we got to the nut of my presentation: minimum spending cuts of $75 billion *per year* that were needed to balance the budget by 1984. And that was based on a Keynesian-oriented Congressional Budget Office forecast; the actual number resulting from a supply-side forecast would be even bigger.

I thought this would have a sobering effect. My message was that far more sweeping and wrenching budget cuts than we had told the public about would be needed. Fraud, waste and abuse prevention was only a small part of the solution. There would have to be major surgery on entitlements and subsidies.

But they didn't grasp that. They didn't recognize that we were in a much tougher fiscal and political equation than they had previously assumed. With the exception of Marty Anderson and Alan Greenspan, no one in the room betrayed any comprehension of what the federal budget looked like or how it was calculated.

The fundamental concept of the current policy 'baseline'—that is, spending going out and revenue coming in with no change in existing policy—was foreign to them. Yet that was the benchmark from which all the domestic 'cutting' and defense 'increasing' was being done.

Likewise, I made the point that the revenue loss from the tax bill was the actual loss. There was no Laffer curve or revenue 'feedback' due to the stimulative effect of the tax cut. That was already built into the baseline calculation.

Again, total puzzlement was the response. These were, admittedly, technical points; but governing consists of technical points. The basic problem, I began to perceive, was that Reagan and Meese still had a one-year-at-a-time frame of reference when it came to budgets. As governor of California, neither Reagan nor his adviser had ever had to deal with 'out-year' projections.

In 1967, they didn't have to worry about what revenues were going to be in 1970. They had only to cope with next year's budget being 'X' percent higher than last year's. That was not a very mysterious, or taxing, concept. The state constitution said balance the numbers, one year at a time.

Now it was essential for them to understand that the whole supply-side revolution was designed to put in place, all at once, a *multi-year* reduction in taxes and spending *compared to existing policy levels* over the same period. That approach required a 'before and after' look at each year's numbers—stretching out to 1986. But we didn't get there.

Right on schedule, the meeting broke up. Meese announced that we would reconvene the budget discussion the following Thursday. The President's parting words were consoling: 'If the mess is really this bad, that's all the more reason why we're here.'

His instincts were good. Yet Reagan seemed as far above the detail work of supply side as a ceremonial monarch is above politics. I was not a knight errant, but I interpreted his words as a blessing to go forth and do what I thought necessary to do battle with the federal dragon.

Back at my office I took a hard look at the timetable to see how much time Meese had allotted in the President-elect's schedule for the budget sessions we would need to have. Suddenly the utter scarcity of presidential time hit home: only four more sessions, totaling six hours, between now and the inauguration. We'd just used up a quarter of that time discussing the administration's highest priority, and we hadn't even scratched the surface.

Since Meese had indicated that our time with Reagan was stretched to the limit as it was, I made a decision that was almost surely unwise, but probably unavoidable. If I spent our time in what few meetings remained trying to educate them on basic budget making, we would never get to the crucial item-by-item spending cuts.

So, I decided that my staff and I would plunge in and start going through the line-item budget cuts contained in my rapidly growing set of black books.

For the time being we would just set aside all the big picture stuff—defense increases, tax cuts, the aggregate budget numbers, and what the economy was going to look like over the horizon. Later, we'd come back and discuss the broader question of how it all added up.

I had no idea at the time that it would take another thirty days before this actually happened. Our warring economic sects—supply siders, monetarists, eclectics—took that long to agree on a forecast, which was what the overall budget numbers depended upon. As a result, the senior staff would not be able to sit down and discuss what it all added up to until February 7 or thereabouts.

That meant, in turn, that the President would not see the big picture until around February 10—three days before the deadline for making the final decisions. But by then they would all be prisoners of my schedule, the February 18 address to the Joint Session of Congress having been publicly announced.

Meanwhile, my revised approach to the presidential budget sessions seemed to work. Going over the cuts line by line proved a much more congenial labor than explaining the economic theory and fiscal math.

During those four pre-inaugural sessions I focused on the dozen or so 'big ticket' items, most of which were culled from the

Gramm–Stockman cut list. Together, these items would save more than $25 billion per year by 1984. They included the outright elimination of four major programs: the CETA* public jobs program; most trade adjustment assistance benefits for workers; and the two special categories of Social Security benefits for college students and those with minimal earnings.

These items were nearly the opposite of the ephemeral 'fraud, waste and abuse' reductions that had been talked about so airily during the campaign. In combination, the four proposals would have terminated public jobs or cash benefits to nearly four million recipients then on the rolls.

I wanted the President and his adviser to know from the start that we would be working toward a huge spending cut total, at least by all prior standards. Raging political controversies and allegations that millions of people would be impacted or 'hurt' had to be expected.

The Reagan economic policy revolution would not be a simple matter of 'limiting the rate of increase in federal spending', as Meese kept phrasing it. It would involve drastic reductions in dozens of programs. It amounted to a substantial retraction of welfare state benefits that people had come to feel 'entitled' to receive.

I was relieved to find almost no resistance to my proposals on the part of the President and his advisers, even after I emphasized that these cuts would cause dramatic legislative battles. Reagan paid close attention to the discussions. He was surprised when I told him, among other things, that college students were able to invade the Social Security trust fund; and that some laid-off workers were getting nearly two years' worth of handouts from the federal government.

Reagan's body of knowledge is primarily impressionistic: he registers anecdotes rather than concepts. I soon learned that it made less sense to tell him that you were eligible for a thirty-five cents-a-meal lunch subsidy if your income was above 190 percent of the poverty line than to tell him, 'The kids of cabinet officers qualify.' He was not surprised by these revelations; they conformed to his *a priori* understanding of what outrages the federal government was capable of perpetrating.

Still, these simplifications undoubtedly had a cost that I didn't

* Comprehensive Employment and Training Act.

recognize at the time. They made the impending bruising political battle to shrink welfare state spending sound too much like nostrums about fraud, waste and abuse. It wasn't the same thing at all.

By the end of the last session, the President-elect had approved, with only minor modifications, all of my dozen big ticket proposals, as well as several other items. Even better, an ethos was forming within the group. It was as if we'd put one of those United Fund Drive thermometers on the sidewalk outside Blair House, and each time we met we were able to paint in the level of mercury higher and higher.

Reagan never flinched. Soon we reached the point where he would respond to one of my explanations with 'No questions about it. It has to be done.'

This attitude went far toward relieving my fears that the White House would resist spending cuts. On the other hand, it tended to bolster their assumption that the budget was swollen with easily justifiable opportunities for major domestic cuts, and that the job of reconciling tax cuts, spending cuts, and defense increases was both feasible and plausible.

'Just keep bringing your black books, Dave,' they would say, firmly believing that I was leading them to the promised land of balanced budgets. I began thinking that our progress was splendid.

A few days after the last session, I chirped enthusiastically to Greider over scrambled eggs and bacon that squaring the fiscal circle wasn't going to be such a political problem after all. The President wasn't backing away from making the tough cuts.

'He's signed off on an awful lot of them already,' I said. 'He just says, OK, let's do it.'

Only later would I appreciate the vast web of confusion and self-delusion I was creating. I instilled so much confidence by appearing to know all the answers, but I was just beginning to understand the true complexities and mysteries of the federal budget.

Yet the blistering pace gave me no time to absorb the lessons I was learning. More importantly, I had no time to teach the others what I did know.

If the Reagan plan had been incrementalist in nature, as almost all presidential initiatives are, then the low level of fiscal literacy among the upper echelons of the new administration might not have mattered. Small changes do not big errors make. The changes would have been made by the budget bureaucracies at OMB and the agencies. But a plan for radical and abrupt change required deep comprehension—and we had none of it.

At the heart of the matter was a startling equation. We were taking the budget we inherited, raising defense and cutting taxes on a multi-year basis. When fully implemented several years later, these changes would amount to over six percent of GNP. How much of the fifteen percent of GNP that went to inherited domestic spending had to be shrunk so that the defense increase and tax cuts wouldn't swell the deficit?

History cannot blame the President for not considering this crucial question; I never provided him with a single briefing on this.

There simply wasn't time, given all the dozens and dozens of individual line-item budget cuts I needed to get through. Instead of giving him a bird's-eye view of the budget, I gave him a worm's-eye view. We sat there happily hacking away at CETA and food stamps, 300 million here, 100 million there. That's all they saw.

What they didn't realize—because I never made it clear—was that we were working in only a small corner of the total budget. Those dozen 'big ticket' items we cut in January came from only twelve percent of the total budget. We hadn't even looked at three giant programs that accounted for over *half* of the domestic budget: Social Security, veterans' benefits, and Medicare. Those three alone cost $250 billion per year. The programs we had cut saved $25 billion. The President and White House staff were seeing the tip of the budget iceberg; they weren't finding out about the huge mass which lurked below the waterline.

Meanwhile no one questioned the schedule. No one raised any questions about what *wasn't* being reviewed and what *wasn't* being learned. The fiscal and economic illiteracy among the core White House group was simply too great to have elicited any doubts. We thus recklessly charged ahead.

My hope for an early consensus on the economic forecast proved to be a vain one. The whole month of January was consumed in a fractious debate. From the outside the supply side was viewed as a sect; but we had sects within sects.

There were three doctrines represented on the forecasting team:

the monetarists, the supply siders and the eclectics. Beryl Sprinkel, an economist of national reputation and now Under Secretary of Treasury for Monetary Affairs, was champion of the first. Paul Craig Roberts and Norm Ture, also Treasury officials, were of the second school; and the new chairman of the Council of Economic Advisors, Murray Weidenbaum, tended toward the third approach.

My own position was a combination of the supply-side and monetarist viewpoints. It was reflected ably in the group by my new chief economist, Larry Kudlow. I had met him during my whirlwind tour of Wall Street on December 18, and had been highly impressed, despite the critical articles on supply side he showed me that he had written during the Republican Convention.

Kudlow insisted that Laffer and Kemp were proposing to sit the economy on a two-legged stool. But 'sound money' and 'sound taxation', he said, were not possible without 'sound budgets'. I rejoiced to hear that. Here, I realized, was a fellow traveller—a supply sider who worked with a three-legged stool just as I did.

Meanwhile, the others could agree on only one thing: that the Congressional Budget Office forecast I had used for the purpose of the Blair House meeting was an ideological abomination. It assumed real GNP growth that was way too low and continued high inflation for years into the future.

So we got our economic shoehorn and tried to jimmy the forecast numbers until all the doctrines fit. It was almost inherently an impossible task.

The essential dilemma was this: real GNP growth plus inflation equals current dollar Gross National Product or 'money GNP'. The Treasury supply siders wanted *the biggest possible numbers for real growth*. That would show the effect of the tax cut. Historically, real GNP growth has averaged about three percent. We therefore had to expect five to six percent. Otherwise, what was the point of the whole miracle cure we were peddling?

On the other hand, the monetarist-oriented members of the team—Kudlow and Sprinkel especially—wanted *the lowest possible numbers for money GNP*. That was the litmus test of sound, anti-inflationary monetary policy.*

---

* The double-digit inflation disaster of 1979–80 had resulted from annual money supply growth in the seven to eight percent range. Under our anti-inflationary

When you brought the two camps back together, it was the inflation number which took it in the neck. We didn't have any pro-inflation faction, and appropriately so. Thus, the ideal long-run economic forecast scenario was this: the Treasury supply siders wanted about five percent real growth; the monetarists wanted about seven percent money GNP growth. Consequently, by the third or fourth year, inflation collapsed to two percent because that's what the arithmetic required.

These economic numbers were a pretty good approximation of the supply-side synthesis. They portrayed a world close to the ideal of inflationless, capitalist growth. By the end of January, we had a tentative forecast along these lines.

Had we stopped right there, we would have been in for a rude shock on the budget numbers. This supply-side/monetarist consensus forecast reduced 1985 money GNP by *$400 billion* compared to the previous high inflation CBO* forecast we had used on an interim basis at the first Blair House meeting.

This meant $100 billion in lower revenues by 1985. Overall, the out-year deficit after the tax cut and defense increase would have been in excess of $150 billion, had we stuck with this consensus. To get a balanced budget from that kind of baseline would have required shocking, draconian domestic spending cuts.

In a sense, we were both purists and greenhorns. We had ended up with a high growth—low inflation consensus forecast on the basis of pure doctrine. Nobody was running the economic forecast through the OMB budget models to see what kind of deficit you got. We didn't learn about that game until much later.

A huge irony was thus in the making. *Had the ideologues stuck with their purist forecast, the Reagan Revolution would not have been launched on February 18—and perhaps never.* The staggering magnitude of domestic

---

policy, that had to come down—to no more than six percent the first year and eventually to about four percent. In all, sound long-run money supply growth would give you an ideal target of about seven percent for money GNP growth.

There was some shorthand arithmetic for the proper money GNP numbers, too. The latter consisted of the sum of money supply growth (how much the Fed creates) and velocity (how fast people spend and respend it). Historically, velocity had averaged about three percent, so you had to take that as a given even though it fluctuated on a short-term basis.

* Congressional Budget Office.

spending cuts necessary to balance the budget would have caused the White House politicians to lurch out of their slumber.

'It can't be done!' they would have shouted. 'It doesn't add up! Something has to give!'

The purist forecast, however, disappeared without a trace during the first eight days of February. But before this accident actually happened, I gave Greider a clear reading on where we were. Over breakfast on January 31, I explained that a high inflation forecast significantly eased the budget equation. Nonetheless, we were sticking with the logic of our supply-side doctrine:

> I don't have to cut as much real stuff out of the budget. In other words, if I forecast twelve percent inflation for the next five years, I could balance the budget even with defense and Kemp-Roth just by holding all domestic programs at a zero real growth level.
>
> But ideologically I'm on the opposite side of my institutional interest. Ideologically, I think inflation can come down pretty fast if you do the right things, and it's necessary if you want to heal the economy. It's really a question of, Are you going to shrink the real size of government or just hold it stable?

This was really the heart of the matter, as I had discovered while doing my pencilwork a few months earlier. With high inflation, the Reagan program amounted to little more than indexing the fiscal status quo; the Kemp-Roth tax cut simply offset tax bracket creep. But by forcing inflation down, the program bordered on a fiscal revolution. It left a huge excess of domestic spending that must either be cut or deficit-financed.

This fundamental point was more important to understand than anything else. But when Greider asked me, 'Where's the President in all this?', I equivocated.

'This is a technician's argument.' It wasn't. But the President wouldn't be apprised of that until much later, and would never comprehend it in any event.

It didn't occur to me at the time that I was making it sound as if we had sat around rigging some budget computer to make the numbers come out right. That wasn't the case. We had actually done almost the opposite.

The economic forecast was in the end drastically changed—and it did improve the budget numbers considerably. But it was the result of somebody trying to be 'realistic', not deceptive. Enter Murray Weidenbaum.

Through no fault of his own, Weidenbaum came on board late in the game. When Lew Lehrman didn't get the post at Treasury, Kemp, the others, and I spent a lot of time trying to persuade Meese and Marty Anderson to give him the CEA job. Eventually, Weidenbaum was named instead—but he got into the crucial economic forecast process only at the tail end and he had to scramble the moment he arrived. Weidenbaum was the picture of the rumpled economist. He had one virtue extremely uncommon among his breed: he spoke in short, English sentences. John Kenneth Galbraith probably wouldn't have been able to understand a word he said.

Weidenbaum had a very easygoing, accommodating disposition. But when he finally arrived on the scene and took one look at the supply-side/monetarist consensus, he roared.

'Nobody,' he said, 'is going to predict a two percent inflation on *my* watch. We'll be the laughing stock of the world.' Ending the conversation with a professorial note, he announced, 'Either we get this forecast mess cleaned up or I'm taking it straight to the President.'

Thus began a one-week march toward 'realism'. I pushed the group toward Weidenbaum's position. I did so reluctantly at first but strongly near the end. My reason didn't have much to do with economic doctrine or the budget numbers; it had to do with the schedule. I needed a consensus, and I needed it fast.

When the first week in February arrived and we still had no forecast, Dale McComber, the chief OMB numbers-cruncher and a thirty-year veteran of the White House budget machinations, finally threatened me.

'If you don't get this forecast locked up within hours,' he said, 'you're going to be sending the President of the United States up that Hill with a blank piece of paper.'

The prospect lacked charm. We now went into a white heat of pressure. The forecasting sessions, which formerly had been crucibles of intellectual and ideological formulations, degenerated into sheer numbers manipulation. The supply siders yielded a tenth of a percentage point toward lower real growth; the monetarists yielded a tenth of a percentage point toward higher money GNP. The supply siders yield another tenth; the monetarists yield another tenth. Round after round it went.

'We've got to get Murray his inflation back,' I exhorted them, which shows I had truly gone haywire. When push came to shove, I was more of an anti-inflationist than anything else; but I wasn't thinking about doctrine any more. I was struggling to avoid a crash landing before February 18.

Passing the tin cup around the forecasting group eventually did not yield a high enough inflation number to satisfy Weidenbaum. So, on February 7, he came by my office and we made the worst possible bargain. If he'd agree to keep the real growth rate 'reasonably high', I would go along with whatever inflation figure he thought he could live with as a professional economist.

He agreed. He would work up a new scenario based on that compromise, and together we would impose it on the forecasters at the next meeting. It would be a *fait accompli*, or as they say in Washington, a done deal.

When the group convened in Room 248 of the Executive Office Building (EOB) for the final meeting, Weidenbaum unfurled his scenario. There was a discontented rumbling from the monetarists and supply siders, accompanied by a few growls. Someone finally taunted the professor.

'What model did *this* come out of, Murray?'

Weidenbaum glared at his inquisitor a moment and said, 'It came right out of here.' With that he slapped his belly with both hands. 'My visceral computer,' he smiled.

Larry Kudlow had warned me that we were making an error by accommodating Weidenbaum's position. But I indicated that all the time for debate had ended. Weidenbaum's forecast was gavelled through.

Never before or since has a single belly-slap produced such devastating results. The new Weidenbaum forecast added *$700 billion* in money GNP over five years to our previous consensus forecast. Nearly $200 billion in phantom revenues tumbled into our budget computer in one fell swoop. The massive deficit inherent in the true supply-side fiscal equation was substantially covered up. Eventually it would become the belly-slap that was heard around the world.

It wasn't really Weidenbaum's fault. He wasn't any convinced supply sider; he'd have gladly knocked down the real growth numbers in order to make room for a 'respectable' level of inflation. The starting deficit we had to contend with would then have been much higher and more realistic.

But all the rest of us knew better than the old greybeard from St Louis. We insisted that we had found the economic Rosetta stone.

The inflation-saturated and battered US economy we inherited in 1981 was going to do what? Why, just leap up on its hind legs and start growing at a five percent annual rate. And it would do so at the same time it was going through the shakes and shivers of taking the monetary restraint cure and experiencing the tremors of disinflation.*

The whole proposition eventually shattered within twenty-four months. The 1982 economic numbers made it clear as a bell. When you added the supply siders' assumption of 5.2 percent real growth for that year to Weidenbaum's 7.7 percent inflation, you got a mountain of money GNP—and phantom tax revenues. The gold standard, hard money crowd ended up forecasting 13.3 percent money GNP growth for 1982; they would have had to put three shifts on the Fed's printing presses to achieve it.

The Fed didn't do that, though. It listened to our words, not our numbers, and throttled back money supply growth. The economy did what it always does in response to the monetary cure for rampant inflation, speculation and debt. It fell down on its knees, suffering the dislocations of recession in order to purge out the monetary cancers of inflation.

In 1982, we didn't get 5.2 percent real growth. Instead, the US

* Various silly rationalizations would later be offered by the supply-side true believers. Some of them said the real world's drastic deviation from our forecast path was due to overly restrictive policy by the Fed in the summer of 1981. But that was nonsense. Our ultimate policy norm was an inflationless, gold dollar economy. Had the gold window actually been reopened in early 1981, the economy's cyclical collapse would have been even more drastic, traumatic and costly. The 'Volcker recession' would have looked like a picnic by contrast.

Others pointed to the slight delay of the first ten percent installment of the tax cut; but while a few percentage points' difference in marginal tax rates may affect long-run supply, it has no bearing whatsoever on short-run demand. You had to be a Keynesian to believe that a slightly larger tax cut could have neutralized the gale forces of the 1981–82 global disinflation engineered by the Fed.

economy *contracted* by a 1.5 percent. And inflation came down to 4.4 percent. The mountain of money GNP thus didn't materialize. The 1982 growth rate of money GNP was about three percent rather than thirteen percent.

Money GNP came in at a staggering $338 billion lower level than Weidenbaum had slapped out of his computer. Tax revenues were thus about $85 billion lower in the final reckoning than we had forecast.

This was just 1982, but the error pattern would persist and widen every year thereafter. In all, it was an accidental case of double jeopardy. The Weidenbaum forecast's money GNP numbers were way too high for our theory and monetary policy; its real growth numbers were way too high for reality.

But both errors threw the budget numbers way out of whack. One inflated the revenue projections and the other deflated the spending projections. The eventual $200 billion annual deficits were buried in the resultant combination.

The table below tells the whole story, proving that our Rosetta stone was a fake. The push-pull hypothesis was upside down. The difference between the explosion of real growth in 1982 that we forecast and the collapse which actually occurred is what sent all the budget numbers spinning.

	Real GNP Growth (%)		
Quarter	Supply-side/monetarist Consensus	Final Weidenbaum Forecast	Actual Outcome
1981:4	4.0%	4.0%	−5.3%
1982:1	9.4%	5.2%	−5.5%
1982:2	7.8%	5.2%	0.9%
1982:3	6.8%	5.2%	−1.0%
1982:4	5.4%	5.2%	−1.3%

The February 1981 economic forecast eventually became known as 'Rosy Scenario'. Weidenbaum wrote the final, specific numbers. But its underlying architecture—the push-pull hypothesis—was ultimately the work of a small band of ideologues. Paul Craig Roberts, Norm Ture, and Steve Entin were in on every play. Throughout the whole process, Jude Wanniski and Art Laffer, Jack Kemp and Lew

Lehrman were close at hand, in constant communication with their allies inside the forecasting group.

By contrast, the newcomers to the supply-side revolution—the President, the Secretary of the Treasury, and the White House senior staff—were almost entirely innocent and uninformed. Fittingly, then, it was the revolutionaries, myself included, who made the forecast on which their supply-side policy revolution was launched. No one else can be blamed.

4

Shortcuts to the Reagan Revolution

Somewhere in all this there was an inauguration.

We were about to become a government . . . finally. Since the election, we had just been a loose group of people bumping into each other in rented rooms.

Senator Mark Hatfield, chairman of the inaugural, had the high-minded notion that everyone seated behind the President on the West Front of the Capitol should wear morning coats. At first I thought it was just an inconvenience; but that morning I understood that Hatfield was right. It helped to create the extraordinary and grave sense that something new was starting. I would be dishonest if I said I didn't get a little choked up when the President, looking out over a crowd of almost ten thousand in the direction of the west from which he had come, said: 'Let us, together, make a new beginning.'

My new office was in the Executive Office Building (EOB), the French Renaissance-style building next to the White House that looks something like an elaborate wedding cake. It is the most stately office building in the world, with immensely long corridors of black and white marble. If you look closely at the marble floor, you can see cochleate fossils, little spiral creatures that lived millions of years ago. Their fate became to be trodden on by presidents, vice presidents, secretaries of state and war, admirals, generals, bureaucrats and buffoons.

My three deputies and I did some gaping that first full day in our new quarters. My office alone was about the size of the gymnasium of my junior high school. It took some getting used to.

We did notice something distressing that first day. The office, cavernous though it was, was filthy.

The General Services Administration, which among other things sees to the cleaning of government offices, has several levels of bureaucratic cleanliness. Level One, for instance, would mean that your office got vacuumed every day. Level Five meant it only got cleaned once a week—something like that.

As head of the Carter White House's administrative staff, Hugh Carter, also known as 'Cousin Cheap', had decided to save money by opting for Level Five. It looked as though he'd opted for Level Twenty. When I picked up my phone, it almost slipped out of my hand it was so greasy.

One of my deputies shook his head. Another, who never passed up a wisecrack, said, 'The reason it's greasy is they spent the last four months of the campaign handing out pork.'

As a cabinet officer I was eligible for the perk of eating in the Executive White House Mess right next to the Situation Room.

Executive Mess privileges were, next to access to the President, the *ne plus ultra* of White House status. It sounded good. But once we kicked the congressional politicians in the shins, I could never get out from under the daily crises. So I had to eat at my desk, only getting to the mess during congressional recesses. When you consider how often they took them, though, I wasn't exactly deprived.

As I started work in my new office, I began fully to comprehend how ill-prepared I was for the job ahead. The realization came late, but these realizations always do: the new ship's captain, biographer or architect seldom, I suppose, feels truly inadequate to his task until it is too late. What lay ahead for me had nothing to do with the elegant theories of my Grand Doctrine; it was all planning, processing, negotiating, deciding, and leading. And I had no experience in any of it.

The one consolation was that the 600 OMB career staff were dedicated anti-bureaucrats. They weren't in the business of giving things away. They were in the business of interposing themselves between the federal Santa Claus and the kids and saying, 'Whoa...'

Governance, I was learning, consisted not so much of a tidal wave but of endless, smaller waves of angry Lilliputians. By Saturday afternoon, January 24, the first wave had arrived.

Just before the inaugural, the President had approved, in principle, a series of symbolic 'first day' directives designed to show that we would 'hit the ground running' and come out slugging the federal monster. Among these were an across-the-board hiring freeze, a fifteen percent cutback in agency travel budgets, a five percent cutback in consulting fees, and a freeze on buying any more furniture, office machines and other such equipment.

Within hours of the first full day I was swamped with urgent demands as to the meaning of these 'directives'. Did the travel cut apply to FBI agents on their way to apprehending a felon? Did the equipment freeze cover the blood-circulating machines essential to coronary bypass surgery? How did the hiring freeze impact the guy promised a federal job in Washington on February 1 who had already moved there from Utah? My staff and I held a desultory debate on it all and ended up exempting as much as we included.

Maddening as these problems were, they were insignificant compared to some of the other things that were fast piling up on my desk, already cluttered with paperwork driven by the February 18 launch date. Following his own naïve plan for cabinet government, Ed Meese had scheduled a full cabinet meeting with the President for *each day of the first week* to continue the review of my budget cuts.

It was a mixed blessing. I was reluctant to put on the table any important items I hadn't already worked out with the relevant cabinet member. But my staff had not yet had time to write up all the easy, non-controversial cuts. We had scores of budget line items that you could table without fear of provoking an outburst, such as killing government publications on how to grow a tomato. We had to scramble all week to find enough of these 'safe' items to fill Meese's cabinet agenda while the 'big ticket' spending cut and economic forecast items receded further and further.

By Friday, the Cabinet was understandably restless. All week it had been forced to sit uselessly around the table mouthing non sequiturs while I ran the show. When I walked in on Friday morning, four or five of them, including Jim Edwards of Energy and Mac Baldrige of Commerce, were huddled in a corner grousing about 'Stockman's high-handedness'.

I grinned sheepishly. I thought they were probably offended by the fact that their briefing papers were still warm from the OMB Xerox machines. We just didn't have time to get the papers to the cabinet members before they saw them at these meetings.

Sensing a revolt was brewing, I hauled the box of black briefing books for that day out into the hall near the Oval Office. With the help of a few staffers, I began frantically removing all the items I thought might cause any controversy whatsoever. I'd already heard enough incorrect and erroneous ideas from the Cabinet that week to recognize that not all of my new colleagues were in the vanguard of the supply-side revolution. Some of them, in fact, sounded like partisans of the other side.

One of the 'safe' items I had left in their books, however, was a brief paper recommending an immediate presidential action: the total elimination of oil price and allocation controls. It was so central to our free market approach that I hadn't imagined anyone would object.

I was wrong. Jim Edwards, dentist and former governor of South Carolina, did. He began with a noisy fuss about 'moving too fast', then built up a good head of steam declaiming that oil decontrol was a 'complex' matter, that consumers wouldn't 'like' it, and that the President himself might be blamed for 'higher gasoline prices'. He also needed 'tools' to deal with future shortages and worried about small refineries losing their access to 'cheap', federally allocated crude oil.

As I listened to this claptrap, I thought, 'Dentist, extract thyself.' Decontrol should have happened six years ago, and here he was saying he hadn't even studied it yet. The Secretary of Energy was missing a point—like the entire free market doctrine on which administration policy was based.

At the same Friday meeting, the Cabinet had pounced on another of the 'safe' items I had left in their briefing books—a requirement that all cabinet agencies clear any new regulations they proposed through the OMB so that OMB could do a stringent cost-benefit analysis of them. Sweeping deregulation was another pillar of the supply-side platform.

'What kind of bureaucracy are you building up over at OMB?' Secretary of Transportation Drew Lewis demanded. I was flabbergasted. This 'regulatory budgeting'—that is, central, systematic review of new regulations—had become an article of faith among conservative critics of the regulatory superstate. He had the equation upside down.

These were the early warning signals. I was faced with cabinet colleagues who were ill-schooled in even the basic tenets of the Reagan Revolution. Most were carrying their own do-it-yourself policy formulation kits. Hence, I could see that getting the program out the front door of the White House might involve a struggle for which there was no time.

The next morning over scrambled eggs I told Greider: 'It'll be the people in the Executive Office versus the cabinet departments like it always is. The cabinet secretaries are getting domesticated by their people, by their permanent bureaucracies.'

My anxiety was compounded by another factor. To be efficient about the budget item-cutting process, the OMB staff and I had created four categories of budget reductions. We had labelled them A through D. 'A' consisted of items that would each save a billion dollars or more per year, whereas 'D' consisted of tiny programs— small 'nicks', as we called them—that each amounted to savings of $25 million per year or less.

Each list was accompanied by a towering stack of papers explaining and justifying every proposed cut. I knew there were tens of billions of desperately needed and philosophically justifiable savings to be gleaned from this awesome pile. But I also saw that the level of detail and the complexity of the numbers were mind-boggling.

The OMB staff papers recommended savings in Uncle Sam's two separate black lung programs*, three different veterans' pension programs, and half a dozen small, overlapping nutrition programs. There were also savings to be harvested from two separate airline subsidies, five different programs to pump taxpayer money into the railroads, and a half dozen mechanisms each for distributing subsidized credit to farmers and small business. The options went on and on.

How was I going to get through all this, I wondered; how would there be time to explain, defend and get all this approved by everyone in the White House? Thus by the end of the first week I confessed to Greider that the process was already out of control and that I was asphyxiating in paper:

> Well the Inauguration disrupted everything. It's just been organized chaos. We're getting the paper done at 9.00 am and I'm rushing into the Cabinet Room at 10.00 and giving the briefings because that's as fast as it can get processed.

* Government subsidized health care for sufferers from coalminers' disease.

Now at my desk over at OMB literally I have a stack of options papers. I'm not kidding, it's two feet high and I'm going through those things, having them revised, modified, rewritten and churned back into the process as quickly as I can but I just can't get ahead of the curve. . .

With less than three weeks left before our self-imposed deadline, a drastic shortcut had to be taken. I settled on two expedients: using something called 'budget plugs', and forming a budget-cutting committee that would be able to make an end-run* around both the Cabinet and the White House.

The budget plugs were placeholders for decisions we would now have to make after the program was launched on February 18. Since we didn't yet know exactly how much the defense budget would be in the out-years, we would insert an estimate with an asterisked line below saying: 'Exact future defense spending to be determined.' Likewise, we would insert in the budget a ballpark estimate of what we expected to save once every single one of the thousands of domestic programs had been reviewed.

Together, the plugs and the committee would tame the chaos sufficiently to allow the President to make his February 18 speech to the Congress. An impressively thick 'White Paper' chockablock with details and apparent precision would give the impression that the economic program was being launched with utter coherence and admirable preparation. In fact, my expedients saw to it that critical loose ends were left unresolved everywhere. They ensured that the whole fiscal plan was embedded with contradictions and booby-trapped with hidden pressures.

The first plug I had to come up with was the one for the defense budget.

By the end of January, Weinberger and his new team were even further behind than I was. The only semblance of a Reagan defense budget was a hastily assembled package of line-item amendments to the already enacted 1981 budget and the 1982 recommendations of the now departed Carter Administration.

That package was called the 'get well' plan. It was a miscellany of

* American football term: a flanking movement.

small fixes: money for spare parts, fuel, pay raises, medical supplies and some new procurement. But in no way did it constitute a complete coherent program from which I could construct a budget 'path' showing how much we would be spending on defense in the years beyond 1982.

Being immersed in the still-unresolved economic forecast and floundering in papers on the domestic savings options, I was extremely loathe to initiate a full-dress White House review of the defense question. For on top of everything else, the White House was now knee-deep in yet another time-consuming distraction from the main business at hand. The national debt ceiling was almost certain to be breached during the upcoming congressional recess, precipitating a cash crisis. Therefore the *current* urgent priority at the White House was to coax the Congress into raising the national debt ceiling.

Bill Schneider, my chief deputy for national security matters, put it to me bluntly. 'If we try to schedule a serious defense review on top of everything else,' he said, 'we're going to blow out the White House circuits completely. If we dump defense on them, they'll be lobotomy candidates.'

Schneider thus began meeting with Weinberger's deputy, Frank Carlucci, to develop some ballpark 'plug' figures that Cap and I could agree on. The good news was that Meese and the other White House senior staff were more than amenable to the idea.

Another element of the administration's fiscal policy was thus being taken hostage by the tax cut. But I didn't recognize it in the slightest. Kemp-Roth and 10–5–3 were radical and novel approaches to tax policy. They would start small and then balloon after three to five years into a massive change in the baseline revenue level. The revenue loss would be about $50 billion or 1.6 percent of GNP in the first year, but $220 billion or 4.5 percent of GNP by the fifth year.

We therefore had to do an extraordinarily foolish thing. We had to make tentative judgments within a matter of two or three weeks regarding every component of the budget—defense, agriculture, Social Security—all the way out to the middle of the decade. This was the only way you could demonstrate the fiscal math of how ends would eventually meet.

And so defense, which was going to cost hundreds of billions more, had to be assigned huge, arbitrary out-year numbers without any debate or review. This permitted us to prove on paper that the tax cut, which would yield hundreds of billions less, was fiscally affordable and prudent.

Still, the Secretary of Defense was 'Cap the Knife' Weinberger. He would find ways to rebuild the nation's flagging defenses at less cost than the arbitrary 'plug' numbers we would temporarily insert in the out-year budget.

I was sure that Cap still had some of the Knife left in him from his own OMB days.

A few days before he and I met, I told Greider that despite our policy of increased defense spending, we had an economy-minded man at the Pentagon. After all, he had even gone along with the hiring freeze without so much as a single grumble.

'Any other Secretary of Defense, Republican or Democrat,' I said, 'would have resisted that stoutly and probably gotten Defense exempted. . . . But Cap (said), "No, go ahead with it." And it's very unusual.'

At 7.30 the following Friday evening, Weinberger, Frank Carlucci, Deputy Secretary of Defense, Schneider, and I gathered in the Secretary of Defense's office at the Pentagon. That office is eloquent testimonial to the fact that nuclear holocaust is not an abstraction. Behind the Secretary's desk is an array of dozens of phones that connect him, instantly, to the commanders of all American forces throughout the world. It is an arresting display.

It was a very unusual Pentagon meeting: no charts, no computer printouts, no color slides, no colonels with six-foot wooden pointers. The only implements we had were my Hewlett Packard pocket calculator and a blank piece of paper. It is somewhat fitting that the largest peacetime defense budget in US history was about to be tabulated on a $70 pocket calculator manufactured by a major defense contractor.

When we got down to the business at hand, a major hindrance was immediately apparent. Real growth was to be the whole point of the Reagan defense program; not budget growth that was going to be eroded by inflation. But we still had no idea what inflation assumptions would be included in our forecast.

In those heady days, however, there was no problem a shortcut couldn't overcome. So we settled on specifying the out-year defense budget in constant 1982 dollars. When the economists finally agreed on a forecast, we'd just add an amount for inflation to each year's number, and presto!, we'd have our defense plug.

The next problem was settling on what the 'real growth' should be since Reagan had been all over the lot on that one. An early campaign manifesto, the 'Chicago statement', had called for five percent growth per year, while the campaign's defense hawks had committed their candidate to eight or nine percent growth.

In a parting 'up yours' gesture at the new administration, the Carter lame-duck* budget had already provided five percent real growth through 1986. But Carlucci now maintained that the Carter lame-duck budget would not provide for the kind of weapons modernization, force structure expansion, and readiness and sustainability funding that was needed. We had to think in terms of the eight to nine percent growth range, he said.

Carlucci's suggestion didn't shock me. Under Jack Kemp's influence, I had become a 'big budget' proponent on defense. Some of my hawkishness had to do with the zeal of the convert, and some was the result of pundit George Will's influence on me; George was adamant on defense. Still more of it came from watching the grim footage of the charred remains of the US servicemen being desecrated by the Iranian mullahs at the site known as Desert One.

But I knew that Marty Anderson, back at the Office of Policy Development, was a flinty anti-spender on everything. If I came back to the White House with the higher figure, he'd go off the deep end. The last thing I wanted was a time-consuming punchout at the White House. So I suggested we split the difference down the middle and go with an interim seven percent real growth increase. A fully developed Reagan defense budget could be worked out later in the spring and then we'd get the real answer.

Weinberger thought about it a moment.

'In light of the disgraceful mess we're inheriting,' he said, 'seven percent will be a pretty lean ration.' But he agreed to go along.

There was one last question about the base year from which you started the seven percent real growth calculation. But by now I wasn't listening very well and simply took Carlucci's suggestion that we start with 1982 level after the 'get well' package had been added. I

* A lame duck is a President who has already been voted out of office but has not yet vacated it.

took out my calculator and went to work. Carlucci and Schneider took down the numbers as I called them out.

When we had finished, Weinberger looked at his watch, yawned, and noted it was not yet eight o'clock.

'I'd call this a good night's work,' he said.

My day had begun at 4.30 am and wouldn't end until after midnight, so to me a half hour was a nanosecond, but I had to agree with him. We'd accomplished a lot in a short time.

Or so I thought, until the constant dollar figures we'd come up with were translated into current dollar values. When I finally took a hard look at them several weeks later, I nearly had a heart attack. We'd laid out a plan for a five-year defense budget of *1.46 trillion dollars*!

As my eyes traced along the computer printout, seeing the 'plug' balloon with each progressive out-year, I could hardly believe what I saw. The number started at $142 billion in 1980, and rose to $368 billion by 1986—an increase of 160 percent over the current dollar defense budget in just six years.

'How can this *be*?' I sputtered to Schneider. Patiently, he walked me back through the numbers, step by step. Gradually, I realized what haste can do.

The GOP campaign proposals for a defense hike of five, seven or even nine percent real growth had been predicated on Carter's 1980 defense budget of $142 billion. But in response to Desert One, Congress had raised Carter's request for defense funds and enacted a 1981 budget with nine percent real growth built into it. The Reagan 'get well' package had further raised that to twelve percent real growth. Then, the second Reagan 'get well' instalment for 1982 had added another fifteen percent real growth increase on top of the big 1981 numbers.

What it boiled down to was a gigantic fiscal syllogism: we had taken an already-raised defense budget and raised that by seven percent. Instead of starting from a defense budget of $142 billion, we'd started with one of $222. And by raising that by seven percent—and compounding it over five years—we had ended up increasing the real growth rate of the United States defense budget by *ten percent* per year between 1980 and 1986. That was double what candidate Ronald Reagan had promised in his campaign budget plan.

I stormed about the office fuming over my mistake, but by then the February 18 budget was out and they were squealing with delight throughout the military-industrial complex.

My second expedient, the end-run around the Cabinet, would eventually prove as consequential as the budget plugs.

By now it was clear that Ed Meese was protecting the President from having to choose sides among his cabinet members. He was seeing to it Reagan never had to make a disagreeable choice in front of contending factions. That certainly kept Reagan above the fray, but presidents have to make unpleasant decisions.

Whenever there was an argument, Meese would step in and tell us to take our arguments to some other ad hoc forum. The President would smile and say, 'OK, you fellas work it out.'

I was a quick learner. If the Reagan political household operated by delegation and consensus among subordinates, I would invent my own version of it. My growing pile of unreviewed budget cuts provided an ideal pretext.

This new round of cuts would have generated significant cabinet dissent. A number of the items, such as soil conservation subsidies, urban development grants, and mental health research funds, were the bread and butter of bureaucratic life in cabinet agencies. If Meese was going to remand every dispute to some conference table far removed from the bubble of obliviousness he was constructing around the President, I would never get through them all.

I took him aside, therefore, and proposed another committee—the Budget Working Group. It would, I explained, review all the remaining budget cuts with the affected cabinet officers *before* they went to the President and the full Cabinet. Not only would that speed up the process, but it would prevent the 'gang-bang' dynamic that had already developed among the Cabinet from getting any worse. If it was consensus Meese wanted, then he would get it.

But it wouldn't necessarily be the kind of consensus he had in mind. I didn't have either the time or inclination to go for Meese's kind of consensus. That's the kind that makes everybody happy because no one has to bite any bullets. We had a revolution to make—and that was all bullets.

While both Baker and Meese would be members of my Budget Working Group, I knew neither of them would attend any of the meetings. Certainly Meese wouldn't. His modus operandi was now established. He spent his days following the President around; no matter how perfunctory or ceremonial the event, he was there. So was Baker—and so was Deaver. They were all busy keeping their eye on each other, making sure no one was whispering in the President's ear about the other. It is a phenomenon peculiar to inner circles, but it suited me well. They wouldn't attend a meeting unless the President did.

Meese agreed to my proposal and permitted, as it were, the President to sign off on it himself. I now had my Budget Working Group, and for all practical purposes, it was a stacked deck. It consisted of hard-core anti-spenders, including Marty Anderson, Transportation Secretary Bill Brock, and Murray Weidenbaum. Don Regan and his deputy, Tim McNamar, were also on it, and they too had been taking a hard line on other people's budgets, even on their own.

I told Greider at our next breakfast that I'd found a foolproof way to make the Cabinet swallow my castor oil: 'It'll be [Energy Secretary] Edwards defending [synfuels] against six guys saying, "By God, we've got to cut these back or we're not going to have a savings program that will add up."'

By early in the week of January 26, we had the new budget-cutting machine oiled and rolling. When we switched off the ignition eight days later, nearly every vestige of cabinet opposition to budget cuts had been run over. The cuts we'd made included everything from education impact aid to subsidies for synfuels, physician training, the postal service, Amtrak, local sewer plant construction, and low-income housing, as well as scores of grant programs for community development and health, education and social services.

My system worked for two reasons. First, Meese and Penn James's White House personnel operation was overwhelmed with several thousand slots to fill. As a result there were empty desks all over Washington. Most cabinet secretaries hadn't even yet got their top policy deputies approved. There was a vacuum in their outer offices; and if nature abhors a vacuum, my Budget Working Group did not.

Not having their policy hands in place, the cabinet secretaries were forced to bring career civil service employees with them when they were summoned to the Group's meetings in Room 248 of the

Executive Office Building. We called it the 'Cutting Room'. It was at these meetings that Marty Anderson came into his glory. Among the whole California crowd, Anderson was the only broadly knowledge-able and sophisticated policy analyst.

He also had a knack for driving a wedge between the cabinet officer and his agency's career bureaucrats. The latter would make a smooth, fact-ridden presentation on why such-and-such a cut was imprudent, always making sure to include a line about how 'we're willing to do our part to hold the budget down, but this OMB proposal goes way too far.'

'Now let's see, Mr Branden,' Anderson would start in. 'It is Mr Branden, isn't it?' This was rather coy, since everyone around the table had a big name card at their place.

'How long did you say you've been at HUD*?' Mr Branden hadn't in fact been asked.

'Twelve years,' Mr Branden would say, with an air of incipient discomfort.

'I see,' Anderson continued. 'And you were at another agency before that? Yes? Fine. Now my point, Mr Branden, is I've heard this same argument ever since I was in the Nixon Administration. Delighted as I am to see it hasn't changed, it's still wrong.'

By now Mr Branden would be slumped down, puffing furiously on his pipe and realizing he'd been shish-kebabbed. Anderson's rap was a nice way of emphasizing that the world of Washington was divided into 'them' and 'us', and that anybody who had been in the bureaucracy that long belonged in the former camp.

It was done not to humiliate the Mr Brandens of the world, but for the edification of the cabinet officers who had brought the Mr Brandens with them. After that, cabinet officers felt a little reluctant about siding with 'them' against 'us'.

The second reason the system worked is that the Budget Working Group consisted of first-rate people.

Marty Anderson and Murray Weidenbaum were first-class free market economists. They knew an unjustified and wasteful economic subsidy when they saw one. They recognized that the vast Great Society–spawned system of federal categorical aid for nearly every imaginable purpose from rodent control to special education

* Department of Housing and Urban Development.

for gifted children was nonsense. The national politicians had simply usurped state and local responsibilities.

Likewise, Bill Brock had been a serious student and critic of the burgeoning US welfare state. He brought more than his share of knowledgeability and principled critique of federal spending excesses to the table. In all, the still green cabinet officers who came to the 'Cutting Room' faced overwhelming analytical and intellectual firepower. They usually conceded after only a perfunctory debate.

After eight sessions in the Cutting Room I had won ninety percent of my proposed cuts outright and had been forced to compromise on only a handful.

But in my frantic—and apparently successful—race against the clock, I was creating a troubling atmosphere of misunderstanding.

The President, having been excluded from the nitty-gritty work of deciding what fat to cut, was unable to learn anything of the substantive content of his radical new program, or about why individual cuts were so important. The fruits of the Budget Working Group labors were presented to him in several hour-long blizzards of paper, with the justification for each cut boiled down to a half-page explanation. When he was later called on to justify the cuts, he would remember only that he was making the cut, not why.

Our controversial and draconian scaleback of middle-income student grant and loan aid, for instance, was based on my general critique of middle-class welfare. It was absolutely the right thing to do if you wanted low taxes, low spending and more justice. Why should some steelworker pay taxes to help his plant manager send his kid to a private school out of state?

But it was now justified, as all the other items were, in a single, abstract paragraph. An abrupt change in national higher education policy that would affect seven or eight million students was thus reduced to a glib attempt at reconciling the 'tight fist' and the 'big heart': we would help the neediest students first.

If the President learned any lessons from the hundred individual paragraphs we presented him with, they were undoubtedly the wrong ones. When he later found himself being challenged by congressmen and senators, I would hear him say again and again, 'The fellas in the Cabinet round-tabled all this and are in one hundred percent agreement that these cuts should be made.'

In fact, they hadn't and they weren't. We had brow-beaten the Cabinet, one by one, into accepting the cuts. It was divide-and-conquer, not round-tabling. In my haste to expedite the revolution, I had inadvertently convinced the chief executive that budget cutting was an antiseptic process, a matter of compiling innocuous-sounding 'half-pagers' and putting them in a neatly tabbed black book.

The members of his Cabinet, meanwhile, were no more revolutionary or anti-statist than they had been before; they had only temporarily acquiesced. We forced health research cuts on Dick Schweicker at HHS.* We stiffed Jack Block with soil conservation cuts at USDA.** We shackled Ted Bell with a sweeping retrenchment at the Education Department.

They all gave lip-service defense to these spending cutbacks during the first season of real-world legislative battle. But in time the original cuts were largely ignored by the 'fellas' who had purportedly round-tabled them.

Yet the supply-side economic policy revolution could add up only if deep dents were kicked in the side of the welfare state. This meant remaining in the political trenches year after year until the middle of the decade. The work of shrinking back the spending boundaries of the state had to proceed in tandem with the automatic fall of its revenue claim on the national economy, as the multi-year tax cuts achieved full maturity.

The Cabinet was not disposed to that kind of patient attack on spending. This first big round of cuts involved the easy ones—and even those left everyone miffed. My Budget Working Group would prove to have succeeded only on paper, not in the real world of politics. The President never had the foggiest notion of why.

The Budget Working Group did, however, face stiff resistance on three matters. Those three battles were instructive and pointed to the real, lasting score in the illusory brave new world of the moment. The first involved Mac Baldrige, Secretary of Commerce, and cutting the Export-Import Bank.

This was an initiative dear to my free market heart. Export subsidies are a mercantilist illusion, based on the illogical proposi-

* Department of Health and Human Services.
** US Department of Agriculture.

tion that a nation can raise its employment and GNP by giving away its goods for less than what it costs to make them. They are nothing less than philanthropy on an international scale. Export subsidies subtract from GNP and jobs, not expand them.

Export subsidies are the classic case of the single-entry book-keeping mentality that has larded the federal budget with so much boodle.* Their champions say, in effect, Give Boeing some money so they can make more planes and create more exports, jobs and tax revenues. But you could give Boeing money to build pyramids and the same thing would happen.

The problem is simple: the interest rate subsidy has to be paid for by taxing someone, or by borrowing. But if you tax someone, or borrow, you reduce economic activity elsewhere in the national economy. You can't ever escape double-entry bookkeeping. The politicians nevertheless keep messing up the economy by pretending they can.

Moreover, in 1981, the Export Import Bank's practice was to bestow about two thirds of its subsidies on a handful of giant manufacturers, including Boeing Aircraft, General Electric and Westinghouse. I had long insisted, to any liberal who would listen, that the supply-side revolution would be different from the corrupted opportunism of the organized business groups; that it would go after weak claims like Boeing's, not just weak clients such as food stamp recipients. Giving the heave-ho to the well-heeled lobbyists of the big corporations who kept the whole scam alive would be dramatic proof that we meant business, not business-as-usual.

But Mac Baldridge was a protectionist leaning manufacturer. He had no understanding of free market doctrine, and no willingness to hear about it. To him, my proposal amounted to 'unilateral disarmament' in the war for export markets. His position, needless to say, boiled down to insisting that if the French were foolish enough to give away great gobs of their national patrimony subsidizing aircraft sales, then we should not hesitate to do the same.

I did win a victory of sorts in the Cutting Room. After two and a half hours of table-pounding and an outpouring of purple rhetoric (from both sides), we compromised and cut the Ex-Im's lending

* Illicit money.

budget by forty percent. The $7 billion that the Carter Administration had proposed was thus cut to $4 billion.

Baldridge was to reopen the Ex-Im issue every year—and Congress raised its budget every year. But I was learning. The Ex-Im subsidies were a fiscally trivial yet symbolically important piece of corporate welfare. They were as deeply embedded in the system as were all the other subventions and illicit gifts to the organized clients of the Second Republic.

I had also set about with considerable gusto in dismantling the Department of Energy's entire technology development budget in one glorious fell swoop, following the guidelines in the Republican platform.

Among the wasteful corruptions of the Second Republic, the Carter Energy Department stood out in my mind as a great, malodorous garbage dump. The Carter budget had allocated $17 billion for the Energy Department over the years 1982–86. What for? So that it could subsidize such economic white elephants as a multi-billion-dollar coal-liquefication plant for the Gulf Oil Company, windmills, fluidized bed combusters, solar-power towers, gasahol plants, shale plants, stirling engines, photovoltaic cells, and countless other experiments in high-cost, unproven energy technologies.

There was nothing wrong with all this experimentation. It's precisely the kind of thing Adam Smith had invented the free market to accomplish. But the federal bureaucracy was neither competent nor called upon to usurp the job.

The sight of lobbyists for oil, natural gas, utility and equipment manufacturers lining around the block at DOE*, drove me up a wall. So, too, did the spectacle of the congressional energy committees— and their members' upturned palms.

And now Jim Edwards the Dentist himself was sitting in the Cutting Room with his upturned palms, mouthing every platitude and confusion upon which the whole foul enterprise had been launched.

The synfuels (synthetic fuel) plants he was fighting to save would 'put a cap on world oil prices,' he said. Never mind that it was not in the power of the US Department of Energy to alter something called the law of supply and demand.

* Department of Energy.

'We can't cut back too far on fossil, solar and conservation programs or we will undermine congressional support for the nuclear development program,' he insisted. Taxpayers were supposed to be paying for those boondoggles*, too?

Such was the extent of the Dentist's commitment to the free market ideology of the Reagan Revolution.

Eventually the debate degenerated into show-and-tell hour, with the Dentist and his DOE bureaucrats explaining how peat moss and garbage could generate steam. Why you could make it out of corn, sugar cane, wood chips, and about anything else which burned. Then there was hardworking, underpaid Exxon. It was on the verge of a dramatic technological breakthrough with its donor solvent process for converting coal to gasoline . . .

I was amazed to hear this from a member of Ronald Reagan's Cabinet. I tried to be diplomatic. But I was still churning inside a few days later when I described the whole sorry incident to Greider.

'The government built [Exxon's] plant,' I told him. 'Now we're spending $60 million per year to help them run it. Well, I'll be goddamned if I'm going to spend $60 million to help Exxon run a demonstration plant. They can run it themselves.'

With Marty Anderson and Murray Weidenbaum strongly behind me, I eventually overpowered Edwards on most of the issues. The February 18 budget recommended the elimination of all six of DOE's synfuels plants, as well as $11 billion—two thirds—of its five-year energy development and subsidy budget.

Edwards left the Cutting Room bitter, spoiling for a fight and waiting to get even. I left the room to the congratulations of my staff, but with the gnawing feeling that my Grand Doctrine was coming up against a truly hostile and unyielding political world. What I did not then know was how little weight the paper recommendations of a presidential budget carry on Capitol Hill—particularly when you've got a whole department full of bureaucrats, including the top one, working for the other side.

It was during the third and final major battle of the Budget Working Group that I really met my match. The results are best expressed in the language of my opponent. I was bureaucratically outsavvied as I obtained my first ocular orientation of the

* Schemes that waste money and time.

de-revolutionary posturization of the governancal process. Translation: I got rolled by Al Haig.

The Gramm-Stockman budget plan had called for deep cuts in foreign economic aid on the basis of pure ideological principle. Both Gramm and I believed that the organs of international aid and so-called Third World development—the UN, the multilateral banks, and the US Agency for International Development—were infested with socialist error. The international aid bureaucracy was turning Third World countries into quagmires of self-imposed inefficiency and burying them beneath mountainous external debts they would never be able to pay.

For the Budget Working Group's session on 'foreign aid retrenchment', I therefore wanted to reduce US multilateral and bilateral aid by forty-five percent—a $13 billion saving over 1982–86. The proposed changes were far-reaching. Carter's $3.2 billion pledge to the World Bank's 'soft' loan program would be cancelled; so would all future US funding commitments to the other regional multilateral banks. Likewise, contributions to the UN agencies would be permanently frozen.

Carter's huge recommended AID* increases would also be eliminated. Just for good measure, the Peace Corps budget would be cut by twenty-five percent.

My recommendations had to be sent to the agencies involved forty-eight hours before the Cutting Room session; they were to be held in tight secrecy by the cabinet secretary and his top policy aides. Yet within twenty-four hours of their transmittal on Tuesday, 27 January, a world crisis was under way.

The entire document—including the black binder cover it had been sent over in—had been reproduced on the State Department Xerox machines in massive quantities. From there, still warm, they had been sent out with a speed to rival that of Federal Express. Absolutely and positively, they found their way into the foreign aid-minded warrens of Capitol Hill, into all the embassies that line Massachusetts Avenue. By the end of the following day it had become a major press sensation. Thursday's front-page story in *The Washington Post* reflected the barometric pressure of the gale:

David A. Stockman has proposed the biggest cutback of foreign

* Agency for International Development.

aid since its inception in the aftermath of World War II. . . Stockman's plan calls for drastically trimming every facet of non-military aid. . . [The] proposals are certain to trigger an outburst of fierce opposition from foreign aid supporters. . .

They did, with a little help from State. All day Thursday I was deluged with phone calls from the Hill. By the end of the day I had even received a copy of a letter to Secretary Haig from Congressman Silvio Conte, a strong supporter of foreign aid and the ranking Republican on the House Appropriations Committee. The letter was a lengthy critique of my proposal. Oddly, it contained language almost identical to the language in the 'confidential analysis' the State Department had just sent to us. Subsequently, I learned that State had instructed US ambassadors abroad to 'generate a reaction' from their host governments.

By the time of the Cutting Room session that Friday afternoon, the issue was so superheated that I decided I had to invite Haig to my office beforehand in an effort to calm things down. But it was not a calm man who walked—stormed—into my office that day. It was General Haig, and he had come, in military parlance, to take names and kick ass.

'I am truly shocked by these leaks,' he began. I was momentarily speechless. The proposition that they had come from me was so preposterous that it worked. I let it drop because I couldn't bring myself to believe that he believed it himself.

Seeing that his opening salvo had produced the desired effect, he ordered a cease-fire. He then told me that while he was not unmindful of the need for budgetary 'restraint', he and no one else was 'in charge of policy'.

For the time being, I could only wonder how he could so easily separate budgetary restraint from policy, inasmuch as the two are inextricably linked. But his main point was coming through loud and clear: he didn't know whether foreign aid was effective or not. He hadn't really studied it, and he didn't really care. The administration, however, had to be 'realistic'. He reiterated: 'The whole international community expects continuity in US policy, and as long as I'm in charge, those commitments and expectations are going to be met.'

In response, I made some stiff remarks to the effect that the

Reagan Revolution in economic policy couldn't just stop at the water's edge. I urged him to look into the can of worms his bureaucracy was rushing him into defending. But he never heard a word of it.

In his mind, the whole issue had boiled down to what is known in Washington as a turf battle. He was the experienced man of war and affairs—the man who had landed at Inchon with MacArthur and who had talked a President into resigning—and now a thirty-four-year-old upstart was telling him what he could and couldn't do.

Instead, he started reciting from all the 'urgent' cables from allies and deploring the uproar of the Hill. He concluded on a quasi-conciliatory note, saying we ought to 'get the issue behind us as soon as possible.' Meaning, Let's have no more of this crap, OK? It was a formidable display of bullying. I agreed to withdraw my proposal and to entertain a private counterproposal from him the following week, laying out a more modest savings plan. Meanwhile, we agreed to use the Budget Working Group meeting for a 'low key' discussion of the 'policy' issues, as he viewed them.

'Low key' it wasn't. Normally ten to fifteen people attended Cutting Room sessions. When we walked into it this time, it was packed to the rafters with Haig's entourage of forty or fifty people from State and the Agency for International Development. Immediately Haig began to complain. To quote his words: 'I can't make decisions in a roomful of people. There are forty people here. I don't know who they are!'

It was . . . surreal. They were *his* people—he had brought them. And now he was saying he couldn't be expected to decide anything in their presence. Not surprisingly, the meeting broke up without having produced any results. Late that afternoon I was back in my office when the phone rang. It was Haig. He was furious.

'You know,' he said, 'I no more than got back to my office and the press was calling me about the outcome of the meeting.'

I was still fuming about it the next morning when I told Greider, 'Well, hell, it wasn't me who called the press about the outcome of the meeting. Jesus Christ, he did it twice!'

Haig and I met again the following week. He quibbled with every single line of the foreign aid budget. Eventually, we ended up with a more modest proposal to reduce foreign aid by $7.5 billion over four years. But when it went to the Congress on February 18, that was the last time the Secretary of State ever paid any attention to the figure. It turned out that 'realism' required an urgent 'supplemental' funding request about every other month.

The policy officials at State and Aid rationalized these requests as a 'politically balanced' program of military aid and Third World welfare. Of course, when it came time for them to write up 'talking points' for the President's pleading session with reluctant congressional Republicans, that rationale was not in evidence.

'Now I've always been against the traditional economic aid boondoggles,' the President would say, after checking his State Department talking points, 'but our program is totally different.'

Well, it wasn't—not in the slightest. But as a consequence of Haig's and State's determination, hardly one dime of the $7.5 billion (over four years) in foreign aid savings ever materialized.

Yet so naïve was I that after the episode I actually bragged to Greider that I had won the fight, and let Haig claim victory. In fact, when Haig and I met, one-to-one, to work out the final compromise, both of us had lost track of the numbers. As a result, the numbers tipped slightly in my favor when they were published in the February 18 'White Paper'. That these paper 'savings' didn't mean a thing, I would not find out until later in the season.

By the first week of February I was an ambulatory bundle of contradictions. OMB was going at seventy-eight rpm to meet the February 18 deadline. I was encouraged by the progress we were making on the budget savings front, especially now that the five dozen program reductions we'd rammed through the Budget Working Group the previous week were added to the big entitlement changes the President had approved before the inauguration.

The savings looked impressive. Our OMB scorecard showed a savings of $26 billion in 1982, rising to $47 billion by 1984. On a cumulative basis this added up to nearly $220 billion for the five-year period. These numbers were way above what had ever been proposed or debated in the Congress. The morale at OMB was fantastic. We were ripping through the stuff. Today the Energy Department, tomorrow Education; the day after, the world! There was a feeling of 'it can be done' in our offices. In a very short time we had built a streamlined Rube Goldberg device: a conveyor belt that led to a chopping block. It seemed like the fiscal equation was really starting to add up.

Despite the sporadic resistance of some of the cabinet members and the screaming and foot-stamping of the Dentist and the General, the White House appeared to be a bastion of support for my work. The President had not flinched on the 'big ticket' entitlement reforms such as cutting food stamps and retirement pensions. Marty Anderson and Murray Weidenbaum had been splendid and constant allies in the Cutting Room. And even the so-called Baker Wing—the liberal saboteurs that the *Human Events* Magazine gang and other right-wingers had been declaiming against—was being cooperative.

I spent almost the whole first week of February on Capitol Hill, briefing clusters of Republican senators and congressmen on the upcoming budget reduction package. I didn't pull any punches as to what we had in mind, presenting them with black binders full of 'two-pagers' on each of the significant spending cuts.

To my surprise, the GOP rank and file was not making any categorical objections to the 'two-pagers' during this process of congressional test marketing.

To be sure, I was picking up a few, well, friendly hints. Senator Jesse Helms, the right-wing firebrand from North Carolina, took me aside after one session. He was very fatherly, soliticitous, and supportive.

'The whole nation is depending on you,' he said. 'Now, you go right to it, boy. But don't let them OMB bureaucrats down there confuse you. The tobacco program doesn't cost the taxpayers one red cent. And it never will as long as I'm chairman of the Agriculture Committee.'

What struck me most favorably that week on the Hill was the favorable attitude of the Senate moderates, the group that we in the Kemp circle had previously looked on with grave suspicion. Budget Committee Chairman Pete Domenici had found nothing in the entire $220 billion reduction package that he seriously objected to. He was already gearing up his staff and Committee to move on it immediately after February 18.

Bob Dole, chairman of the Senate Finance Committee and the Nutrition Subcommittees, which would carry a huge share of the entitlement reduction load, had also been highly supportive. He had told me he was eager for me to spend as much time with his Committee members as possible, laying out the case for each of the proposed reforms.

Even two of the self-anointed liberals had volunteered their best efforts. Public Works Chairman Bob Stafford had agreed to eliminate the EDA* and Appalachian development programs. And subcommittee chairman John Chaffee had declared he would go along with a substantial scaleback of the $4 billion per year sewer grant progam. He asked for only minor changes in our proposal.

On the House side, the reaction had been even more encouraging. I hadn't expected any help, needless to say, from the liberal democrats, but I had agreed to a 'courtesy' meeting with the House Democratic leadership.

I had arrived for that meeting with some trepidation. Tip O'Neill greeted me and ushered me to a huge wing chair. There were two identical wing chairs; I sat in one, he in the other. He took up considerably more of his than I did of mine, so that the overall effect was slightly comical.

Our chairs were arrayed so that they faced a semicircle consisting, among others, of Carl Perkins of Kentucky, chairman of the Education and Labor Committee; Jim Jones of Oklahoma, chairman of the Budget Committee; Dan Rostenkowski of Illinois, chairman of the Ways and Means Committee; Dick Bolling of Missouri, chairman of the Rules Committee; and Jim Wright of Texas, Majority Leader. From my uncertain seat I stared out at the faces of the Politburo of the Welfare State.

Their faces were not implacable, exactly, but collectively they were enough to give pause even to the most self-assured radical conservative. O'Neill, with his massive corpulence and scarlet, varicose nose, was a Hogarthian embodiment of the superstate he had labored for so long to maintain. Carl Perkins had practically created the Great Society single-handedly. Richard Bolling was the liberal master strategist of the Democratic majority. And Jim Wright was a snake oil vendor par excellence, a demagogue of frightening rhetorical powers. When Wright got warmed up, there was no Bible-thumper in the country could touch him. But it was the Speaker who opened the conversation.

* Economic Development Administration.

'We realize some of the old ways have to change,' he said. That disarmed me, all right. 'It's a new day. A different time. But,' he continued ('Here it comes,' I thought), 'we're bothered by some of these social spending cuts we're reading about in the newspapers. We hope it isn't what it sounds like.'

Fair enough. I took a run at the school lunch cut. It was being described in the press as an improvement upon the cruelty of Oliver Twist's overseers. I explained that it did not take a dime from the nine million poverty-level students who were affected, it only eliminated the token subsidy that went to families above *twice* the median income. The Speaker of the House and other members of the Politburo expressed both gratitude and amazement. They hadn't even known that the subsidy was going to children whose parents earned over $18,000 a year.

My session with the Politburo went well. It was a good icebreaker, and O'Neill generously ended the session by saying to his colleagues, 'We don't agree with everything, but this young fellow sure knows what he's talking about.'

For a flicking moment I almost felt badly about the campaign ads that had drawn a huge Tip O'Neill look-alike (the big spending enemy) riding along in a long stretch limousine (the Congress) and running out of gas (your money). Almost.

On Friday of the same week I addressed the House Republican rank and file in a full caucus meeting. The large class of freshmen whooped it up on budget cutting as if the session had been a pep rally for the home team. That Saturday I gave Greider an upbeat assessment of our congressional prospects:

> On the Hill, it's been good. Hell, I went up there to speak to the caucus the other day and they cheered and stomped and said, 'Keep it up!' I think the fact that I came from up there may help sell this program. I mean, it's not coming from some guy they never heard of.

At the end of the first week in February, however, I returned from the Hill to trouble below. The OMB technicians had finally got us some overall budget numbers. They were based on a forecast that wasn't the final slap of Weidenbaum's computer, but it was getting there. The numbers were shocking. And that took some doing, because at the moment I was riding too high to be shocked by anything.

At the Blair House meeting of January 7, I had estimated the budget gap to be $75 billion. That meant we must find $75 billion of domestic spending cuts to balance the budget by 1984. But now OMB was showing that after Kemp-Roth and the 10–5–3 depreciation reform, and the defense buildup, there would be a deficit of *$130 billion* by 1984. The cumulative five-year deficit totalled more than $600 billion.

In those days, a deficit of $130 billion was just not imaginable. No one in the Reagan entourage or supply-side camp had ever seen or expected a domestic spending cut requirement even close to $130 billion. It was nearly double all the back-of-the-envelope calculations that had previously been made. John Anderson's taunt was now an actual challenge far more imposing than we had expected. Suddenly, the ruthless efficiency of my Budget Working Group cutting machine didn't look so imposing at all. We had ended up with only $47 billion in domestic savings for 1984—just one third of what we needed to achieve a balanced budget. We still had a long way to go and almost no time left to get there.

I called Jim Baker and asked him to schedule an emergency meeting of the entire senior White House staff to discuss the gap.

We assembled on Saturday morning, February 7, in the Roosevelt Room. Directly across from the Oval Office, the Roosevelt Room is the functional center of the West Wing of the White House. Teddy Roosevelt's Nobel Peace Prize medallion sits on the mantle. The room is oval and windowless, hung with paintings of American landscapes. Much history has originated in that room. The historians of the Reagan era will judge that our meeting that morning was the point of no return.

I should have blown the whistle and called off the blitzkrieg. But a radical ideologue at the height of his powers does not stop, in mid-headlong rush, to wonder how history will judge him years from then. I had momentum, I had won victories, I would win more. The pace couldn't be slackened for a moment. To falter now would be to leave the Reagan Revolution stillborn and defeated. If there was a problem—and there was—I would come up with new schemes during the two weeks that remained before the launch.

I had already casually moved the target date for a balanced budget from 1983, which Reagan had promised during the campaign, to 1984. There hadn't been so much as a 'What's *that* again?' from anyone in the White House. But then everyone's noses were so deep in paper they simply hadn't noticed.

But that was merely a straw in the wind compared to what would come next. I soon became a veritable incubator of shortcuts, schemes and devices to overcome the truth now upon us—that the budget gap couldn't be closed except by a dictator.

The more I flopped and staggered around, however, the more they went along. I could have been wearing a sandwich board sign saying: *Stop me, I'm dangerous*! Even then they might not have.

During the Roosevelt Room meeting I presented a whole new package of deficit reduction measures. I'd driven my staff around the clock to ready it in the previous several days.

I called it 'Chapter Two', and it encompassed a whole new batch of items from my anti-statist agenda. These included user fees on general aviation and yachters, elimination of tax loopholes like the oil depletion allowance and industrial development bonds, and drastic curtailment of dairy, maritime, water projects, and other business-oriented subsidies. The plan also included a cap on the tax deductibility of home mortgage costs by upper-income taxpayers. We called it a 'mansion tax'.

In all, 'Chapter Two' would have provided more than $20 billion in additional savings by 1984. Philosophically, it substantially broadened the reach of the entire program. By ending subsidies to commercial interest groups and a wide range of middle- and upper-income taxpayers, it dramatized the underlying fairness and justice of the whole supply-side vision.

What it didn't do was come close to raising the savings count to the needed $130 billion.

Bookkeeping invention thus began its wondrous works. We invented the 'magic asterisk': if we couldn't find the savings in time—and we couldn't—we would issue an IOU. We would call it—'Future savings to be identified'.

It was marvelously creative. A magic asterisk item would cost *negative* $30 billion . . . $40 billion . . . whatever it took to get to a balanced budget in 1984 after we toted up all the individual budget cuts we'd actually approved.

The circumstances of this accounting invention were slightly more innocent than what eventually materialized. I'd never believed we could review the entire $740 billion Federal budget before February 18. So I had contemplated two more budget cut packages to be transmitted to Congress later.

The first would consist of all the 'cats and dogs' savings proposals we expected to come up with after a comprehensive scrub of the Carter Administration's official lame-duck budget for 1982. While these would not be big dollar items, cumulatively they would provide a significant additional savings, perhaps $10 billion per year. This additional savings package would be completed within weeks, and was thus known as the 'March revisions'.

The second additional cut package would involve big dollars and the true heavy lifting, politically speaking, of the Reagan fiscal revolution. It would entail sweeping reform of the big middle-class entitlement programs: Social Security, Medicare and federal retirement pensions.

My Grand Doctrine was basically hostile to the prevailing 'social insurance' premise on which these giant programs rested. Stripping out 'unearned' benefits and welfare components from the retirement program and means-testing Medicare would result in huge cost reductions.

Thus between the March revisions package and the big hit on middle-class welfare, I had a theory on where the magic asterisk savings would come from. The problem was twofold, however. First, the budget plan was now getting complicated, with three different layers of savings. There were a lot of cracks in comprehension at the White House between which things could still fall.

Secondly, the framework of the fiscal plan would be unveiled on February 18. But the thing that would ultimately make it add up—sweeping curtailment of middle-class entitlements—would remain shrouded in mystery, at least temporarily. The false impression that you could have huge tax cuts and a big defense increase without storming the twin citadels of the welfare state—Social Security and Medicare—could easily be conveyed.

At the emergency meeting on February 7, I thus warned everyone that a huge budget gap remained to be filled despite our spending cut progress to date. Both 'Chapter Two' and these additional budget cut packages would be needed to close the deficit gap.

To his credit, Marty Anderson immediately expressed serious reservations about the 'future savings' plug. 'If the number ends up too big,' he said, 'you're going to undermine the whole credibility of the program from day one.' He insisted that we needed to spend the whole remaining week, if necessary, digging up further specific itemized cuts that could be proposed on February 18.

Then came a new complication. Despite whatever agreement I had with Cap Weinberger, Anderson insisted we had to come up with at least 'token' savings in the defense area. Now, it was technically impossible to display a 'defense cut' since we were in fact *adding* nearly $150 billion in outlays to the pre-Reagan five-year defense level. I explained this several different ways but it simply failed to penetrate the group's comprehension. Instead, the others present—Baker, Meese, Brock, Weidenbaum, and Regan—all joined in the clamor. We had to have 'defense cuts' too.

As the meeting progressed, the confusion multiplied. All the loose ends that until that point had not been seriously focused upon by the entire senior staff began percolating up to the Roosevelt Room table. That was not surprising, since it was our first look at the overall budget since the fumbling episode at the Blair House on January 7.

Don Regan made a contribution, too. He levied a twenty-five cent fine on me for calling the 'Reagan 10–10–10' tax cut by its former designation, 'Kemp-Roth'. He also warned that the pressure from congressional Republicans to include some of their favorite special interest gimmicks in the President's tax proposal was becoming intense.

But all in all, the meeting was beginning to stumble toward paydirt. We had only eleven days remaining, actually far fewer 'working days' due to the turnaround time needed for document production and advance briefings. A collective recognition was developing that we still faced a jumble of unresolved issues and an overall fiscal equation that was far from adding up.

Nevertheless, the laws of White House bureaucratic life exerted themselves before any real awakening could firmly set in. After two hours or so of deliberations, the discussion came to a screeching halt. Everyone, it seemed, had to be somewhere else in a matter of minutes. So the jumble of problems and possibilities on the table produced no reconsideration of where we were heading.

Toward the end of that black day, I had a long session with Greider in my office. I'd missed our usual breakfast getting ready for the emergency meeting. I confessed to him that the budget gap was still huge and that the tenor of my message at the meeting had been, 'Boys, we're coming up short.'

But I told him I thought we could close the gap in part with a new round of cuts called 'Chapter Two'. They were aimed at middle- and upper-income groups and corporate welfare, and they were hard evidence that we intended to attack weak claims, not just weak clients.

'They signed off on every one of them,' I told Greider. I was confident that the whole Chapter Two package would fly. It would add a powerful new equity dimension to the entire economic program, and would prove a strong antidote to the black eye my cuts had rapidly begun to acquire in the news media. The editorial cartoonists were featuring me either as the Grim Reaper, hovering with a scythe over a shivering huddle of wretched poor, or as Scrooge, merrily depriving cripples of their turkey. In the midst of it all the 'mansion tax', zapping the oil depletion allowance and squeezing yacht owners, would help to even out the picture.

Still, these charges that the Reagan program was anti-poor infuriated me. My Grand Doctrine had to do with just the opposite: it aimed to reverse both the national economic impoverishment and the rampant injustice that characterized the Second Republic's decaying regime. All subsidies were equally bad, whether buried in the tax code or stuffed in the budget, if they caused inefficiency and injustice. The oil depletion allowance wasted economic resources as much as did the CETA public jobs program.

So, rather than viewing the newly expanding and worrisome budget gap as a threat, I saw it as another, unexpected opportunity to force the logic of my Grand Doctrine deeper and more comprehensively into the initial economic program of the Reagan Administration.

'I always wanted to do Chapter Two,' I told Greider.

I had no conception until our numbers started adding short about two weeks ago that I would be in a position to actively, to successfully advance it so soon. I knew you couldn't close the whole gap by cutting marginal social programs or the energy department budget. You could only do it with an unorthodox strategy of equity in the shrinkage process. That was part of my strategy to force acquiescence in the last minute into a lot of things you would never see a Republican Administration propose.

Greider, who knew the instincts of Republican politicians better than I, remained sceptical. He doubted that Chapter Two would survive. But I was now confident that I had allies and that a breakthrough was possible.

Suddenly remembering that I was tempting the national news editor of *The Washington Post* with more explosive information than someone in his position might be expected to keep to himself, I reminded Greider that we were off the record.

'If you tell your guys about this shit, I'll have 160 people calling the White House,' I told him.

Greider smiled. 'You will anyway,' he said.

Two things were certain about the events after February 7. The first was that as we went into the final ten days, the President of the United States was not even given the slightest warning that his economic policy revolution was bursting at its fiscal seams. I'd made perfunctory status reports at a couple of cabinet meetings. For all practical purposes, however, he'd been out of the loop completely since inauguration week. He knew nothing about the forecast debate, the defense plug, the $130 billion deficit gap, Chapter Two or the 'future savings' promises we were building into the plan.

There was an indecent irony to this two-week gap in the President's economic policy log. His architect had been frenetically designing a fiscal house of cards for the New Order. Meanwhile, he had been busily trying to persuade the agog congressional Republicans to support an emergency increase in the debt ceiling to keep the old order solvent. They were kicking and screaming at the idea. But he told them once his new economic plan was enacted, they'd never, ever have to do it again.

'This is the last time I will ever ask you to do this,' he declared, with the air of a parent asking a son to take his dateless sister to the prom. And as far as he knew, it was the last time. What he couldn't know was that he would end up raising the national debt by more than all of his predecessors combined.

The second certainty was that the final week of White House deliberation on the economic plan gave a new definition to the concept of chaos—leaving the notion of confusion with no remaining worlds to conquer.

Symptomatic of this is that we did not have a final economic forecast and final estimate of the budget gap until the *last day for decisions*. The promised additional 1984 saving needed for a balanced budget might be $30 billion, $40 billion, $50 billion. We'd find out at the end.

Still, someone might have asked some basic questions. How many congressional horses do you need to cut $40 billion more—on top of the black book full of cuts already proposed? How many horses do we actually have?

This essential political feasibility question was never asked. Our team had no serious legislative experience or wisdom. Most of them had no comprehension of the numbers, and I didn't really care. Mowing down the political resistance was the whole purpose of the Reagan Revolution.

Moreover, you couldn't even grab that 'future savings' number, stick it up in the wind, and see which way it pointed. The number bounced up and down and all over the place during the last five days.

The OMB numbers–crunchers were already working around the clock, but we were trying to remake a $700 billion budget in two or three weeks. Decisions were being made, unmade, modified, and revised by the hour. There was thus a traffic jam of numbers flowing into the OMB central computer.

I had invented a one-page budget scoresheet to keep everyone posted on the numbers. I knew what it meant, almost. But it was beyond reason to believe anyone else could have.

Nevertheless, on Tuesday 10 February a full cabinet meeting was held to update the President and his team on the budget plan that had to be locked in and finished by Friday.

The scoresheet showed 1984 revenues after the tax cut, and total outlays after the defense increase but before any domestic spending cuts. The difference between those two numbers was the starting budget gap—$129 billion.

The rest of the table was supposed to tell you how much of the $129 billion we had already saved and how much we had left to go. But that's where everything got complicated. Both the haste and my expedients had given rise to four different categories of savings numbers, 'approved savings, Budget Working Group—$71 billions;

pending savings, Budget Working Group—$9 billion; expected additional savings from small programs and accounts (March revisions)—$15 billion; remaining savings to be identified—$33 billion.'

If you squinted hard enough at this complicated scoresheet, you could see something important: we were four days from D-Day, yet we had only $71 billion in firm savings in the bank, or just over *half* of what it took to get a balanced budget. The other three categories were either still up in the air or just air.

But no one squinted hard at the scoresheet or maybe even looked at all. No one said, 'Now just where are you going to get the $58 billion savings in the last three categories? Name names. Kick some tail! Gore some oxes! Slay some sacred cows right here on the cabinet table!'

To be sure, I went over the numbers and tried to convey the meaning.

'We can make it add up, but what remains to be cut,' I told them, 'is nearly as big as what we've already cut. The additional cuts will be far tougher than anything we've already agreed upon.'

There was no dissent. The Cabinet apparently figured there was room in the Reagan Revolution for the Russell Long caveat: 'Don't cut you, don't cut me, cut the guy behind the tree.'

The President nodded. 'We're here to do whatever it takes,' he said. He would make this statement over and over in the future. It was his mantra.

In effect, the President was letting his fiscal architect develop his economic policy revolution for him. He was taking my plan on faith alone, having no reason to suspect that the numbers wouldn't add up.

If there were no questions or dissent at the cabinet meeting, however, there was something much worse: confusion. A number of the cabinet officers complained that the administration was getting a 'black eye' because of the proposed social cuts. I tried to calm them by pointing to the Chapter Two cuts.

'Barge operators, dairy farmers, general aviation, big oil,' I said, rattling off the list, 'they're all going to take their hit too.'

Warming to our defense, I then began to tick off a number of so-called social programs that we hadn't cut a dime out of. Social Security, Medicare, veterans' benefits, Head Start, Supplemental

Security Income for the poor, disabled, and elderly, summer jobs programs for ghetto youth. But—crucial point—it wasn't that we intended to spare those programs; they would have to be cut too if the whole fiscal plan was to work. It was simply that we hadn't yet got around to cutting them.

My own facility for rattling off lists proved to be my undoing. Before I had finished my recitation, there was a clamor around the table.

'That's great!' someone said. 'We've got to get this out.'

Ed Meese immediately threw in that he thought it was a swell idea. I should 'get with' him, Press Secretary Jim Brady, and Dave Gergen right after the meeting to work out a press announcement for the next day.

The whole point of the cabinet meeting had been to inform them we would need *$58 billion in additional cuts*. But—in part through my carelessness—they were now about to fence off enormous chunks of the budget and say, in effect, 'See, we haven't touched these!' We were turning into The Gang That Couldn't Cut Straight.

When we huddled after the meeting, I warned Meese and the others, 'We can't imply that they're exempted from cuts entirely.' At best, I said, we can say we're not going to cut the 'basic benefits' in these areas. 'That doesn't exempt them from serious reform.'

Meese then declared an on-the-spot compromise. The 'sacred cows' list would include the five I had mentioned plus two more for good measure: low-income school lunches and veterans' disability benefits.

I left the Cabinet Room thinking that the 'basic benefits' proviso gave me all the running room I would need when time came to lower the axe. But it was a meaningless proviso.

The lead in the next day's *New York Times* story showed exactly what kind of damage had been done:

> President Reagan's abrupt announcement yesterday sparing seven basic social programs from budget cuts . . .

The fact was these seven programs accounted for $240 billion of baseline spending—more than forty percent of the domestic budget. And we had just neatly built a fence around them. Henceforth people would wave these newspaper clippings in our face over and over.

The next day, Wednesday, brought another bombshell.

Up to now, the President had remained almost entirely passive. At a meeting that day we brought up the Chapter Two tax expenditure proposals, starting with the oil depletion allowance. All of a sudden, the President became animated. Our proposal unleashed a pent-up catechism on the virtues of the oil depletion allowance, followed by a lecture on how the whole idea of 'tax expenditures' was a liberal myth.

'The idea implies that the government owns all your income and has the right to decide what you can keep,' said the President. 'Well, we're not going to have any of that kind of thinking round here.'

Having rendered forty percent of the budget immune from cutting on Tuesday, Wednesday the entire tax code was put off limits.

When I met with Greider to tell him that my Chapter Two cuts—the ones I had so triumphantly said would sail through the White House—had been discarded, I was somewhat sheepish and awed. I told him that an unexpected, and adamant, Ronald Reagan had risen to the occasion. What I didn't tell him because I still didn't realize it myself was that my whole plan was now in big trouble.

> The President has a very clear philosophy. A lot of people criticize him for being short on the details, but he knows when something's wrong. He just jumped all over my tax proposals . . . he doesn't believe in tax expenditures. We didn't even bring up the other proposals. When we got shot down so fast on the depletion allowance, I figured, 'Well, this is futile.'

By Friday 13 February when we met for a wrap-up session, the scoresheet showed that we had backed ourselves into a tight corner. Itemized 1984 deficit reductions would total about $70 billion. The 'future savings to be proposed' would now amount to a negative $50 billion. That was a bigger number than everything then in the budget except defense, Social Security and interest.

Defense had become cockeyed, too. To satisfy the White House staff clamor for defense cuts, I essentially conjured up a mirage. The February 18 budget would now show $6 billion in 'defense savings' as part of the $70 billion cut total for 1984. Over five years, the new defense savings number was $28 billion.

But I had to keep my agreement with Weinberger, too. So I just raised the pre-Reagan baseline by $28 billion, added Weinberger's increase, then subtracted the new 'defense savings'. This two-sided bookkeeping entry left Weinberger happy and everyone else confused. It was only symptomatic.

After the plan had been signed off on Friday, the numbers kept moving all weekend. The exhausted and frantic OMB professional staff struggled to catch up. When I came into the office on Sunday morning, Dale McComber, the *numero uno* of federal budgeteers, was still chained to his desk. He'd been there all night. Dale was scratching his head; he wasn't impressed by the madness that had gone on—and it still didn't add up.

Due to final technical reestimating, the itemized savings proposals had shrunk down to $64 billion. Fortunately, the total budget gap for 1984 had come down, too. Still, to get the budget to balance in 1984, we'd have to put a negative $44 billion in the 'future savings' line.

McComber then reminded me that Marty Anderson and the whole White House senior staff had been adamant. The 'future savings' plug couldn't be biggger than $30 billion. A bigger number might raise 'credibility' problems.

'So what am I supposed to do now?' I complained. 'The first phase of the show is over.'

The collapse of the tax loophole component of Chapter Two had been the culprit. So, I quickly created a second 'future savings' plug worth about $13 billion in 1984. This was to represent what we thought might be saved in the next package of 'cats and dogs' to be forwarded to Congress in March. I buried it way down at the bottom of the white paper appendix table. If you had a magnifying glass, you could read it.

Had I been a standard policymaker and not an ideologue with a Grand Doctrine for changing the whole complexion of American government, I would have panicked at this point and said, 'This won't work.' To close a $44 billion budget gap *after* already cutting the budget by $64 billion would have involved nothing less than trench-style political warfare. But I had my own agenda. Four weeks of nonstop budget cutting, congressional briefings, press interviews, and Washington show stopping had given me an exaggerated sense of power.

I knew that the remaining $44 billion gap was huge. I remembered it was probably going to end up even larger, due to our cockeyed economic forecast. But I saw in this only the potential leverage it provided to further my Grand Doctrine, not its danger to the nation's finances.

The $44 billion in future budget cuts would become a powerful battering ram. It would force Congress to shrink the welfare state. It would give me an excuse to come back to them again and again.

The misdirected and corrupt politicians of the Second Republic would be hammered into the new servants of the public good. This wasn't arrogance of the normal sort; it was grandiosity of the historical variety.

Three days later the President stood before a joint session of the Congress and unveiled his plan for economic prosperity to the country.

'Can we,' he said, 'who man the ship of state, deny that it is somewhat out of control? Our national debt is approaching one trillion dollars. . . Have they [the Democrats] an alternative which offers a better chance of balancing the budget, reducing and eliminating inflation . . . are they suggesting that we can continue on the present course without coming to a day of reckoning?'

Those were our beliefs. But, to extend the President's rhetorical line of question, in hindsight, was the ship sailing with an accurate chart?

A profound question about the chart's accuracy was actually buried between the lines of the very first page of our white paper. On a five-year basis, our giant tax cut and big defense buildup cost nearly $900 billion. Our domestic spending cuts, including the $44 billion magic asterisk, came to only about half that.

So how could you worsen the budget by $900 billion, cut it by $450 billion, and still come out with a balanced budget? The answer was buried in Murray Weidenbaum's visceral computer. We were peering into the veil of the economic future. We were betting the fiscal house of the United States on our ability to predict the precise shape and composition of a $4 trillion economy all the way out to 1986.

One single number that didn't appear in the white paper might have made a profound difference. It blared out a clear message: *Murray, go slap it again. Your first answer doesn't compute.*

If you projected the *inherited* budget policy, Carter's mess, the one which had brought us to 'a day of reckoning', as the President said that night, with our Rosy Scenario economic forecast, what did you get? That was the missing number: a *$365 billion surplus* over five years.

With Rosy Scenario, the old, 1970s tax and spending policy would have projected out over five years to produce an unprecedented surplus without cutting a dime of domestic spending. That's what a mechanical computation of the numbers would have shown.

But how could that have been? The politicians had spent two decades revving up the welfare state. There hadn't been a budget surplus in twelve years. Spending was out-of-control, everyone agreed.

The answer was this: Rosy Scenario, why she was an economic heart-throb. Touch her hand to the deficit-ridden federal budget and the surpluses never stopped.

The idea that we were actually inheriting a huge budget surplus was just plain . . . haywire. Still, that was what our numbers assumed.

5
The Counter-Revolution Begins

The President had made his speech and the Reagan Revolution was now rolling. Unlike other supply siders, I had left myself no theoretical escape hatch. Some of them had argued that deficits could be financed out of national savings, but I believed that that was misguided. The resulting rise in real interest rates would impede real economic growth and thereby fuel the politicians' case for easy money.

Other supply siders had loosely and casually defined the problem away. They had assumed that a strong economy would itself pay for the tax cuts. But I believed the opposite was true. An economy which approached the supply-side ideal of inflationless growth worsened the fiscal imbalance, unless massive spending reductions were made too.

There was no economic magic. The success of the Reagan Revolution depended upon the willingness of the politicians to turn against their own handiwork—the bloated budget of the American welfare state. Why would they do this? Because they had to! In the final analysis, I had made fiscal necessity the mother of political invention.

Still, I did recognize that this political assumption had yet to be tested in legislative battle and proven correct.

That was why the initial attacks of the pundits bothered me. They were always criticizing the plan on the grounds that it posed a great 'economic risk'. They were in effect accusing us of relying only on the Laffer curve. They were saying, 'The napkin is wrong!'

But on February 18, the President went before the Congress with a sheet of paper that essentially showed revenues at $770 billion and spending at $880 (with no cuts). There was no napkin to be refuted. They had no choice but to reduce spending.

A few days later Greider prodded me on the 'economic risk' theme.

'Step back a minute,' he said, 'go back to the original question: Will it work? Talk about the risks.'

> Those are *political risks*. That's what everybody's missed in this whole thing. . . I don't think there is much risk in the economic sense. Can you get it through the swamp up there—Congress? And that's purely a challenge of leadership and creativity.
>
> Politically, the plan is not that radical. We're just repealing about ten or twelve years of accretion in terms of government's share of national income, marginal tax rates and loosely conceived programs that have cropped up all over.

That last remark put the whole issue in a nutshell. If you took the Reagan defense buildup and added it to the 1970 domestic spending burden, it would cost about 18–19 percent of GNP—an amount nearly identical to what we thought federal revenues would bring in after the Kemp-Roth tax cut and the 10–5–3 depreciation bill. That was the basic fiscal math of the thing.

The test now was whether the politicians would shrink the bloated subsidy and welfare enterprises of the Second Republic back to their 1970 levels. Making the supply-side fiscal equation whole was thus a battlefield test of theory against history. Given the inherent odds, it was bound to generate new evidence of an unpalatable kind.

During the March revisions round, I discovered the glory days of the Cutting Room were over. Resistance began to crop up everywhere, both within the Cabinet and on the Hill. In its totality, it amounted to a counter-revolution—a broad range of political signals that the free market and anti-welfare state premises of the Reagan Revolution were not going to take root.

The 'March revisions' were the smaller ('D' list) budget cuts we hadn't got to before the overall plan was unveiled. My target for these savings was $13 billion in 1984 and $62 billion over five years. Now, we had to come up with them.

But almost before we had got started on these new cuts, political reality blew a large hole in the side of the cuts we'd already sent to Capitol Hill—and I barely knew it happened.

One of my basic fiscal principles was that the federal government had no business repairing or building local city streets, country roads, bridges or mass transit systems. They served the local populace and benefited only local economies; the local taxpayers should therefore pay for them. Money that came from Washington on a skyhook had an invitation to indulge in waste and excess written all over it. It was the pork barrel at its grandest and most wasteful.

Mass transit operating subsidies were a special abomination, costing the taxpayers over $1 billion per year. Every study showed that the only effect of these gifts from the federal larder was to raise the already monopoly-level wages of local transit workers—or to reduce arbitrarily the transit fares paid by rich and poor alike.

Similarly, the multi-billion transit capital grants were encouraging the construction of new subway systems all over the country, when there was no hope that these economic white elephants could ever pay for even their operating costs, let alone the billions it cost to build them. But with eighty to ninety percent 'free' financing from Washington, city fathers and chamber of commerce types were tripping over each other to get in line at Uncle Sam's money kitchen.

If there was any single clear-cut case of what the Reagan Revolution required, it was dumping this vast local transportation pork barrel. The federal government had no business whatever fixing local potholes and buying local buses; its only valid role was to complete the interstate highway system and other national highways.

But Drew Lewis, Secretary of Transportation and probably the most astute politician in the Cabinet, turned completely white when I first laid out my plans to scrap the local highway and transit subsidies. I was proposing to touch off a political firestorm by disrupting the flow of $14 billion per year of federal gravy to governors, mayors, contractors, and unions. Nevertheless, attacking abuses in programs for the poor required that we cut the pork out of the programs for the non-poor, too.

Lewis finally said, OK, why not raise the federal gasoline tax modestly and let the states preempt a share of it? He felt this compromise would make it politically feasible to eliminate $20 billion—nearly thirty percent of the built-in spending on these programs—over the next five years.

But when this proposal to buy off local officials with new tax revenues leaked to the press, the White House message was simple:

No one was authorized to talk about tax increases on Ronald Reagan's watch, no matter *what* kind of tax, no matter *how* justified it was.

A few days later, Greider asked about the gas tax's demise, wondering if the White House had stepped on it.

> Marty Anderson was the heavy in this because he is absolutely insistent that there be nothing that smells, looks, tastes or feels like a tax increase in the Reagan program. He thinks that's where [Margaret] Thatcher went awry. So he's just like a guy with a bazooka. When anything comes up which looks like a tax . . . Wham!

I accepted the White House writ philosophically, but in the rush I promptly forgot all the political reasons why Lewis had come up with the gas tax expedient. I just blithely assumed we would keep fighting for the spending cuts I had originally proposed.

Lewis's initial reaction to my attack on the transportation pork barrel accurately reflected the consensus of the politicians. The Republicans on Capitol Hill, led by conservatives like Senator Alfonse D'Amato and liberals like Senator Arlen Specter fought and prevailed on every effort to cut mass transit. And all of the congressional politicians wanted to keep fixing local potholes, roads, and bridges. We finished up saving hardly a dime of my $20 billion.

In the end the transportation sector of the pork barrel never even knew the Reagan Revolution had tilted at it. It was a dramatic case of everything staying the same—but it would be only one of many.

During the March revisions round of cutting from their budgets, the cabinet members started to dig in their heels. They were facing OMB proposals that hit them where it hurt: in their administrative expenses budgets, and in some of the smaller 'motherhood' programs which had been passed over the first time around. One way or another, some of them succeeded in making sure the cuts would never be made, except on paper.

A good example was the roughly $2 billion per year in cuts we requested from Dick Schweiker at HHS—the giant Department of Health and Human Services which accounted for a huge share of the domestic budget. These cuts were to come from overhead accounts and small discretionary programs. The idea was to trim some fat from disease control, mental health, the Food and Drug Administration, local public health programs, and health research and statistics spending. Much of this spending was a local, not federal, responsibility.

What I got back from HHS was a fat protest: 185 pages of bureaucratese on why it couldn't be done. It turned out that all the line-item cuts we had recommended would slash 'top secretarial priorities'.

'Dollars are dollars,' Schweiker insisted. 'I've got to have some discretion in my priorities.'

Dick Schweiker had been in Congress for nearly twenty years— right there on the health and welfare committees. 'My priorities' was a euphemism. The Secretary of HHS didn't want to get skinned alive by his committees; he knew exactly where *not* to cut.

So we came up with alternative savings through new cuts in HHS's entitlement programs. The new entitlement cuts were justified and involved further reforms in AFDC* and SSI** and eliminating the Social Security lump sum death benefits. But that was where I got skinned. Schweiker's substitute entitlement cuts would be needed to shrink that $44 billion when we went after it in the future. If you cut the entitlements now, you couldn't cut them again later.

Likewise, if you spared the local grant programs and overhead accounts now, as he insisted, you would never cut them in the future, either. Indeed, once they were spared, Schweiker would spend the entire next year championing these expenditures as his 'special commitments'. So when I tried to go back at them in future budgets, he insisted that he would be supremely embarrassed to propose cuts in programs he had promoted from coast to coast in the interim. Dick Schweiker was right. By then, they couldn't be cut.

This same 'substitution' syndrome occurred in most of the other departments. Consequently, we created a raft of little impregnable fences all around the small programs that were spared in the trading. What I didn't realize at the time was that the fiscal equation of the February 18 plan was so brutally tight that there was no room for trading at all, not even nickels and dimes with the Cabinet.

* Aid to Families with Dependent Children.
** Supplemental Security Income programs.

*   *   *

This fence-building principle was dramatically illustrated when Secretary Haig once again came into his glory. OMB had found a way of saving a minute $10 million in the State Department's operating budget. The idea was to shave 591 people from the 22,000-person payroll.

Never mind that our plan would amount to a mere 2.6 percent cutback in State Department employees, a much smaller cut than we were asking many of the other agencies to make. The General announced that it was an intolerable abomination and that he would take his case to the President—personally.

When the appointed time for his presentation came, Haig rose martially from the Cabinet table, and strode purposefully toward the end of the room to an easel and a set of charts his staff had set up. He then grabbed a metal pointer from an aide. A little clearing of the throat for just the right effect, and the briefing over this trivial matter could proceed.

'Mr President,' he began, 'if you accept the OMB proposal, your entire foreign policy will go right down the drain.'

'I'm willing to do my part to hold down the budget,' he continued, 'but I've got a foreign policy to conduct. I cannot tolerate being micromanaged by OMB accountants. Now, Mr President, they're simply asking you to rear back and *shove your head right into a pencil sharpener.*'

The full dramatic effect of this memorable oration was slightly diluted by titters from the Cabinet members.

For once, the other Cabinet members sprang to my defense, although not for purely selfless reasons. They maintained that Haig could not be given special status, that every department had to 'take a hit'. But the General would have none of that. The State Department, he averred, could hardly be lumped in with the domestic agencies. Its mission was simply too important.

The debate raged. As it did, I saw the President pick up a piece of paper and scribble some numbers on it. In time I learned that was his practice when confronted with brawling Cabinet officers.

After the last shot had been fired and the smoke had cleared sufficiently to see into the Rose Garden, the President picked up his piece of paper and said, 'Now I've done some figuring here on this 591. Couldn't you fellas live with 295 each way?' Haig professed he could not live with 295 less payrollers, and before the session had ended he had managed to rescue the jobs of another 130 of them without whom, presumably, the foreign policy of the United States would not have survived.

Afterwards, everyone congratulated me for 'hanging in there'.

Unfortunately, as time went on, there was less consensus, more choices to be made, and finally no margin in the budget within which to plod about looking for compromises.

More importantly, it did not occur to me at the time that a bureaucracy which sent its Secretary roaring into the Cabinet Room to rescue a few hundred redundant employees during a period of ostensibly drastic personnel cutbacks would hardly be content to abide by whatever 'compromise' departmental budgets were settled on. Indeed, it was not. By 1986 the State Department budget would be *fifty percent bigger* in after-inflation dollars than the 'compromise' level Haig had reluctantly agreed to in the Cabinet that day.

The Justice Department turned out to be even more intractable than State. On the theory that law enforcement is the primary responsibility of state and local agencies, I had proposed to shave about 2,000 of Justice's 54,000 employees.

Attorney General William French Smith did not think his department was a place to start economizing.

'The Justice Department is not a domestic agency,' he said. 'It is the *internal arm of the nation's defense*. Our budget is less than one percent of Defense's, and dollar for dollar we provide far more actual security to the American people.'

Smith then arrived at the gist of his argument. If anything, he said, the Reagan Administration would have to spend more on law enforcement, rather than less. In time I would discover that Smith, a silver-haired, immaculately tailored conservative from central casting, was an easy mark for every spending proposal that came along.

'Restoring a strong federal law enforcement capacity,' he continued, 'is going to be highly popular with the American people.'

It was time to say my piece. I objected that we couldn't afford—literally—to fall into the old trap of throwing funds at programs just because we liked their purposes, and certainly not because it might be popular. If we wanted to toughen law enforcement, then we should do so by making strong conservative appointments to the federal bench.

I diplomatically reminded everyone that under the Constitution, criminal law enforcement, drug prosecution and other such popular causes were state and local responsibility. Those units now provided about ninety-five percent of the funds the country spent on law enforcement—always had and I hoped always would.

Once again, the President managed to split the difference, but this time he prefaced it with a statement of principle.

'No,' he said, 'Bill is right. Law enforcement is something that we have always believed was a legitimate function of government.'

Of course it was, but given the fiscal austerity the administration was ostensibly ushering in, how much law enforcement could we afford at the federal level?

The answer was that once the Attorney General had christened his agency an 'Internal Defense Department', we would have lots of law enforcement at the federal level, even if we couldn't afford it. Justice's budget would grow and grow as the Attorney General came up with more and more schemes to show that the administration was 'committed' to aggressive 'internal defense'. The thirteen anti-drug task forces Smith created were a good example of how Republicans can fecklessly throw money at problems, too. Keeping drugs off the nation's streets is an admirable goal. But no matter how many Coast Guard cutters or AWACS-type planes we deployed, the stuff still kept coming in, by boat, plane, and even parachutist. Every other week Smith seemed to be off at some warehouse surrounded by German shepherds and big bales of pot. But the inexorable bottom line was that over four years the street price of the stuff never changed significantly.

Within a year we would begin adding to the law enforcement budget nearly every time Smith felt we were about to be 'embarrassed' by congressional Democrats proposing even higher budgets for Justice. Its funding level eventually exceeded our original targets by fifty percent, too. But by then it was no use explaining to those who sat around the Cabinet table that it was we, not they, who had enacted a giant tax cut and taken a vow of fiscal frugality.

Some battles I fought with more zeal than others. If there was a single program in the 1981 budget we inherited that was both a statist abomination and something a Republican Administration had a chance to kill outright, it was the Urban Development Action

Grant Program. It was called UDAG—a sincere-sounding acronym that covered a multitude of sins. PORK would have been more accurate.

It had been started in 1978 by the Carter Administration, and had quickly ballooned to a cost of $650 million a year. During the '80 campaign, the Carter people had used it for blatantly political purposes.

UDAG was a classic example of the single-entry bookkeeping fallacy. The spenders said that by subsidizing downtown hotels and ski resorts, the federal government would 'create' jobs and 'redevelop' lagging local economies. What they didn't say was you would also raise taxes, waste savings and destroy jobs paying for it. On any conservative hit list, this would be right at the top.

Or so I thought. But Secretary of Housing and Urban Development Sam Pierce launched a noisy campaign to spare this turkey, and soon the White House switchboard was flooded with HUD-orchestrated 'distress calls' from local Republican mayors and 'businessmen' who happened to be in the redevelopment and construction business.

With unsettling rapidity, they convinced Ed Meese that UDAG was really a 'Republican program'—never mind that it had been started during the Carter Administration—because the grants had to be leveraged with private capital. I told both Meese and Pierce that this kind of 'leveraging' was an old trick in the federal spending game. Other federal grants could even be used to 'leverage' UDAG deals. It was a good case, in fact, of the double-fleece.

To no avail. Meese ordered me to restore the program and told me in no uncertain terms that taking it to the President would be no use. It took some time for it to sink in that the Counselor of the most supposedly ideological conservative President of the twentieth century had decided not to touch perhaps the most ideologically offensive and wasteful bit of federal spending on the block.

So, to make ends meet, we saved Jimmy Carter's UDAG program and cut Nixon's Community Development Block Grant program instead, even though the prudent—and necessary—step would have been to eliminate both. Four years later the Reagan Administration would be able to tell the American taxpayers with pride that their hard work had gone toward the construction of twelve new Hilton Hotels, six Hyatts, five Marriotts, four Sheratons, two

Ramadas, one Albert Pick, and a Stouffers . . . in a pear tree.

For my part, if I was really the 'wunderkind' the press was saying I was, how was it I didn't realize that if the administration couldn't turn down something like UDAG, it wasn't about to cut all the less ideologically obnoxious programs necessary to balance the budget?

Getting the $13 billion in 1984 savings for the March revisions turned out to be much tougher than I anticipated. The stray cats and dogs on the 'D' list didn't want to be rounded up, as I found out in trying to eliminate the Job Corps. Orrin Hatch of Utah, chairman of the Senate Human Resources Committee, had already told me about the virtues of the Job Corps—perhaps owing to the fact that one of the Job Corps' major facilities was in Utah.

But I didn't see any of its other virtues. The Job Corps was charging the federal government $12,000 for each trainee—more than it would have cost to send them to Harvard for a year. Moreover, there was no convincing evidence that this $600 million per year program worked. The youths it spent so much money on would probably have got jobs without it. The program inherently self-selected the most motivated among underprivileged youth. As with so many of the Great Society programs, the ones who profited from the Job Corps were the people who ran it.

Shortly after sending this proposed cut to the Labor Department, the White House switchboard had gone tilt. I explained the episode with some chagrin to Greider:

> One of our great conservative friends, Orrin Hatch, put through seventy-five calls—well roughly that—within a day and one-half after he got wind of this, begging not to cut the Job Corps. I just thought it was interesting that even the hardest of the hardliners picks up a whiff of this from the options paper and he's all over this place. . .

Reluctantly I agreed to go along with Hatch, thinking—naïvely— that I would be able to revisit the Job Corps the next year. This time I'd have my long knives unsheathed. What I did not yet understand was that if a program is spared once, it takes on a nearly sacrosanct status. The *Mañana* Syndrome that I had acquired obscured my vision as to the real prospects for the revolution's success.

By March of 1981 I had been a witting accomplice in a rash of protective fencemaking all around the budget. But I resolutely refused to believe they were there, assuming that the world started fresh every morning at 5.00 am just as I did. I thus led myself to believe that for purely political reasons we had left only two sacred cows unscathed: the tobacco program and the Clinch River Breeder Reactor.

They turned my stomach, these two; they were the epitome of the Second Republic's wasteful and unjust economic socialism. What I didn't see was that these two self-acknowledged 'exceptions' defined the rules of the game.

The tobacco program actually proscribed under law the right of free American citizens to grow tobacco without a license from the state, a license worth upwards of $1,000 per acre. If you presented a hypothetical case of that kind to a conservative, he would either retch or denounce it as some nefarious scheme of the Soviet Agriculture Minister. Starting with the so-called acreage allotment, every aspect of the tobacco industry was regulated, including prices, with a thoroughness and high-handedness that, indeed, would be the envy of the Soviet Agriculture Minister.

The most perverse part of it all was that this system was justified on the grounds that it protected the 'little guy'. Here was the big lie in its baldest formulation. Every independent economist who had studied the matter had concluded that the value of the government subsidies ultimately went to the landowners who rented out the allotments. The 'little guys' were latterday sharecroppers who sweated in the fields for comparatively meager earnings. There was nothing to be said for this corrupt state enterprise except: Eliminate it.

As a result of a 1980 campaign commitment that had been made to Jesse Helms about his beloved tobacco subsidies, however, I had to chomp down on my tongue whenever its defenders said in public that the program didn't cost the budget 'anything much'. I knew that was beside the point but didn't realize how much so.

True, it was one small bite for Helms, the only one he ever asked for. But it turned out to be one giant bite out of the budget. The tobacco program itself 'cost' only a mere $50 to $100 million a year. But it was a potent carcinogen when it came to the occupational disease of the politicians: *malignant precedentitis*. Other Republican stalwarts never ever failed to cite it when their own 'life and death' programs were being 'unfairly' brought under the knife.

They had a point. What kind of revolution was it that left the most corrupt symbol of the old order standing untouched? It was as if we'd left the Bastille intact, royal banners still streaming in the smoke-filled air. Weary but not appreciably wiser, I moved on to the next chapter of great exemptions—the Clinch River Breeder Reactor.

Back in November 1980, Howard Baker had actually written a letter to Reagan opposing me for OMB or any Cabinet job that superintended his cherished Clinch River project, a subsidized nuclear-power demonstration plant which I had often spoken out against. When Baker had subsequently changed his mind about my OMB appointment, I changed my position on his pet porker. He didn't even have to ask.

The trouble was, no one else would accept the fact that I had declared my previous wisdom on the matter 'non-operative', as they said in the Nixon White House. Ted Kennedy even took to reading my old speeches in the Senate. It was the only time that the leftish senator from Massachusetts ever agreed with me, and I couldn't even say: Right on!

Greider, who was now having a not too hard time of it playing the role of a gleeful Torquemada, smiled and said, 'Let's talk about nuclear for a minute.' I suppressed a groan. 'What,' he said, 'does that do for your free market premise?'

'Oh,' I said wanly, 'it shoots it full of holes.' I explained that I hadn't waited to get rolled, I had just moved out of the way. 'This package will go nowhere without Baker, and this Clinch River is just life or death to Baker.' I felt compelled to add: 'Very poor reason, I know, but that one wasn't worth taking on.'

But there was an even bigger nuclear boondoggle: the Barnwell reprocessing plant for which the Dentist over at Energy also had a sweet tooth. Yet there was not a gram's worth of economic justification for it. Barnwell required a large breeder reactor industry to sustain it economically by buying its product. Only there wouldn't be a breeder reactor industry for fifty years, if then, since the world's plentiful supply of cheap uranium made conventional nuclear plants far less expensive.

Moreover, we had almost $13 billion in non-nuclear energy cuts pending before the Congress—cuts in fossil, solar, synfuels, and conservation projects. To come in now with an even bigger nuclear boondoggle than Clinch River would consign the non-nuclear cuts to the ash heap. Given the Noah's Ark mentality of the congressional committees, if you had two big nuclear projects you would end up with at least two of every other energy source.

Thus even as we were struggling at the end of February to come up with the March revisions, the Dentist was submitting a huge proposal for new nuclear spending initiatives. He demurely explained that projects like Barnwell and others would add 'only' about $500 million to the 1982 budget, which was like saying your child's college tuition will cost only whatever they charge for freshman year. The out-year price tags on each of these projects was in the billions of dollars. When I realized what Edwards was up to, I resolved to come to the presidential appeals session loaded for bear.*

The appeals session with the President was notable for turning quickly into an ugly confrontation leavened with rampant confusion. Edwards arrived with a list of exotic nuclear projects that no one in the White House had ever heard of.

The President said that he wanted to 'do something' to support the nuclear industry. I railed on, saying that *none* of the Dentist's projects made any sense because none of them could stand the test of the marketplace. Unfortunately, Meese and the President had both been persuaded by the specious argument that if it weren't for the regulatory costs and other barriers imposed by the federal government, nuclear energy would be competitive.

This was not even remotely true, but the damage was done, and the Dentist got approval of several of his projects. He also received a 'presidential mandate' to launch a crusade to revive the nuclear industry with federal boodle. In the end, the Barnwell project was remanded for 'further study' only because Edwards could not quite explain how we were going to 'acquire' it but not 'buy' it. As I described the scene to Greider:

All of a sudden, all the voices around the Cabinet table say, 'Oh, you want to try that one again? Run that one by us again. . .'

* Ready for action.

'Well,' he says, 'instead of the government buying it, a number of private utilities would, and those utility purchasers would give it to the government.'

But why would the utilities . . . give it to the government? Because it's a big tax write-off!

What did become clear, however, was the appearance of a double standard on energy subsidies. If the market needed help on nuclear, why not solar, fossil, and all the others? We had no answer, which is why today the non-nuclear energy budget is *five times larger* in real terms than our original Reagan budget permitted. Sacred cows run in herds—that's the part I didn't understand.

When Greider pressed me on my new 'nuclear deviation'—to be added to my 'tobacco deviation'—I inadvertently made an admission that the requirements of congressional coalitions rendered my whole Grand Doctrine on which the Reagan Revolution was based a Grand Impossibility. The reason was politics.

'Well,' I rationalized,

there's going to be *one chink* in the armor. You can't be perfect. Political democracy is turbulent, and is complicated by all the interests that have built up inside the system over the years. How could somebody be a hundred percent consistent and still function in the system? You couldn't. But I've been about ninety-eight percent consistent, which is amazing to me. I'm surprised I've got this far.

Of course, I hadn't got nearly as far as I thought, because the whole Reagan Revolution in fiscal policy was still only a paper plan. But I believed, despite these few setbacks, that the Reagan budget plan was a political master stroke.

As forwarded to Congress on March 10, it included both the first and second round of budget cuts. Listed in microscopic print were more than three hundred programs that I had persuaded the White House to cut, reform, or eliminate over a fifty-day period.

'Nothing has been spared,' I thought. 'We've taken on the rural electric co-ops, the barge industry, airline subsidies, mass transit boondoggles, synfuel subsidies to the big oil companies, the dairy lobby, the health planning bureaucrats, home-builder subsidies, water projects and on and on.'

When he learned about my plans to zero out one of the more outrageous water projects, Max Friedersdorf, chief White House congressional lobbyist and a seasoned veteran of the pork wars, nearly checked into a cardiac arrest unit.

'I don't question you on the merits of the Red River Barge Canal,' he said, 'but how am I going to handle Senator Long? No one's passed a tax bill without him in the last twenty years.' But it was too late to back off: word of this cut was already on the street.

It was agreed, however, that Senator Russell Long and his Louisiana colleague, Senator Bennett Johnston, should be given their day in court before the budget was officially published.

The two of them arrived at the White House in early March. I was worried. They were both veteran warriors, these two, though their styles were quite different. Long, nephew of legendary Louisiana Governor Huey Long, was a sixty-three-year-old good old boy who had a pronounced mumble. He was hard to understand, but I have a feeling it was deliberate; his success derived from never communicating exactly what he meant. Johnston, by contrast, was a clear-speaking corporate lawyer, very articulate, very smart—the ultimate New South politician. I didn't know how well the President would be able to stand up to this pair, especially given what kind of bad news he had for them.

After they sat down, Johnston said, 'Well, Mr President, we're all for your program. Ninety-nine percent for those budget cuts. And we want to help on the tax cut. But, boy, we need your help on this Red River. This is number one. This is a must.'

The President didn't so much as flinch. He said, 'We've got huge reductions to make in the budget and they have to be evenly distributed around the country. This isn't a good project, and I can't take the cut out.'

I was ecstatic. But when I told Greider about the incident, he merely smiled, ever the cat toying with the mouse, and said I was being too enthusiastic. The real day of reckoning, he said, would come on the tax bill.

'You're right,' I responded. 'You won't know until the final closing days of the conference on the tax bill. Then you'll find out. Then I'll find out.'

I did find out. Red River flows on and so does a lot more pork just like it. But in March I thought Greider was dead wrong. People had made careers out of underestimating Ronald Reagan, and many of the worries I had about the budget gap were subsumed by a growing belief that the President could overcome virtually any obstacle ahead. He had backed ninety-eight percent of my recommendations and was now rising to the occasion as the critics began to turn their fire on us.

Near the end of February, all the nation's governors came to the White House to discuss the economic program. There was a lot of rubbery political talk, though the message was clear enough: They were opposed to any cuts that affected them.

Hugh Carey of New York got up to speak. Carey was a kind of poor man's Tip O'Neill. He stood for everything O'Neill did, but he had about one fifth of O'Neill's charisma.

'Mr President, I hear your theory,' Carey said, 'but I don't see the evidence that we can afford this big giveaway to the rich. Do you realize how many needy people are going to be hurt? And you're going to have deficits that no Democrat ever dreamed of.'

The President had by now been listening patiently to the governors for half an hour, not saying very much. But as soon as Carey sat down, he came down on him like a ton of bricks. The color came to his cheeks, the passion to his voice; his fists clenched.

'I'm not going to sit still for the notion that we're hurting anyone,' he heartily declaimed. 'We've tried your way for decades and millions have been hurt by runaway inflation and unemployment.

'We didn't invent deficit spending,' the President continued. 'We didn't advocate tax-and-spend until the economy was a mess.

'The American people want a change,' the President reminded Carey, 'and to say our tax cut benefits only help the wealthy, well, that's a deliberate distortion and I'm not going to put up with hearing it!'

It was magnificent. He needed no one to come to his defense that morning. I had to restrain myself from applauding at the end. After it was over, all Hugh Carey could do was gather up what remained of the New Deal, stick it in his briefcase, and shuttle back to New York, whupped.

With the release of the March budget revisions on March 10, the fiscal equation was supposed to have been nearly completed. But between February 18 and March 10, the budget numbers got a lot worse despite our whole new round of cutting in the March revisions.

The authentic detailed estimate of the budget is made by a thousand green eyeshades out in each department who specialize in all the accounting ins-and-outs of individual programs. It takes them two or three weeks to do the job after the White House gives them the economic forecast assumptions.

When we finally heard back from the agency green eyeshades, it turned out that baseline spending was $9–10 billion per year higher than we had estimated in the February 18 white paper. There was another $10 billion of deficit baked into the cake that would now take even more spending cuts to eliminate.

This $9–10 billion growth in the budget estimates wasn't unusual or even unreasonable in a $740 billion budget (with no spending cuts). It was only a 1.4 percent error. Not bad for government work, as the saying went.

But the 'overrun', as it was soon christened, gave me my first glimpse into just how tightly wired our budget plan was. When the smoke had finally cleared from the second round of budget cutting within the administration, you could go back to the crucial question. How much domestic spending did you have to cut to get a balanced budget in 1984 after the tax cut and defense increase? The answer was $118 billion. Thus, the score on March 10 was $74 billion in cuts *proposed*, $44 billion in future savings *promised*.

I now realized it was going to be a white-knuckle operation all the way. So, when some of our 'allies' on the Hill started to descend on me demanding concessions, I resolved not to give in to them one dime's worth. We couldn't afford any more slippage.

But when these political messages came in, I translated them into dozens of individual ideological errors that had to be put down. I didn't add up the political pattern; instead, I subtracted brownie points from all the people who were deviating from the doctrine.

One of the more relentless pests was Senator Jack Schmidt of New Mexico. He was a famous astronaut who had walked on the moon and he had never quite got over it.

He professed to be one of the most militant tax- and budget-cutting Reaganites in the entire Senate. He was always trying to show that he was more-conservative-than-thou, but when it came to his moon complex there was no limit to what he wanted to spend.

Within hours of the March 10 budget release, Schmidt called me to demand 'a fair amount of your time to clear up some misimpressions you have about the space program'. We had cut the Carter NASA budget by about $600 million, or nine percent, by cancelling a number of lower-priority space science projects and applied technology programs.

I was as much of a space buff as the next person, but I have always found NASA's line about the 'technological spinoffs' that make life here on earth so much better appalling. It was true that on the way to the moon the space program produced everything from Tang to Teflon to medical telemetry systems. But the way to improve medical telemetry or anything else was to reward private inventors, entrepreneurs, and investors with lower taxes. NASA was in effect claiming that the way to build a better mousetrap was to go to Jupiter. At any rate, NASA was hardly suffering. Even with the cut, its 1982 budget would be eleven percent higher than 1981.

Needless to say, Schmidt was appalled by my arguments, and called them 'excessively ideological'. The whole economic future of the United States depended on rapid technological advance, he said, with NASA in the vanguard. This was even more urgent, he warned, because of the ambitious French space program and the rapid pace of Japanese technological advancement. I was not aware that either the French or the Japanese had yet landed on the moon, but I took the occasion to remind him that technological advancement was a gift of the marketplace, not of government bureaucracies.

To this he replied, 'Technological progress is too important to be left to the free market.' Here was the premise of the Second Republic in a nutshell. Progress of *any* kind was too important to be left to capitalists. Only Washington could do it. That was the argument for solar-power towers, synfuel plants, and the budget-bleeding European Supersonic Transport.

Seeing that I was an unpersuadable ideologue, Schmidt concluded the meeting by saying, 'I can't imagine that the President or anyone else in the administration holds that view,' and left.

He turned out to be right. We would end up adding billions to our original five-year space budget. The administration's 1986 funding request for NASA exceeded our original after-inflation spending target for that year by seventy-five percent.

I got another political signal one day when Bill Timmons brought one of his lobbies, the barge operators, to see me. He'd told me over the phone they wanted to 'reason' with me about our proposed $300 million per year user fee. He introduced them, then sat back and twiddled his thumbs, his job already done.

The gist of their elaborate presentation was that they didn't object to our cutting off their subsidies . . . as long as we cut off the railroads' subsidies, too! Item by item they ticked off the 'unfair' largesse that the government handed out to the railroads.

Finally I reassured them that we planned to cut off *everyone's* subsidy, giving them a lecture about economic efficiency as I went along. They pretended to be pleased, and declared that was, after all, only 'fair'. They were also gravely pessimistic about whether this logical solution would ever transpire. It wouldn't.

Even the most blatant boondoggles we had proposed to cut or eliminate were producing stout champions, and each time I looked out the window I saw more of them gathering, sharpening their own blades. One day after a White House meeting, Senator Strom Thurmond of South Carolina, a man not known for liberal leanings, took me aside and with a gentle smile said, 'Now, we're all behind the President's program, yuh heah? But you take good care of those REAs. Them's some real *fine* people.'

The whole rural countryside had been strung with electric wires by 1950, bringing the original mission of the Rural Electric Administration (REA) co-ops to an end. But the co-ops had never quite got over the thrill of cheap electric power. So when the lights were turned on in the last barn in America, they went into a new line of business—building power plants with even bigger federal subsidies. They could have bought their power from private utilities, but preferred yeoman socialism instead.

At the time Thurmond accosted me, I thought he was simply discharging a local political obligation. He would then tell the locals: 'Yes, suh. Talked to the budget director right in the White House.' Upon that, we would get on with cutting the REAs. That proved how much I knew. Four years and about $15 billion wasted REA dollars later the fight would still be going on.

Hard on the heels of the March 10 budget release, I had back-to-back meetings with the Congressional Rural Caucus and the Northeast-Midwest Coalition. Neither of them said they were opposed to spending cuts. No. The Rural Caucus had produced an instant analysis showing that our budget discriminated in favor of the northeast and midwest urban areas. The Northeast-Midwest Coalition had produced an instant analysis showing that our budget discriminated in favor of the rural southwest and the great plains states.

Both of these caucuses were 'bi-partisan', meaning it was hard to tell who was Republican and who was Democrat, and the meetings with them worried me. But never mind. There was yet time, I believed, for both education and persuasion.

The worst nonsense of all in the budget, of course, was farm subsidies. The nation's agriculturalists had never been the same after the New Deal turned the wheat, corn, cotton and dairy business into a way of life based on organized larceny.

The Reagan Budget of March 10 cancelled nearly every single farm subsidy program. Whereas the Carterites had spent over $30 billion propping up agriculture, we would spend less than $10 billion over five years in comparable dollars of purchasing power.

Within weeks, however, our free market farm program was in big trouble on the Hill—for a curious reason. No one in our potential GOP–Boll Weevil* coalition was objecting to shrinking the subsidy payments by two thirds. Instead, they got into a crossfire about what they were pleased to call 'farm bill philosophy'.

The Democratic Boll Weevils came from the less fertile, less productive, and less affluent farm areas. They wanted a strong government hand in there to help their dirt farmers survive. That could be done by giving them a lot of subsidy money, but big spending was now passé.

Instead, the Boll Weevils wanted to help the farmer 'make a profit in the marketplace' by having the government control production and marketing. Let the farmer make his income from the market, but make it a Soviet-style market, one in which you can't plant, harvest or sell your wheat without permission from the state. As Charlie Stenholm of Texas said to me: 'We'll hit your low budget numbers, but we're going to flush your free market ideology right down the commode. You can't get farm income up without production controls.'

The farm belt Republicans, on the other hand, centered in the northern and midwestern states, represented the more productive and affluent farming regions. They were totally against production

* The conservative Southern Democrats.

and marketing control because they had the lowest costs and could usually make a decent profit, even if the prices were low.

But the farm belt Republicans had another angle. They wanted subsidized export financing in order to expand overseas demand. They insisted the export subsidies would pay for themselves in higher farm income.

So there our coalition was, yelling at each other about philosophy, pretending you could keep all the nation's excess agriculturalists propped up without costing the budget a red cent. One faction wanted to subsidize less and regulate domestic production even more; the other wanted to regulate less and subsidize foreign markets. Neither approach would work, and a hybrid of the two would be a fiscal nightmare. I knew we were heading for trouble. I just couldn't fathom how much.

By March, our free market farm program was getting such a poor reception on the Hill that Jack Block was growing desperate. He started pleading for 'some running room'.

I agreed to give him some limited flexibility in negotiating with our coalition on the farm bill. Block professed to be a stout free marketeer and I believed him. But once Block got his 'running room', he never stopped running—backwards. The GOP–Boll Weevil coalition never stopped arguing farm bill philosophy. One thing led to another.

We ended up signing a new five-year farm bill that amounted to a smorgasboard of everything—production controls, price supports, subsidy payments, export financing. The agriculturalists turned the USDA's welfare handouts and market-rigging schemes into awesome surpluses of cheese, wheat, corn, rice, cotton, even mohair and honey. We ended up spending $60 billion over five years rather than $10 billion. It was another case of missing the revolution by a country mile.

But the most troubling development, both philosophically and strategically, became clear at a Cabinet Council meeting on Tuesday 3 March. Only thirty minutes had been allocated for this particular meeting. There hadn't even been an agenda circulated, so I figured it was going to be some kind of jawing session.

Drew Lewis was the first to speak, and what he had to say made my jaw drop. The time had come, he said, to 'keep faith with our campaign pledge' to restrict Japanese auto imports.

This preposterous idea was so philosophically inimical to what I thought we stood for that for a few moments I just sat back, concussed. Free trade is merely an extension of free enterprise; free markets don't stop at the border. But here was a Cabinet officer talking protectionism in the White House, not two months into the administration.

After Lewis had said his piece, a drumbeat started. Mac Baldridge talked it up for import controls on Japanese autos, too.

After Baldridge, Brock spoke. He didn't speak, he echoed. Then Labor Secretary Raymond Donovan was recognized, and he started echoing. It was a Swiss chorus.

Finally Jim Baker realized what was going on and stepped in, saying, 'This meeting's over, but we haven't even heard from the other side.' The Cabinet Council meeting, in fact, had been rigged by Lewis. He didn't plan to hear from the other side.

Lewis had also already figured out the White House decision-making system. If you got a consensus among the key advisers, it was a done deal.

So he'd prearranged a meeting for the coming Friday with eight auto state Republican governors, including Bill Milliken of Michigan, Jim Rhode of Ohio, and Jim Thompson of Illinois. This time the President would attend.

This session would be as rigged as the Cabinet Council meeting. The governors would make their pitch for Japanese auto import quotas. The President would listen as they sold him this bill of goods, then stand up and say he had decided to come to the rescue of the US auto industry.

But now a roadblock had been thrown in front of Lewis's plan, thanks to Jim Baker's alert intervention. Don Regan, who was a stout free trader, was as mad as I'd ever seen him. Steam was coming out of his ears. Murray Weidenbaum didn't show any steam, but he was upset, too.

At the governors' meeting, the President indicated he was undecided but said something that made my free enterprise flesh crawl. It meant they had already got to him.

'Yes,' he said, 'we believe in free trade, but there's something different here. Government regulation is responsible for this.'

I should have known then that the game was lost. The President was a strong free trader, but he was also a politician, and his political antennae could be tuned to the desired frequency. In this case, Lewis and the others had cooked up a theory that the auto industry had been so overregulated and crippled by air bags, pollution control devices, safety standards, and other government-imposed Ralph Naderite schemes that it was now up to the government to undo the damage. And since the President had always opposed, rightfully, these excessive environmental and safety regulations, it was plausible to him.

This cover-up for protectionism really frosted me. Overregulation had absolutely nothing to do with Detroit's being uncompetitive. Under US law, Japanese-made cars had to be equipped with tail-pipe controls, the proposed air bags and all the rest of this junk, too. It was a wash. Yet now the President was being convinced that the government *owed* it to Detroit to get back at Ralph Nader by attacking the Japanese.

At the time, I considered Lewis's auto import gambit a serious but correctible bump in the road. Lewis hadn't been drilled in the catechism yet. We would teach some lessons and give him some education. He would then stop whispering non sequiturs in the President's ear and the crisis would pass.

I told Greider in early March that the Lewis caper was a good example of why you had to be vigilant in protecting the agenda. 'Here's what happens to an administration when you allow one of the parochial players too much free rein,' I dreamily concluded, 'but we've been going to war against it ever since.'

'Going to war' meant it was time to call Bob Novak, the Prince of Darkness. The Evans and Novak syndicated column was a kind of supply-side dartboard. You could use it to stick somebody in the forehead fast, if you had to. So after my 8.00 am breakfast at the Hay-Adams with Greider, I had a second (lighter) breakfast at nine with Novak.

What resulted was a column which appeared in hundreds of papers across the nation saying that the administration was going astray on a fundamental supply-side principle because the Secretary of Transportation's chief adviser was a leftover Carterite. He'd written the infamous Goldschmidt Report, a statist tract urging a tripartite—government, industry, and labor—pact to rescue the ailing auto industry.

It was one of those pernicious seeds that could grow into the concept of 'industrial policy', the euphemism such people as Gary Hart preferred to use instead of 'socialized industry'. The concept was an insult to every principle of capitalism. And Drew Lewis had fallen for it hook, line, and sinker.

When he found out I was responsible for Novak's column, Lewis went into orbit. As I described it to Greider: 'He called me up . . . raving about "What are you doing? We have to solve these things privately in the White House! Why are you stimulating stories against me?"'

In response I told him, 'OK, then let's have a full debate on it, not one of your rigged Cabinet meetings.'

Lewis agreed to stop 'backgrounding' the press and telling them that the President had already decided in favor of import restraints, and I agreed not to have breakfast with the Prince of Darkness for a while.

But at the March 11 meeting of the White House Auto Industry Task Force, there was no meeting of minds. Lewis had been a brilliant success in business at rescuing failing companies. He viewed the auto industry's problems in the same light. If everyone put something in the kitty, including the federal government, then the industry could be made whole again.

Still, no matter how antiseptic, Republican, and voluntary it could be made to sound, it led in only one direction: to the irreparable impairment of the engines of capitalist prosperity.

It was an attempt to impose political solutions on economic problems, and as such was reactionary. Industries rise and fall, and in so doing bring about growth, technological advance, and rising general living standards. This is the phenomenon Joseph Schumpeter called 'creative destruction'. But the politician is by nature opposed to the cycle of creation and destruction of industry. He wants everything to be level, smooth and unchanging.

Industrial policy therefore sought to use the subsidy, trade and legal powers of the state to sustain industries that could no longer sustain themselves. Industrial policy replaced the test of the marketplace with raw political power. It locked in obsolete labor and capital to unproductive use. It impoverished society. It was the antithesis of supply-side.

For a while I thought that Regan, Weidenbaum's and my free trade counterattack would work. But I hadn't reckoned with the fact that Ed Meese preached Cabinet government but practised something entirely different. While the Cabinet task force was arguing feverishly, Meese was trundling around the White House, quietly pounding square pegs into round holes, convincing himself and the President that all we had to do to maintain our free trade position was to convince the Japanese 'voluntarily' to restrict their own exports.

Under the Meese formulation, our hands would be clean; the Japanese would do the dirty work to themselves. It was another case of not knowing the difference between campaigning and governing. In the latter what counts is outcomes, not positions.

Thus, at a task force meeting on March 19 attended by the President, the scheme was laid on the table. Our ambassador to Japan, Mike Mansfield, would be instructed to 'talk turkey' in private with the Japanese, and warn them of the building momentum on the Hill in favor of the Danforth auto quota bill. He could tell them that it was up to them: that if they wanted to head the bill off at the pass, they must impose export restrictions on themselves. Otherwise it would be done by the US Congress.

I hadn't yet given up the fight. So much depended on it. I told the President that if he was against the Danforth bill, then all he had to do was to signal, in no uncertain terms, that he would veto it. He would tell the Congress that the bill violated every free market principle we held.

What's more, it would be a serious political mistake to grant special relief to one industry and region of the country. All that would do was encourage the fiercely parochial instincts of the Congress, the same ones that were already causing such havoc with our spending cuts.

The President replied that he would not signal a veto in advance. My heart sank when I heard that. Studied silence on our part on the matter of this horrendous piece of legislation would itself be an unmistakable signal to the Japanese: unless they imposed their own 'voluntary' restrictions, we would serve them up to the tender mercies of the auto belt politicians.

Sure enough, after Mansfield and Brock had held a few 'consultations' with the Japanese, they did mysteriously 'volunteer' to limit their auto exports to 1.68 million vehicles—right on the eve of Prime Minister Nakasone's visit in May. And so the essence of the

Reagan Administration's trade policy became clear: espouse free trade, but find an excuse on every occasion to embrace the opposite. As time passed, we would find occasions aplenty.

But I consoled myself with the illusion that the auto imports episode was just another aberration, and told Greider the following Saturday that it would *never* happen again.

The President had a 'campaign commitment', I told him. It was a 'one-time response', not a 'strong policy thrust'. The administration had stumbled 'onto a rotten policy for extraneous reasons. . .'

'It's fuzzed up so much,' I said, 'that it's going to be hard to make any generalizations from it to the next issue.'

That was the essential problem. The generalizations indicating that the Reagan Revolution was not destined to succeed were already in place. I was just refusing to make them, fuzzing up the counter-revolutionary patterns with rationalizations that couldn't hold.

Victories and the Hour of History

One blitzkrieg followed another as the revolution moved up to Capitol Hill. I had become the Fastidious Accountant, who could not tolerate losing one dime of the $74 billion in 1984 spending cuts we now had pending because there was still another $44 billion in savings which we would have to come up with later. Congress thus had to enact every jot and tittle of the administration's proposed cuts.

There was a reason for this. Politically, these were the most palatable cuts available; philosophically, they were the most justified reductions to be had in the entire budget. The next $44 billion would be getting closer to the bone—and much tougher.

My fixation on the exacting math of the program implied a stunningly radical theory of governance. The constitutional prerogatives of the legislative branch would have to be, in effect, suspended. Enacting the Reagan Administration's economic program meant rubber stamp approval, nothing less. The world's so-called greatest deliberative body would have to be reduced to the status of a ministerial arm of the White House.

That theory ordinarily would never have had a chance of being proven even in the Republican Senate. But Senate Budget Chairman Pete Domenici and I came up with a procedural innovation that resulted in the appearance that the US Senate had indeed rubber-stamped the Reagan Revolution.

He and I agreed early that the tax cut would be in deep trouble unless we first passed the sweeping budget cuts. Our innovation thus brought before Congress a large share of the Reagan spending cuts for an immediate 'yes' or 'no' vote in March in a single omnibus package. Called 'Budget Reconciliation', this vote would essentially be a mandate from the full Senate to its committees to start cutting *all* the programs the administration had recommended for surgery. My aim in this tactic was to take the Hill by storm before the interest group opposition to spending cuts congealed.

What I didn't quite understand at the time was that Domenici had embraced the same strategy for the opposite reason. He was a Hooverite. He believed that budget expenditures needed to be drastically reduced and the budget balanced quickly. But he also thought the administration's tax package was far too big and risky.

Domenici believed that consideration of the Reagan spending reduction package first would prove the tax cut was *unaffordable*, the opposite of my lesson. He would show that even after a 'best efforts' housecleaning of the budget, you still couldn't get to a 1984 balanced budget with the full Reagan tax program. Thus, he saw reconciliation as a way station to a tax bill compromise, whereas I saw it as a precondition for a tax bill victory.

Under the normal Senate procedure, you couldn't have avoided a debate about so fundamental a policy question as whether the Reagan spending reduction package would prove that the tax cut was unaffordable. The normal procedure is to start with a Budget Resolution, which establishes the overall policy blueprint and the basic architecture of the entire fiscal plan. You debate and establish the economic assumptions, tax policy, defense policy, the deficit or surplus targets—everything which shapes the massive federal budget.

By contrast, our omnibus reconciliation bill shoved the fiscal blueprint aside and put the Senate to work laying some of the bricks first. The measure that would be brought to the Senate floor would say just one thing: cut domestic spending by these precise amounts. There would be no taxes, economic forecast, or even defense issues to palaver about.

Back then, I wanted to shut off the debate, thinking that I knew the answers and the senators didn't. If we succeeded in avoiding debate and starting fast, we could gain early momentum for the entire plan.

Reconciliation almost foundered, however, on the very first day of 'mark-up'—the Senate Budget Committee's line-by-line review of the draft of the budget plan, which took place in mid-March. Domenici was sensitive to charges that he might try to 'sabotage' the tax cut by not coming up with enough budget savings. So at least for the first year—1982—he vowed to equal or exceed the administration's total.

But he and his committee Republicans were having a hard time swallowing some of our line-item cuts in everything from education for the handicapped to the pregnant mothers' feeding program to the Export-Import Bank cuts. So they proposed instead to save $6 billion by limiting the cost of living adjustments (COLAs) on all federal pension programs, including Social Security. Then these savings would be used to protect their favorite programs.

As my script had it, Social Security had to be kept in the bull pen during this first budget-cutting go-round. The $6 billion COLA savings and a lot more would be needed in later innings to get the $44 billion we still owed.

Worried, I immediately called Jim Baker and told him about this. He went in to a red alert. From the beginning, he had thought of Social Security as Ronald Reagan's Achilles heel, and was determined to keep the President as far away from it as possible. The trouble was that neither he nor anyone else in the White House realized what the $44 billion we had plugged into the March 10 budget under the line 'future savings to be identified' really meant. It was nothing more than a euphemism for, 'We're going to go after Social Security.'

The White House staff then had some vague idea that we could close the $44 billion gap without sweeping Social Security reform. We hadn't got around to discussing it yet, but the notion was dead wrong. The budget math gave you no alternative—since Social Security accounted for more than one third of all domestic spending. Ships were already passing in the night.

But this was not yet apparent because at the moment there was a common tactical objective. We had to stop Howard Baker and Pete Domenici from cutting Social Security. Jim Baker arranged for the President to go up on the Hill the very next day and try to talk them out of it. We briefed the President, telling him that he must tell the senators he wanted *his* cuts, not theirs.

A warm fire was crackling in Howard Baker's cavernous office when we arrived at 9.30 am on March 17. The Senate Republican leadership and Budget Committee members were already assembled. I called them privately the College of Cardinals because many of them had taken on an air of self-importance and imperiousness owing to all their new power and committee chairmanships.

Reagan led off with an Irish joke, and the meeting got down to business: their proposal to attack nearly one quarter of a trillion dollars in indexed pensions, affecting roughly 36 million Americans.

Nearly to a man, the GOP stalwarts insisted that balancing the budget was impossible without curtailing the entitlement COLAs. They were absolutely right in insisting that this step would eventually be necessary. But there was also a hidden agenda in all this breast-beating, a lot of parentheses and footnotes to their bold talk about entitlements. They wanted those entitlements cut so they could preserve their energy projects, soil conservation grants, EDA projects, highway funds and education aid. Those were the mother's milk on which Republican politicians lived—self-professed conservatives as well as moderates—no less profitably than their Democratic colleagues.

'The budget's out of control due to entitlements,' they argued almost in unison. 'Now, are we going to have the guts to face up to it, or just keep nickel and diming these small discretionary programs?'

They had a point, but it led to the wrong outcome. After the senators put their favorite charities back into the budget, the tax cut would have to be diluted because that wouldn't be enough spending cuts to keep the budget equation balanced. I just wasn't going to let that happen.

'Fellas,' the President finally said, 'I promised I wouldn't touch Social Security. We just can't get suckered into it. The other side's waiting to pounce. So let's put this one behind us and get on with cutting it.'

Howard Baker responded by saying, 'Mr President, we hear you loud and clear.' The meeting was over.

The issue had only been postponed, really, but for the meantime I had gained my objective. Social Security was safe on the pantry shelf, awaiting the carving knife that would have to be applied to it later.

And the Senate Republicans were in a bind. They had publicly vowed to start the ball rolling fast and were now in a drama of high visibility, a drama in which they had to deliver on their pledge or be embarrassed. Once blocked on Social Security, they didn't have any choice except to swallow nearly the entire package of the White House's budget cuts.

In the next several days the Budget Committee did just that. The rubber stamp had worked its first test.

But, in truth, a great confusion had been born. The message, both public and private, that had issued from the emergency meeting in Howard Baker's office was unmistakable: *Reagan vows no Social Security cuts*. Such messages, once issued, stick like glue. That lesson would be coming soon.

In the meanwhile, I saw nothing but success. Due to reconciliation first and Social Security later, the whole fiscal policy debate had been drastically narrowed, at least for the moment. The Senate Budget Committee had been transformed into an item-by-item domestic budget-cutting machine. And as a result, the big picture question—Does it all add up?—was postponed to another day.

Under the cool and resourceful leadership of Baker and Domenici, the full Senate proved just as pliable as the Budget Committee. Nevertheless, Domenici kept worrying about a 'run on the bank' in the form of a spending amendment. He understood the precedentitis disease well. If one interest group got spared, discipline might collapse entirely. An amendment offered from the Republican side of the aisle by John Chaffee of Rhode Island thus became a crucial litmus test. It sought to restore $1 billion in funding for normally irresistible programs: elementary education, heating fuel assistance, weatherization funds for the poor, UDAG* grants, community and mental health service and mass transit.

But sixteen Democrats joined with the Republicans and defeated it, 59–41. The moment they did so, the battle for the Reagan budget was won. A subsequent amendment to restore an infinitesimal $6 million with which to inoculate children against disease was defeated by a wide margin, leaving veteran observers to shake their heads in disbelief.

The subsequent passage of the President's budget by 88 to 10 created a grand illusion. It appeared that the senators who passed it had changed their political spots. It looked as if the Reagan Revolution were an unstoppable force.

* Urban Development Action Grant.

VICTORIES AND THE HOUR OF HISTORY

I thus told Greider in early April that the defeat of the Chaffee amendment had been nothing less than a political watershed.

'It could well be the turning point in the whole process,' I said. 'It was the kind of amendment that should have passed. A little for education, a little for heating assistance, a little for nutrition. It was the classic spending constituency coalition. . . The fact that it didn't win tells me that the whole political logic has changed.'

Once our 'Reconciliation First' strategem had won Senate approval the first week in April, the bricks were laid. Then the Senate Budget Committee went back to work on the Budget Resolution—the blueprint and architecture—for 1982 and the out-year's budget. Once it did, all the doubts, reservations and outright complaints the Committee had about our economic program bubbled right up to the surface, in a rather public way, too.

As a group, the Senate Budget Committee was not exactly in the vanguard of the Reagan Revolution. Disagreement among its members was rife. The GOP moderates on it, such as Nancy Kassenbaum of Kansas and Mark Andrews of North Dakota had long laundry lists full of objections to the $74 billion in cuts we had proposed. And that was to say nothing of the additional $44 billion we would eventually need.

Worse, neither of them had any use for the Kemp-Roth tax cut. In that they were not alone. Their disdain for it was shared by freshman Slade Gorton of Washington. A brilliant iconoclast, Gorton wasn't opposed to spending cuts but was rabid anti-free-luncher when it came to the 'does it add up?' question.

Then there were Bill Armstrong of Colorado, Chuck Grasley of Iowa and Steve Symms of Idaho. They were hard-core conservatives who believed in the old-time religion of balanced budgets. The latter two had unhorsed archetypal big-spending liberals, and had arrived in Washington raring to attack the federal deficit. They were hardly the kind to be impressed with our promise to find $44 billion in 'future savings'.

On top of that, the Committee's GOP ranks contained incipient divisions on the matter of our defense increase. John Tower of Texas, who was also chairman of the Senate Armed Services Committee, was the real architect of the proposed buildup, and Bill Armstrong of Colorado, for all his right-wing nature, was sceptical of every kind of spending and not persuaded that so many defense dollars were actually needed.

Since the Republicans had a slim majority on the Budget Committee—twelve to ten—the administration's overall fiscal plan couldn't be approved without absolute Republican unanimity. We would get no comfort from the Democrats who sat on it. Even those of them who favored budget reduction, such as Fritz Hollings of South Carolina, dripped with contempt for Kemp-Roth.

There was still another problem on the Senate Budget Committee. Multi-year budget making was something entirely new to Congress. Domenici and the other senators would thus be even more reliant on their staffs than usual. And Domenici's chief aide and confidant was Steve Bell—an avowed opponent of supply-side economics.

Both Domenici and Bell felt that Rosy Scenario was off by a mile and were determined to force the administration to compromise on the tax cut once Domenici had delivered on the 'Reconciliation First'.

But I'd seen them coming, too. After countless meetings with Domenici, I had brow-beaten him into accepting most of Rosy Scenario's predictions instead of the Congressional Budget Office (CBO)'s economic forecast, which would have brought our total 1984 deficit to $80 billion, once you added the $44 billion in additional cuts we owed. And that would have been the end of the Reagan Revolution right then and there.

So far so good. But then, a week before the Committee was scheduled to start mark-up on the 1982 Budget Resolution, we heard that Bell and his staff were planning to add $16 billion to our deficit estimate on account of technical quibbles. The worst news was that they were going to refuse to display the $44 billion 'future savings to be proposed' as a 'cut'. Instead, they insisted upon calling a deficit a deficit. They were going to put it on the bottom line and blow the 1984 balanced budget sky-high. By the time they had finished with their reckonings, the administration's budget for 1984 would show a $60 billion deficit—a horrendous prospect.

I began agitating the Legislative Strategy Group at the White House, and another emergency meeting was called for April 2. The Senate leaders and heavy hitters from the White House were there.

Pete Domenici spelled out the situation. 'The Budget Committee is not going to buy a "pig in a poke",' he said. The pig was our $44 billion in budget savings; the poke was the 'savings to be proposed' aspect of it. Unless we were prepared to say *right now* where the $44 billion was going to come from, he would flatly refuse to insert this 'future savings plug' into the budget. Rather than 'undermine the integrity of the budget process', he was willing to take the risk of presenting to his Committee a budget plan that was as much as $60 billion out of balance by 1984.

I told Domenici that he had a perfectly valid point, but that we couldn't solve the problem all at once. We couldn't identify every single cut we were going to make over four years right away. Social Security was due for reform; the defense increase numbers had to be trimmed; and all the major entitlement programs would have to fall under the axe. But for the moment the issue was where to put the $44 billion. We could put it 'above the line' as a future savings amount we were pledged to come up with, or 'below the line' as a deficit. We owed the money—that much was certain.

But, 'It would be a drastic mistake,' I concluded, 'to let mere accounting quibbles thwart the President's program at this critical juncture.'

We supply siders had all along considered Bob Dole highly unreliable as far as our tax cut was concerned because he tended to be of the traditional Hooverite persuasion. But as soon as I finished my pitch, he turned to Domenici and said, 'Put it above the line, Pete. Otherwise, you're going to hand the Democrats an easy shot at the tax bill.'

Dole hadn't suddenly changed his mind about so fundamental an issue as the Kemp-Roth tax cut. He was simply asserting his territorial right. *If there's any compromising to be done on taxes, he was telling Domenici, he — the chairman of the Senate Finance Committee — would take care of it in due course.*

It remained only for the Senate Majority Leader somehow to resolve the question of where to put the $44 billion. Howard Baker, master of timing and conflict management, accepted his responsibility with some reluctance. He agreed with Domenici on the policy, but with Dole on the politics.

So, in an attempt to defer rather than solve the fundamental issue, he cleared his throat and said, 'Gentlemen, I'm tempted to designate this $44 billion with a magic asterisk. But I won't.'

There was a pause. 'But,' he continued, 'come to think of it, that's our only choice. And so I will.'

Which was how the $44 billion magic asterisk was officially baptized by the politicians.

For the 'next little while', Baker said, the $44 billion would be counted as a future savings, not a deficit. It was a typical Baker formulation—nothing was ever final—but for the time being, it would do. At least our gimmick had acquired an aura of seriousness. It was no longer the asterisk that dared not speak its name. Having come up with the closest thing to a Solomonic solution, Baker adjourned the meeting on a note of cordiality.

The 'next little while' turned out to last four days. Domenici's staff was outraged by the decision to affix the magic asterisk to the $44 billion. Bell confronted Domenici: 'Do you really want to go down in history as the Budget Chairman who couldn't add?' The very next week, April 6, Domenici's draft budget included the administration's full tax cut *and* whopping deficits in 1984 and beyond. It was bad news, I thought, but correctible bad news. There would be time to reinsert the magic asterisk.

But I had underestimated Domenici. His stratagem had exactly the desired effect. As soon as the Republicans on the Committee saw the deficit figures, they panicked. By Wednesday afternoon, two days later, they were in open rebellion.

Domenici called me that afternoon and told me, 'You better get up here right away. We've got a lot of unhappy Republicans that don't want to vote for this resolution.'

I rode up to the Hill that night to see what damage control I could do and realized very quickly there wasn't much I could do at all. Tempers were already at 105 degrees Fahrenheit.

We met in Domenici's office in the Dirksen Building. All the Senate Budget Committee Republicans were there, sprawled in chairs randomly placed about the room, as if to testify to the group's present state of disorder.

The talk went in circles—furious circles—as everyone gave his or her speech about why they were so angry at the other, or at the White House. Tower was furious because Armstrong had knocked defense. Domenici attacked Armstrong over his opposition to the deficit. Everyone was sitting there shouting at each other.

I realized there weren't any solutions to be had that night. I urged them to cool off during the recess and finish the budget when they returned.

They did neither. Domenici's staff had turned the heat up on the debate and weren't about to lower it. The next day, Domenici pushed the Committee to a final vote. The Reagan plan—our 'resolution package'—was voted down, 12–8. The critical votes against us had been supplied by the Armstrong anti-deficit faction.

The press seized on the vote as evidence that the Reagan bandwagon had skidded into the ditch. It looked as if the politicians were not going to be made to play my rubber-stamping game after all. It was certainly unmistakable evidence of the split in GOP ranks on Kemp-Roth and the economic plan's fundamental architecture. Explaining what had happened a few days later to Greider I fingered the anti-tax cutters.

> Domenici's staff saw this as an opportunity to force a change in tax policy by saddling conservative Republicans with those big deficits... Many in the Senate want that. In front of other members, they're very cagey about what they say about Kemp-Roth. Privately, they're just scathing, some of these guys.

I now thought that we might have to phase in the tax cut more gradually to satisfy the Kemp-Roth haters. No matter. It would be a small price to pay for getting a deep, permanent tax rate reduction into the statute books.

But I was determined, fiercely, not to permit even a hint of compromise to waft up from the Senate side until after we had seized control of the House floor by means of our Boll Weevil–Republican coalition.

Strategically, it was a matter of playing one weak reed against another. The instant the GOP–Boll Weevil coalition discovered that compromise on the giant tax cut was possible, there would be a stampede to water down the spending cuts, too. It was obvious that was what many of them really wanted.

This meant I had to keep the House GOP–Boll Weevil coalition pinned to the mat until we won the Budget Resolution test in the House scheduled for early May. If Domenici would not assume his appointed role of blocking any compromise, we would play rough until he saw the light.

So, I posted a message on the Bob Novak bulletin board and had a little conversation with my friend Bob Bartley, editorial page editor of *The Wall Street Journal*. The next day there appeared on that gray, dignified page a searing editorial entitled 'John Maynard Domenici'.

It accused the Senate Budget Chairman of single-handedly attempting to destroy the Reagan Revolution out of a benighted affection for the failed Keynesian policies of the now medieval past. Domenici was alarmed by this jeremiad. His staff immediately produced a lengthy letter to the editor 'proving' that the Senate Budget Chairman was not, in fact, a Keynesian deviant. My missile had hit its mark.

Domenici had nowhere to turn. By now he was getting phone calls from the President, still recuperating from an assassin's bullet; also from Vice President Bush, Howard Baker and Bob Dole. The message was the same in every case: Get back on the team lest the Republicans prove they aren't fit to govern less than four months after taking power.

In the end the combination of attacks and entreaties worked. Domenici lost his nerve, if not his convictions, and for the moment beat a tactical retreat. He ordered his staff to work out some variation of the magic asterisk solution with me during the recess.

The revolt of the Senate Budget Committee had turned out to be yet another signal from the political system that I refused to heed. It wanted a smaller tax cut; it wanted to compromise. But as I saw it, their job was to drastically shrink a bloated and economically debilitating welfare state budget, not to play politics-as-usual.

Nevertheless, for the moment the budget balancers got back on board. All amendments that might have altered the resolution were handily defeated, and on May 12, the Senate approved a 1982 Budget Resolution that contained nearly one hundred percent of the administration's entire economic program, by a vote of 72–20. The politicians had flinched. They had rubber-stamped the Reagan Revolution.

There was one discordant note, however. My former rabbi from Cambridge, Senator Daniel Patrick Moynihan of New York, had turned against my plan with a vengeance. During the voting he delivered himself of a flamboyantly theatrical speech.

'Free Stockman!' he shouted, while beckoning with both arms toward the Republican side of the aisle. 'Free Reagan!

'Can we not,' he intoned, 'free ourselves from a very momentary aberration not very far from the free coinage of silver?' My old friend and mentor was busy attacking the Laffer curve; unfortunately, that was not the real problem, either.

Cheered by our ninety-seven percent victory in the Senate, no one in the White House wanted to compromise when the fight moved on to the House. They never questioned my go-for-broke strategy. If we could turn *both* houses of the Congress into ministerial arms of the White House, getting them to rubber-stamp every detail of our spending reduction and tax cut program, so much the better. The only problem was, nothing resembling a majority of support existed in the House of Representatives.

Of the one hundred and ninety Republicans in the House, a good forty to fifty had substantial reservations about the pending $74 billion budget reduction package; all Republicans had objections to something significant in it; and none had ever seen the $44 billion in additional out-year cuts that we still owed, nor were they anxious to find out.

At the same time, the thirty to fifty southern conservative Democrats—the so-called Boll Weevils—were everything but supply-side revolutionaries. They were Hooverites: budget balancers, first and last. They talked a good budget-cutting game, but they loved even more their own regional pork, which wasn't insubstantial.

So the Boll Weevils viewed the Kemp-Roth tax cut as an unessential luxury to be implemented at some distant future date. After the spending cuts were watered down, the tax cut would be slimmed down to fit a balanced budget, even if the tax cut didn't amount to much.

The Boll Weevils had endorsed the administration's economic program, but in a curious way. On March 5, they had come to the White House for a highly publicized breakfast with the President in the East Room. With their bellies full of grits, they had stood, one by one, to praise the President. They were with him 'all the way', as G. V. 'Sonny' Montgomery, a senior Mississippi Democrat and chairman of the House Veterans Affairs Committee, put it. The only fault Montgomery found with the program was that it had 'not gone far enough'.

'We want to cut even more than you have proposed,' he told the President.

The President responded warmly. 'That's OK with me. That's what we're here for.'

It was a classic exchange of political fuzzy talk. The President thought Montgomery wanted him to make even deeper spending cuts. Not at all. Montgomery had been proposing a bigger reduction in the 1982 *deficit*, even if it meant forgoing part of the Kemp-Roth tax cut. Long after the Boll Weevils had demonstrated beyond a shadow of a doubt their tepid enthusiasm for spending cuts, the President would continue to speak glowingly of 'our breakfast with the Boll Weevils' as evidence of strong congressional support for our cuts.

We were thus at least one hundred votes short of the House majority needed to implement every item on the budget reduction package. Under normal circumstances, a major compromise would have been in order. But revolutionaries do not compromise. I was determined to keep the Kemp-Roth tax cut alive and to balance the budget. Any slippage from rubber stamp approval of the $74 billion in cuts we had pending would threaten one or both objectives. The Senate had been made to swallow the whole pill. The House would thus be forced to do the same.

Jim Jones, chairman of the House Budget Committee, desperately wanted to compromise. A short, balding, extremely intelligent and articulate Oklahoman, Jones was to the right of the Democratic majority. He was a practical conservative who wanted to cut the budget substantially, as well as reduce federal taxation, especially on business.

He had told me he would go along with seventy to eighty percent of the new Reagan budget package, asking only that we dilute some of the sensitive, low-income cuts such as food stamps and child nutrition, and implement the entitlement cuts over a longer period. Jones had said that he felt the new House could be dominated by a coalition of conservative and middle Democrats, and Republicans. The left-wing Democrats would be isolated, hanging out on a limb with no place to go.

I never considered Jones's overtures for even a moment. I was the Fastidious Accountant, and we weren't playing horse shoes. Close didn't count.

In fact, Jones was an outspoken opponent of the Kemp-Roth tax cut. He advocated reducing it to a single ten percent, one-year cut, putting the remainder in limbo until it was 'affordable'.

That position drove me up a wall. The thirty percent tax cut was not a negotiable part of the revolution. The truth was that Jones and his like-minded colleagues would never enact the remaining twenty percent. They would cut spending only modestly, then plead the fiscal case for keeping taxes high.

There was another reason for resisting compromise with Jones: my profound distrust of the senior Democrats who controlled the standing committees wouldn't allow it. It is no exaggeration to say that flat out. These standing committee chairmen *were* the Politburo of the Welfare State. There was literally nothing that they would willingly cut out of their budgets. And their capacity for sabotage and accounting gimmickry was nearly limitless. Big spending–cut targets and small reconciliation mandates to reduce federal spending laws—in other words, just promises—were all that Jones could deliver. My exacting fiscal equation would be in tatters by the time the President was actually presented with a reconciliation bill under any arrangement with him.

There was only one way to beat the institutionally entrenched potential saboteurs of the Reagan fiscal revolution. That was to set off a demonstration bomb on the House floor by administering a licking to the Democratic committee chairman. The President would mobilize an ad hoc coalition of Republicans and Boll Weevil Democrats on the first test of power—the budget resolution. Then the Politburo would know that it could not later sabotage the reconciliation bills with impunity.

I told Greider on April 4 precisely how I intended to make the budget resolution a decisive power play, explaining that 'My counter strategy is to win on the Floor of the House in order to establish Administration control over the democratic committee chairman who can murder us in the remainder of the process. The way you avoid that is to remind them that if they deviate too far from the program, they'll face the same thing again.'

My intransigence and my strategy, needless to say, did not go down well with Jones and his capable and shrewd moderate Democratic colleague, Leon Panetta. In fact, they were now livid.

My refusal to deal had made their situation utterly, utterly miserable. They had begun as leaders of a broad and unbeatable

middle-to-right bipartisan coalition. But now they were left standing
in between a rock and a hard place, on the rightmost fringe of the
Democratic remainder. This meant they were left having to work up
a budget that would satisfy everyone from Ron Dellums to Phil
Gramm. Since Dellums was somewhere to the left of Ho Chi Minh
and Gramm was somewhere to the right of me, this was no fun at all.
It was sweat, pain, travail and sheer unpleasantness.

While he was courteous enough not to denounce me by name,
Jones publicly vented his resentment during the House Committee
mark-up.* His remarks to a newspaper reporter showed the extent to
which my intended *coup d'état* had stirred up deep grievances.

'The Administration said that it can accept no amendments, that
its budget is untouchable,' he said. 'No Administration has ever
made such demands, and no Congress has ever accepted such
demands. It's not the job of the Congress not to think. What we are
seeing from some Administration spokesmen is a bunker mentality
stemming from a gargantuan sense of egotism.'

Jones was right about what I was demanding from the House
politicians. It amounted to surrender.

With the battle lines drawn, the struggle became a contest between
Jones and the Administration for the bloc of thirty to fifty Boll
Weevils whose votes would make the crucial difference. Jones and
his Democratic colleagues manoeuvered assiduously and deftly to
keep them on board by lowering the projected 1982 deficit from $45
billion to $25 billion. They even proposed to balance the budget by
1983, one year earlier than we did. They also accommodated
practically the entire Reagan defense increase. They knew that low
deficits and high defense numbers were the key to holding onto the
Boll Weevils. For the House Ho Chi Minh faction, they also added
back nearly one quarter of our social spending reductions.

The problem was that there was really no honest way they could
put together a budget that had low enough deficits, high enough
defense numbers, sufficiently restored social spending, and a decent
tax cut. Once we had denied them any Republican votes by refusing
to compromise, it was impossible. The 218 votes they needed for a
majority simply weren't there.

* A preliminary reading of a bill.

But Jones and his group were so mad, they were determined to win. So they resorted to a rash of gimmickry that has plagued the budget process ever since. They artificially raised revenue estimates, fudged the defense expenditure figures, and counted up a phantom savings of $6 billion from rooting out fraud, waste and abuse without any serious recommendations as to how this could be achieved.

In the end, Jones and Panetta's attempt to win back the Boll Weevils by reducing the whole issue to 'Who's got the smallest 1982 deficit?' backfired. The real issue, and their strongest case, was the out-year budget gap—the architecture of the Reagan Revolution's fiscal plan. That was the reason the middle Democrats were so fundamentally sceptical of our tax cuts. They thought they would create intolerable, permanent deficits, and they were right. But now everyone's attention had been refocused on 1982, and a one-year deficit numbers game. Jones thought he had put an ace in his hand, but it was a joker.

Gramm and I were not about to see the Reagan Revolution defeated by accounting gimmickry. So we adjusted the administration's budget to incorporate all the 'smoke and mirrors' the Democrats had produced.

Indeed, the four people who knew more about the budget than anyone else in the House—Jones, Panetta, Gramm, and I—spent the entire month of April rigging the numbers to the point that even we couldn't understand them.

It is perhaps tragic to consider that such competent and well-intentioned men should have conducted themselves as we did. But in the midst of a skirmish, the whole battlefield is often obscured. Gramm and I fought the Democrats on the ground they had chosen. One gimmick followed another; numbers were written in sand.

More importantly, once the numbers and policy choices became nearly meaningless, the decisive battle for the Reagan Revolution got reduced to an image contest between the Speaker and the President, a question of hope versus nostalgia. Would you go with the President's brave new gamble or stick with the Speaker's failed tax-and-spend policies of the past? That's what the members were finally called upon to decide.

In that context, the Democrats seriously underestimated the resilience with which the President bounced back from the assassination attempt. From his remark to the First Lady in the emergency room of the George Washington University Hospital, 'Honey, I forgot to duck', to his triumphant speech to the Congress on April 28, the momentum was all ours. Indeed, for a while the President acquired heroic aura—and the polls reflected it. By the time the House voted on the budget, his already imposing strength in the Boll Weevils' districts had reached never-before-recorded levels.

Thus, while Jones and his middle Democrats were offering the Boll Weevils a marginally lower deficit for 1982, the White House was framing the question in far more politically compelling and dramatic terms: *Are you with Ronald Reagan or against him?*

Jones tried floating a trial balloon by incorrectly saying on a Sunday television news show that the administration had told him, 'They are willing to compromise.' It couldn't have been more untimely. Dave Gergen's smooth White House press apparatus handled Jones's remark deftly. Jones had tossed a slow pitch across the center of the plate and the President knocked it out of the park. Even before saying 'Good morning' on his first day back at work—so the story went—the still-bandaged President had turned to his senior staff and said, 'No compromise!'

'I'm convinced,' said the nation's leader just two weeks after a bullet had ripped into his seventy-year-old body, 'that the American people strongly support my program and don't want it watered down.' Within two more weeks, those wavering Republicans and Boll Weevils were convinced themselves.

By the time of the final showdown in late April, the Democrats had seen the writing on the wall. Upon returning from a global junket—of the kind that are customarily called 'fact-finding missions'—the Speaker of the House threw in the towel two days before the actual vote.

'I can read Congress,' Tip O'Neill told the press. 'They go with the will of the people and the will of the people is to go along with the President. I've been in politics a long time. I know when you fight and when you don't.' To which O'Neill added a coy footnote: 'Time cures all ills.' For all his sins, the foxy old Speaker knew something I didn't. *We'll wait this thing out*, he was saying, *then we'll get back to business as usual*.

On the eve of the vote, the House Rules Committee, a wholly owned subsidiary of the Democratic leadership, agreed to a procedure that virtually ensured easy passage of our budget. It decided to permit (thumbs) 'up or down' votes on the two budgets, Reagan's and Jones's. The up or down vote thus reduced the decision on US economic policy for the 1980s to a political question: 'Whose side are you on?'

Even so, Gramm and I had left nothing to chance. During the gimmick wars with the House Budget Committee, we had produced our own 'bipartisan substitute' plan, which we eventually called Gramm–Latta.* It was this document that the house would approve on the day of the vote.

It contained only three substantive concessions on half a billion dollars in cuts relative to the precise fiscal blueprint I had produced in February, and the most important one went to the pivotal Boll Weevil, Sonny Montgomery. If he abandoned the Democratic leadership—a move which could threaten his chairmanship of the House Veterans Affairs Committee—then Gramm and I were convinced that the other senior southern Democrats would follow him. Thus when he indicated that he wanted $400 million in Veterans Administration health care cuts restored, we were more than willing to accommodate him. 'I'm not going to break my sword on a few thousand extra VA employees,' I told Greider. It worked. Montgomery's defection created a small stampede—or fluttering, as the case may be—of Boll Weevils.

Even so, the Boll Weevils were not altogether ready to defect to the Reagan White House. Democrats did not lightly vote Republican. They needed one last shove—and Phil Gramm provided it.

On the day after Jim Jones's House Budget Committee released its alternative plan, the Boll Weevils held a strategy session in Montgomery's office. The group's chairman, Charlie Stenholm of Texas, asked the members for their opinions of it. One by one they said that it was a *reasonable compromise* and that it would allow them to work with the Democratic leadership while at the same time promoting President Reagan's goals.

Gramm waited until everyone had said his piece. Then he stood up and told them that he could not support it.

---

* Congressman Del Latta, the senior Republican on the House Budget Committee, was the other co-sponsor. Latta was one of the few stalwart anti-spenders among the House GOP—and the only one who never asked me to spare something for his district!

The Boll Weevils, he reminded them, had earlier established firm guidelines. They would accept no deficit greater than the Reagan budget deficit, no defense figure less than the Reagan figure, and no cuts in entitlement programs less than what Reagan had proposed. In his view, the Jones budget clearly flunked the test.

Gramm then said it was 'time to draw the line in the sand' and see who truly desired to rebuild the national defense and revitalize the economy. He told them he was going to offer an alternative budget—'even if I'm the only person in the House to vote for it.'

It was clear to him, Gramm said, that if William Barrett Travis, commander of the American forces at the Alamo had asked for a debate instead of drawing the famous line in the sand, then 'there never would have been a battle.'

This was followed by five minutes of shouting. Jack Hightower of Texas pointedly reminded Gramm that everyone who crossed the line at the Alamo died. There was a murmur of assent at this.

'Yes,' said Gramm, 'but the ones who didn't cross the line died, too. Only no one remembers their names.'

It worked. Scratch a Texan and you'll find a defender of the Alamo. No sooner had Gramm said it than Marvin Leath, a Texas member who rarely said anything at these meetings, jumped up. Everyone in the room knew 'damned well' that Gramm was right, he said. Gramm wouldn't be the only one to vote for his alternative budget because, 'by God, I'm going to vote for it, too!'

That meeting turned out to be the pivotal event; it turned the tide and kept the administration's economic plan in contention all spring and summer. The big tax cut never would have happened without the Boll Weevils crossing the line on Sonny Montgomery's carpet. The irony was staggering: nearly to a man the Boll Weevils were opposed to Kemp-Roth, the half-revolution that eventually destroyed their hopes for a balanced budget for the remainder of their careers. But that strange day they were the ones who made it all possible.

There were others in the coalition with initially even colder feet. Between thirty and fifty 'soft' Republicans badgered Minority Leader Bob Michel relentlessly to restore this cut and that cut. Day after day they came at him with their laundry lists until, his patience sorely tried, he exploded during an eleventh-hour hand-holding session with them.

'Geeminnie Christmas!' he pounded the table. 'When are you guys going to recognize that this is only a Budget *Resolution?* It doesn't cut anything. It's all assumptions! If you've got problems, write 'em down and send 'em to me. We'll take care of them later.'

Most of the nervous GOP pols* went along with the administration's budget on Michel's assurance that *it could all be changed later.* After twenty-five years of being in the minority party, the Republicans still had not adjusted to the fact that they were now the governing party. Michel was saying, in effect, 'This budget is going to lose, just as all our budgets have lost. So don't worry about the cuts. This will have no effect on the real world.'

He was wrong. Their laundry list could *not* be taken care of later, not if we were going to eliminate the $44 billion magic asterisk. The budget plan would have an effect on the real world; but he and the others would only realize that after it was too late.

It remained only for the President, riding a wave of popularity due to his recovery, to drive home the final victory. On May 8, in the hall of the politicians, his plan for an economic policy revolution was officially endorsed, with sixty votes to spare. The real issues that the Reagan Revolution posed, however, had never been seriously debated.

It was the Democratic budget, in fact, that should have won. Behind all its trumped-up numbers, it embraced two propositions that represented the overwhelming bipartisan consensus of the House politicians. They and the Democratic budget acknowledged that high inflation had pushed people into higher income tax brackets long enough. If enacted, the Democratic budget would have brought about a de facto tax indexing, the antidote to bracket creep. But it included no deep tax cut like Kemp-Roth.

The Democratic budget also demonstrated that the Congress would never—ever—go along with the kind of drastic spending cuts that the Reagan Revolution depended on. Despite the big spending cuts promised in the Democratic budget, it only *mandated* through reconciliation bills about $25 billion in 1984 savings. Thus the real spending cuts that the politicians were willing to commit themselves to amounted to less than one fourth of what the Reagan Revolution

* Politicians.

required, even under the optimistic economic assumptions then available.

But since the Gramm–Latta budget actually won the vote, a radical fiscal policy framework had now achieved powerful political sanction. The huge multi-year tax cut was more than halfway home. The massive, parallel spending cut promise that the politicians had also endorsed without comprehending it, however, would suffer a thousand overdrafts.

In the final analysis, the political assumption at the center of the Gramm–Latta budget was still haywire. It trusted the politicians ultimately to retrieve from the electorate nearly as much in welfare state benefits as the plan proposed to give back in one-time tax reductions. This was an inherently foolish proposition, though I had no grasp of it at the time.

The next Saturday, May 16, savoring the victory, I told my sceptical interlocutor at the Hay-Adams that the vote confirmed that a true sea-change in American politics had occurred. A new era had dawned. Something incredible had happened: Presidential power had been restored, and with it, the opportunity for radical change. 'I never expected that to happen,' I told Greider.

> They bought the whole loaf. I guess it's because I grew up in this town when you had a President that didn't have any power. I underestimated what a popular or effective President could do to mobilize the Congress. . .
>
> The 1980 election apparently rattled the politicians more than I really understood at the time. . . There hasn't been a President for decades that's got reinforcement on the Hill. Carter's energy plan, Ford's everything, Nixon's life and limb . . . all failures because everything they tried to do was resisted.
>
> Now what you have going is a process that we haven't experienced since 1965. The President came up with a plan and the Congress said, 'This is the right thing to do at this hour of history.'

7

New Lessons: The Politics of Taking

'We're a little ahead of schedule politically, and a little behind schedule financially,' I told Greider during one of our breakfasts in late April.

Things did look grand on the political side. Congress had all but ratified the sweeping Reagan Revolution blueprint for inflationless capitalist growth.

The financial markets had naturally been following these developments with a keen eye, and they had issued a clear reaction: *panic!*

After my visit to Wall Street in December, I had told Greider that the crucial referendum on our economic program would occur in the bond markets. But between January and April 1981, the inherited, debilitating fifteen percent bond yields had not improved one bit.

The bond markets and the growls of Wall Street bears stung me to the quick because they amounted to a mortal threat to my 'push-pull' theory. That was the foundation upon which all of the budget numbers rested. It was the only scenario by which you could avoid having the economy dumped into recession and the balanced budget dumped into an ocean of red ink.

Greider inconveniently reminded me of my theory of efficient markets and said the markets themselves were voting against the Reagan program, even as I was manoeuvring it toward victory on the Hill.

But I insisted that the situation in the markets was temporary and reversible. The markets didn't believe we were serious about closing the $44 billion gap.

'Yeah, Henry Kaufman does have a point,' I agreed. 'The bond markets have behaved exactly in line with what he said. But,' I told Greider, 'they haven't seen all our cards yet.'

Inwardly, I now realized the whole plan had been put together too quickly. The $44 billion magic asterisk was a time bomb—it raised serious doubts about the plan's whole architecture.

'For about a month and a half we got away with it,' I said to Greider. 'Now the veil is being pierced and people are looking behind it. We have to recalibrate the policy.'

At the time, I didn't see that that should be very difficult. It would involve three modest fixes.

The tax bill would have to be adjusted slightly so as not to reduce revenues quite so drastically. Defense would have to be trimmed in order to get the out-year spending numbers down. And last but hardly least, we would have to move immediately on a major Social Security reform plan.

That shouldn't be a problem, I thought. Jim Baker, Ed Meese, and the rest of the senior staff had been badly shaken by the revolt of Domenici's Senate Budget Committee earlier in the month.

For the first time since we had launched the program on February 18, I was able to get them to focus on just how dire the $44 billion gap was. Baker and Meese wanted to know why it happened. 'Let me give you a half-hour briefing,' I told them.

As I described the briefing to Greider:

> So I put together a list of twenty social programs that would have to be zeroed out completely—the Job Corps, Head Start, women, infants and children's feeding programs and on and on. And another twenty-five that would have to be cut by fifty percent. . . And then the huge bits that would have to be taken out of Social Security. And it *still* didn't add up to $44 billion.

At the LSG* meetings, I warned further that 'We are thirty to forty-five days from serious legislative setbacks and loss of Presidential policy control on the entire economic recovery program—*unless a strategic plan is quickly developed to handle the following major threats or challenges* . . .' And: 'The out-year revenue losses from the current tax plan are probably too sudden and too severe.'

* The White House Legislative Strategy Group.

By late April I thought we had an LSG consensus along the lines of my three-point recalibration plan. Unfortunately, events now began to move so swiftly that it was never presented to the President in one sitting as a coherent, comprehensive, strategic adjustment. Instead, we gave it to him one piece at a time. He decided on each element according to his own judgment based on the narrow circumstances at hand. But the recalibration could not be reduced to constituent parts. It had to do with a big hole in the entire dyke.

And just how badly I underestimated the difficulties that would be involved in making the adjustments was revealed by what I described to Greider on 25 April 1981.

'Hell,' I told him, 'all you've got to do is take $4 or $5 billion off Defense, $8 or $10 billion off Social Security, $5 or $6 billion off a $150 billion tax cut in the out-years, plus a lot of incremental changes all over the budget, and you've solved the problem. It looks big, but there are a lot of pieces to shrink.'

No problem.

No single issue was as critical to the success of the Reagan Revolution as Social Security reform. Spending on that program alone consumed nearly $200 billion per year, just under one third of the entire domestic budget. It was therefore impossible to suppose that we could cut enough out of the budget to make our equation balance without touching it.

On April 9, Congressman Jake 'J.J.' Pickle of Texas, chairman of the House Social Security Subcommittee, introduced a Social Security reform bill. It had his committee's bipartisan backing, and it would cut, ostensibly, several billion out of Social Security spending each year.

This action appeared to be consistent with my planned solution to the magic asterisk, but there was one giant problem with Pickle's initiative: the savings amounted to only a tiny fraction of the administration's out-year budget gap. While I did not hope to cut the entire $44 billion per year out of Social Security, I did desperately need a reform plan that saved a lot more than Pickle's paltry proposal.

And so the next day I set in motion a plan to get a lot more savings. What was about to happen had already happened consistently before. It was time to deal with the basic architecture of the Reagan

Revolution, not just details, so a frontal assault on the very inner fortress of the American welfare state—the giant Social Security system, on which one seventh of the nation's populace depended for its well-being—was in order.

Social Security had been born during the New Deal as a minimum, state-insured retirement pension. That idea was noble. But over the decades the system had evolved into a capricious hybrid of out-and-out welfare benefits and earned pension annuities, which were hopelessly tangled together and disguised under the fig leaf of social insurance.

The pure idea of Social Security as an earned pension rested on an exacting discipline. Actuaries could add up the approximate present value of a lifetime of payroll tax contributions and calculate what the resulting pension annuity should be. And under any actuarial system for determining the pension, the two had to equate. Period. The only argument was over what interest rate to use in the calculations.

But that was not what Social Security had become. Social Security, as it had evolved, had come to rest on the myth that everybody earned his or her Social Security benefits and was entitled to them. The truth was that the politicians had sweetened nearly everyone's earned pension with extra dollars for dependants, low earnings and numerous other concepts of 'need' that had nothing to do with what a worker had put into the fund.

The problem with all this closet socialism was that it tempted the politicians with something close to original sin. Unearned benefits severed the exacting actuarial linkage between what you put into the fund and what you got out of it. Once the linkage was gone, the politicians were off to the races, adding promise after promise of unearned benefits to those who retired by mortgaging the incomes of workers not yet born. By 1980 Social Security had become a giant Ponzi* scheme.

The reason was as simple as it was fundamental. Over time, the natural demographics of an affluent industrial society automatically produces a declining ratio of active workers to retired workers. That natural ratio decline is no problem in a system based on earned pensions: each retiree has, in effect, already contributed the nest egg

* An investment swindle in which early investors are paid off with money put up by later investors.

out of which his pension checks are drawn. But it becomes a ticking
time bomb when the state lavishes upon the retired benefits
disproportionate to their contributions. To subsidize those benefits,
the state has to reach out, so to speak, and put the touch on an
ever-expanding pool of resources. But since it cannot manufacture
more workers, it must accomplish this by steadily raising the payroll
tax rate.

Some basic figures go far toward illustrating just how expansion-
ary the apparatus has become over recent years: in constant dollars,
Social Security costs had been $48 billion in 1962 but were projected
to reach $210 billion by 1986. After twenty-five years, the
after-inflation cost of the system would be *four times greater*. Here was
mathematical testament to the necessity of sweeping Social Security
reform.

The major sources of this fabulous growth defined the case for
what needed to be done to reform Social Security, and to contain the
explosion of unearned benefits.

Out-and-out redistributionism was part of the problem. Some
workers got back ninety cents on each dollar of taxes and some got as
low as fifteen cents for most of what they'd put into the fund. This
was supposed to help the poor, but that was the job of welfare
programs.

Dependants' benefits were even more arbitrary and costly. Two
workers who spent thirty years at the same machine, with the same
wage and identical contributions to the fund, could get checks
differing by as much as eighty-five percent. It all depended upon
whether you had a spouse and minor children, not upon what you'd
paid in.

Another gusher of cost was the open-ended and lax disability
benefit program that had been grafted on in the mid-1950s. There
was a case for it, if the qualifying standards were strict and the
benefits not overly generous. But that wasn't what we had by 1981.

Some disability beneficiaries got up to eighty-five percent of their
prior wage on the basis of 'vocational' and 'psychological' disabili-
ties. It was a powerful temptation to the shiftless, a 'moral hazard',
as the experts called it. In twenty years the after-inflation cost had
exploded from $1 billion per year to $20 billion, and was heading still
higher.

In the 1960s another costly liberalization had occurred. In return for a twenty percent penalty, workers were given the right to retire three years early, at age sixty-two. Now seventy-five percent were taking the option. This was depriving the economy of productive labor and making the ratio of workers to retirees worse, thereby further straining the system's solvency.

Finally, in the 1970s another giant error had been made. It was called wage indexing of earnings records, but it amounted to the biggest and most costly freebie of all. If you had worked for thirty years and productivity growth of the US economy averaged two percent annually over that period, wage indexing threw into the calculation of your pension an extra two percent each year beyond what you had actually paid in taxes (in after-inflation dollars). It was a nice bonus for the millions who got it, but who was going to pay for it? The retirees certainly hadn't.

Against this background, the Pickle bill's modest increase in the retirement age was at best a tepid and inadequate palliative. It created the illusion that Social Security reform was a matter of marginal tinkering when what was needed was something far more radical.* If it succeeded, a once-in-a-century opportunity would be lost. Ronald Reagan had arrived in Washington vowing to reduce the size of the welfare state. 'If not us, who? If not now, when?' The de-welfarization of Social Security was the ultimate consequence of those questions.

The problem was that by April 1981, the helpful but extremely limited step of raising the retirement age had become everyone's favorite Social Security reform fetish. This was true even among conservative politicians who had the guts actually to face the issue, such as Barber Conable, Bill Archer and Bill Armstrong. All three were on the key congressional committees.

But if the three of them got hooked on Pickle's retirement age increase, that could close the door on serious reform. So the moment I heard about the contents of the Pickle bill, I was determined to derail it. My strategy had been to herd the politicians into the sweat

---

* The only structural change the Pickle bill proposed was raising the normal retirement age from sixty-five to sixty-eight; but not until 1990, and even then it would be phased in so gradually that the change would not become fully effective until the year 2000. It was essentially a slightly stingier version of the status quo, leaving the arbitrary income redistribution, the wage-indexed pension and the entire structure of unearned benefits intact.

room and force them to make the tough decisions on Social Security reform. The impending insolvency of the retirement fund would be a handy cattle prod.

On April 10, a meeting was convened in the Roosevelt Room to review the options to counter the palliatives offered the day before by the Hill. The group agreed only that we had to come up with between $75 and $100 billion over five years in order to keep Social Security solvent.

There were essentially two ways to do it. The 'expansionist' approach was to raise the money through additional payroll taxes. While Ronald Reagan had not won a landslide on the promise of increasing taxes on ninety million workers, there was a sneaky way to accomplish the same thing: bringing uncovered federal, state, local and non-profit workers into the system. The 'contractionist' solution was not to raise $75 to $100 billion over five years but to reduce Social Security spending—'outgo', in the stultifying idiom of Washington—by that amount.

Secretary of Health and Human Services Dick Schweiker and I might as well have been standing on different planets where these choices were concerned. Schweiker had been a middle-of-the-road consensus politician throughout his career. If he had swerved, ideologically, it had been slightly to the left of the center line.

As a moderate, labor-oriented senator from Pennsylvania, he had been an ingenious political counterweight to Reagan's 1976 candidacy. Subsequently, Schweiker acquired a little right-wing gloss by coming out against gun control and abortion; but when it came to the welfare state, he hadn't really changed his spots at all. As with most quasi-conservative politicians, he accepted all the welfare state's premises, merely trying to pinch a few pennies from the resulting costs when the opportunity arose.

Rather than charge in and attack the fundamental welfare state flaws of Social Security, he wanted to go the expansionist route; that is, rope up the uncovered government and non-profit workers and drag them into the system, too.

In the Social Security Ponzi scheme, this had always been an attractive option. It would bring in new revenues, and the newly insured workers who'd pay them wouldn't start collecting for twenty or thirty years. Schweiker's tax proposal would raise $75 billion for the trust fund over 1982–86, nearly enough to close the gap.

'Our job,' I said, in attacking his suggestion, 'is to shrink the Social Security monster. Not indenture millions more workers to a system that's already unsound.'

Marty Anderson and several others supported me, but Schweiker did not retreat. He had one good point on his side, and he wouldn't let go of it: as it was, many government retirees were getting Social Security coverage late in their careers by working a while in the private sector.

'They're milking Social Security already. By God they can pay for it!' he said over and over.

I kept counter-attacking that we had to come up with a solution that addressed the false premise of the system and attacked unearned benefits. But I met a stone wall of resistance.

'Removing unearned benefits is justifiable,' Schweiker's Social Security Administration adviser cautioned, 'but you'll be perceived as attacking the fundamental basis of the system. I doubt it would ever fly on Capitol Hill. Besides, if you're going to change benefit entitlements, it should be done prospectively, with ample transition time before anyone is directly affected.'

Don't rock the boat, build a bigger one, was one of the bureaucracy's standard themes—let's phase it in over the next four hundred years. But if Social Security reforms were phased in over a ten or fifteen year period, the initial savings would range somewhere between negligible and nonexistent.

By the end of our meeting with Schweiker, Marty Anderson and I had prevailed. The HHS technicians were instructed by the White House to come up with several options packages. Each one had to be aimed at reducing unearned benefits and the redistributionist elements of Social Security. In deference to Schweiker, coverage expansion proposals would also be included in the packages, but would not be the major element. And each had to produce near-term budget savings in the range of $100 billion.

During April, the pressure from the Hill for an administration plan continued to mount. The ad hoc Social Security Working Group thus hastily reconvened again on May 1 in the midst of the House Budget Resolution battle and other distractions.

Sure enough, Schweiker and his people came up with forty options presented in monkish texts that were so dense and unreadable that neither Meese nor any of the other White House staff who were just now focusing on the nitty-gritty of Social Security had the faintest idea what the real issues were. You had to learn a whole new language even to speak up about the Social Security behemoth: PIAs (Primary Insurance Amount), AIMEs (Average Indexed Monthly Earnings), bend points, bands, replacement rates, megacaps, insured status—it went on and on. Which was precisely what the Social Security priesthood wanted. The only White House staffer who understood any of it was Marty Anderson; and like me he was an ideological libertarian who wanted to contract the system as extensively as was politically feasible and then some.

Over the next week the working group thrashed through the ever-growing list of options nearly every day. In response to my heated and not overly courteous attacks, the Social Security bureaucracy apparently decided to empty the attic on me. By midweek the extremely complex list of reform options had swollen to over a hundred items.

Frankly, I was happy as a pig in mud. I had some really sharp people on my OMB staff who gave me crash tutorials in the arcana, and by dint of night after night of long homework sessions, I'd mastered the obscure jargon and logic of the system.

Marty Anderson and I had not let the pressure up. We had pushed Schweiker steadily in the direction of fundamental rather than cosmetic reform. By the end of the week, we had reviewed nearly $150 billion worth of potential reforms.

As a matter of highest priority I had wanted to get at whittling down the bonus benefits provided through wage indexing. The Social Security bureaucrats finally came around, even offering a sneaky, back-door method to accomplish what it called 'freezing the bend points'. This step alone would cut long-run pension costs by five to ten percent.

Likewise, more than $30 billion in savings was achieved through tightening up the runaway disability program. We also eliminated some minor, unearned dependants benefits, and capped the amount of these extra benefits that could go to each household.

On the final issue of early retirement the Working Group reached an absolute impasse. Schweiker had represented steelworkers and coal miners and knew whereof he spoke. Heavy industrial workers wanted out at sixty-two years, period, he insisted, and in many cases had more than ample health justifications. I argued that those cases were precisely what the disability program was designed to handle. I wanted a stiff increase in the early retirement penalty that would save six times more than the token reform proposed by Schweiker. So the issue was left open for debate at the session with the President.

All of the consensus proposals plus the early retirement options were then summarized in a cover memo which explained almost nothing. To it was appended a thick volume of explanatory tabs written in perfectly incomprehensible Social Security Administration format and jargon which obscured almost everything.

Nevertheless, we were on an exceedingly fast track owing to the drumbeat from the Hill for an administration plan. So by May 9, on a Saturday afternoon, this sweeping and political explosive package had circulated through the West Wing of the White House in preparation for the 10.00 am meeting the following Monday with the President.

Only sixty minutes had been allotted for that meeting on May 11 with the President—not much time for him to review a plan which in both philosophy and detail reversed forty-five years of Social Security history. But since only three people in the room— Schweiker, Marty Anderson, and I—understood the issues, I assumed that an hour would probably do it.

The President quickly vetoed Schweiker's proposals to expand the payroll tax as a matter of principle.

I then presented my case for a stiff increase in the penalty for early retirement.

I reminded the President that the early retirement feature of Social Security hadn't been part of the original New Deal plan at all. It had been grafted much later when the system appeared to be flush with funds. That carried the day.

'I've been warning since 1964 that Social Security was heading for bankruptcy,' he said, 'and this is one of the reasons why.'

After a short burst of confused debate, Schweiker finally agreed to compromise at a penalty of forty-five percent (instead of the current twenty percent) for retirement at age sixty-two. But one key aspect had been left undiscussed: whether to make the new early retirement penalty effective immediately or a few years down the road. We had a mountain of material to get through in the few minutes remaining, and the detail got lost in the shuffle.

NEW LESSONS: THE POLITICS OF TAKING

Marty Anderson knew Ronald Reagan had a deep disdain for the Carter Administration's 1977 'rescue' of Social Security, which had already proven itself inadequate. So he now reminded the President that we had to do better.

'They gave us the largest tax increase in history and said it [Social Security] would be sound until the year 2030,' the President remarked. 'Now we're here four years later and it's already bankrupt. It just proves what we've always said.'

Marty Anderson was shrewd, and he knew that the moment the meeting had broken up, Jim Baker and perhaps Meese and almost certainly Mike Deaver would gather around the President and try to insert a ten-foot pole between him and Social Security. The remark he made was a masterpiece of preemption.

'That's right,' he said. 'You'll be the first President in history to honestly and permanently fix Social Security. No one else has had the courage to do it.'

The President pronounced himself enthusiastic about the final package and approved it all on the spot. It was one of the rare instances in which this ever happened. By way of concluding the meeting he said, 'Our people on the Hill want this. It represents exactly what we have always said should be done. Let's go forward with it.'

There was one other person in the room who understood the plan, and claxons were going off in his brainpan—Dick Darman. By now Darman had become the White House's chief legislative strategist and Jim Baker's political right hand.

Darman did not particularly object to the substance of the reform package. But he objected mightily to the haste and stealth with which it had been assembled and to the fact that the Social Security Working Group had considered questions of political feasibility only in passing. He told Baker that we had strayed far beyond the boundaries of politically safe reform measures, and that the package we were going to present to the President could well ignite an inferno on the Hill. That was all Baker needed to know.

He and Darman did not raise these political feasibility questions in the session with the President. There wasn't really time, with everyone drowning in paper, options and the foreign-language jargon of Social Security. Besides, they knew the President was philosophically inclined toward our recommendations.

So, instead, they called a LSG meeting for two o'clock that afternoon, in order, they said, to discuss the logistics of how the now presidentially approved plan would be 'put out'.

As soon as we had gathered, Baker said, 'Look, we've all agreed around here that the economic program is number one, top of the list. So let's be a little concerned about whether we screw up the agenda.'

This package, he said, was going to be an HHS package. It would be something HHS had 'generated' as a kind of ministerial response to the Ways and Means Committee's request.

'To be precise,' he said, as if anyone had any doubts, 'this isn't Ronald Reagan's plan. It's Dick Schweiker's.' There was a pause as it sank in. 'Has everybody got that?'

Schweiker sat up, his face reddening. He had been around long enough to recognize the sound of a limb being sawn off, especially when he was sitting on it.

Suddenly, after weeks of antagonism, Schweiker and I became allies. It was time to make a few hard points about 'the facts of life', as I called them.

'This isn't extraneous to the President's economic plan,' I piped up. 'It's integral to it, because it doesn't add up without it.'

Schweiker said that he was willing and able to carry the ball, but, 'If there's *any* doubt as to where the President stands, this'll be dead on arrival when it gets to the Hill.'

Darman stepped in and tried to smooth over the impasse by asking what reception we were getting from the Hill. Both Schweiker and I had to admit that we'd been so absorbed in getting the package together, we hadn't focused on that.

Schweiker argued hard for the package that contained so many reforms he had initially opposed. He now had a proprietary interest in it; moreover, he told Baker and Darman it could be sold because it was the best choice available.

'By damn,' he said, showing a few BTUs of temper, 'I've spent twenty years on the Hill and I know when something will fly. So let's not start on the defensive. This is a plan we can be proud of.'

But Baker wouldn't budge. The plan had to be announced at HHS, not the White House.

'Why not Baltimore?' said Darman.

Baker grinned and said, 'That's too close.'

I was furious, but there was nothing I could do. Baker was Chief of Staff.

'OK,' I said. 'Announce it wherever you like, but this has to go out as an administration plan, not a departmental initiative. Is everybody going to agree to that?'

Baker grumbled, but shook his head in assent. I should have realized that such rubbery gestures meant nothing given Baker's determination to keep Social Security away from the White House.

Within two days I knew we were in deep trouble. That morning I was the featured speaker at the weekly breakfast held by SOS, a kind of secret society of influential House Republicans. No sooner had I finished the final sentence of my opening remarks than Congressman Carrol Campbell of South Carolina lit into me like a junkyard dog.

'You absolutely blind-sided us with this Social Security plan,' he seethed. 'My phones are ringing off the hook. I've got thousands of sixty-year-old textile workers who think it's the end of the world. What the hell am I supposed to tell them?'

I was surprised to hear this coming from Campbell. He was an extremely conservative, serious-minded, and smart member of the House Ways and Means Committee, who had been one of the original Reagan supporters in the House. He wanted sweeping changes in Social Security every bit as much as I did.

After cooling down, he added, 'Most of the package is sound and I could support it. But you've screwed it up completely by making the early retirement reduction effective immediately. That's going to bring the whole thing down in flames.'

I was . . . stunned. I didn't know what to say, because I didn't grasp what had happened.

A few hours later, I understood. At the May 11 meeting with the President we had run out of time before nailing down the date on which the new forty-five percent early retirement penalty would take effect. The HHS technicians had presumably inserted 'January 1, 1982' in the blank. This meant that someone planning to retire in nine months who thought he was going to be getting $650 per month would now be getting $450. The cut was tough—but the lack of warning was devastating.

'Sabotage!' I fumed to my staff back at the office. But there really wasn't any basis for my reaction.

By making it effective so soon instead of phasing it in over several years, millions of workers had in effect been told that the early retirement they had planned on would now be entirely disrupted. I didn't want to wait 400 years for the reforms to take effect, but I just hadn't thought through the impact of making it effective immediately.

Yet this confusion turned out to be the least of the problems. The real trouble was the White House staff. The whole package had come zinging at them out of the blue. They didn't understand the whys and wherefores and had no plan ready to cope with an adverse political reaction.

After the Schweiker press conference of May 12, the reaction hit with gale force. Congressman Claude Pepper, the eighty-year-old folk hero of the liberal and radical senior activist groups and chairman of the House Aging Committee, had three words for the plan: 'Cruel and insidious'.

House Speaker O'Neill, licking his wounds from the administration's House Budget Resolution victory, roared that the package was 'despicable' and a 'rotten thing to do'. Organized labor had the usual denunciation. So did Save Our Security, an umbrella organization of senior citizen and labor organizations dedicated to forestalling so much as a penny of cuts in Social Security.

The general sentiment among House Democrats was probably best expressed by Jim Shannon, a member of the Ways and Means Committee and a protégé of O'Neill's.

'He [the President] has gone too far,' he said. 'It's time we stood up.'

After this, only nerves of steel at the White House could have saved the May 12 package. With a matter as inherently combustible as Social Security, there could be no signs of vacillation or retreat. But as the initial adverse wave of reaction built up, White House spokesmen began to refer to the package on background as 'Schweiker's Folly'. That attitude took about five minutes to reach the Hill. So there were saboteurs—but not just some bureaucratic monks at HHS.

By the time the Democrats banded together in defiance of the package on the Senate floor of May 20, it was too late to salvage anything. In the interim I had argued that we had to fight tooth and nail, to get the President out front, even have him give a nationwide speech on TV in order to calm the political uprising. It was crucial.

The package we had devised would save $50 billion over 1982–86, nearly a third of our budget gap for those years. We couldn't afford *not* to fight.

It was all to no avail. The White House would cut its losses, quickly, completely, efficiently—and ironically, because the Social Security reform plan was the one aspect of the Reagan Revolution I had fashioned that the President understood instinctively and was more than willing to fight for. But during the crucial ten-day period between Schweiker's announcement and the Senate's *coup de grâce*, his managers ran up a white flag and kept him in the dark.

The notes that my deputy, Ed Harper, took every day at the 8.00 am White House senior staff meeting show just how that process evolved.

The purpose of these meetings was to formulate the daily 'line' on any significant topic in the morning's newspapers—El Salvador, unemployment, whatever. The 'line' was then conveyed to the President by the troika—Baker, Meese and Deaver—when he arrived in the Oval Office at nine.

On Friday 15 May, three days after the Schweiker press conference, Harper's notes from the meeting read: 'Social Security—need strong efforts to inform people about the *President*'s proposals.'

The following Wednesday, the line had become: 'We're not backing off on this, but the President will *not* lead.'

The next day, May 21, ten days of history had been revised with such alacrity as to make a Soviet historian envious: 'Social Security—need to get this off the front page. Only submitted to Hill in response to a request from a Congressional Committee for a position.'

At the bottom of Harper's notes is the underscored line, '*No Presidential involvement.*'

In the days ahead, I didn't press for a showdown. I wasn't in a position to, having committed the unpardonable political blunder of taking the world by surprise.

So when my former rabbi, Senator Moynihan, led the charge in defense of the status quo on Social Security with a resolution denouncing our package in its entirety, I simply went along with the decisions of the May 19 LSG meeting. Max Friedersdorf was instructed to work with Howard Baker and Bob Dole to fashion some kind of face-saving alternative to the Moynihan resolution.

If it ended up being a face saver, it was hard to tell. The Senate voted, ninety-six to zero against any proposal to 'precipitously and unfairly penalize early retirees' or to reduce benefits any more than 'necessary to achieve a financially sound system and the well-being of all retired Americans.'

The next day's *Washington Post* front-page headline planted a permanent political axiom in the Reagan White House:

SENATE UNANIMOUSLY REBUFFS
PRESIDENT ON SOCIAL SECURITY

At the time, I was still viewing political history as a kind of blackboard. There wasn't any mistake that couldn't be erased if right reason required it. Much later I would come to appreciate better what this headline really meant. The truth was, from that day forward, Social Security, the heart of the US welfare state, was safely back in the world of actuaries who had kept its massive expansion quiet over the decades. The centerpiece of the American welfare state had now been overwhelmingly ratified and affirmed in the white heat of political confrontation.

If my recalibration plan made no headway on Social Security, it wasn't the last of the bad news. Next, the huge spending cuts which had been promised in the budget resolutions got lost in a fog of numbers and a raging political conflagration over the reconciliation bills designed to implement them. Phil Gramm had aptly stated that the reconciliation bills would involve 'shooting real bullets'. But even this metaphor turned out to be an understatement because changing the laws which authorized the welfare state's vast spending projects proved far more complicated and difficult than establishing a blueprint to cut the budget.

The problem started with the budget numbers. The basic fiscal math of the Reagan Revolution was by now clear. You had to focus on the out-years, not on 1982, because that's when the full budget cost of the Reagan Revolution came out of hiding. You also had to focus on the total fiscal blueprint: the $118 billion in domestic spending cuts needed to close the budget gap by 1984.

But the congressional politicians intuitively did the opposite: they looked only at the numbers for 1982, and they focused not on the full blueprint but on the last benchmark that had accidentally landed on the table.

And it was on the matter of the benchmark that everything went haywire. The 1984 cut needed to balance the fiscal equation of the full Reagan Revolution was almost *three and one half times bigger* than the $35 billion reconciliation target that had been established for 1982.

This disconnect had first arisen back in early March, when the administration fiscal plan landed on Capitol Hill. But since a sweeping exercise in plenary budget subtraction had never been conducted before, there were no accounting rules or procedural customs that told which of this pile of items should be included in the reconciliation mandate to the committees and which should be excluded. So the Senate staff did what I was always doing: it came up with a hasty expedient that no one else could understand.

The expedient basically consisted of two ad hoc rules. A large number of the 300 line-item cuts were just nicks, such as a $10 million cut in some research grant program that required no earth-shaking reform of the existing way of doing business. These were the kind of two-bit savings the appropriations committees would be assigned to achieve by snipping off some money in their regular annual funding bills. So the Senate staff excluded most of these small cuts from the reconciliation mandate, dubbing them 'unreconciled cuts'.

The second ad hoc rule involved a peculiarity of the legislative calendar. Most programs get funded one year at a time through the annual appropriations process, but some are authorized by the standing legislative committees for three to five years at a time. The latter custom saves work and also allows for a periodic spending banquet when the multi-year authorization has to be renewed.

But now we had a five-year fiscal plan, and in the course of those five years, numerous programs would reach the end of their multi-year authorization cycle, technically expiring. To be sure, nobody in their right mind expected the farm pork barrel, for example, was going to cost zero in 1982 just because it would technically expire. History proved it would be reauthorized. Still, that immediately became problematic for reconciliation: How could you mandate a committee to reform a 1982 spending law, for example, that technically didn't even exist because it had expired in 1981?

So, in a fit of logic, a second batch of the 300 line-item cuts was excluded from the reconciliation mandate, and dumped into the 'unreconciled' category instead. This included all programs we were proposing to cut but which technically expired in 1982 or the out-years.

That left only ninety-three line items to be included in the reconciliation bill. They were called 'instructions'. On an aggregate basis, the reconciliation instructions added up to budget cuts of $35 billion in 1982, $46 billion in 1983, and $56 billion in 1984, for a three-year total of $137 billion.

But the fiscal blueprint of the Reagan Revolution required total budget cuts of $44 billion, $92 billion, and $118 billion, respectively, for 1982 through 1984. That three-year total amounted to $254 billion.

When you combined the Senate Budget Committee staff's rules for reconciliation with my $44 billion magic asterisk for additional cuts, a great misty swamp suddenly appeared in the out-year numbers for the overall fiscal plan.

On a 1984 basis, the Senate 'unreconciled cuts' amounted to $18 billion and my future savings plug to $44 billion, for a total of $62 billion. By about March 15, then, well over half of the cuts required to close the $118 billion 1984 gap were not even on the reconciliation table.

So when the whole budget-cutting process started in the Senate in mid-March, the fiscal architecture of the Reagan Revolution had been turned into a complicated layer cake by virtue of the scramble and haste with which it was being launched. The potential was awesome for spending cuts to be lost, thereby worsening the out-year deficit picture.

By early June, fifteen House committees were laboring in involuntary servitude under their reconciliation mandate to change spending laws in the face of outright hostility from the interest groups which dominated their meeting rooms.

To remain consistent with the architecture of the Reagan Revolution fiscal plan and stay on track toward the $118 billion 1984 domestic spending cut, there were four things you could not do:

• You couldn't follow the example set by GOP senators in March, when they had tried to cut Social Security and other big middle-class entitlements in lieu of the line-item cuts. Every dime of these prospective entitlement savings was needed for the $44 billion magic asterisk.
• Likewise, you couldn't adopt one of the $18 billion in unreconciled cuts and substitute it for one of the reconciled cuts, because *both types of cuts* were required by the Budget Resolution.
• The third thing you couldn't do was to rely on bookkeeping tricks and phony cuts.
• Finally, you couldn't make out-year spending-cut *promises* in the reconciliation bill. The cuts had to be real, reliable, and in good faith.

What happened in a nutshell was that the House politicians resorted with reckless and joyful abandon to the four things you couldn't do, all the while refusing to recall what it was they were supposed to be doing.

When the committees got down to the reconciliation 'lick log', as Howard Baker aptly put it, the only thing they could remember was the reconciliation mandate number for 1982, the $35 billion spending cut that had been parceled out to the fifteen standing committees. The exacting, multi-year and larger spending-cut requirements of the Gramm–Latta Budget Resolution of early May they lost sight of. The Reagan Revolution's fiscal blueprint of March 10 had become ancient history. The four rules for what was a legitimate cut and what was not got trampled on by the distraught herd.

This collective amnesia was given a big boost by the hirelings at the Congressional Budget Office who were supposed to be the official scorekeepers. Their House political masters came to the CBO scorekeepers with numerous questions about what 'counted' as a cut. But the scorekeepers knew better than to bite the hand that fed them.

The House politicians thus asked their hired scorekeepers if they could count unreconciled cuts. Fine. They asked if they could take a little nip out of Medicare (slated for the magic asterisk savings) and substitute it for one of the mandated cuts. Fine.

They asked what about putting a lower funding cap on an entitlement program like food stamps, but leaving all 23 million beneficiaries on the rolls and not changing one comma as to the amount each was eligible for? Would that count as a savings? That's a fine cut, too, the CBO scorekeepers said. Indeed, that's all the House Budget Committee watchdogs and the CBO scorekeepers said for weeks. Fine. Fine. Count it all.

By the end, 'anything goes' had gone wild. Some of the House Committee bills made Billie Sol Estes* look like a petty thief.

The House Agriculture Committee, for example, had been given credit for $6 billion in three-year food stamp savings, just by using the previously mentioned authorization ceiling trick. It wouldn't have saved a red cent.

The House Agriculture Committee also claimed $2.5 billion over three years by counting savings from the dairy program. But the dairy program was an 'unreconciled cut', not even included in their instructions. This particular scam presented a double problem. The overall fiscal plan required 'unreconciled cuts' in the dairy program of $4.5 billion during the next stage of the legislative process—the reauthorization of the expiring farm bill. So the Committee jumped the gun and came up with only half the dairy cut they owed. They then put that in the reconciliation bill and used the savings to substitute for pork barrel items that were supposed to be cut under the reconciliation mandate.

This kind of math produced cheers in the committee room. The dairy lobby applauded, having wriggled out of half the cut intended for it. So did the folks trying to hang on to subsidized loans for grain storage bins, farm operating credit, rural water and sewer funds, subsidized foreign grain sales, rural fire stations, and soil conservation subsidies. These were all spared completely, even though the reconciliation mandate said cut them by $2.5 billion. By counting the dairy savings which were unreconciled, the Committee got away with cutting almost nothing it had been mandated to do in the reconciliation bill.

When I told the elderly, schoolmarmish Republican congress-

* Texan criminal whose large-scale fraud had links with Washington.

woman from Nebraska, Virginia Smith, that all this wasn't kosher, she had an answer.

'Now, David, you mind your P's and Q's on the numbers. It's our job to take care of the policy. Our good Nebraska farmers are all for the President, but they can't do without those storage loans.'

Overall, the House Agriculture Committee bill was a pathetic farce. The Budget Resolution required $14 billion in three-year savings from programs in its jurisdiction. It came up with barely $3.5 billion in savings that were even remotely reliable and meaningful. But under 'anything goes', the CBO scorekeepers certified that it had *exceeded* its reconciliation target.

Committee after committee played the same havoc with my exacting rules. The Armed Services Committee counted $1 billion in savings without even cracking open the statute book on military pensions, the mandated object of its knife. An obscure provision of law said that if and when the civil service pensions were shifted from twice per year COLAs to once per year as we had proposed, the military pension COLA would automatically follow suit.

So the Armed Services Committee simply 'assumed' the Civil Service Committee would take care of this 'if and when'. But being a wholly owned subsidiary for the federal employees unions, the Civil Service Committee had no such intention of tampering with the civil service COLAs at all. It didn't. The $1 billion savings from the military pensions was all air.

The House Banking and Urban Affairs Committee was at least as creative. Under anything goes, the Committee exceeded its $4.4 billion savings target. But this was accomplished with a whopping fib: the Banking Committee averred it was just going to up and put the whole Ex-Im Bank out of business in 1983, thereby saving the entire $4.4 billion in one slice.

Never mind that the Banking Committee was a hotbed of support for the Ex-Im Bank, more zealous in its loyalty than Chicago Cub fans. Nobody was going to really let the Ex-Im Bank go out of business. But when they scribbled a new expiration date in the pro forma authorization statute, CBO said: *Wonderful—You have made a big cut!* Meanwhile, one of the most crucial entitlement reforms in the whole fiscal plan—reforming the subsidized housing program—got spared completely. The builders' lobby cheered. The tenants' lobby cheered. No savings were had.

The Commerce Committee achieved a $10 billion savings by the expedient of putting the Strategic Petroleum Reserve (SPRO) program off-budget. The latter was the fiscal equivalent of prohibition. You would keep on spending just the same as before, but now it would be illegal to count it.

The most preposterous savings claim was surely the one made by the Civil Service Committee. The Committee members had been instructed to save $15 billion over three years by putting a cap on federal civilian employee pay increases. And they did. But they also decreed that the President could not actually impose the cap until he also implemented comprehensive wage and price controls on the entire US economy. Not one day sooner. Never mind that wage and price controls were as likely under Ronald Reagan as unilateral disarmament.

The Public Works Committee won the chutzpah award. This gang of porkers counted billions in out-year savings for water projects, mass transit, highways and other prized slabs of bacon. How were all these billions going to be saved? Why the porkers sent the Budget Committee a letter promising to do it in the bye-and-bye.

The Ways and Means Committee bill provided a final case of the fiasco which emerged from the House committees. Its reconciliation mandate included eighteen specific instructions for savings in programs ranging from AFDC* to extended federal unemployment benefits. Altogether these reconciliations in instructions would have saved $30 billion over three years.

When the dust had finally cleared, it had achieved only $16 billion, or half of the instruction savings. Yet it claimed $27 billion or eighty-five percent of its target. The $11 billion difference was made up by counting unreconciled savings and by reaching into the Social Security and Medicare savings needed in the future for the $44 billion magic asterisk.

Unlike most of the other committee bills, Ways and Means had resorted to no gimmicks or smoke and mirrors. But it still had undermined the three-tiered layer cake needed to get the full $118 billion in 1984 spending cuts. You couldn't cut the same dollars out of Medicare twice in order to avoid cutting something else.

Thus the reconciliation process flushed out of the system all of the

* Aid to Families with Dependent Children.

confusion, misperceptions, and cynicism that had built up over the prior four months. It underscored the complexity of altering the dozens of different kinds of federal spending mechanisms that had evolved over the decades. And it showed that the institutional management and scorekeeping tasks of plenary budget subtraction were nearly insuperable.

In combination, the fifteen committee bills amounted to a calamity. They claimed 1984 savings of $55 billion, of which precisely $25 billion was actually valid and taken from the ninety-three line-item instructions in the reconciliation mandate. That amounted to less than *one fourth* of the $118 billion in cuts needed to achieve a balanced budget in 1984. And even the one-quarter loaf would be true only if Rosy Scenario held up—which she wouldn't.

I had been keeping abreast of these wretched developments by means of the OMB 'boiler room' operation, which had been set up in late May. We had a desk assigned to keep track of what each of the fifteen House committees was doing—and every day the news seemed to be worse.

Phil Gramm had been keeping tabs on this savaging of the Gramm–Latta Budget Resolution as well. When we concluded that the bills the committees were writing were beyond repair, we decided the only thing to do was to fight back with another showdown on the House floor. We would write our own bill, a 1,000-page substitute for the abomination the committees would shortly deliver.

I ordered my OMB staff to start preparing 'Son of Gramm–Latta' in early June—in secret. No one in either the White House or the Congress was to know about it until I could lay the groundwork. The last thing we needed was for Congress to hear that the White House was writing its own reconciliation bill.

Son of Gramm–Latta was an even more radical usurping of the House's prerogative than the original Budget Resolution. But if the politicians were not going to fall voluntarily into line with the Reagan Revolution, then they would be forced to. The strategy was to bring all the power of the Great Communicator to bear on them and shove our budget cuts down their throats by orchestrating another up-and-down vote on a valid version of the whole reconciliation bill.

This was a risky undertaking. It was a planned cataclysm, really. An insurrection on top of a revolution.

'That offends a lot of sensibilities,' Greider warned. 'Anybody can look ahead to the day they're a subcommittee chairman and say, "Do I want to go along with *that* precedent?" That's a real Robespierre, isn't it?'

I got the chance to spell out the catastrophe that we were facing a few days later on June 2 when the President held a meeting with the Republican congressional leadership.

I made a pretty lurid presentation on what the House committees were doing, and it got their attention. Minority Leader Bob Michel agreed to have me come up to the Hill over the next week and let me present the administration's view of just how flawed the various reconciliation bills coming out of the House committees were. We would do it on a round-robin basis, meeting with the Republican members of each committee, one committee at a time.

This turned out to be virtually a solo mission, since the other members of the White House LSG team were now utterly preoccupied with the tax bill. I kept them posted on my mission, but they did not focus on the need to have a comprehensive substitute of our own—Son of Gramm–Latta. I nevertheless assumed they had agreed to it in principle at the June 2 meeting.

Bob Michel was in a quandary. The last thing he wanted was to appear peremptory by inviting the OMB director into his neighborhood in order to tell everyone to clean up their act. He insisted, therefore, that my attitude during my round-robin sessions with the GOP committee members should be that an administration substitute bill would only be considered as a last resort. The final decision on whether to offer it wouldn't be made until the committee bills had been reported to the House on June 12 and the parliamentary procedure under which they would be considered had been determined. He would let me make my pitch to the members, but he didn't want me giving them the idea that if they didn't do anything about this calamity, we would.

In his heart of hearts, Michel believed that the committees would make the necessary adjustments themselves. That was not a very practical assumption, frankly. The Republicans were by no means the innocents in this game of sabotage. Moreover, Republicans were the minority party. How were they supposed to get the Democratic-dominated committees to rewrite the bills?

The fact remained, of course, that the Republicans still had no real idea just how far out of line the bills were with the Budget Resolution fiscal plan they were supposed to be implementing.

Their conventional wisdom was nicely summarized in a quote given to *The Washington Post* in early June by Ralph Regula, a moderate from Ohio and a senior Republican on the Budget Committee: 'We've been pleased with the results so far. The indications are that most of the committees are coming up with real cuts . . . they're seriously trying to reach the targets.' Regula was probably the single most knowledgeable, hardworking and broadly respected Republican on the Budget Committee.

The Congress felt that as a co-equal branch of government, it had the right to 'mix and match' as long as the savings came out to the only number it could remember—the $35 billion reconciliation target for 1982. What they didn't realize was that the Gramm–Latta budget and the Reagan Revolution had all along required of them one thing: surrender. The fact of life was that there was no possible way to close the $118 billion gap without precise, lockstep conformity to the half-finished budget blueprint I had laid out for the Congress in March. The Congress had to forfeit its independence and accept the role of rubber-stamping parliament if the whole plan was to work.

For the meantime, my veiled threats of usurpation of the rights of Congress did not stir up too many tremors of resistance. For one thing, Tip O'Neill had led with his considerable chin, announcing that the Democrats were not going to 'roll over and play dead' as the reconciliation bills slashed away at long-treasured Democratic programs. O'Neill's statement sounded like a flat-out admission that the Democrats had no intention of going along with even the inadequate and *illusory* budget cuts they were virtuously proclaiming they had made. The Democrats, he was saying, were going to offer amendment after amendment when the reconciliation bill came to the House floor.

For the moment, this didn't sit well with the Republican–Boll Weevil coalition. Aside from being an admission of bad faith, it had a troubling practical ramification. They were practical politicians and, as all of them do, they hated nothing more than line-item floor amendments. Why? Because it forces them to vote against their constituencies in the full light of day.

If Tip O'Neill was really going to play that 'salami tactic'* game, the Republicans and the Boll Weevils were at least willing to entertain my notion of an up-and-down vote on a substitute package.

A second reason my godfatherly offer-you-can't-refuse did not stir up resentment in early June while the carnival was still under way in the committees had to do with the bald-faced cynicism of some of the 'savings' the committees were cooking up each day. The Republicans were angry, for instance, over such ploys as the Civil Service Committee's claim that it had saved $100 million per year by shutting down the nation's 10,000 smallest post offices. This was a deliberate swipe at rural Republicans and Boll Weevils, yet everyone knew it would never be implemented.

The super-liberal Education and Labor Committee had perpetrated an even more flagrant ploy. In order to protect the big CETA public jobs program, child nutrition and other programs dear to the heart of Chairman Carl Perkins, the Committee had deeply slashed a dozen smaller 'motherhood' programs that enjoyed wide bipartisan support. These had not been slated for deep cuts at all and they included Head Start, Meals on Wheels, vocational education, the foster grandparents' program, and others.

Perkins and his Democratic cronies slashed all of these programs, knowing full well that once their proposed cuts reached the floor, there would be an overwhelming drumbeat to put them back in. And so there would—but by then the other programs they wanted to protect would be safe. No one would be able to come after them to make up the loss in savings.

Once I had spent a week with the Republican and Boll Weevil members of the various committees, I thought I had laid sufficient groundwork to be able to unveil Son of Gramm–Latta. But my pitch for this comprehensive substitute to the Committee reconciliation bills elicited a torrent of criticism. Charlie Stenholm of Texas led the charge.

'With all due respect to the Budget Director,' he said, 'we're being asked to tear up our voting cards and become White House robots.

* Dividing things up into small slices.

Well, I don't know about the rest of you, but I'm right proud of the Ag Committee bill. We got our numbers. This is just an attempt to dictate phee-losophy.'

I was livid, and I let him have it. The Agriculture Committee bill was the biggest fraud in the lot—and it had plenty of competition. It had barely achieved ten percent of what it had been instructed to cut.

'If that's what everybody around here thinks,' I shot back at him, 'then we're heading for an absolute fiscal disaster. This isn't politics as usual. The Ag Committee bill is a travesty. It didn't change *one comma* in the Food Stamp law. You slopped down the dairy farmers, busted the budget and then have the nerve to call it a savings. You stuffed money back into every pork barrel in the whole USDA, and that's no small feat. How in the world does anybody around here think that we can afford a tax cut if everybody's going to turn tail and run when it's time to bite some real bullets on spending? We're at the Rubicon, and you-all better decide which way we're going.'

Stenholm backed down, and some of the others were aroused, especially Jack Kemp. Up to now, he had been disinterested in the budget-cutting aspect of the economic plan. But the tax cut was his baby—his reputation was riding on it—and the news that it was in jeopardy alarmed him. He weighed in on my behalf. So did Gramm and Trent Lott of Mississippi, Minority Whip.

'Are we gonna continue to be mossbacks,*' demanded Lott, 'and keep doing things the way they've been done since time immemorial, or are we gonna change things? I say we're here to change things, and as tough as this is, it's gotta be done.'

Michel concluded the meeting by saying that OMB should continue to work on its substitute bill, but he insisted that it still be kept quiet.

'We can't have the appearance that this is being written downtown,' he said. He told his aide, Billy Pitts, to mobilize the minority staff on each committee to begin drafting a substitute bill to cover each of their jurisdictions.

'Make sure OMB has complete input,' he admonished Pitts, 'but it's got to be written on *our typewriters*.'

It was a start, but his orders were ambiguous. The committee staff could—indeed, would—deduce that it was a mandate to draw

---

* Dyed-in-the-wool conservatives.

up the bill their way, as long as they let OMB put in its two bits.

But Michel and his colleagues were determined at all costs to keep up appearances. Congress wasn't a mere rubber-stamping operation, it had its pride. Michel was struggling mightily to avoid a clash between the Reagan Revolution and the Republican rank and file. The trouble was that the very nature of what was required meant that a clash was inevitable.

Bolstered by the apparent shift in sentiment among our coalition's leadership, I assured the LSG that my Son of Gramm–Latta strategy was falling into place.

On the morning of June 11, I addressed the entire House Republican Caucus as part of my campaign to get them to discard the work of the House committees completely. The people who attended these meetings were usually the younger, eager beaver members, especially this particular meeting because it was held at 8.00 am. All the old bulls were still sleeping off the previous night's Capitol Hill Club festivities. The current class of Republican freshmen were called the 'Reagan robots', and I encountered no argument from them about the *coup d'état* I had in mind.

The lines were drawn. All that week the atmosphere was charged in anticipation of the pitched battle on the House floor between the Reagan coalition and the Democratic majority.

By Friday evening, June 12, all of the reconciliation bills had been reported by the fifteen House committees. I ordered the OMB staff to work around the clock over the weekend, to get out their magnifying glasses and go through the 1,000-page legislative opus that the fifteen committees had combined—conspired—to produce. Early the next week we would have a bill of indictment readily showing that the committees had wantonly violated their instructions.

On Saturday morning Phil Gramm arrived in my office in bluejeans and flannel work shirt, ready to join me in the final preparations for battle.

By the end of the day, Son of Gramm–Latta was finished. It went back to the letter of the Gramm–Latta fiscal plan, dropping all the phony savings and unreconciled cuts in the House Committee bills. It provided instead ninety-eight percent of the exact savings required by the ninety-three reconciliation instructions.

NEW LESSONS: THE POLITICS OF TAKING

If we could manipulate the parliamentary procedure into an up-and-down choice between Son of Gramm–Latta and the House bills, the Reagan Revolution would storm the gates of the Second Republic.

Everything was in place. Admittedly, there were a few pockets of resistance among the GOP–Boll Weevil coalition, but I was confident they would subside in the heat of battle. The President would take his case to the American public in a nationwide speech, and the politicians would once again be forced to show whether they were with him or 'agin' him. On June 13, I told Greider he was about to witness a major event in US history.

Greider then asked, 'Where is the President in all this?'

'They're preoccupied with other crises and the tax bill,' I said. I confessed that I had been on a solo mission the last two weeks.

'He's kind of on the margins of day-to-day involvement. There are all these other issues popping up right now. We're going to give him a full briefing next week.'

The following week, the cornered and intimidated politicians struck back and stopped the Reagan Revolution dead in its tracks. In a single week of raw confrontation and emotions, the democracy defeated the doctrine. The American welfare state emerged from the ordeal largely intact, and from then on the politicians would be in unchallenged control.

8

Collapse of the Reagan Coalition

At the time, only a temporary retreat seemed in order. Only over the months ahead would I realize that everything really had ended between Monday 15 June and Friday 19 June 1981.

On Sunday 14 June I leaked to Bill Greider the ten-page bill of indictment against the House committee bills that Phil Gramm and I had spent the prior day assembling.

On Monday, the front page of *The Washington Post* carried the headline.

OMB INDICTS DEMOCRATS

The week was starting as planned, but reactions came in fast.

Budget Chairman Jim Jones called my charges 'science fiction'. His colleague Leon Panetta militantly insisted that 'the President had gotten all the cuts he had asked for.' The press bought this preposterous claim that the administration was just nitpicking hook, line and sinker.*

The reporters were simply echoing the line being put out by the House committees. The bills themselves were a miasma of confusion, and neither the Congressional Budget Office nor the House Budget Committee had blown any whistles on the doctored-up numbers the committees had produced. Once the big picture had been obscured, the only objective in clear sight was $35 billion in 1982 — period.

The politicians were thus able to manipulate the process and the

---

* Thus *The Wall Street Journal* story read: 'Congressional committees are winding up their budget cutting work and seem certain to meet — if not exceed — the $36 billion in cuts the President wants.'

public's perception so as to create a completely misleading frame of reference. They had one sanction in doing this, and it was not inconsiderable. The majority of the politicians in both parties who had been elected by the American people the previous November wanted it that way, because their constituents wanted it that way, too.

The Great Society may have faded into the past, but its promoters were still in business. And its gifts were flowing out to millions of citizens. The media had portrayed the November election as a sea-change in American politics, but if there had been any movement of the waters it had not been as profound as everyone had been led to believe. The tide had come back in.

Phil Gramm's and my protests that the Congress was pursuing a reconciliation process that would lead, ultimately, to fiscal madness were quickly drowned out by a concerted congressional attack. Gramm and I were accused of being dictatorial, dogmatic. They made us, not the numbers, the issue. And in a way they were right in doing so because we were trying to dictate a sweeping change in welfare state spending that no one else wanted to see happen.

Rules Committee Chairman Dick Bolling said that our bid amounted to 'incipient tyranny'. Tip O'Neill weighed in with 'I don't know what I like less—the arrogance of David Stockman in sending up this package, or the godfather tactics of his right-wing allies . . . I feel sorry for Bob (Michel). As I see it, he has just been given the paper and told, "Here, pass this."'

The sympathetic reference to Michel was a shrewd divide-and-conquer ploy. The Speaker was in effect suggesting that the GOP leadership had forfeited its political manhood by going along with us, and was now attempting to goad it into standing up—like real men.

On Tuesday morning, I got my first chance in two weeks to tell the President how threatened his whole economic program was. There was to be a press conference that night. To prepare him for it, I gave him a three-page briefing paper which said that the committee bills were 'riddled with gimmicks' and would make our 1984 balanced budget 'nearly impossible to achieve'.

He looked disgusted, and said, 'We can't let them get away with that.' He readily agreed to my suggestion that he include a strong denunciation of the House bills in his opening statement that night, along with a warning that he was prepared to offer a complete substitute bill of his own.

The President had by now spent a good amount of time in meetings with Tip O'Neill, and these had become increasingly abrasive. He had come to resent Tip O'Neill's refrain that he was simply an advocate for the wealthy and utterly insensitive to the needs of the common man. He saw O'Neill as the embodiment of what had gone wrong with government over the past forty years.

So when a reporter put the question to the President that night that O'Neill was charging, 'you have just a bunch of selfish and wealthy advisers,' the President answered hotly and accused the Speaker of 'sheer demagoguery'. His own origins had been working class, he said. He was not insensitive to those in the 'working group'.

The President's direct hit on the Speaker provoked a furious reaction. Majority Leader Jim Wright, one of the premier practitioners of demagoguery on the American political scene, brought a rousing ovation from the Democrats as he neatly turned the truth inside out:

> The President is responsible for all those cuts and now he has the audacity to blame us . . . This is the President's bill. Here we are in the position of doing all the hard work and he's blaming us for doing what he asked us to do.

His next remark was a real beauty.

> It's a lot like a young person murdering his mother and father and then throwing himself on the mercy of the court as an *orphan*.

Wright's combativeness infected the ranks of the sixty-three Boll Weevils who had previously voted for the Gramm–Latta Budget Resolution. Except for the half dozen hard core who had rallied to Phil Gramm, the rest weren't even remotely genuine fiscal conservatives. Most of them were simply muddle-minded pols who had been scared by the President's popularity in their home districts. But now the federal trough was being threatened, and they sprang to defend it.

Boll Weevil Bo Ginn of Georgia was quoted by *The New York Times* as saying, 'We were tired of being manipulated by the White House.'

Wes Watkins, a hot-tempered, pugnacious Oklahoman whose demagogical skills were exceeded only by his inclination for pork, was moved to tell the press that 'We have given the President ninety percent of what he wants.' He warned of dire consequences if the White House was presumptuous enough to 'pick a fight'.

What the White House did next was to shoot itself in the foot. Dave Gergen's press operation was busy publicizing some of the phony House committee cuts, gleaned from the long list I had given them. Three examples they fastened on were the 10,000 rural post offices, and the Meals on Wheels program for the elderly and Head Start.

I had put these three on the list because they were perfect examples of the cynical devices the committees had used. But the White House press office got that wrong and made it sound as though these were programs the President was determined to *defend* from the dastardly congressional budget cutters.

Not surprisingly, this infuriated a lot of people on the Hill. We had been lashing them for weeks and weeks to make tough cuts, and here the White House seemed to be saying it would fight to the death to save these programs. So now we were becoming The Gang That Couldn't Reconcile Straight.

Once the politicians thought the White House was manoeuvering for selfish political reasons, the revolt on Capitol Hill rapidly spread. The Gypsy Moths—the moderate to liberal northeastern Republicans—quickly joined its ranks.

'I think we've been overlooked,' huffed Margaret Heckler of Massachusetts.

I had done my best not to 'overlook' the Gypsy Moths. They had a list a mile long of cuts they wanted restored, and I had accommodated them where I could. My notes from a meeting with about thirty of them the week before shows just how expensive the session had been.

- Conrail—work out to the satisfaction of Lee, Lent and Madigan.
- Amtrak—add back $112 million.
- Low-income energy—add back $400 million.
- Elementary and special education—add back $300 million.
- CETA* youth and training—add back $200 million.

- DOE weatherization—add back $200 million.
- Medicaid cap—increase to six percent in FY 1982.
- Guaranteed student loans—$100 million add back, plus rewrite formula for families above $25,000 income.

Gramm and I had faithfully put all that back into Son of Gramm–Latta, but now it was no longer to any avail. With the Boll Weevils in open revolt, the Gypsy Moths wanted much more than mere millions. So did they all.

For victory on the House floor the magic number was 218. We needed that many votes, and not one less. With none to spare, each vote became all the more precious—and all the more expensive.

All of a sudden the game of budget subtraction turned into something rather different: an open vote auction. Every concession we made quickly turned into a demand for more concessions. My compromise with the Gypsy Moths on Amtrak quickly ricocheted across the Capitol to the Senate, leading to the uncancelling of a train route in Oregon.

For their part, the Gypsy Moths, now being spurred on by the governors of their states, found that the more liberal cap on Medicaid I had agreed to was unsatisfactory. Now they wanted no cap at all.

Other Gypsy Moths wanted Jimmy Carter's solar energy bank restored. Congressman Bill Green, who represented the New York City's Upper East Side (the 'Silk Stocking District'), was the chief troublemaker of the lot. He even threatened to vote against the entire substitute bill unless we restored $50 million in funding for the National Endowments for the Arts and Humanities. It was hard to keep the auction from getting out of hand.

One smoldering hotbed of the revolt was the Republican committee staffs. Despite Bob Michel's instruction to them to work closely with OMB, they had gone off on their own. By the middle of the week, their versions of the substitute bill were as bad as the Democratic committee bills they were designed to replace.

The worst saboteurs turned out to be the staff—and Republican members—of the Public Works Committee. They had already totted up billions in utterly phony savings, for highways, water

* Comprehensive Employment and Training Act.

projects and mass transit in the out-years. Now they turned their attention to rescuing the $600 million per year Economic Development Administration EDA from its planned and well-deserved demise.

As the Republican agitation for EDA intensified, I came to see that particular boondoggle as the test for fiscal reform in general. If this demonstrably useless program couldn't be killed, then the chances that the other, larger cuts were possible seemed depressingly remote.

As I explained to Greider, this would be the test of whether we could accomplish anything at all.

> EDA is supported by just a bunch of guys like Don Clausen and Bud Shuster who have been on the Public Works Committee since time immemorial, and they're not about to give up on it. They're all coming at Michel saying, 'You can't let Stockman rule the roost! EDA is a good Republican program because it creates jobs and investment.'
>
> But I'll be damned if they're going to get it back.

Here was the nub of the problem: each committee had its pet project, and each bloc of GOP or Boll Weevils had enormous leverage on us. Each one could be the crucial bloc to put us over—or under—the magic 218.

By midweek the situation was at a boil. It was then that the Democratic leadership did several very shrewd things which cut the ground right out from under Gramm and me.

The Republicans had been outraged by certain egregiously cynical elements in some of the reconciliation bills such as Head Start and Meals on Wheels cuts. One of these 'poison pen letter' cuts, as we called them, in particular was a masterpiece. It claimed substantial savings by elminating funding for 'suppers' at child care centers. But a little fine print later on in the bill provided that 'lunch' could be served at any time of the day or night.

These kinds of horror stories were fiscally insignificant, but they had strong anecdotal value. They were memorable little rotten eggs, and they gave the committee bills a distinctly suspect aroma.

So at midweek the Education and Labor Committee suddenly decided to reconvene, despite the fact that the official deadline for reporting its bill had passed. Why had it reconvened? To restore $1.75 billion in funding for Head Start, Meals on Wheels, foster grandparents, impact aid—the works. The GOP–Boll Weevil coalition took note of this, shaking their heads in approval. *Now that's more like it!*

At the same time, the House Budget Committee suddenly exercised its authority to remove a few other rotten eggs. Funding for the 10,000 rural post offices was restored. The GOP–Boll Weevil coalition approved. *That's even better!*

The final move came when Tip O'Neill reversed himself on parliamentary procedure and ruled that the voting on reconciliation would be yes or no. No amendments would be allowed; no one-program-at-a-time plank would have to be walked; no one would have to vote against his constituencies. The GOP–Boll Weevil coalition approved heartily. *Now we're home free!*

They had wanted to avoid amendments at all costs, and now the Speaker has said, Fine.

Thus by Wednesday evening the atmosphere among our troops had dramatically changed. The bills hadn't changed at all except for pure cosmetics. The Democrats had only defumigated them.

The majority thus played a clever game of appearing reasonable. Bob Michel seemed to sum up the House GOP's new what's-all-the-fuss-about attitude when he told the press, 'Let's face it, we've come a long way from where we were several weeks ago. I'm not hung up on saying we've got to have everything we want.'

It was a disastrous attitude, of course, but I couldn't talk him out of it. Nor, as it turned out, could I convince the White House.

The LSG gathered on Wednesday evening, June 17, to hear Max Friedersdorf's grim report. The votes for Son of Gramm–Latta or any White House substitute simply weren't there, he said. Friedersdorf's scorecard showed ten to twenty possible Gypsy Moth defections, and that we would only be able to count on ten hard-core Boll Weevils. That left us with under 190 votes. We weren't even in the competitive range.

Jim Baker and Dick Darman were worried, but for another reason. Darman's theory that Ronald Reagan had to be perceived as a success was now in trouble. Something else was at stake here—Jim Baker's reputation. Since Don Regan, who was now in 'command' of the tax bill, was not competent to handle the legislative battle alone, Baker had become heavily involved in backstopping him.

Baker also saw the President more than anyone, and he knew by now exactly what aspect of the revolution the President felt most strongly about: the tax cut. For Baker, therefore, the stakes were high. He didn't want to become known as the man who fumbled Kemp-Roth.

Whatever was going on deep down in Baker's mind that night, it was clear he wanted to go along with the House committee reconciliation bills in order to pacify the Boll Weevils and Gypsy Moths. He was adamant that if we pressed on Son of Gramm–Latta and lost, 'Then you can kiss your tax reduction bill goodbye. The Weevils and the Moths will flake off for good.'

In response, I told him that there was something else we could kiss goodbye if we didn't challenge the House bills—a balanced budget and any hope of keeping the fiscal plan intact.

'If we cave on this,' I said, 'you're putting the House committees and all the hypocrites in our coalition back into the saddle. Once we blink, they'll spend us into disaster. There *isn't* any choice. The numbers in the House bills are so bad that we've got to go for broke. Put the President on the tube and beat them into submission.'

Baker and I were at an impasse. He didn't want to do anything; I wanted to do everything. As usual, it was Darman who saw a way around it.

He had noticed that I had been especially insistent about going after the entitlements, such as food stamps, guaranteed student loans, the Medicaid cap and Social Security minimum benefits. We had only one shot at these reforms, because entitlement programs run literally on automatic pilot.

The remainder of the cuts in the reconciliation mandate involved 'discretionary' programs. Those we could go after every year when Congress voted on the appropriations bill, vetoing them if necessary. It was the wrong way to go, because you would have to fight to cut these programs five years in a row, rather than just once in the reconciliation bill. But it was theoretically possible if you thought you had that much political staying power.

So, said Darman, why not try for the entitlement reforms now, but put off the discretionary reforms for later? We'll live to fight another day.

It was a solution, but I didn't like it. There was a large element of *mañana* in it. However, there was no other way. It had been a solo mission, and now I was realizing just how alone I was.

The next morning, Thursday 18 June was warm and humid. Baker had laid on a meeting with the President to brief him in on the recent developments.

'The committees have broken faith with the Budget Resolution,' I told the President. 'It could jeopardize your entire economic program.'

Baker now came out sounding like he was against challenging the Hill on *any* of the spending cuts, even the entitlements. It was as if last night's LSG meeting hadn't taken place.

'We have to understand,' he warned Reagan, 'that we're running a very great risk here. If we throw down the challenge and lose, it'll sap our momentum.'

Then Dave Gergen supported Baker, saying we didn't have enough time to build a public campaign with which to pressure the Congress.

It was time to hit the bottom line. 'Mr President,' I said, 'if you can't get even those entitlement cuts, it'll produce huge deficits in '83 and '84. If you want to balance the budget, you can't live with the meager cuts they've made.'

There was no more blunt way of putting it. The President asked for the numbers, and I handed him the paper. As he read it, the muscles in his jaw started to grind.

'Well, if that's the case,' he said, after studying them, 'we can't accept it.' I had won, for the time being. The White House moved into action.

Hours later all the key players were in the Cabinet Room for a strategy lunch: the President, senior White House staff, Bob Michel, Trent Lott, Phil Gramm, Del Latta, Charlie Stenholm, Sonny Montgomery, and Kent Hance.

Not surprisingly, only two people in the group aside from me were in favor of a complete challenge to the House committee bills: Gramm and Latta. The others wanted to go the face-saving route, especially Hance.

Hance had been an obscure congressman from Texas and a junior member of the Ways and Means Committee, but now he had new luster. He had become the Phil Gramm of the tax cut issue. The names on the marquee were CONABLE-HANCE, and Kent Hance didn't want to jeopardize his top billing by challenging his colleagues on this other matter of spending cuts.

'If we go too far in upsetting our Boll Weevil friends,' Hance told the President, 'our tax bill is going to be in a heap of trouble. I know what the Budget Director is telling us, but most of the Weevils think their committees did a right good job on reconciliation. We need to be careful about that.'

The President's jaw muscles started grinding again. Hance had got to him.

A feeling of dread came over me. It was June 18, and the President still had only the vaguest idea of how exacting the fiscal equation was. I had simply failed all along to reckon with a crucial fact of life: the President would inevitably be called upon to make on-the-spot tactical decisions and compromises. But if he didn't understand the big picture, how would he make the right decisions?

'No,' he said now in answer to Hance, 'we can't do anything to jeopardize the tax bill. I've retreated too far on that already.'

He turned to Michel. 'Bob, what do you recommend?'

Michel had spent the previous weeks being pummeled by House Republicans demanding the usual concessions. He was smoldering with resentment at the OMB dictator, and he let it all out.

'Mr President,' he began, 'I'm doing everything I possibly can for you.' He continued addressing Reagan, but his eyes went to me. 'But some of your *people* down here have got to learn they can't have their way a hundred percent of the time. You can't treat the House like it's a rubber stamp. Many of these committees busted their buns trying to come up with their savings.'

Then he used a familiar metaphor. 'Sure, you've got some smoke and mirrors in there. But this isn't the last inning in the ballgame. I think we better decide five or ten things we have to have, and go along with the committees on the rest. Shoot, the Senate bills are hitting their mark. We'll get some of that in conference.'

Whatever resolve the President had had during our morning meeting in the Oval Office vanished over the bean soup and swordfish. He could resolve conflicts of great principle sometimes, but those between people almost never. It was agreed that the White House would work with Michel to fashion a limited substitute focused on selected entitlement reforms. It would be called Gramm–Latta II. But it would incorporate as many of the committee bills produced by the House Democrats as possible.

The lunch group adjourned. The President had ratified a decision by the politicians of Capitol Hill directly inimical to the require-ments of the Reagan Revolution, yet he had not even a dim apprehension of what he had just agreed to. We were about to restore budget cuts that were by themselves insufficient to balance the budget in 1984 in order to improve the chances of enacting a massive tax cut. We would take a giant leap backward in order to take a giant leap forward. It made that much sense.

Michel and I went straight from lunch to his office to preside over one of the most expensive sessions I have ever attended on Capitol Hill. I lost $20 billion in proposed three-year budget savings in four hours—$5 billion per hour.

Michel and I crammed into Gramm–Latta II some of the worst features of the committee bills. Hour by hour I back-pedalled. At the insistence of Charlie Stenholm and the GOP farm bloc we put in the $2.5 billion phony dairy cut, as well as all the lesser pork in the Ag bill. So too with the entire Public Works Committee bill. Democracy had made the world safe again for EDA.*

The Banking Committee had cut almost nothing real, so we incorporated what they had. The phony SPRO cut, $9 billion worth, went into Gramm–Latta II as well.

When the dust settled at the end of the afternoon, most of the 1,000 pages the committees had written had been incorporated into Gramm–Latta II. We had reduced our challenge to nine entitle-ment reforms and a handful of cosmetic reforms called 'block grants'.

The politicians had thus been rewarded for their obstruction and timidity. They were now in control of policy, not the White House. I became their accountant, sitting there at the table totting up the bill on my pocket calculator.

Under the House's anything goes arithmetic, Gramm–Latta II didn't look bad. The cut arithmetic added up to $38 billion in 1982 savings, with over $50 billion by 1984. But these numbers counted phony cuts, promised cuts, unreconciled savings and middle-class entitlement reforms outside the scope of the ninety-three reconcilia-tion instructions. On the basis of the true fiscal math of the Reagan

* Economic Development Administration.

Revolution, Gramm–Latta II provided well under one third of the cuts needed to hit the $118 billion savings target for 1984.

The dusty papers from June 1981 now make it clear that the Reagan Revolution was lost. But the same numbers didn't then. I was working off two sets of books—the immediate and the future—and I rationalized. The difference between what we needed to cut and what was actually in hand would shrink if we could get the entitlements and block grants enacted. We'd live to fight for all the rest another day. The President would be using his veto unstintingly, year after year. Somehow the equation would balance, if we just worked at it long enough.

Even this watered-down version of Gramm–Latta II got off to a shaky start. The next morning, Friday, the President put in a call to Tip O'Neill to pave the way for when the bill came before the leadership-controlled Rules Committee.

'I want a chance to send some substitute language up there on the budget,' the President told the Speaker. 'The House has worked hard and done a good job, but it hasn't gone far enough, and I—' Reagan's face suddenly clouded.

O'Neill had interrupted him to say, 'Did you ever hear of the separation of powers? The Congress of the United States will be responsible for spending. You're not supposed to be writing legislation.'

The two old Irish pols squared off.

The President interrupted O'Neill's lecture in Government 101. 'I know the Constitution,' he snapped.

'Can you be specific about what you're going to send up?' O'Neill asked. 'You always talk to me in vague generalities. I don't want to see the Republicans trying to shove something through without full consideration.'

'Oh, come *on*,' Reagan taunted him. 'I was a Democrat myself, longer than I've been a Republican, and the Democrats have been known to make a few power plays.'

O'Neill cooled off. 'OK,' he said, 'we'll have a look. Have your people talk to Jones and Bolling. I'll get back to you.'

I'll get back to you is the moral equivalent of, The check is in the mail. O'Neill never did 'get back' to the President.

Gramm–Latta II was officially launched that afternoon, June 19.

To my dismay, it became almost immediately clear that we would
have to mount an all-out campaign if even this incredibly weak
version was going to suceed.

Among the nine major entitlement reforms contained in Gramm–
Latta II, two of them—the Medicaid cap and the elimination of
Social Security minimum benefit—accounted for one third of the
extra savings compared to the committee bills. They were critical
tests.

Elimination of the Social Security minimum benefit would not
have deprived the genuinely poor elderly at all. They would automatically qualify for a dollar-for-dollar increase under the means-tested
Supplemental Security Income program. The only ones who would
lose were double-dippers and others who shouldn't have been receiving the minimum benefit in the first place. It was, in short, the
cleanest, simplest and most justified entitlement reform there was.

The House did approve that reform when it approved Gramm–
Latta II a week later. But within thirty days, the politicians had
been seized with abject panic. They were suddenly faced with doing
something they had never done before: cancelling checks that went
out to several million people.

Throughout July, before Gramm–Latta II went to Senate-House
conference for final approval, the Democrats began an attack *on a
reform they had already approved*, charging that this was just evidence
that the Republicans were planning to dismantle the whole Social
Security system.

By late July, the reconciliation bill was nearly law. But then,
before the ink could even be put to the parchment, Majority Leader
Jim Wright offered a resolution on July 21 that would commit the
Congress to repealing the minimum benefit reform as soon as the
reconciliation bill became law. It passed by a vote of 405 to 13. Only
ten Republicans, plus Phil Gramm and two of his faithful Boll
Weevils, voted against it.

At the time, I dismissed the vote as a gesture, a symbolic
sense-of-the-House resolution. I believed, incredibly, that the 405
stampeding congressmen could be corraled before they did any real
damage.

Now I see it in a different light. The vote was historically
significant: it was the *coup de grâce*. If the politicians could not bring
themselves to make even that adjustment to Social Security, then

the $44 billion magic asterisk was just that: magic.

We also lost the cap on Medicaid payments—but that only took about six days.

As we moved into the final, climactic week of June, the Congress was still up in arms about the dictator at OMB. Gillis Long of Louisiana, a senior southern Democrat on the Rules Committee, thundered at even the tepid challenge posed by Gramm–Latta II. It was further evidence the White House was trying to turn the House of Representatives into a 'second-rate legislature'.

Even our principal allies were in a sullen temper as we moved into the final critical days. *The New York Times* noted that 'Even Representative Bob Michel of Illinois, the Republican leader, rebelled against the demands of David A. Stockman, the Budget Director, snapping, "We don't have a dictatorship up here yet."'

Given the mood up there, we desperately needed very strong signals from the White House that the President was behind Gramm–Latta II all the way, or as George McGovern said of his proposed running mate, Tom Eagleton, 'a thousand percent'.

I had been confident that the President would do what he did best and make a nationwide address on TV about the importance of Gramm–Latta II. But now that was cancelled.

Jim Baker and Mike Deaver had a policy called the three network 'blockade'. If all three networks didn't agree to televise a presidential address, then there would be no address.

In the end one of the networks refused, but there was also another reason for no TV speech on the crucial budget-cutting bill. Ironically, they were 'saving' the President for the big upcoming push on the tax bill that we could no longer afford.

So when the President failed to show up on prime-time TV putting in a good word for Gramm–Latta II, the congressional politicians deduced that the White House's support for it was tepid, and concluded it was just another *putsch* come to shove by Stockman and Phil Gramm.

On Tuesday morning, June 23, just two days before the vote, the President held a breakfast for the sixty-three Boll Weevils who had voted for the Gramm–Latta budget two months earlier. Less than forty showed up. There was a mad scramble at the last minute to fill the empty places with White House staffers in order to avoid embarrassment at the opening 'photo op'.

As unity breakfasts go, this one was a fiasco. Many of the breakfasters went directly from their grits and coffee to the cameras outside, telling the assembled reporters that by gum, they thought the House committees had done a pretty fair job and they were going to stick with them. The whole episode gave Jim Wright more than enough ammunition for gleeful, disparaging commentary.

The discontent of the Boll Weevils spread to the ranks of the Gypsy Moths. Soon they were caterwauling to remove the Medicaid cap entirely, and to restore funding for a dozen other, smaller programs.

By Wednesday, June 24, the vote count was bleak. The President and his senior staff left on a speaking tour. It had been previously scheduled, but it amounted to a symbolic evacuation of the premises before the mortar assault from Capitol Hill.

Only a staggeringly dumb political blunder later that day by the Democratic leadership reversed the deteriorating situation.

The Rules Committee refused to permit a yes or no vote on the Gramm–Latta II amendments attached to the 1,000-page commit-tee bill. They decreed that it must be broken up into five separate amendments. This meant that our Republicans—and Boll Weevils—were going to be forced to vote against food stamps and Medicaid and Social Security, out loud and one at a time.

They didn't like it. It got their partisan dander up, and for the first time in weeks they felt that the enemy was the Democrats, not me. This was the kind of contest House Republicans loved: a procedural fight against the so-called 'gag rule' issued by the majority.

The five-separate-vote rule on Gramm–Latta II was actually the opposite of a 'gag rule'. The term usually refers to a rule which prohibits separate votes on parts of a bill. But the GOP–Boll Weevil coalition was gagging so hard at the Speaker's proposed rule that they simply called it the first thing that came up their throats.

Max Friedersdorf, our congressional liaison and a canny, experienced expert at the peculiar political chemistry of the House GOP's minority culture, instantly realized that Gramm–Latta II had suddenly been given a chance of making it.

Over the weekend, he and Baker had pretty much decided Gramm–Latta II didn't stand a chance. But this tactical blunder by the Democrats changed all that. Indeed, it changed the nature of the battle itself. Now the real vote on Gramm–Latta II wouldn't be the vote on Gramm–Latta II itself, but on the 'gag rule'. Among the 193 Republican members of the House, there was nearly complete unity on defeating it. If we could prevail on procedure and get the rule changed back to up-or-down, then we might win the main event as well.

Friedersdorf called Baker in Los Angeles and told him to get the President on the phone to the swing votes as soon as he was finished with his speech at the Century Plaza.

He did. The President spent two and a half hours stalking votes that night.

But the real breakthrough came when two Boll Weevils, Billy Tauzin of Louisiana and Ralph Hall of Texas, agreed to vote against the Speaker's rule if we would agree to divide Gramm–Latta II into two separate packages. One would cover everything under the jurisdiction of the House Commerce Committee—on which they sat—and the other would cover everything else.

The chairman of the Commerce Committee was John Dingell of Michigan, and he was ruthless. He could make the life of any of his Committee members who went against him exceedingly unpleasant. Tauzin and Hall were not anxious to have their lives made unpleasant.

Friedersdorf and I jumped at the offer, but I knew these two votes would not be cheap.

The next morning, Thursday 25 June word spread that Gramm–Latta II would be divided into two amendments—if our coalition prevailed on defeating the 'gag rule' vote, scheduled for later that day. The Commerce Committee amendment would be called the Broyhill amendment, after the ranking Republican on the committee.

As I suspected, there was an immediate run on the savings bank. Michel's office was soon aswarm with Gypsy Moths, flapping their wings and demanding every concession on the Broyhill amendment they could think of and then some.

Michel called me in a state of near-panic.

'Better get up here,' he said. 'It's crazy.'

By the time I arrived at the room where Michel's staff had herded them all, it was pandemonium. The session lasted for two and a half hours, during which the 'gag rule' was being noisily debated upstairs on the House floor.

It was a small, narrow room, packed to the rafters with staff and at times up to forty-five Republican members, all clamoring for bacon. By contrast, the pit at the Chicago Commodities Exchange resembled Aunt Tilley's afternoon tea party.

Some of the GOP members had come only for last-minute clarification and assurance on Gramm–Latta II. But a good dozen or more had come to deliver outright threats. Unless the Medicaid cap, the health block grant funding levels and a number of other provisions were changed *on the spot*, they would vote with the Democrats on the rule, ensuring Gramm–Latta II's defeat.

I used yet another metaphor when I laid out the scene for Greider:

> They were just like piranhas. All the leadership—Bob Michel, Broyhill—were down there, so nobody was up on the floor defending us. The Democrats were having a field day, because we're all packed into this little auction . . . The rumor mill was just running rampant. Somebody comes dashing in and says, 'Now is it true that we're cutting out the rail crossing in Schenectady, New York?'
>
> The thing was really getting out of hand. The place was full of lobbyists, all whispering to them about this or that dire consequence that would occur due to the Broyhill amendment. I mean, it was such a high pressure cooker, emotionally, that they couldn't behave.

In fact, we were tacking on adjustments to the Broyhill amendment faster than they could be recorded. It was a mess.

Bill Green of New York wanted the Medicaid cap raised—first by one percent, then by two percent, then by three percent. Then he wanted its calculation base changed. I gave it all to him, thereby eliminating all but an insignificant portion of the savings. Scratch another entitlement reform.

Carl Purcell of Michigan wanted $30 million for nurses' training. He got it.

Jim Leach from Iowa wanted the $100 million family planning program pulled out of the health block grant. He got it.

Norm Lent of New York wanted still more money for Conrail. He got it.

On and on it went, until everyone was satisfied. In order to buy two Democratic votes, we spent almost as much on Republicans as we had tried to save by means of Gramm–Latta II. That was the GOP–Boll Weevil coalition's bottom line. It was a firing squad deployed in circular formation when the hour of reckoning finally came.

It should have been evident to me, as I walked out of that paper-strewn room, exhausted, spent, voices ringing in my ears, that a coalition so indisciplined and divided could never, ever be expected to perform the kind of budget cutting down the road that the magic asterisk required.

But politics has . . . odd effects on a man. Sometimes you can't see the war for the battles. My blood was pumping fast. I was smelling political gunpowder. The bizarre session left me more determined than ever.

I raced back to my office, planning to begin working the phones in order to get the last votes we needed to defeat the rule.

When I walked in the door, one of my deputies waved me over. Bill Thomas was on the phone. Thomas was a conservative Republican member from California, and one of the craftiest GOP tacticians and head-counters on the Hill.

'We ain't gonna make it,' he said. 'Not unless you open the soup kitchen.'

In the Congress, the 'soup kitchen' is what you throw open in the last hours before a vote to get people off the fence. At this point, democracy becomes not a discussion of the ideals of Jefferson or the vision of Madison. It becomes a $200,000 feasibility study of a water project; the appointment of a regional director of the Farmers' Home Administration in western Montana.

Bill Thomas had spent some time practising this art in the California state legislature, and he was now the official cook of the GOP soup kitchen. And he was good at it. If someone came at him and started talking about the plight of the elderly or an end to hunger on the planet, Thomas would hold up his hand and say, 'Don't give me all that bullshit . . . '

And of course it had *nothing* to do with the plight of the elderly or an end to hunger on planet Earth. It had to do with reelection. The deals that were dished out in the soup kitchen were the irreducible minimum, the quarks of politics.

Thomas ticked off half a dozen deals he had already made with various Boll Weevils and wobbly Republicans. 'Give the word and they'll vote with us,' he said. 'But don't think about it too long. We've got about forty-five minutes before the vote and I've still got to find them all and say OK.'

What deals they were. They ranged from things that turned my stomach to things that made me only faintly ill, from reviving the sugar quota program to exempting state-owned cotton warehouses in Georgia from the new inspection user fee.

Only in hindsight would I realize that Bill Thomas's summons to start ringing the dinner bell caught me by surprise. I had devised a grand and infinitely detailed ideological theory for radically reshaping the nation's fiscal policy, but I hadn't fashioned even the rudiments of a theory of political compromise. And in this promiscuous democracy, the former was unattainable without the latter.

My Grand Doctrine was missing the single most important chapter of all. Any serious analysis of the costs and consequences of legislative compromise would have utterly invalidated the fiscal equation of the Reagan Revolution from day one. But that analysis I'd never made.

So, lacking a basis for any other response, I told Thomas, 'Do it.'

Less than an hour later the Democrats' 'gag rule' was defeated by a hair, 217 to 210. That ensured the anticlimactic victory the following day of Gramm–Latta II. The administration had triumphed, winning a close but decisive victory. So it was said.

It was nothing of the sort, and perhaps a remarkably cynical but apt statement made by John Breaux of Louisiana crystallized the utter deception of our victory. He had been the shakedown artist* on the sugar import quotas. What he said was that he had been 'rented, not bought'.

He was right, because all those votes we had either rented, bought, traded or begged would never be there again for us. And if we were to do what was necessary on spending cuts to avoid the fiscal disaster implicit in the giant tax cut, we would need to rent not a dozen votes, but 200. It couldn't be done, and it wouldn't be done.

The postscript irony to the harried events of 25 June 1981, was that all that renting and hog-slopping I had done to rescue the Broyhill substitute went for naught.

---

* Con man.

After the rule had been defeated, the GOP–Boll Weevil leaders finally succumbed to battle fatigue. Without even checking with the White House, they huddled briefly on the floor and decided to dump the Broyhill amendment entirely—and with it the Medicaid cap and health block grants that only hours earlier they had won the right to offer.

By then the cumulative wear and tear on the frail GOP–Boll Weevil coalition had passed the breaking point. All day long they had been taunted and pelted with Democratic accusations which were a parody of the real truth unfolding.

Bruce Vento, a tough, militant liberal from Minnesota, had ridiculed the Republicans on the floor. 'When Commander in Chief Stockman says jump,' he roared, 'you do not ask why. You do not even ask if it will be good for your district. You only ask how *high* and how *often!*'

Banking Committee Chairman Freddie St Germain called the tattered remains of Gramm–Latta II 'a prime example of David Stockman's monumental hubris, which turns the slightest deviation from the OMB computer printouts into a disaster for the nation.'

What survived of the original Gramm–Latta II, in the end, was minimal. There were some honest reforms in the food stamp and child nutrition programs; tenants in public housing would now have to pay thirty percent of the rent instead of twenty-five percent; and military and civilian retirees would receive a cost of living allowance once a year instead of twice. The Aid to Families with Dependent Children and the guaranteed student loan programs would undergo slightly more significant reforms than they would have under the House committee plan; and the Social Security student benefits would be phased out a little more quickly than otherwise.

The total of these and Gramm–Latta II's other measures amounted to the grand sum of $16 billion more than committee bills—over three years. To balance our budgets over that same period we needed to cut $256 billion.

But for the time being it looked like a victory. Taking their cue from Cole Porter, our anything goes scorekeeping rules said we had cut $38 billion from the 1982 budget, and more than $140 billion over three years. The extent to which this victory was comprised of promises and paper savings would only become apparent later.

Even I overestimated how much had actually been cut, and I had been onto the politicians' racket from the very beginning. No one understood this new, multi-year bookkeeping, however, and the word went out that a sweeping fiscal retrenchment had begun.

From California, *The Washington Post*'s correspondent Lou Cannon captured well the false euphoria the White House had concocted from its unknowing defeat. 'Reagan today looked forward to a new coalition dedicated to further reductions in the size and scope of government.'

For a time, I too half-believed our press clippings. We would get those $118 billion in cuts for 1984, somehow.

Over the past three weeks I had had every political deal imaginable shoved down my throat, but I could not bring myself publicly to acknowledge it.

It seems strange, perhaps, but that was incompatible with my revolution. Revolutionaries don't cut deals—they cut heads! My mind formed a retroactive syllogism: The fiscal equation would not work if we made deals; therefore we had made no deals. QED. That perhaps accounts for the astonishing statement I made the next day.

On Friday morning, the day Gramm–Latta II was officially passed by the House, I attended Godfrey Sperling's Friday morning breakfast for the press. This is a weekly on-the-record event in Washington.

There were about fifty reporters there, and they gave it to me pretty good. You didn't make any history up there yesterday, they said. You made deals. It infuriated me. What were they talking about? I was not a politician; not one of *them kind*. Finally I shot back at them the ludicrous asseveration that 'no deals were made'.

This elicited a roomful of guffaws. They were a hard-boiled bunch of reporters, and they feasted on this remark of mine much more heartily than they went at their breakfast.

'You think,' I shot back, referring to the politicians, 'they have turned into pure, public-minded citizens up there who vote strictly on the merits?'

Well, there it was, out on the table with the cold eggs and bacon. I had squared the circle. OK, OK, I had said, so I'm a ninety-five percent revolutionary. We had to throw in a few sweeteners to go the last five yards.

The New York Times headline that resulted from the breakfast accurately conveyed the impression I still had as of June 26, 1981:

COLLAPSE OF THE REAGAN COALITION

REAGAN AIDES SAY A BALANCED BUDGET
IS NOW POSSIBLE BY 1984

My parents came to town for the Fourth of July, and I slept in until seven and took the day off, the first in a long time. I played tour director, taking them to see the things that people come to Washington for: the parks, the monuments. It was a chance to clear my head of some of the brambles that had accumulated over the past six months. From this point on, my head would continue to clear, and by July 18 I would finally be confessing to Greider that no, I wasn't sharing in the general euphoria—I had at last realized that the Reagan Revolution, and the nation's economy, was in deep trouble.

Another episode that occurred during the intervening period brought me to that point.

A conference was scheduled to resolve the differences between the House and Senate version of the reconciliation bill. Since the bills were enormous, the conferencing of them would also be enormous. And dangerous.

There was a way out, however. A conference could be avoided if one house set aside its version of the bill and adopted the other's. In this case, I felt that there was not enough at stake between the House and Senate versions to risk a conference.

Because the Democrats were the majority party in the House, a conference would put the House committee chairmen—the same ones who had worked such mischief and whom we had, through herculean effort, twice defeated—right back in the saddle. It would give them still another chance at diluting the spending cuts. A conference would also mean 150 legislators gathering in little rooms all over the Capitol. Who knew where that would lead?

So I persuaded the LSG and the President to ask the Senate to adopt the House version. That would mean no conference, and Gramm–Latta II could be sent down for the President's signature. They agreed. I asked the President to call Howard Baker himself and make a direct request.

I arrived in Baker's office at 9.30 am on the morning of July 9, carrying a fresh batch of OMB computer printouts so I could explain precisely why it made sense to adopt the House version. Domenici had already arrived.

I had never seen two more furious human beings. The woodshed was nothing compared to what greeted me that day.

Domenici's face was light reddish, the veins in his neck pumping very warm blood.

'It's about time,' he said heatedly, 'you learned this is a democracy around here.' He pointed to my computer printouts. 'And you can shove that pile of paper right back in the OMB garbage can where it came from. From now on, we're doing it *our* way!'

Domenici, of course, was right. He and his senators had worked hard on their bill. They had resorted to their share of shortcuts, but had done a far more creditable job than the House committees.

But there was an even more important point. Each Senate chairman had wired tiny little favors and compromises into the fine print in order to accommodate his Committee members. They just couldn't walk away from all this legislative lubrication without a fight. This imperative inherently meant more dilution of the spending cuts, but it was simply one more element of the political equation that I had neglected to consider in designing the fiscal plan.

And so a clamorous and unmanageable conference got under way. It was pretty clear that I and my computer printouts were not welcome. Indeed, OMB was so unwelcome that some of my staff who had been assigned to monitor the fifty-eight-ring circus were bodily removed from the conference in order 'to make room for others who wanted to attend' (ie., lobbyists).

Nonetheless, determined that we not lose another dollar of budget savings, I doggedly ordered OMB to draw up a seventy-five-page study that showed, with crisp precision, which of the two bills most closely followed the original reconciliation instructions. I sent it up to the Hill to guide the conference in its deliberations.

Nothing was too small to overlook because by now I knew we were slipping into desperate trouble. Thus, in the case of the tiny $55 million per year National Health Service Corps, the missive noted that both the Senate and House bills exceeded the budget resolution. 'The original Administration level could be achieved by accepting the House extension language, but adopting a $38 million funding level.'

The conferees were not amused by this suggestion on how to save $17 million more nor with the dozens of similar suggestions in the document. In fact, it brought another explosion of wrath. Most of the time, Baker and Domenici's staff pretty much dictated the stories of

The Washington Post's Hill reporter, Helen Dewar. Thus the day after my list arrived, the staff sent me a response via Dewar's story:

> . . . the White House, never shy about sharing its budget preferences, is circulating on Capitol Hill a seventy-five-page list of recommended compromises for the House–Senate conference . . . circulation of the document, covering nearly every major point of dispute in the conference and many minor ones, is the latest example of budget director David A. Stockman's fastidious pursuit of Reagan's budget priorities in Congress. . .
>
> Republican politicians grumbled privately that the Office of Management and Budget can 'never leave well enough alone,' as one of them put it.

Things had come to an ironic pass. Someone else had been excluded from the conference: Phil Gramm.

Phil had brought the House down on him by rallying the Democratic Boll Weevils to the Reagan Revolution. So the Democrats wouldn't take him into the conference with them. And the Republicans pretended they couldn't take him in—after all, he was a Democrat. Gramm was left in no-man's-land. The irony was that both parties had taken great delight in excluding from the final process the co-architect of the very plan they were deliberating over—the only member of the Congress who understood it.

For two weeks the politicians haggled happily away, and when it was over they had done exactly what I knew they would. The conference produced valid budget savings lower than both the Senate and the House bills. The resulting 1,000-page document was replete with every loophole, every cut corner, every perversion of fine print in the considerable repertoire of the professional staff that dominated the conference.

Finally Stockman was beginning to understand. National governance was not as simple as in those heady days of early February when I had brought the hapless Dentist from South Carolina to the Cutting Room and beat him into submission.

Now it was my turn. I was being banished from the game. For six months I had defied the rules of democracy, and the politicians had finally said, enough. They may not know what to do with dairy subsidies, but they do know what to do with implacable ideologues and absolutists.

A final accident of the reconciliation battle tells the lasting story. On 26 June 1981, Rita Seymour and her telephone number (255–4844) were voted into law by an amok House of Representatives. Ms Seymour was only a low-level Congressional Budget Office staffer. But in frantically trying to add up the spending-cut numbers the brawling Representatives were about to enact her name and number got scribbled on the margin of the reconciliation bill and so she got mistakenly enacted along with the budget figures.

At the time, the phone number set off much tongue-clacking among the Democrats and other critics of the administration's program. It was proof that Reagan's robots had done it again.

They had enacted sight unseen the largest spending reduction bill in history, a sweeping measure so hastily assembled and patched together that it was as if the White House surgeon had left his tools inside the patient's tummy.

But Ms Seymour's accidental memorialization was actually symptomatic of an altogether different reality. In fact, at the eleventh hour a panicked herd of GOP and Boll Weevil politicians had taken control, rather than an overpowering and dictatorial White House. The Reagan coalition had come eyeball to eyeball with the Reagan Revolution. In the political white heat of the hour it had wavered, complained, rebelled, then broken into a chaotic and disorderly retreat. The Seymour phone number was only a snippet of the debris that resulted.

So 26 June 1981 marked a historical moment, but not the one which has been ascribed to it. It was the day on which the United States Congress reached the limit of its ability—and willingness—to reduce spending.

The borders of the American welfare state had been redefined, but they had been only slightly and symbolically shrunken from where they had stood before. The half trillion dollar per year domestic budget which remained now had incredible staying power, because in surviving the White House assault it had gained renewed political sanction.

9

New Lessons: The Politics of Giving

July of 1981 was an eventful and paradoxical month—the period when the Reagan Revolution reached both its culmination and its nadir. It was a month that saw the completion of our spending reduction package and the passage of our tax bill. It was also the month in which the Congress effectively took over both programs. If I had entered the White House with the intention of launching a *coup d'état*, six months later I would find out exactly who *couped* whom.

What the Congress did in July to the tax bill was much the same as what it had done to the spending 'reduction' package. It brought the turbulent reality of politics again crashing down on the ideological orphan in its midst. That started a bidding war, and once the war started, we became ensnared in its logic. If it was logic, it was that of the alcoholic: one more couldn't hurt, given all that had gone down already.

I worried and warned, Cassandra-like, all the way to the end. But too much was happening at once. Like most of the others, downtown and on the Hill, I was now wearing blinders.

Over the days before the House voted to approve the tax bill on July 29, the only real numbers being counted were the votes. Questions of tax policy and fiscal impact had long since been forgotten. When the final showdown came, it took the form of a raw struggle for political power and control of the House—and the nation's revenue base was the incidental victim.

But one fact was more important than any other: the tax cut was one of the few things Ronald Reagan deeply wanted from his presidency. It was the only thing behind which he threw the full force of his broad political shoulders.

Getting the tax cut passed was one of the few episodes involving domestic policy and legislative bargaining in which he firmly called the shots. By intimidating and overpowering the whole lot of the nation's politicians, he got what he wanted. It was at once awesome and tragic.

Nearly to a man, the Democrats had been bitterly opposed to Kemp-Roth from the very beginning. They were not enamored of its principal sponsor, to say the least, and it was both a political and an ideological threat to them. So against it were they that, for a time, resistance to it became almost a test of traditional Democratic ideology.

Like everyone else, the Democrats did not have a clue as to what the budget numbers would be three to five years down the road. But politicians comprehend without analyzing. They knew that a thirty percent cut in the federal income tax base amounted to a drastic change in the fiscal status quo—a radical and alien idea. They wanted nothing to do with this uncongenial supply-side notion that the betterment of the common man did not depend exclusively upon their own largesse; that the politically brokered redistributions of Washington were the problem, not the solution. Nor could they abide the proposition that social progress might come about as the result of the invisible exertions of workers and entrepreneurs down in the anthill of a $3 trillion capitalist economy.

Many of the incumbents in their ranks had also been battered by Kemp-Roth in the 1978 and 1980 elections. It was something that Republican challengers, not yet housebroken in the ways of Washington, instinctively embraced and championed. Kemp-Roth gave these nettlesome upstarts the chance dramatically to seize the political high ground and to link their otherwise hopeless candidacies to the powerful currents of tax revolt that were swirling through the electorate in the late 1970s.

The Democrats had lost no sleep over scribblers like Laffer and Wanniski or backbench hot shots like me or even Kemp. But Howard Jarvis's California Proposition 13 (a property tax cut by statewide referendum) had put the fear of God into them. Anti-tax, middle-class populism was a mortal threat to the middle-class welfare state. A lot of GOP congressional candidates had caught on to this hot new political theme, and soon Democratic incumbents were on the defensive—for the first time in decades.

The Democrats had therefore determined to discredit and defeat Kemp-Roth. If supply-side ideology was allowed to sink deep political roots, their own ideological foundations could crack.

Kemp-Roth did not rate much higher support among the traditional Republican politicians of Washington. Endorsements ran a mile wide, but convictions were an inch deep. The GOP rank and file may have considered it a handy platform to campaign on, but not an appropriate policy to govern with.

In order to get enthusiastic about Kemp-Roth, you had to be distinctively unenthusiastic toward—even disdainful of—the myriad busybody projects that make up daily congressional life. You had to believe that the vast expanse of federal problem solving didn't really solve very much after all. You had to believe that, in principle, it was wrong. More to the point, you had to have no compunctions about starving the budget beast.

Most of the Republican politicians in Washington were ex-lawyers, bankers, farmers and businessmen. They had heard the supply-side music, perhaps had hummed a few bars of it on the campaign trail. But they couldn't read the music, and anyway, they didn't have much use for it. They had come to Washington as ideological neuters, wrapped warmly in the cozy fog of country club republicanism and faithfully murmuring its nostrums.

They were easy marks, quickly coopted by the congressional culture and welfare state apparatus. It may have taken a term or two, but soon most of them were busily and earnestly promoting the 'good work' of the subcommittee they landed on. They became patrons of pork.

They listened to one another's causes in the cloakroom, the gym, the Capitol restaurant, and on the subway to and from the House chamber. Collectively, they disseminated and absorbed the policy folklore of the Second Republic. By a gradual but certain process, they became the legislative chambermaids of the welfare state.

All that really stood between them and the Democrats was their content-free rhetoric about 'private initiative' and 'fiscal responsibility'. In the end, the majority of congressional Republicans were nonplussed by the radical and alien premise of the supply-side ideology.

When it came to taxes, the GOP's idea of a tax reform consisted of opening up loopholes in the IRS code. They preferred to pump up the welfare state from its back end by means of tax subsidies rather than direct expenditures. Some championed the utility industry; others shilled* for smokestack manufacturers. Still others promoted tax breaks for the thrift industry, equipment leasing, small business, cattle feedlots, pharmaceuticals, waste water recycling plants, and countless more.

Tax subsidies were another misguided way of doing good. All claimed their favorite tax breaks would promote jobs and economic growth someplace or other in the land. But few of these tax breaks helped the nation as a whole, because all were premised on the Second Republic's fallacious single-entry bookkeeping.

But they boasted one extremely attractive feature: they had constituencies who rewarded those who promoted them. The hundreds of political action committees that have sprung up over the past decade were in charge of the payback.

All in all, the Congress of early 1981 was exceedingly inhospitable terrain upon which to champion a supply-side-oriented tax cut. Shortly before the assassination attempt on the President of March 30, the pundits had all confidently predicted Kemp-Roth's imminent demise.

'Is the big tax cut dead?' headlined a *Newsweek* story. It distilled the prevailing atmosphere succinctly: 'Ronald Reagan's $48 billion package of budget cuts is steaming through Congress, but his three-year ten percent tax cut proposal seems to have run aground.'

This climate encouraged the new chairman of the Ways and Means Committee, Democrat Danny Rostenkowski of Illinois, to believe that his tax bill mark-up strategy would 'get Kemp-Roth out of the way' on the first day. Then, he said, the Committee could explore on a 'bipartisan basis' what it really wanted in a tax bill.

This brisk dismissal was no partisan wishful thinking. The Democratic leadership knew that most of the rank and file, including the Boll Weevils, was biding its time, waiting to be rescued from the unpleasant thing called Kemp-Roth. Tip O'Neill echoed Rostenkowski: 'There's no support out there, even among the Republicans, for Kemp-Roth.' O'Neill had seldom been so truthful. 'The Senate Republican leaders would be delighted to get off the hook.'

* A shill is a decoy who works with a con man.

During a meeting late in March, the Boll Weevils told Don Regan the exact same thing. They weren't going to swallow the full thirty percent rate cut. They had their own more traditional plan: a tax package consisting mainly of estate tax relief, savings incentives, and capital gains tax reduction.

Speaking for the Boll Weevils, Phil Gramm put it in plain English. 'The President's budget is on the road,' he told Regan, 'but the administration is in the ditch on tax cuts.' And Gramm was one of the few true believers in a supply-side tax cut. The outlook, obviously, was bleak.

A measure of how dispirited the atmosphere at the White House was could be seen in our response to the gauntlet that Rostenkowski had thrown down. Don Regan was stirred to issue the formal rejoinder. Thundering it was not.

At a hastily assembled press conference, the administration's spokesman for the very centerpiece of the Reagan Revolution blew a trumpet that sounded more like a piccolo. Kemp-Roth 'is far from dead,' Regan declaimed. *Next question?*

Barber Conable, Mr Republican Tax Policy, was rushed down to the White House for a lengthy meeting with the President. Despite the dirge Conable delivered on the subject of Kemp-Roth's prospects, the President said he was determined, nonetheless.

'I can't turn tail and retreat on this,' he said. 'I promised it during the campaign. There is a long road ahead. We can't start to back away now.'

Conable wearily agreed to stay on board—at least for the time being. But he had a supple mind and he could damn by faint praise better than anyone. After the meeting, he told reporters on the White House driveway, 'I shall do my duty.' His use of the word 'duty' had a Tennysonian *Charge of the Light Brigade* ring to it.

By April Fool's Day, with the tax cut's champion in the hospital recovering from a bullet wound, there was not much zeal left in the issue. Among people with enough clout to make any difference, only Jack Kemp and I still carried the flame. Don Regan did, too, but his enthusiasm derived entirely from the man in the Oval Office. If the President had lost interest in Kemp-Roth at noon, on any given day, Regan would have had it buried by sundown. He had no strong ideas of his own.

Subsequent events have tended to obscure this near-demise of the tax cut, as my own efforts in late March to breathe life into it show.

On March 26, I had spent hours testifying before the House Budget Committee, taking a lot of heat on Kemp-Roth. The only stirring defense for it on the Committee came from a not surprising source—Jack Kemp.

Finally, Dick Gephardt of Missouri, an old colleague from the House and a rising, astute Democratic politician, took pity on me and tried to offer some friendly solace. He noted that I had made a 'valiant' defense of supply-side tax cutting, insisting nevertheless that no one was buying. It was time, therefore, for the White House to drop a lost cause and turn to something more viable and practical on the tax front.

'If I read the tea leaves correctly,' he mused out loud, 'Congress will pass a one-year tax cut.'

One year when we wanted three!

That may have been the prevailing consensus, but it amounted to a repudiation of the entire Reagan Revolution. I came down hard on Gephardt's remark.

'The President will veto a one-year tax cut,' I shot back. 'And we'd have to go back to the drawing boards [and start all over]. So I would strongly urge Congress not to do that.'

This defiant warning produced headlines the next day and squeamishness at the White House. Both Baker and Darman felt that the only chance to get even part of Kemp-Roth passed was to make a deal with Rostenkowski, and veto threats wouldn't help that already tenuous prospect.

So they went to the President and convinced him that I had violated his general principle of not announcing vetoes in advance. The White House had to disassociate itself from my remark. Larry Speakes was subsequently instructed to do just that.

Speakes informed the press corps that the President would not decide to sign or veto tax legislation until it reached his desk. The budget director had only been expressing a 'personal opinion', he added; but, of course, my recommendations would be given 'great weight'.

The Washington Post put it more directly:

WHITE HOUSE BACKS OFF TAX VETO THREAT

I was furious. This wasn't just any piece of legislation, some bill on preschool education grants or Meals on Wheels. This was the heart of the Reagan Revolution.

What Gephardt had been talking about was a one-year, ten percent *average* tax cut, with the relief heavily tilted toward the low end of the income spectrum. The bill, moreover, would have been decked out with tax breaks for failing industries and two-wage earner families, and with savings incentives. There wasn't a trace of supply side to it.

Which was exactly what the politicians wanted. They were going to kill the Reagan Revolution in its cradle so the Congress would be safe for business-as-usual. If they were to take us seriously, we had to make an explicit, advance veto threat. But things had deteriorated so far that even the White House lacked the will to do that. It looked as if Kemp-Roth was dead.

There were two miraculous recoveries in April—the President's and his tax cut's—and the former had everything to do with the latter. On his first day back on the job, still too weak to leave the third-floor residence, Ronald Reagan summoned Baker, Meese, and Deaver. The President was 'concerned and agitated—he was irritated,' they later told the press, about the assertion that his administration had signalled its willingness to compromise on the tax cut.

Marvelous though the President's resolve and involvement were in principle, in practice they were disastrous. The problem was that the President did not have great depth of understanding about the tax code. The complexities, intricacies, and mysteries involved in the tax breaks that the Congress wanted were simply beyond him. In essence, he didn't understand the link between the federal tax structure and the budget. He could not grasp that to fiddle significantly with the former was to change the numbers in the latter—and for the worse.

So the strategy that Ronald Reagan played on behalf of his tax cut was one of brute political force. As between a zero and a thirty percent tax rate cut, he had drawn his own line in the sand somewhere near the upper end. But he would rely on his advisers to settle all the other tax bill matters that came along.

The four of us, Jim Baker, Dick Darman, Don Regan, and myself, were an odd lot. Each of us had a different philosophical and operational vantage point. Baker and Darman were guided by the 'governing' principle. Their idea was to achieve as much of the policy as you could without sacrificing the President's continuing capacity to succeed. As non-ideologues, they would have been happy to settle for a half loaf on the thirty percent rate cut—as long as it could be arranged so as to look like a 'win' for the President. But they were never given that kind of latitude, and so were forced into a riskier game.

Regan operated on the 'echo' principle. Whatever the President insisted on, he would try to get—without regard to the price. He had been a Marine, and this was the moral equivalent of taking a hill. However admirable an ethos, it involved a curious inversion of the normal role of the Secretary of the Treasury.

From the beginning of the Republic, secretaries of the Treasury, Democrat and Republican, have been the watchdogs of the revenue code. It is only natural, given that one of the principal functions of the Treasury Department is to finance the nation's massive public debt.

Secretaries of the Treasury, therefore, have a built-in allergy when it comes to turning the congressional politicians loose on the tax code. Their dual institutional responsibilities of collecting the taxes and borrowing the shortfall instill them with a keen sense of the dangers of such political raids on the revenues.

But Regan had no such allergy at all. He got plenty of warnings from his professional tax policy staff that most of the 'ornaments' that the Congress wanted to add to the tax cut constituted abysmal tax policy. His Assistant Secretary for Tax Policy, Buck Chapotin, was a brilliant and doughty warrior when it came to sound taxation. He would fight almost every single one of the congressional tax ornaments up to the last moment.

Yet Chapotin did not have much leverage. Regan backed him up on the individual items of tax policy, but not on overall strategy. The Treasury generally never established a limit as to how much the politicians could dump into the tax bill—for one very simple reason. The captain of finance at Treasury was not about to be bested by the whiz kid at OMB. If I had got ninety-five percent of the President's budget cuts, then he would deliver that much or more of what the President wanted on Kemp-Roth.

That made Regan no bulwark against fiscal recklessness. By July, he would be sitting happily in the middle of the tax trough, preening, delighted at his political prowess in having got so many of the politicians to join in the feeding.

My own vantage point was ideological, and therefore not very reliable either when it came to adding up the numbers. Of the four of us, I was the only one who had an actual passion for a supply-side tax cut. To me, the issue was meta-numerical. It was critical to my view of the world. As I saw it, supply siders were dedicated to capitalist wealth creation whereas the politicians were dedicated to socialist wealth redistribution. That was the fundamental axis of the struggle for the Reagan Revolution.

And now the doctrinaire liberals and New Deal Democrats on the Hill were trying to steal the supply-side tax cut right out from under our noses. They were willing to go for an income tax cut, maybe even as high as twenty percent—*if* it were limited to those with incomes no higher than $50,000. Therein lay the Catch-22. The income cap proposal killed the supply-side idea with a single sentence.

What liberals have never been able to bring themselves to admit is that capitalism is the product of capitalists. It is the prospect of getting rich and keeping the rewards that drives invention, innovation and entrepreneurial risk taking. It produces intellectual capital as well, which in turn brings about more and more output and wealth from the farms, factories, and workers already there. The idea that our supply-side stimulus to capitalists had to be polluted with redistributionist political ornaments was profoundly offensive to me.

As I saw it then, that was precisely what a deal with the House Democratic leadership would have meant. The Speaker was beyond salvation; on the matter of taxes, he was a fly in New Deal amber. Tip was still fighting the good fight against FDR's mythical 'economic royalists'.

Jim Wright, the Majority Leader, was even worse. He was as misguided as O'Neill, and he had more energy. He practised the politics of envy, pure and simple: the deliberate inciting of middle- and lower-class resentment against the rich. By 1981, the Jim Wright philosophy of taxation had prevailed so many times over the years that the federal income tax bordered on an out-and-out soak-the-successful scheme. Nearly forty percent of all federal income taxes were being paid by the five percent of taxpayers whose incomes were above $50,000. To the congressional Democrats, all of whom, not incidentally, earned above that sum, $50,000 of income was the Great Divide. If you earned more than that, then you were not entitled to fair treatment. You were, in a sense, automatically suspect.

Shortly before the bidding war began in earnest in early June, Wright offered an olive branch of compromise for the last time. But it was no compromise at all, because it limited the tax cut largely to lower-income taxpayers.

While I was ready to go all-out for the supply-side tax cut, I was by now not unmindful of the threatened fiscal equation. I was confident that the $44 billion gap could be closed by having the thirty percent tax rate reduction cut back to twenty-five percent and by substantially diluting the overly generous provisions of the 10−5−3 depreciation reform. After all, the latter wasn't even a supply-side concept. It had simply been the political price we had to pay in 1980 in order to maintain a semblance of GOP unity on tax policy. Together, at any rate, these two adjustments to the February tax plan would help ease the threat of out-year deficits significantly.

Now everything began to happen quickly, one thing leading to another. The turning point was Gramm's 'Alamo' Budget Resolution speech to the Boll Weevils. The ensuing May 7 stampede of the Boll Weevils to Gramm−Latta amounted to a crushing defeat of the House Democratic leadership. That, in turn, suddenly made us realize that we now had both leverage and momentum. Now we held the good cards, not the Democratic leadership. The LSG immediately swung into action, and it did not take long to come up with a deft and subtle strategy.

None of us believed a deal could or should be made with the House Democratic leadership. But we all thought there was a chance of separating Rostenkowski and the other middle Democrats from O'Neill, Wright, and the hard-core, redistributionist liberals.

If Rostenkowski was prepared to agree to multi-year, across-the-board rate cuts—even if they were significantly less than thirty percent—we were all prepared to recommend it to the President. The magic, after all, was in the supply-side aspect of the cut, not the thirty percent.

We were hopeful. Rostenkowski was much less ideological than the Democratic leadership. He was a reasonable, decent man who wanted to be a successful Ways and Means chairman—in sharp contrast to the disastrous regime of his predecessor, Al Ullman.

Rostenkowski was from Chicago. He had been trained in the Mayor Daley school of politics, and he liked to be where the action and power was, not off somewhere orating and bellowing out slogans left over from the 1930s. We would offer him the chance to cut a deal with the mayor of the nation—the President.

In order to gain leverage, however, we would first explore an alternative deal with the Boll Weevils. If Rostenkowski couldn't be tempted far enough in our direction, we would show him that we were prepared to offer the Boll Weevils one or two goodies on their own tax cut wish list. If he still wouldn't move far enough, then, as a last resort, we would attempt to rally the Gramm–Latta coalition behind a 'bipartisan' supply-side tax bill on the House floor.

Even with the new momentum that our Budget Resolution victory had given us, this was still a strategy based on bluff. Rostenkowski had spent the whole spring warning about the economic perils of locking in a multi-year tax cut. The Boll Weevils were still lukewarm (or lukecold) on Kemp-Roth. It was never quite clear in our minds how we would leverage one faction against the other. But within a few days of the House Budget Resolution victory, we launched our gambit. Max Friedersdorf and Baker hauled in the press and confidently started playing poker in public.

'If I were Danny Rostenkowski,' Friedersdorf said, 'I would be coming in to talk to the President about his tax program and get the best deal I can before the tidal wave rolls over him.'

Well, no *tsunami** was looming at the moment, and it was doubtful that even the Great Communicator could stir one up. There was, however, a small thunderstorm brewing in Texas and it turned out to be a very fortuitous one.

It came in the person of Kent Hance. He was one of the Boll Weevil regulars, and to look at his record up to May 1981, no analyst would have marked him as the man who would soon put the torch to the US revenue code. He was a junior Democrat from Lubbock, Texas, a homespun good ol' boy. Supply-side economics was not the

* A giant tidal wave.

first idea he had accidentally run into and not understood. But he was ambitious. His brilliant Texas colleague, Phil Gramm, had made it look so easy. Gramm had become a Washington household word overnight—and Hance decided he was going to become the 'Gramm' of the tax-cutting game. Unlike Gramm, however, he brought more politics than vision to the role he was about to assume.

Notwithstanding, he plunged into the task of lining up his Boll Weevil colleagues with great energy and enthusiasm, and by early May he had got ten or twenty of them at least to consider supporting a modified version of Kemp-Roth—if the first-year cut were delayed until 1982 and reduced to five percent, from ten. The Boll Weevils also still insisted that estate tax reduction and savings incentives be part of any compromise package.

It was a start. On May 12, the LSG met with the President in the Oval office. Keeping secrets in the White House is usually a fruitless endeavor, but every precaution was taken to keep even the fact of this meeting a secret.

It was Don Regan who told the President what the LSG wanted to recommend to him. 'Let me call a spade a shovel,' Regan began. 'Kemp-Roth can't pass. We think it's time to start seriously exploring a compromise.'

Regan, Baker, and others then explained our strategy of playing Rostenkowski against the Boll Weevils. Darman called it 'bait and switch'.

'We dicker with the Boll Weevils,' Darman explained, 'in order to put the squeeze on Rosty.'

As Regan and the others talked, I studied the President's face. He looked pained. Obviously he hadn't anticipated that his own advisers would be counseling him on the need to compromise on his most cherished reform. But Ronald Reagan was a politician. He was willing, up to a point.

'Going with some of their ornaments,' he pondered. 'Well, yes. I've always been for getting the estate taxes back to reason. But on the rate cut, we have to draw the line. Twenty-five percent is as low as we can go. I don't want you fellas asking me to go under that figure. We'll take it to the people if we have to.'

That presidential admonition became the LSG's negotiating charter in all the negotiations that followed. It became known as 'twenty-five percent plus ornaments'.

For the time being, I was delighted. I assumed—naïvely—that the 'ornaments' would come cheap and that the five percent lower rate reduction would reduce the $44 billion magic asterisk.

My complacency was anchored in the LSG's belief that our 'bait and switch' strategy was going to work. Somehow we were certain that in the final crunch, Rostenkowski would accept the President's terms. Once a deal with the Chairman of the Ways and Means Committee was cemented, passage of the bill in the House would be a cinch. The supply-side, across-the-board rate reduction would be enshrined in law.

When I met with Greider on May 16, I was a fount of optimism. True, the financial markets were still in bad shape and no evidence of economic recovery was in sight. But our secret instruction to compromise the tax bill would be the elixir Wall Street needed.

'Well,' I said, 'that's the last pound of flesh that they want. They've got everything else. By pound of flesh I mean they're deeply sceptical and it takes a series of things to get them to believe and a tax compromise would be the last of them.'

But now Greider had heard me make repeated, erroneous predictions of a financial market turnaround. But I was convinced that all of my fixes—defense, Social Security, and now the tax compromise—were falling into place.

The specter of deficits, I said, was the central threat to our whole Grand Design for economic rejuvenation, but it was being cured even as we spoke.

> The markets fear the prospect of huge deficits because they see the deficit as a kind of leading indicator of monetary policy. They know that if huge deficits are unavoidable or inevitable the Fed will cave to those or behave erratically—just continue to gin up the volatility and uncertainty that's in the markets today.
>
> I never believed that just cutting taxes alone will cause output and employment to expand. I think the thing that's strangling the economy right now is the financial market. You have to get interest rates visibly moving down. Without stabilization of the financial market you're not going to get any supply-side expansion.

*   *   *

Then Greider asked me precisely what kind of compromise we had in mind. All our conversations were strictly off the record, and I had been telling him absolutely everything now for months. But suddenly I went catatonic.

'I'm under constraints not to talk about it,' I demurred.

Greider teased, 'But is the blueprint already there?'

'I can't talk about that,' I blurted.

The reason for my sudden demureness had to do with an extremely unpleasant episode of a few days earlier, in which I had been caught, red-handed, in the act of leaking. Actually, I had been doing no such thing; it just looked as if I had been. But the incident proved to be a decisive—and fatal—turning point in the tax bill saga, because it gave Don Regan undisputed command of the entire operation. From that point forward, he started throwing his weight around with a new officiousness and self-confidence.

Here is what happened to bring that about. At the end of the crucial meeting with the President on the tax bill compromise, the need for secrecy was so great that we had all practically raised our right hands in an oath of silence. We could hardly execute a 'bait and switch' strategy if the parties involved knew what we were up to; or if they knew how much ground we were willing to give up.

Later that same day I held a previously scheduled 'backgrounder' with reporters from *The New York Times*. To my horror, they already had the whole story of the 'secret' Oval Office meeting, a mere seven hours after we all had taken the oath. They wanted me to confirm it.

I could have easily denied the story. But when I was confronted with the truth, I sometimes had a hard time with the ritual lying which is part of the game—especially if the reporter was four feet away, looking me straight in the eye. So, taking a deep breath, I confirmed the story on background.

Next day's *Times* story fingered me but good. It quoted a 'senior White House official' as indicating that the President had decided to compromise significantly on Kemp-Roth. That wasn't me, but there, a few paragraphs down, was a quote by David A. Stockman on a matter wholly unrelated to the tax bill. It was an unfortunate juxtaposition.

Don Regan flew into one of his trademark Irish temper tantrums.

NEW LESSONS: THE POLITICS OF GIVING

According to his staff, he spent the whole morning screaming and fuming about 'the kid'—no matter that he had no proof that I had been the source of the *Times* story.

Larry Kudlow of my own staff had got a temperature reading from Buck Chapotin, whose advice was for me to call Regan and try to make amends. I called him, and inadvertently handed him the smoking gun he was looking for.

As soon as he picked up the phone, I started by saying, 'Don, I just wanted to explain the *Times* story. I talked to them, but . . .'

Before I could complete the sentence with a 'they already had the story', there was a roar on the other end of the line. I thought the Merrill Lynch Bull was going to come crashing right through the receiver.

'*God damn it!* This is the final straw,' he bellowed. 'You're not going to get away with this. I'm going straight to the President.'

He even slammed his fist on his desk so hard it seemed as if it were my own.

'This is the last time you're going to undercut me!' he fumed. 'I've had it up to my ears. We're going to settle right now who's in charge of economic policy.'

There was no calming the man down; and he immediately called the President of the United States to tell him that it was I who was responsible for the *Times* story and for undermining the administration's entire strategy.

A few hours later my secretary came on the intercom. 'The President is on the line,' she said.

I had expected trouble—though nothing like this—and I had already composed my defense. But the President initially gave me no opportunity to deliver it.

'Dave, I've got a big bone to pick with you,' he said. 'Don tells me you leaked to *The New York Times*.'

His voice was stern and threatening. It was the only time I had ever heard it that way. And it was sobering. 'I can't have this,' he continued. 'We all took an oath of secrecy. I won't tolerate this kind of thing again.'

With sweaty palms, I then told him that I hadn't leaked the story, that the *Times* already had it. I also pointed out that the on-the-record quotes were unrelated to the tax bill. 'Mr President,' I said, 'it wasn't me who spilled the beans.'

Apparently he had the article in front of him, because after a moment he said, 'Yes, I see your point.'

My palms dried, and my body relaxed. I think he did, too. We both agreed that you can never be too careful. 'The press will sabotage you every time,' he said.

The President concluded the phone conversation by saying, 'Well, we all have a big job to do. I want you to keep working on the budget cuts. But we've got to make it clear that Don's in charge of the tax bill. That's his department.'

Over at Treasury, meanwhile, Regan was wasting no time making sure everyone now knew exactly who was in charge. He got a White House OK to call in several key economics reporters.

'*This* is where you will hear administration tax thinking,' he pointedly told them. 'If you hear something different from someone else, then it's wrong.'

Regan's press aides took the line and were soon promoting it as a 'second-half' comeback story. The photo that ran in an early June *Time* Magazine profile on him was captioned: 'The marine has landed.'

'This is my great outing,' Regan preened. 'I'm enjoying it.'

In early June of 1981 I was discovering that the big leagues really were different from the political back benches. Governance was not a realm of pure reason analysis, and the clash of ideologies. It really did involve the brute force of personality, the effrontery of bloated egos, the raw will-to-power. My Grand Doctrine was looking more Utopian every day.

It had started to dawn on me that maybe we were not all crusaders on the road to Jerusalem. I had known all along that Regan was jealous, but I hadn't sought the magazine covers I had landed on — I viewed this as a by-product of the hot seat I was in. I didn't employ a cadre of public relations flaks to sit around and cook up ways to get me on the seven o'clock news. Regan did. My crew worked like dogs on substance.

Even my press secretary, Ed Dale, was an old journalistic warhorse whose passion was solely for facts. He was too seasoned, too thrilled by the policy battle ever to think about 'profile building' for his boss.

I had always wished Regan would stop blaming me for being

inadvertently more conspicuous than he. There was no need for all these stories of supposedly intense rivalry between us. But I had blamed them on his staff of profile builders.

Until now. Now the scales had fallen from my eyes. I was finally beginning to see that raw hunger for power was as important a part of the equation as pure ideas.

This late discovery of mine had very practical implications for the revolution, too. The blueprint required hundreds of things to be done *just so*. There was no room for error born of weak comprehension. But how could we maintain this precision drill if the field was full of inflamed egos?

If my idealism was beginning to yield to a more rational view of what drives politics, it was for the better. I was seeing things not as I wanted them to be, but as they were.

So was Dick Darman, only with him the pedagogical technique was more gentle. I now had to stop by his office periodically to be briefed on the latest tax bill machinations on the Hill. His embellishments, however, made it as good as the real thing. At first I had not liked him that much. He was always asking inconvenient questions, or seemingly preoccupied with the process—tactics, trades, players, deals, winning. I later realized he saw these as inexplicably linked with substance, but I didn't like the connection at the time.

To one who thought in terms of ideology, these seemed almost coarse concerns. Ours was not a natural basis for an alliance, but he was stuck with my ideology—it was *the* official administration policy, at least on paper. And as we got deeper into the decisive legislative battles of June and July, I came to admire his hard-headed, cogent and zestful approach to political strategy.

There was a curious antecedent to all this reeducation I was getting in Darman's West Wing basement office. Pat Moynihan had occupied the same office during the Nixon Administration; it was the exact spot where all those memos which had introduced me to the inner sanctum of American government had actually been written.

'Do you realize one of my greatest gurus used to hold court right here?' I told Darman one afternoon, as he was waxing about his theory of governance and public interest.

Darman never missed an inconsistency. 'You mean the guy who is saying that supply side amounts to the free coinage of silver?' he said with a wry grin.

That stopped me for a moment, but I had an answer which betrayed the trouble I knew was brewing. 'Well, Moynihan's got a problem,' I replied. 'He went off and got himself elected Senator from New York. He just can't get away with holding a sound view of economic policy. New York *is* the welfare state, you know.'

Darman had an unfair question. 'As long as we're counting the votes, how many other states end up in that category?'

Darman was a complicated embodiment of the reality principle. He found my doctrine about free markets, capitalist dynamics, and economic justice appealing. He was too much of an intellectual with a high-minded view of the public interest to make excuses for the raw pork barreling that dominated the Congress.

He had thought about the big picture and comprehended the historical significance of the Reagan Revolution. His was the only office in the White House where you found a whole table stacked with serious books that the occupant had actually read. He knew which side Hayek was on and which side Beveridge was on, and didn't disagree with my choice. Yet he still thought it was better to lean toward where you were going than try to get there in one leap and risk falling flat on your face.

But for the moment there I sat amid the echoes of Pat Moynihan's typewriter and Darman's memorabilia from his salad days with Elliot Richardson.

All of this was disconcerting, but I kept coming back.

By June, our close working relationship had turned into a friendship. I confess that some of the cement had probably been our low regard for Regan's competence, as well as mutual disdain for his overbearing manner. One day we dubbed him the 'chancellor of the exchequer', and the label never came unstuck.

Both Darman and I worried about what was going on at the Treasury. But through the LSG meetings and Darman's daily sessions with Regan, Baker, and various delegations from Capitol Hill, we did our best to steer the process. Up until the final weeks of July, we were for the most part successful.

In the meantime Darman was good therapy. We had long conversations and debates about ideology and politics. I continued to learn—from him—that I didn't have as many answers as I thought, that I had built an edifice of doctrine, but not a theory of governance.

Once the President drew the line in the sand at twenty-five percent, a deal with Rostenkowski was never remotely possible. His Democratic colleagues on the Ways and Means Committee could never have been made to swallow it. It was still Kemp-Roth, and they said to hell with it. Nevertheless, a game of cat and mouse between Rostenkowski and the Boll Weevils went on for several weeks. The end was already scripted, though. We would cut our deal with the Boll Weevils, and wage the tax policy battle on the House floor. And then the bidding war that would help plunge the country into record deficits would begin.

Only the President could have stopped it. Or maybe Don Regan, but Regan, not knowing any better, never advised him to reduce his terms. Jim Baker made a few private runs at the President. But Baker knew a Rock of Gibraltar when he saw one, and nothing was to be gained by running his boat up against it. The President had made up his mind to stake his presidency on getting the whole supply-side cut. Baker concluded early on that this was a genuine presidential decision—beyond the ministrations of even the Chief of Staff.

The first week of June, Rostenkowski's impatient Democratic colleagues called off our bluff and threw down the gauntlet. This was their final offer: a two-year, fifteen percent (total) tax cut. And oh what a variety of ornaments. Blinking lights!

'Not good enough,' the President responded.

The response of the Ways and Means Democrats was plain enough. They declared war on the White House.

That's how it looked then, anyway. Now I realize the sequence was different. We had already declared the war in February. It wasn't until June that they finally decided to fight back.

There is something about having war declared on you that breeds easy camaraderie. Our 'Situation Room' was Baker's table at the Executive Mess, right next to the real thing. On June 3, the day the war began, Baker, Regan, Darman, Freidersdorf, Gergen and I huddled over our food. We all knew that the battles we had already been through were going to seem like spring training compared to what was coming next.

'Well,' declared Darman, with his disingenuous, nervous laugh. 'I believe this is it.'

Darman had a way of getting efficiently to the essence of things, at the same time leaving you to speculate as to whether he anticipated disaster or triumph. His face was a cross between the Sphinx and the Cheshire cat—knowing, with a trace of mischief.

One feels a certain gravity—and grandiosity—sitting in the bowels of the White House, and the metaphor of that day's lunch menu was 'Crossing the Rubicon'. Again and again it was trotted out, along with its companion, 'The die is cast'. I had now been around the White House long enough to have heard these metaphors applied to some pretty quotidian stuff; but for once our collective sense of inflated self-importance and conviction that we were 'dueling with destiny'—as I think Gergen put it—seemed actually warranted. We had got wet crossing something, and it looked, smelled, and felt like the Rubicon. But Caesar knew what his action would bring; we did not.

In any event, there were no doubts. No one suggested taking the issue back to the President. Our job now was to win the battle. Tactics became paramount on this the first day, as they would until the bitter end of the tax bill episode.

Later that same afternoon, nine of the Boll Weevil leaders were hastily summoned to the White House to meet with Baker, Regan, and Friedersdorf. By then, most of the details of what would become known as the 'Conable-Hance' tax reduction bill had been worked out. It was now just a matter of cementing the alliance. Gramm, Hance, Stenholm, Montgomery and the other Boll Weevil leaders signed on, and on June 4 a new GOP–Boll Weevil coalition announced its 'bipartisan' tax reduction bill in the Rose Garden. The first shot had been fired.

I was enthusiastic about Conable-Hance. It reduced revenue losses in the out-years almost precisely in line with my game plan—by about $8–10 billion in 1984. That was no small help in closing the $44 billion gap.

Moreover, Buck Chapotin had come through in cutting down the excesses in Conable's 10–5–3 depreciation plan. Utilities and industrial structures were put in a less generous write-off category, and the double declining balance method of write-off was eliminated. Those and other steps were consistent with good tax policy and also reduced the revenue loss by tens of billions of dollars in the out-years.

More importantly, I thought these changes showed that the politicians were capable of discipline. The Boll Weevils had been reluctant to accept even the twenty-five percent tax cut because they were worried the revenue losses and deficit would be too high. In crafting the compromise, we had solved some of their deficit worries by diluting the politicians' plan, 10–5–3, not just the supply-side cut. Thus, it was reasonable to think that just the opposite of a bidding war was under way. We had trimmed the tax bill in a way that would ease the fiscal equation and strengthen political discipline in the battle with the Democrats on the House floor.

The compromise, I told Greider showed how serious we were about bending the budget equation into shape, despite interest group politics.

But Greider wasn't buying. 'Where,' he asked, 'is Charles Walker in all this? Won't he come at you?' Charlie Walker was the quintessence of K Street,* the super-lobbyist of the corporate tax world who had actually helped Conable organize the 10–5–3 business tax coalition in support of generous write-offs.

My stubborn refusal to recognize what my own theory deplored—the power of interest groups—was evident in my pat dismissal of Charlie Walker:

> I don't think he has so much influence with us. As long as you keep the Congressional champions of depreciation reform happy, the compromise will hold. Conable has gone along. He's the father of 10–5–3. If he can live with it, Walker can squawk all he wants.

Within days of that confident statement, Walker, the Chamber of Commerce, and most of K Street would come at us like a battalion of tanks. The firing lasted four days, then abruptly stopped. Walker got everything he wanted: with a couple of years delay in the effective dates, the business community pushed the compromise bill all the way back to where we had started. For the years after 1984, we had an undiluted 10–5–3, no reduction in the revenue loss, no help on easing the budget equation at all.

* A street well-known for its lobbyists' offices.

One element in our defeat here was the White House's own Office of Public Affairs, then headed by Elizabeth Dole. She and her deputy, Wayne Valis, had spent practically the entire spring rallying the business community lobbyists on behalf of the administration's economic plan and the budget cuts. Once the tanks started crashing through the White House grounds, Dole and Valis practically tackled and hog-tied Jim Baker in his own office. 'Treasury's pulling out the rug on 10–5–3 is intolerable,' they told him. 'Our supporters feel betrayed. They moved heaven and earth to pass Gramm–Latta. Now they feel entitled to fair treatment and consideration.'

'Fair treatment and consideration' is polite Washingtonese for 'they want theirs'. And they got about as close to all they wanted as you could get. The original 10–5–3 plan had reduced revenues by $162 billion over five years. Our compromise would have lowered that revenue loss by one third. But after Jim Baker and Regan ordered Buck Chapotin to retreat, all but $2 billion of the revenue loss was restored.

Even so, I was not as alarmed as I should have been. The deal with the Boll Weevils hadn't seemed that expensive, and much of it consisted of surprisingly sound tax policy. One element of it called for reducing the top rate on investment income from seventy percent to fifty percent—immediately. That was even more supply side than Kemp-Roth.

The Boll Weevils had also insisted that Conable-Hance include a major reduction in the gift and estate tax. That was all to the good, too. The punitive taxation of estates and a lifetime's accumulation of wealth were among the worst anti-capitalist propensities of the Second Republic.

Most of the other items were gimmicks, such as the marriage penalty relief provision and raising the contribution ceiling on individual retirement accounts. But one of the Boll Weevil 'ornaments' would lead to madness.

The Boll Weevils had insisted on delaying the first instalment of the Kemp-Roth tax cut until January, 1982, and I had vehemently opposed that. I was willing to give up on our original idea of enacting the first cut in July of 1981. After all, supply side was a long-term, incentives-oriented proposition, not some Keynesian booster shot to pep up the economy by the next quarter.

But I saw a huge danger in stretching out the implementation dates of the three tax cut instalments too far into the future. It would give both the politicians and inflation too much time to fiddle with them and whittle them down.

I was even at loggerheads with my buddy Phil Gramm on this. He wanted to 'backload' Kemp-Roth, that is, let the big tax cuts take effect later rather than sooner. His reasoning was that this would keep up the pressure on the politicians to keep cutting spending halfway through the decade while avoiding the risk of a temporary deficit increase.

I decided it was time to post another message on the Bob Novak bulletin board as a convenient way of telling people they were getting out of line. In late May, my note ran under the Evans and Novak by-line:

> The supply siders want a 'front-loaded' tax cut [i.e., 1981]. The [Boll Weevil] alternative [i.e., backloaded] entices senior Reaganites, but—contrary to fears of edgy Treasury . officials—not Stockman. As budget director, Stockman naturally is interested in any deficit-reducing scheme. But as a supply sider and Republican politician he sees dangers in what Hance and Gramm propose.

It worked. Hance eventually came around and agreed to a 1 October 1981 date for the first tax cut. Naturally, there was a *quid pro quo*, but it seemed incredibly cheap. All he wanted was a tiny, $2,500 per year tax credit for small oil royalty owners against the windfall profits oil tax. It would only cost the Treasury $700 million per year. That was barely coffee fund money, even for smallish oil companies. Carter's windfall profits tax was then fleecing the industry of nearly $20 billion per year—almost thirty times the amount of Hance's little gratuity.

I was more than inclined to go along with it for ideological reasons as well. I considered the whole windfall profits tax an abomination. Plucking some loose change from this illicit revenue pot seemed a fitting way to close the deal on Kemp-Roth. I remember marvelling that Hance would give in on something so profound for so little.

But it did not take long to realize that Hance had poisoned the political well. During my numerous meetings the next week with

Gypsy Moth Republicans on the budget reconciliation bill, all I heard about was the oil royalty owners credit provision.

Their vision wasn't obscured by ideology. They saw Hance's 'little gratuity' as blatant, parochial favoritism. And it set all their anti-oil industry bile juices pumping. Carter had done a good job of inflaming the country against the oil companies. Now they were thinking as clearly as a lynch mob, and if Hance 'got his' on oil, well then there was no limit to what they were going to ask for. Hance's $2,500 tax credit had triggered a trillion-dollar bidding war.

By the middle of June, I was in a sober frame of mind. 'We weren't going to get involved with tax bill brokering of special interest claims,' I told Greider.

> But then we made a compromise. My fear now is that if we do that too many more times it becomes clear to the whole tax lobby constituency in Washington that we will deal with them one at a time. And we're going to end up back-pedaling so fast we'll have a Christmas tree before we know it.

As I look back on it, I realize that Conable-Hance was a calamity from the very beginning, both symbolically and operationally. Hance was a textbook politician who had got his name on the marquee only because he had 'got his' first. The lesson was not lost on the others.

Barber Conable, by the same token, had been the good shepherd to all the non-Kemp-Roth tax schemes of the GOP rank and file. Now they were counting on him to champion their bill when the nut cutting began in earnest. He had no disposition to betray them.

During the next thirty days, therefore, the process of one thing leading to another rapidly gathered momentum. I started to get nearly a daily lesson on the fundamental defect of our blueprint for the Reagan Revolution. That is to say, it had no room for politics.

The fact was, there wasn't a semblance of a Reagan ideological coalition in the Congress to support the revolution. The Republicans and conservative Democrats amounted to a frail, faction-ridden, and unstable political gang, saturated with fierce sectional and parochial cross-pressures.

The latent GOP–Boll Weevil parliamentary majority, in terms of gross vote numbers, was nearly meaningless. An actual majority for any specific bill had to be reconstructed from scratch every time. It had to be cobbled out of a patchwork of raw, parochial deals that set off a political billiard game of counter-reactions and corresponding demands. The last ten or twenty percent of the votes needed for a majority of both houses had to be bought, period.

The payments inherently shattered the fiscal equation. They caused the budget reduction package to shrink and the tax cut package to expand. Winning any battle, perforce, meant losing the war.

By the middle of June, I could finally sense this coming. I worked the House reconciliation bills all day and tracked the latest twist in the tax bill saga at early evening LSG meetings. It was evident that the politics was pulling the two sides of the budget in opposite directions.

But I still had a blind spot as to the precise and fatal implications of this for the budget numbers. The problem was the February economic forecast. I did not yet realize it was totally out to lunch.

The problem was, the whole out-year trend of the February budget numbers was drastically wrong. Under the actual economy which materialized, the GNP shortfall due to lower than forecast inflation and real growth was cumulative. It got larger and larger each year. That meant the deeper you got into the out-years, the worse was the underlying deficit position.

But since the politicians feared the near-term deficit, they designed their ornament proposals in the opposite manner. They phased them in gradually, thereby 'backloading' the revenue loss into the foggy future two or three elections down the road. This was the patented formula of 'Buy now, pay later.'

Even the sparse ornaments of Conable-Hance exhibited this pattern. They cost $4 billion in 1982, but $25 billion by 1986. Thus, as the underlying real-world budget position deteriorated in the post-1984 period, this new backloaded revenue haemorrhage generated by the Congressional politicians made the situation even worse. But I missed the danger of 'backloading' ornaments entirely.

After Walker and the Chamber of Commerce won back the full shot of 10–5–3, I also gave up any hope that the tax bill would ease the near-term problem. The $44 billion magic asterisk savings in 1984 would have to be worried about later.

This was an even more foolish assumption than not worrying

about 'backloading' the tax bill. With the Social Security package shattered, defense officially locked in at the high February numbers, the reconciliation bills shrinking by the day, and no help from the revenue side, I should have known that the 1984 balanced budget was already pie-in-the-sky. I should have insisted that both the near-term and the long-term cost of the tax package be reduced. But I still believed that in the fall and in subsequent years we would launch new drives to hammer the fiscal equation back into place.

During the remainder of the first round through August, therefore, damage limitation would be the objective. If the final tax bill revenue loss was no larger in 1984 than had been our original proposal, no ground would be lost. The total budget gap would still be $118 billion; the magic asterisk would still be $44 billion. We could find some way to push through the budget cuts we had pending and come up with some of the $44 billion we still owed.

When Greider asked me in mid-June about what the incipient bidding war might do to my fiscal equation, I had an answer:

> My objectives are purely pragmatic. I'm not really that concerned about 1985. If you shift the budget structure towards balance in 1984, it will automatically carry into 1985 and the years beyond that.

The next round took place in the Senate. The Finance Committee was no hotbed of support for supply-side tax cutting. All its Democratic members opposed Kemp-Roth, and its Republican ranks were filled with sceptics. Republican Senators Chaffee, Packwood, Durenberger, Danforth, Heinz and Dole were all in that category: and they made up six of the eleven who sat on the tax-writing Committee.

All spring the Committee's Chairman, Bob Dole, had been walking a tightrope, desperately hoping someone would let him off the high wire on Kemp-Roth. He wanted to bring the tax bill to the Senate floor, but the battle looked futile. The Senate has no rules on limiting floor amendments, and the filibuster privilege can turn any senator into a temporary majority of one. Consequently, there was no way for Dole to bring a tax bill to the Senate floor and avoid ambush from all directions—unless the Finance Committee was united behind it. A bill brought out of Committee with nearly unanimous vote and with the Committee's determination to oppose all floor amendments can sometimes safely run the gauntlet of the full chamber. A little luck helps, too.

But Dole didn't have even eleven votes for Kemp-Roth. There was simply no room in the tax package for all of the items his colleagues wanted, needed, or demanded because Kemp-Roth alone would bring about all the tolerable revenue loss just by itself.

Dole remained pessimistic until the early June deal on the House side with the Boll Weevils. That broke the Senate logjam. The 'clean bill' the administration had all along been demanding was suddenly unimportant. Tax ornaments were now fair game, so getting the votes was a more realistic prospect.

When Dole finally succeeded in getting the bill out of the Finance Committee by a vote of nineteen to one on June 27, the limbs of the Christmas tree were pendant. There were new ornaments for the savings and loan industry, small business, research and development, stockbrokers, the oil industry . . . you name it. Even the original Conable-Hance oil tax sweetener got sweetened further.

The whole prior policy on IRAs* was also changed to make the 35 million workers who already had employer pension plans eligible for the retirement savings deduction too, at a cost of $8 billion over five years.**

And the decorating spree was still not over.

Dole had wanted the Senate's package to be no larger than the administration's. He was going to get Ronald Reagan his twenty-five percent income tax cut *and* take care of his Committee colleagues sufficiently to get a vote of nineteen to one. His term for that nearly unanimous tally was 'floor insurance'.

As of June 27, I was convinced he had come through. By raising some new revenue and diluting 10–5–3, he had limited the total package's loss in revenues for 1984 to $149.2 billion. Our target had been $150 billion, so Dole's figure was, as they say, close enough for government work, especially given all the new ornaments he had had to include.

---

* Individual Retirement Accounts (an American investment vehicle for retirement purposes).
** In fact, the revenue estimating technicians totally blew this one, failing to reckon that millions of people would switch their existing stock of taxable savings into the new IRA deduction. The actual five-year cost turned out to be $32 billion—a figure fiscal light-years away from where the whole IRA game started.

I shook my head admiringly. 'Dole's something close to a miracleworker,' I told Darman. 'The nineteen to one committee vote will shut off floor amendments, we've lost no ground on the budget, and we got 5–10–10.' ('5–10–10' was the new shorthand for the President's three-year tax cut: five percent the first year, then ten percent each year for two years.)

Unfortunately, Bob Dole was not quite the thaumaturge* I thought he was. By mid-July the tax bill was still on the floor of the Senate when the bidding war broke out on the House side, and there is no impermeable membrane between the two houses. Dole's nineteen to one 'floor insurance' policy quickly became null and void. The Senate instantly began adopting multi-billion-dollar sweeteners as fast as they could even be proposed in the House Ways and Means Committee debate.

Also, Dole had not really taken care of all his Finance Committee colleagues. When his pot of tax cut money ran out, he had begun issuing a kind of legislative scrip. Certain Finance Committee members would have the right to offer floor amendments. Dole, meanwhile, would reserve his right to oppose them vigorously.

This was how tax indexing was born, courtesy of Senator Bill Armstrong of Colorado. He was a low-church supply sider, and one of the few consistent anti-spenders in the entire Senate. Armstrong's case for tax indexing was at once appealing and powerful. If the politicians refused to control their spending, then why should they be bailed out every year by the automatic increase in revenue that resulted as inflation pushed people into higher tax brackets?

Practically speaking, indexing the income tax in a high inflation economy amounted to permanent Kemp-Roth, because it eliminated bracket creep forever, rather than just the next three years. The problem was the combination of Kemp-Roth and tax indexing in a *low inflation economy*. That was a far more radical proposition. Under these circumstances, Kemp-Roth would be a deep and permanent cut in the revenue base.

Dole was inclined to agree, but he issued scrip to Armstrong to offer it on the floor, anyway.

'Armstrong doesn't have the votes on the Senate floor,' the Senate's best vote-counter told Jim Baker. 'We'll bury indexing in an hour.'

* Performer of miracles.

But Dole had also not taken care of the Senate's all-time maestro of tax politics, Russell Long of Louisiana. He had been chairman of the Finance Committee for more than a decade and now found himself in the unfamiliar and forlorn position of playing second fiddle.

But he consoled himself by continuing to champion his favorite tax charity—Employee Stock Ownership Plans (ESOP). ESOP was an absolutely harebrained scheme. The idea was to make mini-capitalists out of millions of workers by subsidizing their acquisition of stock from their employer. To do that, more of an employee's total compensation was exempted from the income tax. That in turn narrowed the tax base and was therefore the kind of thing that made tax rates so high in the first place. If workers really wanted to own a piece of the Rock, they could buy it on the stock market with after-tax dollars along with everyone else.

Both Long and Armstrong took care of themselves on the Senate floor. Despite Dole's expectations and assurances, tax indexing passed by a margin of fifty-seven to forty. Long's ESOP amendment sailed through, too. And between the two, the 1986 revenue base was reduced by nearly $25 billion. After Senate floor discipline broke down completely, billions more in out-year revenue losses were added on top of that.

Ironically, it was our Pyrrhic victory in the House on the Gramm—Latta II reconciliation bill that touched off the final, most costly round of the tax-bidding war. We had gained not much at all from Gramm—Latta II, and had left behind raging bitterness among both the Democratic leadership and much of the rank and file.

Our defeat of the House Democrats on the Budget Resolution in early May had not unsettled them too severely. A budget resolution only set targets. But the Gramm—Latta II reconciliation bill had put a burr under their saddles. It involved real legislation, real money, and in one fell swoop it smashed their control. We had beaten the committees. In a very real sense, we had politically unmanned the Democrats.

About a week after Gramm—Latta II passed, they rallied. It was pure partisanship that brought them together—a fierce determination to recoup their threatened parliamentary power.

On the eve of the vote on the tax bill, Tip O'Neill presided at a pep rally, officially designated as a caucus, and defined the spirit that had dominated the Democrats the entire preceding month of July.

'If we win this one,' he boomed, 'we're still running the show. But if we lose, we might as well turn over the House to the White House.'

That would have made my life considerably easier, but here was the essential, tragic irony of all my efforts. In my frantic endeavor to get the Democrat-dominated House to reduce spending, I had (a) not succeeded, (b) annoyed them, and (c) produced in them an irrational, desperate sense that they were engaged in a life-or-death struggle for power with the executive branch. As a consequence, the Democrats abandoned every principle, policy, prejudice, or even mushy sentiment they possessed about the federal tax code. When they returned from the Fourth of July recess, they put the nation's entire revenue system on the auction block in preparation for the final showdown.

'I don't like this poker game of calling and raising,' Jim Wright protested wanly. He then promptly added, 'Frankly, we'll put anything in the bill if it will buy votes.'

And they did; they put a 'sweetener in every pot', raising Hance's royalty credit gratuity ($10 billion) to win back the Boll Weevils. Then they restored the commodity straddle loophole and increased the proposed marriage penalty deduction (at $5,000). Finally, to please Gypsy Moth Republicans, they added new tax breaks for mass transit systems, hiring unemployed youth, and rehabilitating old 'frost belt' industrial plants.

These champions of the little guy also raised the tax exemption for US citizens living overseas to $100,000 per year; added a new tax break for utility dividends; and exempted nearly all estates from federal inheritance tax (only the 7,000 largest out of 2 million per year were not affected).

While they were at it, the House Democrats also tacked onto their own tree some of the ornaments the Senate had put on theirs: tax-free savings certificates, IRAs (for everybody!), special write-offs for trucking companies suffering the trauma of deregulation, bigger pension plan write-off allowances for professionals (Keogh plans), and new research and development credits.

Every imaginable category of middle-class voter got something, too: small businesses were practically exempted from corporate taxation; child care deductions were raised substantially; farmers got new tax benefits. By the time the Democrats had finished their bill, one disgruntled liberal, David Obey of Wisconsin, accurately observed that 'It would probably be cheaper if we gave everybody in the country three wishes.'

To pay for all these new arrangements, the Democrats scaled back the business and supply-side tax cuts. This gave them a powerful competitive advantage going into the final showdown on the House floor. No one could accuse them of fiscal irresponsibility, at least under the Monte Carlo standards then prevailing. Why, their bill would cost no more than the original administration plan or the Senate Republican bill!

The House Democrats' tax bill was more appealing than the other two. It had more where it counted—a little bit of ideology and a whole lot of parochial and regional politics. There were things in it designed to cause defections up and down the entire GOP–Boll Weevil coalition.

Back at the White House, the situation was pronounced grim. 'Conable-Hance isn't competitive—not even close,' said Ken Duberstein. He was Friedersdorf's assistant in charge of the House side, and an unfailingly accurate vote-counter.

A good part of our problem had been the Ways and Means Committee Republicans. They had voted for a number of the Democrats' new ornaments during the Committee mark-up, because some of them had begun as Republican proposals and they didn't want to abandon their own stepchildren.

Other elements were at play now, too, especially the natural jealousy and mutual suspicion between House and Senate Republicans. These animosities went back a long way, and they were deep. That there was less substance to it all than Redskins-Cowboys rivalry mattered not at all.

By the week of July 20, the Senate floor consideration of the tax bill had got out of control. Every day, some Republican senator was walking off the floor with a new tax break in his pocket.

As an example of how far things had gone, only the threat of a liberal filibuster had prevented a bipartisan coalition of senators from the south and west from dismantling the windfall profits tax entirely. This abortive attempt, however, only inflamed the anti-oil Gypsy Moths on the House side. And so the week before the House tax bill vote, the GOP–Boll Weevil coalition amounted to a seething gang of contending factions. Everyone was accusing everyone else of greed, and in the same breath shouting '*What's in it for me?*' Beside all this, supply-side theory was, well, as relevant as love at an orgy. The only unifying principle, in fact, was a resurgent Republican partisanship born of the GOP's resentment at the Democrats for trying to reclaim their power by blatantly and cynically auctioning off the tax code.

At a White House strategy meeting, Minority Whip Trent Lott summed up the mood: 'Everybody else is getting theirs, it's time we got ours.'

The political equation was thus saturated with kerosene. The only remaining question was whether the White House and leadership of the GOP–Boll Weevil coalition would light the match.

We did. The fateful moment came on Thursday 23 July in the Cabinet Room. It was a meeting, but it could also be called a banquet, though that is putting it perhaps more delicately than it deserves. The day that 'Conable-Hance II' was born was a day that will go down in fiscal infamy.

Try as I have, it is virtually impossible to discern rationality in the behavior of any of the principal players. They were: the President, Regan, Baker, Michel, Lott, Conable, Hance, and a supporting cast of GOP Ways and Means Committee members and Boll Weevils. Let me quickly add my own name to that list, though I cannot claim to have sat at the table with the big boys. In my new capacity as participant rather than principal, I sat against the wall. The view, though not as good, offers perspective. It is also difficult to ascribe individual culpability for what occurred during those four or five hours on July 23.

The meeting was actually the culmination of a process that had begun forty years earlier, when Ronald Reagan, as a working actor, had learned that it was economically fruitless to make more than four films a year. Then, on the eve of his victory in the 1980 New Hampshire Primary, he had learned about something called the Laffer curve; a little over a year later supply side had become the centerpiece of his economic revolution. A few months after that, he had agreed to adjust the curve, slightly. Just one month later, the Congress began their counter-revolution. And because it had all taken place within a democracy, we had come, finally, to the bargaining table. But the President was not about to abandon his revolution.

He was entitled to a Treasury Secretary who would do his bidding, and in Donald Regan he had one.

To his credit, Regan had struggled manfully throughout the ordeal to limit the congressional ornaments. His philosophy of tax policy was no more coherent, to be sure, than his understanding of the supply-side catechism, and that was not an asset. But he had been a stout warrior against the grotesque excesses of the politicians. He was familiar with their handiwork because it concerned his own professional field. For years they had foisted multi-chambered segmentation, regulation, and protectionism on the financial industry, creating a tangle of irrationality, inefficiency, and injustice that remains very much in place today.

Regan learned from this only one lesson, but it was the right one. Capitalism requires a level playing field. He transferred the principle to tax policy, and he was right there, too. But at every step of the way, Regan had been crushed on his own level playing field. Politics is not a level field. It systematically disrupts the natural economic terrain, using the fiscal and legal powers of the state to grant privileges, subsidies, protections, and advantages unattainable in the competitive market. This is why the tax code defies every economist's calculus of rationality.

Political necessity had been defeating Regan all summer. His attempt to excise the blatant excesses of 10–5–3 lasted four days. He waged a spirited fight against the all-savers certificate boondoggle of the savings and loan industry—to no avail. The Senate adopted it. The House Democrats included it. The July 23 group would now do the same. That was the pattern. It would happen with item after item.

The President was also entitled to a budget director who could tell the meaning of the numbers he was counting, and that he did not have on July 23. Budget numbers are the final inexorable arbitrator in the fiscal equation of democracy. They measure the quantitative effects of the behemoth's giving and taking. Someone has to assess—coldly—the balance; someone has to stand astride the bottom line as the politicians pour on the red ink; someone has to shout 'Stop!' I had tried, and failed, and now, with my back literally to the wall, I did not raise my voice and shout again. I sat quietly and watched passively as the politicians and the President and the Secretary of the Treasury stumbled in the trough.

But I had less excuse for complacency about the afternoon's madness than they did. I was playing from a fuller deck. My version of the supply side was not based on a four movie anecdote like the President's. It was not a content-free fiduciary commitment like Regan's. And there was no Laffer curve running through it. I knew both sides of the giving and taking equation had to add up to the same number, and within a reasonable interval of time. I was beginning to suspect that they weren't even close before the afternoon started, and I should have screamed bloody murder long before it ended.

But despite all the evidence, I said nothing about the problematic numbers because I couldn't let go of the Reagan Revolution fiscal plan and the doctrine it embodied. As far as July 23 was concerned, it all reduced to a single number. Whatever happened, we couldn't let Conable-Hance II cost, by 1984, any more than what we had said our tax cut would cost by then back in February: $150 billion.

Thinking about how I stalked about the Cabinet Room that day, I am reminded of the drunken businessmen in the opening scene of *The Graduate*, one of whom corners Dustin Hoffman so he can give him just one word of advice: 'Plastics.' Perhaps I seemed even more ridiculous, going from ear to ear saying, 'Hundred and fifty billion.'

Fittingly, Barber Conable sat across the table from Jack Kemp. These two pols were the antipodes of the GOP spectrum, the one orthodox, the other radical. Jack was not by nature quiet, but Conable did all the talking. Kemp had already won the policy argument about the supply-side tax cut. He had but one vote, but it was the only vote that counted in that meeting. The President sat at the middle of the table as an omnipresent reminder that the line had been drawn at twenty-five percent.

Conable was resigned to that, if not convinced of its wisdom. But he had come with a different mission. His purpose that day was to take care of his brood on the Hill, to explain to the President how the battle could be won, and what it would take. They wrangled over several issues.

Conable insisted that tax indexing be incorporated in Conable-Hance II. Both Don Regan and I fought that one, but Conable and his GOP colleagues persisted. We solved the impasse by delaying the effective date of tax indexing until 1985. That didn't reduce the risk a wit—it just shoved it one year beyond my 1984 ceiling of $150 billion in tax cuts. Another bill to pay on the first day of the next billing period. But Bill Gradison, an influential Republican on the Ways and Means Committee, and the GOP faction favoring tax indexing was brought on board.

Small business had to be taken care of, too, Conable insisted. The National Federation of Independent Business and other small business lobbies had a strong following within the coalition and they wanted theirs, too. In due course, about $6 billion of small business odds and ends were added to the Christmas tree.

The Gypsy Moths were also coming unstuck from the coalition. 'Repelled by the smell of oil,' Conable explained. So we replaced that smell with the aroma of crackling cedar logs. An important new innovation in the war against energy shortage would be granted a fifteen percent tax credit subsidy: the wood-burning stove.

Nothing that might win a vote was too big or too small. Perhaps the most absurd moment of the entire session came when child care agencies were exempted from the windfall profit tax. How many nurseries owned shares in an oil well? That was . . . unclear, but it couldn't hurt.

More had to be done for savings incentives. The bill already contained the IRA-for-everybody and Keogh plan proposals that would end up costing $90 billion in lost revenues over the decade. But now a fifteen percent interest deduction was also added at a cost of tens of billions more.

Ultimately, the Ways and Means Democrats also trumped the original Conable-Hance on estate and gift tax relief. It was part of their strategy to bring the Boll Weevils back into the fold.

One of the noisiest repentant strays among the Boll Weevils had been Ken Holland of South Carolina. Pointing to the estate tax relief and other items targeted at the upper-income brackets in the Democratic bill, Holland had insisted that the Democrats wanted to help the wealthy, too. 'Under our proposal, those people can buy a Mercedes Benz in only four years,' he said, shedding some clarifying light on the debate.

Conable-Hance II, therefore, would incorporate everything the Democrats had proposed on gift and estate taxation *and* a few new ornaments as well. As with the others, the changes would be phased in over six years.

I was now contemplating another curve. These estate tax provisions cost only $114 million in 1982. By 1990, the cost would be $11 billion per year—100 times more. A sharply ascending curve, clearly.

The limbs of the tree were already at breaking point, but no one in the room understood. How could they? By now they couldn't even count all the ornaments. It was a white heat of largesse.

'What's the stacking order for ISOs?' someone shouted. By now all heads automatically swiveled to Buck Chapotin.

'That's incentive stock options,' he responded in his flat Texas drawl. 'The answer to your question is, first-in, first-out.'

All heads nodded agreeably.

'What about the ITC lid on used machinery?' Dick Schulze wanted to know. 'Are we going with the $150,000 or not? That's pretty important to me.'

Regan fumbled through his bulging notebook and came up with no answer. The President looked perplexed. He didn't know that ITC meant 'investment tax credit' either.

'Buck, I thought we had the used machinery people taken care of,' Regan finally replied.

'Well, sir, we've said we'll go to 125, but they want 150.'

Regan then turned to Schulze, 'What about 125 through '84, then 150 after that?'

'Done,' Schulze replied.

Even Tip O'Neill in all his glory had never spent $1.6 billion that fast.

Conable got his, too. 'Now my sense, Mr President,' he said, 'is that we have a fairness problem out there in the country. These federal programs need to be cut, but we've got to indicate some sensitivity.'

Conable was pushing an above-the-line charitable deduction for non-itemizers. It was absolute heresy at the Treasury, contradicting the whole rationale for the standard deduction. 'You're talking Girl Scouts and the Salvation Army here,' said Conable. 'Besides, Danny's [Rostenkowski] got in his bill now.'

Of course he did. Conable put it there: a billion-dollar ornament.

Sitting along the wall, I scribbled a half-prophetic note and passed it to Darman.

(Left) The Japanese mysteriously "volunteered" to limit auto exports on the eve of Prime Minister Naka-sone's visit. Free markets don't stop at the border. This cover-up for protectionism really frosted me. *(Center)* Energy Secretary Jim Edwards, a dentist before becoming governor of South Carolina, was opposed to the elimination of oil and price allocation controls. It was so central to our free market approach that I hadn't imagined anyone would object. *(Right)* Among the whole California crowd, Marty Anderson was the only broadly knowledgeable and sophisticated political analyst.

Jim Jones, chairman of the House Budget Committee, wanted to make deals. But when I refused, he accused me of a bunker mentality stemming from a gargantuan sense of egotism. Jones was right about what I was demanding from the politicians: surrender.

28

I had come nearly to idolize Howard Baker. I believed he would outclass Lyndon Johnson as the greatest Senate Majority Leader of all time.

Marvelous though the President's resolve and involvement were in principle, in practice they were disastrous. Ronald Reagan proved to be too kind, gentle, and sentimental to lead a revolution. 29

30

As a Senate moderate, Pete Domenici had been viewed by us with grave suspicion. But eventually he performed a heroic political act when he begged the President to let him vote against the tax cut he knew we couldn't afford.

31

Majority Leader Jim Wright was a snake oil vendor par excellence, a demagogue of frightening rhetorical powers.

32

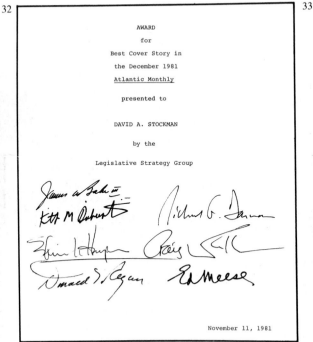

```
                    AWARD

                     for

             Best Cover Story in

              the December 1981

               Atlantic Monthly

                presented to


             DAVID A. STOCKMAN

                   by the

          Legislative Strategy Group


                                November 11, 1981
```

A response to the *Atlantic* cover story signed by the gang. The press made this into a roaring overnight scandal. I was the Judas. The reality inside the Oval Office was quite different.

33

William Greider was my intellectual sparring partner. He captured a glimpse of the staggering confusion and disorder in which the Reagan economic program was born.

34

"Just keep bringing your black books, Dave," they would say, believing I was leading them to the promised land of balanced budgets. I began thinking that our progress was splendid. Only later would I appreciate the vast web of confusion and self-delusion I was creating.

35

There were demonstrations and wild charges of unfairness and hardships due to budget cuts, especially surrounding my attacking the welfare state flaws of Social Security.

36

"Defense is not a budget issue," the President said repeatedly. "You spend what you need." But there was no tribunal of wise men to objectify and precisely quantify the "need." The Bradley Fighting Vehicle cost $1.7 million per copy. We were planning to buy 7,000 of them. It was a battlefield bull's eye, too vulnerable to fight in since one direct hit would take out a whole squad.

37

George Shultz, the new Secretary of State, suggested a flat tax to the President while they were golfing.

38

Max Friedersdorf was our congressional liaison and canny political expert who sensed Gramm-Latta II could survive because of the Democrats' staggeringly dumb political blunder.

39

The President triumphantly drew a happy sketch on the tally sheet of congressional votes that gave him the largest tax cut in history. It was a Pyrrhic victory.

My original comrades in the revolution, economist Arthur Laffer *(left)* and peripatetic polemicist Jude Wanniski *(right)*, weren't very good-natured about my eventual apostasy.

Raw hunger for power was as important a part of the equation of government as pure ideas. So Don Regan worked on the "echo" principle: whatever the President insisted upon he tried to get for him. He helped me see things not as I wanted them to be but as they were.

43

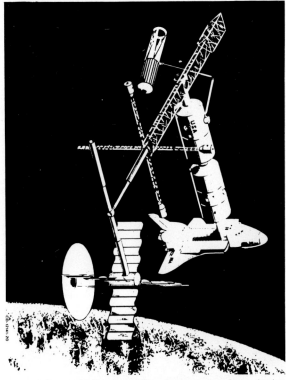

Space stations are high-tech socialism, but it was time for an election year showcase. Big spending to me, sound investment to NASA administrators.

44

Lowell Weicker, one of the biggest spenders to bother calling himself a Republican in this century, voiced a key concern about me: "How long are we going to allow this little pissant to dictate what we do around here? He's had his head up his ass from day one."

45

Dick Lyng, now Secretary of Agriculture, was the political engineer who ran up massive USDA budgets.

Social Security, the centerpiece of the American welfare state, was overwhelmingly affirmed in the white heat of political confrontation. *(Left to right)* Claude Pepper: Eighty-year-old folk hero of radical senior activist groups. Bob Michel: He tried to keep the Republicans on board but couldn't. Tip O'Neill: He helped the intimidated politicians stop the Reagan Revolution dead in its tracks. Senator Moynihan: My former rabbi led the charge in defense of the S.S. status quo. This was truly the triumph of politics.

46

When I finally left the White House, in August 1985, the President had accepted but never understood the revolution I had brought to him on the eve of his election. And he had no idea of the failure I was leaving behind.

47

'I hope they're enjoying this,' it said. 'They've just put themselves out of business for the rest of the decade.'

Actually, it was worse. They had just put the Ways and Means Committee in the tax-raising business for years to come. And that would not prove nearly as much fun.

The final session with the Republicans lasted about two hours.* By the end of it, both Darman and I were shaking our heads. We wanted to win—if for different reasons—but neither of us had expected it would come to this.

The Boll Weevils assembled in the Oval Office later in the afternoon, and they had one thing on their minds—oil. By the time the dickering was over, Hance's royalty owners' gratuity had swollen to $13 billion.

Until then, the oil war had not bothered me in principle, although I cringed at the revenue loss. But Conable-Hance II now included something truly offensive under the heading of Oil Tax Break. The oil depletion allowance would remain frozen at twenty-two percent rather than be phased out, as the existing law called for.

That was the straw that finally broke my back. The $4 billion price tag was bad enough, but the principle was even worse. The depletion allowance was an unjustified and wasteful tax subsidy, a symbol of the corrupt political system the Reagan Revolution was challenging. And now the revolution had embraced even that in order to win.

Later that afternoon, Darman and I stood alone in the West Executive parking lot, numb. We were trying to make sense of the afternoon's events.

'I'm worried,' Darman said. 'Maybe we should take a dive on this.'

The tax battle still had not been won. More deals would have to be made over the remaining week before the vote in order to glue the GOP–Boll Weevil coalition back together again. We would have to make some of them. We didn't know if we should. And now Darman was proposing we sabotage ourselves by not cutting them.

'Yeah, I can hear Bill Thomas now,' I said. '"Time to open the soup line."'

---

* There had been preliminary sessions without the President that morning and in prior days.

It wouldn't be hard to cause the whole endeavor to collapse at the eleventh hour. All we would have to do was refuse a housing project here, a railgrade crossing there. Maybe even one water project feasibility study would do it.

We paced around the parking lot some more. 'I don't know which is worse,' Darman said, 'winning now and fixing up the budget mess later, or losing now and facing a political mess immediately.'

'I vote against both options,' I said, hoping to spur Darman into coming up with another of his clever stratagems. 'What's your write-in candidate this time?'

For a moment Darman got more serious than I had ever seen him. I thought he was about to unload a whole new game plan to rescue the tax bill from the insanity which had just been reached. Then he shrugged.

'Welcome to California!' he deadpanned. 'I believe it finally has come down to the White House versus the Democrats, to us versus them.'

Suddenly he was all business.

'Let's get at it,' he urged. 'We win it now, we fix it later. I can think of worse choices.'

'Like what?' I countered.

'Like what Eisenhower said when asked about Nixon's qualifications for President,' Darman responded. '"Give me a couple of weeks and I'll come up with an answer."'

It had been tempting, given the consequences we knew were in store if this bill went through. But in the end we chickened out. Calculated sabotage of our President's most cherished initiative was beyond the pale. We resolved to do whatever we could to help the White House and Treasury teams round up the necessary stray votes.

True, Conable-Hance II went 'whole hog' in 1985 and beyond. But the magic $150 billion 1984 ceiling had been breached by only a few billion. I thought I could live with that. And for Darman, there was no advantage in defeat. According to his theory, Ronald Reagan had to 'govern'. The Democratic bill was just as irresponsible as ours, and a 'win' for the Democratic leadership would only strengthen their hand in future battles, when the choice might not be merely between the lesser of two evils.

*   *   *

The following Monday evening, the President addressed the nation on TV. He delivered a masterpiece of propaganda.

Reagan's White House media men had got it all boiled down to two lines on a chart: It was 'our bill' versus 'their bill'. Our line went down and stayed down. Theirs went down and then came back up.

If presidential speeches were covered by a full disclosure law, the true meaning of this one would have caused an absolute panic. Conable-Hance II—'our bill'—was going to reduce the federal revenue base by *two trillion dollars* over the course of the decade.

There was not a hint, not one scintilla, about what all this fabulous 'giving' actually meant. The tens of millions of Social Security recipients, students, farmers, government pensioners, and other beneficiaries of federal largesse watching that night received no warning that their benefits would have to be deeply and suddenly slashed in order to keep the budget equation whole. The speech was an exercise in pure single-entry bookkeeping. It implied that a new era in free lunches had arrived, something more wonderful than anything the congressional politicians had ever before even imagined.

The President concluded his address with a summons to the public for support for this great boon: 'I urge you again to write to your senators and congressmen—you will make the difference again . . . Let us not stop now.'

We hadn't stopped, and now neither would the public. The letters and telegrams began arriving—bags of them descending upon congressional offices. And in the final two days before the vote, the tide began to shift our way.

Even so, a little last-minute lubrication was demanded. The Georgia delegation notified Ken Duberstein it was 'for rent'. I knew this was coming, and I gagged at the prospect. They wanted us to stop our attempts to abolish the peanut subsidy program.

I could have fought it; I probably could have stopped it. This was no nickel and dime program. It involved big money and a big principle: our free market farm policy.

The peanut growers had, in effect, a government-subsidized producer's cartel. It was a close second cousin to tobacco, and it was a pure corruption of·state power.

But Darman and I had made our decision. It was too late not to win. I agreed to the proposal and informed Jack Block later.

The peanut factor had an instant, decisive effect on the vote. Once the peanut district Georgians had gone over to us, it was OK for a few other urban Democrats in the delegation to do the same. There was safety in numbers.

Eight of the ten Georgia Democrats ended up voting for Conable-Hance II. The 'en bloc' switch of the Georgia Democrats in turn broke the back of the House leadership's fierce campaign to bring the Boll Weevils back into the Democratic column.

'We have wiped them out in the heart of Dixie,' Duberstein declared. More Boll Weevils got off the fence and crossed over to our side. Most had something in their pockets as they arrived.

What had been required to get them off the fence guaranteed that the massive tax cut enacted on 29 July 1981 never stood a chance of being paid for by a commensurate shrinkage of the welfare state. The critical votes that would bring about the former were bought by preserving the first programs that should have been excised from the latter.

Later on, I would come to understand the political equation of the American welfare state better. It would become clear to me how the peanut deal and other events of the last several days before the House showdown symbolically sealed the doom of the Reagan Revolution. They guaranteed that there would be only a half-revolution—and a fiscal disaster.

The peanut program is a wasteful boondoggle. By every surface measure, it should have expired for want of votes long ago. It is of consequence in only a few dozen counties in Georgia and Texas—out of the nation's 4,000 counties. Only a dozen congressmen care about it, along with a handful of senators.

But despite its midget constituency, it survives handsomely because there is always an opportunity for deals. It means almost everything to its handful of legislative guardians and almost nothing to everyone else. No one can resist the temptation to trade—even I couldn't.

The peanut program's survival nexus has profound implications. If it couldn't be eliminated, then almost nothing in the budget could. Almost everything else that costs serious money has a stronger case and a broader legislative base.

There were other signs over those last two days that the process of governance had gone haywire. On the day before the vote,

Democratic Congressman Norm Dicks of Washington announced his support for Conable-Hance II. Jim Wright must have gone into a cold sweat on hearing it. Dicks was a Democrat's Democrat, and his defection was, at the level of legislative politics, fatal. But in the larger scheme, it represented much more. Dicks was an articulate (Senator Henry) Jackson Democrat, supporter of a strong defense and a robust welfare state.

Jackson Democrats *had* to be implacable foes of Conable-Hance II, because the bill was the ideological opposite of what they believed in. The final version of the tax bill would reduce the federal revenue base to seventeen percent of GNP. But the defense budget that Scoop Jackson wanted, combined with the welfare state that Norm Dick's mentor, Senator Warren Magnuson, had built, cost twenty-two to twenty-three percent of GNP. The equation fit as snugly as a square peg in a round hole.

Even worse, Norm Dicks was one of the most astute, intelligent, and responsible younger Democratic politicians in the House. He was no snake oil vendor like Jim Wright; he knew the budget had to add up. But he was the opposite of a fiscal radical. There was no room in his political or ideological scheme for the draconian spending cutbacks the tax bill required.

In short, Norm Dicks's defection to Conable-Hance II was crazy. It didn't add up any more than our budget would. There was something in the air that final week that caused reasonable, intelligent people to take leave of their senses. And when it came time to perform the equally radical task of cutting the budget to fit the tax bill, those 236 congressmen who voted for our bill wouldn't be there. It was a coalition built on sand.

One final stray cat that wandered onto our side was Mario Biaggi of New York, and his defection was as instructive as Dicks's. An urban Democrat who knew nothing about the fiscal equation, Biaggi's snout was always buried up to his eyes in the trough. He announced his support for Conable-Hance II on the grounds that the President had promised him to support restoration of the Social Security minimum benefit. That was the ultimate fiscal contradiction, even if Biaggi had overinterpreted the President's assurances.

Paying for Conable-Hance II required taking checks out of the mail in the amount of hundreds of billions of dollars over the decade. When it came to cancelling entitlements, among all the choices available, the minimum benefit was the single most easy to justify.

Thus, again, one of the last votes for the tax cut was traded (if only in the mind of the trader) for preservation of the first spending dollar that had to be eliminated. American government had come unhinged.

Books such as this invariably assign a great deal of blame, to say nothing of indulging in a little bit of blame avoidance, but any objective history of the Reagan era will show that it was the White House which started the tax-bidding war in the summer of 1981.

Once we refused to compromise on a supply-side tax cut that had no real support among the politicians, the die was cast. We then had to storm the House floor again in order to win. Yet going for broke inherently threatened the majority Democrats with yet another humiliation.

But the Democrats had had enough. They turned the tax bill into a grudge match. If, as the majority party, they did not reclaim their power to control the House floor, they would be permanently under the heel of the Reagan coalition. Or so they thought.

Looking back, it is clear that the House Democrats in fact panicked unnecessarily. The GOP–Boll Weevil coalition had already been broken during the crucible of budget cutting. And the economy was sliding into recession. Given those two developments, the House Democrats would have been back in the saddle soon enough.

They launched their comeback effort just one month too soon. Had they waited, they would have saved themselves great effort— and the country much fiscal grief. But they did not, and the consequence would make them, as well as everyone else, miserable for a decade.

The freak accident of fiscal governance that decimated the nation's fiscal equilibrium and economic stability in July 1981 was thus a consequence of the clash between the Reagan Revolution and political reality.

The Kemp-Roth tax cut standing alone never had a chance. Only its merger with the business coalition's 10–5–3 depreciation liberalization bill and the cornucopia of tax ornaments generated in June and July by the congressional politicians made it legislatively viable.

NEW LESSONS: THE POLITICS OF GIVING

Due to all the 'backloaded' congressional ornaments, the size of the tax cut just kept growing beyond 1984. It was like a fiscal volcano rising steadily against the distant horizon.

Nearly a trillion dollars in tax revenue had to be spent on the business coalition plan and the congressional ornaments in order to pass a supply-side rate reduction costing almost an equal amount (see below).

Year	Kemp-Roth*	Business Coalition Bill (10–5–3)	Politicians' Tax Ornaments	Total Cost	Percentage of GNP
		Cost of the 1981 Tax Reduction Bill (billions)			
1982	$ 25	$10	$ 6	$ 41	1.3%
1983	58	18	17	93	2.9%
1984	87	26	24	137	3.8%
1985	100	36	33	169	4.4%
1986	113	50	48	211	5.0%
1987	127	61	63	251	5.5%
1988	142	65	76	283	5.8%
1989	158	66	92	316	6.0%
1990	173	70	109	352	6.2%
Total	$983	$402	$468	$1,853	–

* As modified to 5–10–10.

Note: Priced out at 1985 income levels. As estimated in July 1981, cost figures were slightly higher due to assumption of higher inflation. July 1981 estimates, for example, priced out 1984 revenue loss at $149.5 billion.

Years later, in 1985, my old rabbi, Pat Moynihan, would say that we had pushed through the tax cut to deliberately create this giant deficit. In truth, not six of the 600 players in the game of fiscal governance in the spring and summer of 1981 would have willed this outcome. Yet caught up in the powerful forces unleashed by the dangerous experiment of a few supply-siders who had got hold of the President's good ear, they let it happen just the same.

10
The Morning After: The Final Lessons

The President was stunned. I'd just shown him that our economic program might result in huge deficits. His response was an irritated stammer.

'Dave, if what you are saying is true . . . then Tip O'Neill was right all along.'

'Mr President, oh no!' I almost yelled, 'I'm not saying that at all. Not in the slightest.'

It was August 3. The battles were over, and we had gathered for a working luncheon in the Cabinet Room. The cuisine was lean—the country's top officials were trying to cut their own fat perhaps more vigorously than they had the government's—but it was de luxe, even sumptuous, and served with clockwork efficiency by the White House stewards.

Whenever the President attended these occasions, the table was full. His presence always guaranteed a big turnout. Baker, Deaver and Meese couldn't afford not to keep an eye on each other during such sessions.

At this particular session the top economic policy team—Regan, Weidenbaum, Marty Anderson and I—was also in attendance. So were the other key White House staffers, including Dick Darman, Craig Fuller, Dave Gergen, Larry Speakes, and a few others.

The luncheon was the first opportunity we'd had in weeks to assemble the whole team around one table and take stock of where we were. Since early June, the White House had been at the vortex of all the pandemonium, and there had been little time for reflection.

We had had massive tax and spending reduction bills moving through the Congress simultaneously. Each cog in the great machine of government had been fully engaged. Crises had been occurring every single day, involving the White House in a nonstop fire drill. Nearly every day there were LSG meetings, hurried (and harried) tactical consultations, and a continual flow of congressmen and senators in and out of the Cabinet Room and Oval Office. At times there had been more Republicans in the West Wing lobby than in the Capitol Hill Club bar. Which is to say, a lot.

By August 3, this swirl of events had finally quieted. The Sunday papers the day before had been filled with heady stuff. The Reagan team had defied all the odds, had driven through the Congress in only five months the most sweeping and radical change in national economic policy since the New Deal.

The 'think pieces' by the same reporters and pundits who had been so sceptical at first contained a note of awe and grudging admiration. The nation's economic policy was now in the hands of a determined and effective White House team that knew what it wanted and how to get it. That was the theme that ran through all the stories on what we had done.

The luncheon should have been a victory celebration. But I was worried to death about where my numbers were going. If the President and Cabinet had been paying attention, I would have already scared the hell out of them with my numerous warnings, especially the most recent one on July 13.

It was then that I had reminded everyone of the 'growing budget squeeze' and a dramatically 'worsening out-year problem'. To balance our 1984 budget, I repeated, we would have to make draconian, bone-wrenching additional cuts in the domestic budget—twenty-five percent cuts in everything from the FBI to food stamps, farm subsidies, education aid, the National Park Service, and the Washington Monument. *One fourth.*

My July 13 numbers and warnings, however, had floated out the Cabinet Room windows and into the Rose Garden. They had been accompanied by a tabulation of all that we were on the verge of accomplishing in the pending tax and reconciliation bills. As a consequence, the good news had blacked out the bad.

So today I had come with the whole can of worms, deliberately prepared to ruin everyone's lunch. I was going to shock them into recognizing that the budget picture was bad going on awful.

At the end of the dessert, I passed out a stack of thick black binders, each one forty-two pages long. Groans around the table—another Stockman paper flood.

I didn't usually prepare opening lines for these occasions, but I had given careful thought to these. What I had settled on was not Churchillian, perhaps, but it was designed to get their attention.

'The scent of victory is still in the air,' I began, 'but I'm not going to mince words. We're heading for a crash landing on the budget. We're facing potential deficit numbers so big that they could *wreck* the President's entire economic program.'

The chatter suddenly stopped. Even Mike Deaver, as I recall, stuck his spoon back in his sherbet and started listening.

'It's going to be harder than hell to get to a balanced budget even by 1986,' I continued. 'On the margin, every single important number in the budget is going in the wrong direction.

'So I want to beg your indulgence for about thirty minutes. We have to systematically walk through this step by step so everyone understands it.

'Then we're going to have to take a hard look at the options. We've reached the point where we have to make strategic choices, fundamental choices.'

For dramatic effect, I finished my introduction with a little flourish. 'This seems like a day of victory. In reality, it's a day of reckoning.' Definitely not Churchill, but they were listening.

I quickly took them through the black books containing all the bad news. During past briefings some people would listen to me and ignore the books, others would read ahead and not listen at all. Usually by the time we came to the discussion period, everyone was all over the lot—a UN meeting without translators.

So I had spent hour after hour working on the format of this particular briefing. It had to be a masterpiece of clarity. The diagnosis of the problem and the options for a solution had to leap up off the pages and shake them by the lapels.

The first page highlighted the basic ideas:

The long-term outlook is grim. We face a minimum budget deficit of $60 billion for each of the next four years.

The briefing book then systematically demonstrated that this was a best-case outlook, even if we got *every dime* of the spending cuts we had proposed in February and March. The more likely case was a deficit somewhere in the $100 billion range. Unless a *major, new mid-course correction plan* was launched by the administration, the budget deficit was positioned to soar out of control.

I reviewed the history of the last six months with them: no progress on the $44 billion magic asterisk; the huge extra cost of the tax-bidding war; the technical errors in the budget estimates; and the numerous spending cuts which were in deep trouble on the Hill.

Finally, I brought in a new element.

Our whole budget plan, I told them, depended on the accuracy of 'Rosy Scenario', the five-year economic forecast we had fashioned in February. All spring and summer, however, I had been hounded by Jerry Jordan, one of the three members of the Council of Economic Advisors, and Larry Kudlow, both of whom insisted that the blatant inconsistency between our monetary policy and the forecast needed urgent correction. The original budget numbers were misleading us. The briefing paper laid out the problem squarely:

> Most economists believe that our mid-session GNP forecast is *incompatible* with the Fed's announced goals . . . This anomaly must be soon corrected. But the consequence will be . . . lower revenue estimates.

For the purposes of the August 3 briefing, I had continued to assume an early, powerful supply-side expansion—five percent real GNP growth. Nevertheless, page twenty should have been an eye opener. It showed that even with a forecast more compatible with the monetary policy actually in effect, the deficit would rise to $81 billion in 1983—and reach $112 billion by 1986.

When I had finished with this part of the briefing, I turned to look at the President. He looked . . . not very well, and it had nothing to do with his health. That was when he said I seemed to be agreeing with Tip O'Neill. Ed Meese jumped in, as he usually did when he saw that his boss was discomfited and at a loss.

'What about the revenue feedback from the tax bill?' he asked. 'You haven't taken account of that in these scary numbers.' His tone was slightly annoyed.

Meese's remark about the revenue feedback referred, of course, to the Laffer curve. The whole California gang had taken it literally (and primitively). The way they talked, they seemed to expect that once the supply-side tax cut was in effect, additional revenue would start to fall, manna-like, from the heavens.

Since January, I had been explaining that there is no literal Laffer curve. 'Higher real GNP and employment growth will not increase projected revenues by a dime,' I reiterated. 'Remember, we're putting the squeeze on inflation at the same time. That will bring down the growth rate of money GNP *and* federal revenue. The budget benefit of the combined anti-inflation and tax cut program comes entirely on the *spending side*. We get lower *outlays* for unemployment related programs and indexed entitlements. But there is *no* revenue feedback. What you see is all we've got.'

I had repeated this little lecture until I was blue in the face. But they never stopped asking about the magical Laffer curve. So, confident that the question would come up again in the face of my dire warnings about deficits, I had prepared a special tab in the new briefing book showing why there was no Laffer curve when you were trying to cure a high inflation, low growth economy.

The tab contained two multi-year budget scenarios. One showed the effect of higher real GNP and employment growth in a zero inflation gold standard economy. In that scenario, money GNP growth and real GNP growth were the same because you had zero inflation. As a consequence, more real growth gave you more money GNP, higher revenues, and lower unemployment related outlays. The deficit plummeted. It looked just like Professor Laffer's napkin.

The other scenario showed the effect of our program in a high inflation, low growth baseline economy that looked just like the 'mess' we had inherited. Then, you superimposed on the baseline a steady reduction in money growth. By the fourth year out, the revenue number declined by $141 billion from the baseline level. This reflected the effect of lower inflation and money GNP.

Next, you superimposed a supply-side tax cut. By the fourth year, the outlay number dropped by $89 billion from the baseline. This reflected the effect of more real growth and less inflation in the total money GNP. Outlays came down because you spent less on indexed entitlements and unemployment benefits.

But when you looked at the net effect on the deficit, it was higher by $52 billion. Hence, the dilemma we faced was clear. Making the real-world economy 'well' would not improve the deficit numbers *compared to the projections we had inherited.*

As I looked around the table, it was evident that I had accomplished . . . nothing. Those who already understood this (Anderson, Darman and Weidenbaum) nodded their heads. The others were puzzled, bored, or annoyed.

I pushed on, turning to some possible solutions. I would just have to keep chipping away at the Laffer curve until everyone finally understood.

'We've got all the benefit of the economic recovery built into the numbers already,' I repeated. 'So the only way to reduce these red ink projections is by cutting more spending or raising some new revenue. That is the strategic choice we now face.' There was some shifting in the seats.

One option was to abandon our 1984 balanced budget target and just hope we would get there by 1986. But Weidenbaum strongly objected to that idea, as did a number of others.

'No,' said the President, 'we can't give up on the balanced budget. Deficit spending is how we got into this mess.'

The next option was to slow the defense buildup. Due to the February miscalculation, we now had a real growth rate for defense spending of 9.5 percent built into the budget. If we slowed that to seven percent over the next five years, it would reduce 1984 spending by $16 billion. And the savings would double that by 1986.

The President didn't wait for the others to respond to this one. He was very firm: 'There must be no perception by anyone in the world that we're backing down an inch on the defense buildup.

'When I was asked during the campaign about what I would do if it came down to a choice between defense and deficits,' he continued, 'I always said national security had to come first, and the people applauded every time.' While that position was plausible it was not compatible with ruling out the idea of accepting a deficit.

So after again insisting that strategic choices were necessary, I moved on to the next option. We could raise $15 to $20 billion per year through a tax on imported oil, alcohol, and tobacco; and by imposing some new user fees.

I quickly added, 'This option *in no way* contradicts our supply-side income tax cut. There are some ways to raise revenue without hurting the economy.'

Don Regan pounced.

'I strongly object to that kind of tax increase talk,' he harrumphed. 'We've just worked our fanny off to give the American people a *tax cut*.'

He trotted out his favorite analogy. 'You can raise the water level or lower the bridge. Our job is to do the latter—to cut the spending.'

No one contradicted him. That left us with only one solution—further deep cuts in domestic spending. My list was draconian: ten million food stamp recipients at the upper end of the eligibility scale would lose their benefits. Two million elderly people would have their SSI* benefits cut by twenty-five percent—in order to protect the blind and disabled and still get a ten percent overall cut in the program. Several million pensioned veterans would face a twenty percent cut in benefits. Farm subsidies, mass transit grants, small business aid, Export-Import Bank loans, and dozens more programs would have to be eliminated entirely.

I had been in favor of such action all along, but I had grown wary of all the fuzzy, abstract White House talk about spending cuts.

None was fuzzier than their talk about an option I had included to reduce federal civilian employment by eight percent. Inclusion of this minor proposal was a big mistake. It started them on a new round of chatter about 'excessive overhead' and 'bureaucratic waste'. Unfortunately, we weren't going to solve a $60 to $100 billion deficit problem by dumping a few thousand useless federal employees, which would reduce the federal payroll by only $3 billion. There just weren't enough of them to amount to serious dollar savings. I had had a chart prepared to show why. Among the roughly one million non-Department of Defense civilian employees, a handful of essential agencies accounted for more than half. The FBI, Customs Service, State Department, Social Security Administration, Immigration Service, IRS,** Veterans Hospital System, and the FAA† Air Traffic Control System employed about 450,000 people. There was room for trimming in these agencies, sure, but dramatic sums couldn't be gained from it. They had to look at the tough program cuts I had outlined instead.

But the group in the Cabinet Room never got that far. Meese

* Supplemental Security Income.
** Internal Revenue Service, the tax collecting agency.
† Federal Aviation Administration.

warmed up to the employment reduction idea immediately. He reminded everyone of how much had been accomplished by trimming bureaucratic overhead in Sacramento. Heads nodded.

I had tried, over the past six months, to educate Meese to the fact that the federal budget was different. It consisted mostly of entitlement payments and subsidies. Paying the salaries of bureaucrats was irritating, yes, but it was essentially irrelevant to the big picture. Still, Meese never shook his old illusions.

Nor did the President. 'The federal government's lathered in fat when it comes to employment,' he insisted. 'We should tell all the agencies—to the rear, march.'

Before long, we were out of time as usual. Nothing had been decided. But at least I had created a new air of urgency about the deficit threat among the White House senior staff. I had tried to create terror; I would have to settle for discomfort.

I thought, afterwards, that I had made some progress in getting the White House group to understand the severity of the deficit problem. I believed they were beginning to recognize that we had implemented only *half* of the Reagan Revolution with the giant tax cut. The job of drastically paring down federal spending to match the new, lower federal revenue level had only just begun.

In fact, I had made no progress where it counted—with the President. My anxious response to this 'Tip was right' remark shows what stood at the heart of the problem: me.

I knew a dozen precise reasons why the numbers were getting worse. What I did not yet realize was that the fundamental plan was fatally flawed. I had been warning about the problems but went on stoutly defending the basic design. It was a schizoid message, and as such, one the President would never respond to.

On the one side of the fiscal equation, the President saw the long list of budget cuts; on the other, the tax cut. The latter, he felt, would somehow take care of itself. Some people would start making more than four movies a year; others would produce more of everything else that the US economy produced. The new revenues to balance the budget would be there.

To be sure, he believed the spending cuts were important, too. We should press ahead and cut wherever we could. We should get rid of useless bureaucrats.

But a drastic shrinking of the welfare state was not his conception of the Reagan Revolution. It was mine.

The President had a half-revolution in his mind. I had put a whole revolution into his budget plan. The August 3 briefing didn't penetrate the disconnect at all.

Jim Baker called an LSG meeting the next day, August 4, to consider the 'next steps on the budget'. I used the occasion to present a strategy paper that contained a bold idea on how to proceed.

We couldn't afford to wait until January 1982 to submit a new budget as part of the normal cycle. When Congress returned after Labor Day, the alarming deficit projections I had warned about in the Cabinet Room yesterday would be all over the streets. The Congressional Budget Office did a routine update during August, and they would come up with essentially the same numbers.

I told the group that if the administration appeared not to have an *immediate* plan to cope with the new distressing picture, the repercussions could be awful. Our already frail congressional base could be hurt. Worse, the financial markets might lose what confidence they had in our plan.

What I proposed, then, was to submit our 1983 budget not in January, but during a 'September Offensive'. It would have to cut the whole range of federal domestic programs to the bone. But beyond that, there were three additional things we had to do: launch a new offensive on the Social Security reform plan; fashion a 'Reagan populism' with which to counter all the predictable demagoguery we would hear about the new budget cuts (that would mean taking a hard 'crack at selective tax loopholes'); and finally, scale back defense. This last was going to be the tough one. The President did not like to hear talk about scaling back defense, but we had to try. Both the numbers and the politics made it unavoidable.

This time what I had to say fell on receptive ears. Meese, Baker and Regan all thought the proposal sound. Apparently, the grim implications of my Cabinet Room briefing had sunk in overnight.

We had to get this whole effort moving fast, so Meese and Baker agreed to schedule working meetings with the President later in the month out on the west coast. I thought, 'Great. They really understand this can't wait.'

Looking back, I don't know why I was so optimistic. All I wanted to do was knock on the same doors—Social Security, defense, tax loopholes, and new domestic spending cuts—that had been slammed in my face earlier. So what was it that made me think the September Offensive was going to work? Just my own stubbornness.

I wouldn't take 'no' for an answer. Never mind that the 536 politicians who had actually been elected by the voters weren't interested in my revolution or my theory.

I would spend the next two months learning that all the doors were shut. In fact, most of them had been locked from the start.

For the moment, however, I was eager and ready for a new budget blitz, and getting the defense numbers back into line would be the first order of business. The professional defense staff at OMB were delighted at the prospect. They had been shocked and incredulous in February when we handed over $1.46 trillion to the Department of Defense (DOD).

Here it is necessary to backtrack a little in our story. We had been heading towards this showdown for months. After I had discovered my horrifying calculator error made in the late January Friday night session in Cap Weinberger's office at the Pentagon, I had naturally assumed that the White House would make the necessary downward adjustments at the earliest opportunity. It was obvious that the numbers we had in the budget were flagrantly excessive as a matter of pure fiscal affordability. But caught up in all the other battles of the spring and summer, they had actually done just the opposite.

Weinberger had decided to consider our back-of-the-envelope scribblings as writ in stone. It was, to say the least, an extremely ex post facto interpretation, since we had all been clear that Friday night that our calculations were very tentative.

Nevertheless, every dime of the $1.46 trillion had, in effect, been dumped into the Pentagon's vast and awesome budget-making machinery. By late April the military bureaucracy had cranked out a budget based on them. The Pentagon had already figured out how to spend every single dollar—tanks, ships, so many million gallons of olive drab paint.

Weinberger had settled for a 'one-option' defense program. There had been other numbers than $1.46 trillion that could be put into the overall DOD* pot and other ways to allocate them among the

* Department of Defense.

'requirements'. But the service bureaucracies had come up with a single plan and Weinberger had become their trustee.

It was ironic in the extreme: the Secretary of Defense of the most tight-fisted and anti-bureaucratic administration of this century had produced a $1.46 trillion budget by delegating the job to the world's largest bureaucracy. Cap the Knife had become Cap the Shovel.

As the hectic days wore on, the Defense spending issue kept slipping through the cracks, even as fixing the $44 billion hole in our budget became more urgent. Through it all, however, I went on warning the LSG whenever I got the chance.

By the middle of May I had sufficiently alarmed Meese that he organized a private luncheon in the Roosevelt Room.

There, I once again outlined the problem: the budget would not add up if we didn't reconsider the February numbers.

I also told them that it had to be brought to the President's attention as soon as possible. The Pentagon's self-generated $1.46 trillion budget would be complete within weeks and circulating throughout the system. Changing it after that would be tough and potentially embarrassing.

Meese volunteered to arrange a meeting with the President and Weinberger. I'd wanted an informal meeting—one in which we could discuss the unplanned jam we had got into, and quietly figure out some way to extricate ourselves.

Meese, however, misunderstood the kind of meeting I had in mind and had agreed when Weinberger told him he would use the meeting as an opportunity officially to present his '1983–87 Defense Policy Guidance'. So Weinberger used the 'informal' clear-the-air meeting I'd asked for to get the President to sign off on the bloated February numbers—once and for all.

'The horse is being let out of the barn, Ed,' I pleaded.

Meese said not to get alarmed; he never did. Besides, he said, 'Nothing is forever.' We'd be able to 'revisit' the problem later.

The time to revisit a decision that had already been made by the President was now. Nevertheless, by midsummer the OMB staff had thoroughly analyzed the Pentagon's plans for spending this fabulous sum of money, and they had practically as many suggestions about how to trim the 'top line' as Weinberger's budgeteers had shopping lists. We soon had a detailed program of line-item adjustments that, taken together, would have scaled back the real growth in DOD to the figure that I proposed in the August 3 budget briefing.

Over five years, the savings would go far toward reducing the out-year deficits. We called our OMB plan the Slower Growth Alternative (SGA), and it was an apt, if not very catchy, name for what we had in mind. What we were proposing was hardly traumatic. In fact, the savings were minuscule compared with the massive, original defense budget numbers we had erroneously calculated in Weinberger's office.

Instead of $1.46 trillion in defense spending over five years, our Slower Growth Alternative provided $1.33 trillion. You practically had to look at the difference closely in order to avoid a rounding error. Weinberger could keep ninety-two percent of his budget. It seemed more than reasonable.

We had taken the utmost care to ensure that SGA conformed to the administration's highest defense priorities—to the extent that these were ascertainable. No cut was proposed at all, for example, in any of the basic strategic modernization programs.

The Pentagon's proposed funding levels for the B-1 bomber, the MX missile, the Trident submarine, a new sea-based strategic missile, and the cruise missile program would all remain unscathed. Those programs would receive more than $150 billion over five years.

Likewise, SGA accepted most of the Pentagon plans for modernizing key conventional weapons systems. It preserved funding for 5,000 new army tanks over five years, compared with the 1,800 that had been built during the previous five years. The Carter lame-duck budget had proposed funding 500 new Air Force fighter aircraft over five years. SGA provided for 1,000, only slightly less than the 1,190 DOD wanted.

With ships, it was much the same. The Carter lame-duck budget provided $55 billion for new surface combatants, attack submarines, aircraft carriers, and other support ships over five years. The OMB plan raised this to $81 billion and 122 ships, three fourths of the way toward the $95 billion and 145 ships the Navy was insisting on.

The OMB plan also provided for substantial military pay increases, as well as a big increase in operating, training, spare parts, repair, and readiness funds. Our plan called for an annual real growth of eleven percent in military operating budgets, compared with the paltry three percent of the Carter era.

The bottom line was that you could do a *lot* to strengthen the military with $1.33 trillion. Every aspect of our capabilities would be given a big-bucks boost. What the Slower Growth Alternative called for was, mostly, trimmings and gleanings. In only one or two instances did it challenge basic defense policy.

The Pentagon was lousy with civilians, for instance. If more manpower was needed to support the buildup, it was painfully clear it could be had by redeploying some of the 914,000 civilian employees already on the Pentagon payroll. The 75,000 new people Weinberger was demanding simply were not needed.

Procurement of 'administrative vehicles' was scheduled to jump from 2,000 to 18,000 per year. Did the military truly need nine times more passenger sedans than it had the year before? Similarly, Army ammunition procurement was scheduled to rise by 166 percent in two years. Purchases of such war machines as earth movers, trucks, fire engines, pumps and compressors, and welding gear were scheduled to rise by 130 percent over the same period.

The OMB proposal did, on the other hand, propose to cancel a handful of major conventional weapons systems—out of the dozens and dozens called for in the Pentagon's five-year plan. One was a $3 billion aircraft carrier.

The $3 billion was just for the carrier, mind. The aircraft it would carry and the escort ships to support and protect it cost another $15 billion.

The carrier was part of Navy Secretary John Lehman's plan for a 600-ship fleet. A naval aviator himself, Lehman was partial to that branch of the service. At the heart of his big Navy were the so-called carrier battle groups—the aircraft carriers and their flotillas of escorts. Lehman wanted to increase the number of these carrier battle groups from thirteen to fifteen.

The expansion was based on the theory of 'getting in harm's way' by attacking the Soviets' arctic ports in the event of war. I asked a lot of experts about this strategy, and I couldn't find one outside the Pentagon who didn't think the idea was absurd. Soviet land-based aircraft would wipe out the carriers long before they got there.

So, I pressed, what *else* can you do with two extra $18 billion carrier battle groups? The answers all came out in a fog about 'deployment rotation cycles' and 'showing the flag'. OK, OK. What do the carrier battle groups stationed in the Mediterranean do if war breaks out in central Europe?

'They get the hell out into the deep Atlantic as fast as they can,' my Navy expert answered.

So I came out against the additional $3 billion aircraft carrier. I did not dismiss the possibility that there was a valid military case to be made for it; but it could only have been marginal compared with the severity of the deficit we faced. Aircraft carriers would not do a country much good if that country were bankrupt.

It was much the same in the case of the new armored personnel carrier the Army wanted to buy. It was called the Bradley Fighting Vehicle and cost $1.7 million per copy. We were planning to buy 7,000 of them.

The Bradley was a bizarre hybrid—a combination battlefield taxi for transporting troops and mini-tank with light armor, a 25mm gun, and TOW missiles. As a taxi, it was way too expensive, nine times more per unit than a modernized version of the old Army personnel carrier (the M-113) that was then being sold to NATO allies.

But that wasn't all. Its armor was not heavy enough to go up against Soviet tanks, yet the Army's theory was that the infantry would fight from inside the Bradley, shooting through portholes. The OMB military analysts were not convinced that the belly of a Bradley would be a very safe place to hide in a battlefield full of Soviet tanks. One direct hit would take out a whole squad.

The case against the Bradley was fairly clear-cut: It was too expensive to ride in and too vulnerable to fight in. Before we bought 7,000 of them, in lieu of far less expensive, traditional battlefield taxis, the case *for* the Bradley ought to be demonstrated rigorously.

Another candidate for cancellation was the F-18 fighter/attack plane. This had been an economizing brainchild of the Carter Administration. The same plane would perform four military missions: as a light attack and fighter aircraft for the Navy, and as the same for the Marine Corps. In this configuration, the F-18 made good sense. At $17 million per plane, it was also cheap, relatively speaking.

The Reagan defense budget bonanza put an end to the four-mission theory straight away. The Navy decided it would meet its need for additional fighters by using a different plane, the F-14. It was much more capable, but it was also more than twice as expensive. Under the F-18 four-mission scenario, production of the F-14 was supposed to stop. But now the Navy had the F-14 back in the budget, several more hundred of them over the five-year plan.

Likewise, the Marine Corps now assigned its light attack mission to still another plane, the AV-8B. It was a brand-new aircraft, and the Marines wanted 228 of them.

Thus, the F-18's four missions had shrunk to two, and we now had three planes in production instead of one. One thing, however, had not changed. The DOD budget still called for the eventual purchase of a thousand F-18's, at a cost of $30 billion. That was the same number called for in the original economy-minded four-mission plan, except now the element of economy was long gone. That was what happened when you set $1.46 trillion on a stump near the Pentagon and turned your back for a moment.

Another system on our hit list was the Army's DIVAD, or 'Sergeant York' gun. It was a new, divisional air defense gun that cost more than $4 million per copy. My analysts believed it was too complicated to work reliably in a battlefield environment, since it was designed to rumble along over rough terrain at high speeds carrying the latest in computerized electronics.

Its chief virtue was that its gun was radar-guided. However, its range was less than that of the radar-seeking missiles of Soviet attack helicopters and other aircraft. It was a battlefield bull's-eye that couldn't shoot back. To us at OMB, it did not seem like a good trade-off between budget dollars and military capability.*

All in all, our Slower Growth Alternative was a pro-defense budgeteer's approach to the administration's massive, planned military buildup. After all the marginal trimming, the Defense budget would still be *fifty-two percent* bigger in after-inflation dollars by 1986 than in 1980. Indeed, the Pentagon's budget would still be nearly twenty percent bigger in after-inflation dollars than it had been at the peak of either the Korean or the Vietnam wars. Given the frightening deficits that were now looming, I didn't see how my proposal could seem anything but commonsensical. This time I was confident I had my ducks all in a row.

*   *   *

* DIVAD was finally cancelled in 1985 after more than a billion dollars had been spent on it.

THE MORNING AFTER: THE FINAL LESSONS

On August 18, Ed Harper, Bill Schneider and I headed out to California for a meeting with the President later that day. It was to be a budget planning session for our September Offensive—and the subject was defense.

The meeting was being billed as a 'showdown' between me and the 'other side'. Weinberger had some pretty good support on his side of the OK Corral: State, CIA, the National Security Council and the Joint Chiefs of Staff. In a fitting gesture of economizing, however, both sides flew out on the same Air Force plane.

Ed Harper had the toughest job on my team, at least as far as getting us to the Los Angeles Century Plaza Hotel was concerned. We had put the whole briefing on about three dozen huge poster-board charts. He and Schneider had drawn straws to see who got to carry them; Ed won the honor of lugging them around.

By now graphics and display had become a fetish with me. We had worked on the poster-board charts all weekend. Somehow, I had to get this mountain of budget numbers and welter of policy issues into a format that they could understand. Multicolor bar charts, bold lines going up, down, and sideways, arrow-headed pointers, boxed-in highlights—anything to simplify the issues.

It was Jim Watt, the Secretary of the Interior who had impressed on me the importance of being explicit.

'The only way you can solve the big, complicated issues,' he joked, 'is to elevate them to the highest possible level of incompetence.'

Much as I hated to admit it, I knew that was exactly where I was headed. No one who might potentially be on my side—Meese, Baker, Deaver, Regan—knew anything about the defense budget at all. Come to think of it, Weinberger didn't know that much either; in his present capacity he was a salesman. But he'd have plenty of heavy artillery with him—Al Haig, Frank Carlucci, and Admiral Bobby Inman, deputy director of the CIA.

I walked into the meeting knowing I would never be able to persuade the President directly.

'Defense,' he had said repeatedly, 'is not a budget issue. You spend what you need.'

Just possibly correct. The only problem was there was no tribunal of wise men who could objectively and precisely quantify the 'need'. In fact, DOD arrived at the conclusion that it needed a quarter of a trillion dollars per year for defense by means of a subjective and approximate process. The theory was that you started at the top by defining broad national security objectives, such as deterring a nuclear attack. Then as you moved down the pyramid, you determined missions and capabilities; then force structure, weapons, and resources; then procurement rates and operating tempos. At the bottom of the pyramid was a vast array of clerks counting up how many repair kits, screwdrivers, and paper cup dispensers would be needed to deter a Russian first strike.

That, anyway, was the theory of defense budgets. The way it actually worked was rather different. The process really began at the bottom of the pyramid. The clerks decided what they wanted, their superiors decided what they wanted; the colonels what they wanted; the generals what they wanted . . . and what ended up on the Secretary of Defense's desk was a wish list a mile long. 'Need', therefore, as defined by DOD was an unscientific melding of the wish list that rose up from the bottom and the policy guidance which came down from the top.

The proposition that I was about to put to the meeting was simple enough: what the Pentagon 'needed' we could not afford. In my analysis, defense spending was not exempt from budgeting. It was, in fact, a difficult, complex exercise in just that science.

But since I knew all this was not going to penetrate through to the President, I decided to use a very carefully planned approach. I thought of it as a kind of jujitsu. I would present my case in such a way as to get the top White House people to use their weight against DOD, and DOD to use its weight against itself.

My opening proposition would be that the 1984 deficit had to come down by at least $75 billion. That proposition, I assumed, would be accepted with acclaim.

The second proposition would be that the $75 billion could not be cut exclusively from domestic spending. That might be philosophically justifiable, but it would never fly on Capitol Hill. Against the chance that someone might say, 'Why not?', I was prepared. It was all laid out in political Technicolor: 'Cut AFDC twenty percent . . . cut school lunches forty percent . . . triple Medicare deductible . . . cut Indian education 50 percent . . . eliminate public housing subsidies.' That was 'all' we had to cut to save $75 billion.

Which would force the White House staff to lean hard into the defense budget. If that's what it would take, they would hardly let the Pentagon get off scot-free. The gap would have to be closed with a combination of defense and domestic cuts.

My third proposition would be that my Slower Growth Alternative represented the *true* seven percent real defense growth policy. Yet the $17 billion in 1984 defense savings meant that we could take some of the worst 'screamers' (the President's term for politically difficult budget cuts) off the hit list.

Weinberger, Haig and the others would now be leaning hard the other way, against the lower defense budget. But I would be ready. Just a slight flick of the leg and they would come crashing down.

The first thing Weinberger would say was that a defense cut would be a bad signal to the Soviets.

I had two charts to trip him up on that. One highlighted the strategic weapons program, the area of most concern, given the Soviet challenge. It had a bar for DOD's proposed strategic weapons budget (the MX missile, the B-1 bomber, the Trident sub, etc.) and a similar bar for SGA's proposals. They were the *exact same size*. The only difference was their color. That meant no cut was involved.

The other chart showed bars representing the US defense budget when the Soviets invaded Afghanistan, and the out-year US defense budget under SGA. The latter was 160 percent higher.

Still, I knew someone would say, 'But the Soviets have 45,000 tanks and we have only 10,000. We can't cut the conventional modernization program.' Here Ed Harper (a certified black belt) would be ready to lay the M-1 tank chart on the easel. The DOD bar for tanks showed '5,270' on top—that was how many they planned to procure. The SGA showed '5,270', too.

We also had two bars for military pay increases, both showing the same levels. Weinberger was always talking about how under Carter pay policy, half the Navy was on food stamps. Not with SGA. We'd even come with backup charts in case we needed them, all with bars for all sorts of defense items. You could construct a lot of equal bars when you were spending $1.33 trillion.

By the end of the match—that is, meeting—all the players would be on the mat. I had anticipated every move, and at the last there would be nowhere to go except my way. The President would experience *satori** and order a defense budget compromise.

*   *   *

* A Zen Buddhist term meaning enlightenment.

Riding the elevator to the top of the towering Century Plaza Hotel, I couldn't wait to get started. I smiled to myself thinking about Jim Watt's advice. The issue was being elevated to a very high level of incompetence indeed.

Within a few minutes, my plan was in pieces.

I had just finished Proposition One, explaining that our minimum 1984 cut target had to be $75 billion. 'And that will only give us one chance in five of getting a balanced budget,' I said. 'The baseline deficit could easily be much higher.'

I heard hooves pawing the ground. Then a snort. 'Wait a minute here,' said Don Regan. 'We at Treasury don't accept these big deficit projections.' I was slightly taken aback by this, since I had never heard him say it before.

Regan turned, the better to address the President.

'Mr President, I want to remind you that your program hasn't even taken effect yet,' he said. 'That happens on October 1. After that, we think these deficit numbers are going to come out a lot lower.'

My swelling deficit projections had nothing to do with the effective date of the tax cut, which seemed uppermost in the mind of the Treasury Secretary. I was still assuming five percent real GNP growth starting in the fourth quarter of 1981 precisely as we had forecast. To be sure, there was no sensible basis for this assumption. But I wasn't even challenging it.

It was a colossal non sequitur, and he was scoring a point with it. He was also undermining the entire exercise. If you didn't need to save $75 billion, well, why fiddle with defense? Or anything else?

I moved on to Proposition Two, that we couldn't cut $75 billion from domestic spending alone, and here too I ran into something I had not anticipated—essentially a problem of the dangling digression.

I was explaining that if we were going to get the full $75 billion from domestic spending cuts alone, we would, for instance, have to squeeze $6 billion per year out of Medicare by tripling the deductible for hospitalization from $200 per admission to $600.

In future, I would never use the word 'Medicare' again unless it was absolutely unavoidable. It had always started the President on a discourse about how the whole $60 billion program had been a big mistake. And it did so now.

'It used to be that doctors had a charity list,' the President said. 'They knew who couldn't afford the regular price and charged them what they could afford.'

Once the federal government had gone into medical care, all that had gone by the wayside.

'We warned about this at the time,' he continued. 'Supported another bill that only helped the needy.'

I couldn't have agreed with the President's philosophical instincts more. But Medicare was a fact of life that would soon cost $75 billion per year. The problem was how to overcome the entrenched political forces that didn't want it cut at all. Several more illustrations of the political difficulties with relying exclusively on big domestic spending cuts produced several more philosophical digressions.

Warily, now, I moved on to defense. I had established neither that we faced a minimum $75 billion deficit cut nor that we couldn't get it all out of domestic programs for (obvious) political reasons. Moreover, I had spent a lot of time *not* making these points. Some of those who had come for the main event were getting impatient.

My key defense chart had six bars designed to show clearly what an error had been made that night in Weinberger's office in January.

As I was explaining all this, I noticed Cap Weinberger fumbling with his briefing book (I had prepared briefing books as well as big poster boards so that no one would get lost). Soon he was whispering quite audibly to the President, who was sitting next to him.

'Do you want to raise a question, Cap?' I said, thinking I had better get to the bottom of the disturbance.

'These aren't DOD numbers,' he said. 'I've never seen them before. We can't deal with incorrect numbers.'

All right. I explained that since I had been trying to make a point about *real growth rates*, I had converted the DOD budget levels into 'constant 1984 dollars'. In terms of the purchasing power after inflation, my numbers represented the exact same budget DOD had developed.

Nevertheless, Weinberger persisted in complaining about the numbers, implying that I was misleading the President. In desperation, I turned to Frank Carlucci to provide assurance that my numbers were OK.

That put Carlucci, of course, in a spot. He wasn't anxious to contradict the Secretary of Defense in front of the President, even though he knew there was nothing wrong with the numbers. You could have converted the DOD budget to constant *1954* dollars and it still would have shown the same front-end balloon in real growth. Constant dollars were just an index to show the change in real purchasing power; the base year didn't matter.

'Well,' Carlucci equivocated, 'I can't tell for sure. We always use constant 1982 dollars at DOD.'

It was a cop-out, and it muddied the waters even further. Most of the others didn't even comprehend the concept of constant dollars in the first place. 'So much for the "true" seven percent real growth story,' I thought to myself.

I turned next to the fundamental point that $1.33 trillion would buy an awful lot of defense capability. The OMB plan would save money, but it wasn't going to slight anything really important. It would still mean a substantial shift in federal budget priorities toward defense. The DOD share of total federal spending would rise from under twenty-five percent to more than one third.

Suddenly the President broke in. 'This is just the point we need to get out,' he said. 'People keep forgetting that defense was forty-five percent of John Kennedy's budget. We're not even close to that.'

This started everyone on a round of discussion about runaway entitlement growth, the theme of which was that you couldn't blame the deficit on defense. Its share of spending was way below past levels.

The point about Kennedy's defense budget was true enough, but Medicare, Medicaid, and the Great Society didn't even exist back then, which made the connection they were trying to make a bit difficult.

We were off the beaten path again, getting further and further into thickets of irrelevance. History was all well and fine, but what confronted us was the future. The question wasn't what JFK did. It was: Did the Reagan Administration need, and could it afford, the nearly ten percent real growth rate locked into the DOD's five-year budget plan? Somewhat desperately, I struggled to get the group back on track.

I skipped to the part of the briefing that showed the marginal items which would have to be cut from the Department of Defense plan. We had arrived at the bitter pill, but I had utterly failed to establish that the patient was ill.

Then the bell rang, and the match was over. No one was on the mat. It was time to move along to lunch and a press photo op. Ed Harper started dutifully stuffing all the unused poster boards back into the carrying case.

'We will have to continue this discussion at the earliest convenient time,' Meese concluded.

As I shuffled disconsolately on to lunch, my mind wandered back to the first Blair House briefing eight months earlier. It seemed a long, long time ago. But nothing had changed.

Still, I kept pushing. The follow-up meeting on defense was held a week later at the Biltmore Hotel, near Santa Barbara. This time the President didn't attend. Meese was in charge, just as he had been the night two of our Navy fighters were attacked by Libyan planes and shot them down over the Gulf of Sidra.

Weinberger flew all the way out to California to deliver a brief message to the group at the Biltmore: he wasn't going to budge. Not by an inch. Not a dollar. We all could have saved the taxpayers thousands of dollars in jet fuel.

But right after the meeting Meese pulled me aside. 'Hang in there,' he said, 'the President would like to see a compromise worked out on this. I'll quietly work with Cap through Labor Day. He'll come around.'

It cheered me up considerably. Defense was the political lynchpin. If we didn't get the cuts where needed, the September Offensive wouldn't make it five yards up Capitol Hill.

So I went merrily back to work on the other elements of the Offensive. I knew that whatever Weinberger came up with in the way of cuts, they wouldn't amount to much, but at least we'd have broken the 'not one dollar' barrier. The President would get some choices in DOD's own handwriting, and that would be a start.

The senior White House staff were obviously under the impression that the President was willing to compromise on defense. Just prior to Labor Day, Jim Baker told some reporters 'on background' that the $20 to $29 billion would be cut over three years. That sounded pretty close to the $30 billion OMB wanted cut over 1982–84. And once you knocked down the budget levels in the immediate years, the out-year savings automatically became much larger.

Baker's statement stirred continuing press speculation. Since Weinberger had been taking a very public stand for months about the inviolability of the original Reagan defense budget, this incessant speculation in the press did not make him look good. It seemed he was being overruled by OMB and the White House, and it made him furious. He, Carlucci, and the rest of the Pentagon high command steadily worked themselves up into a raging boil. National security policy was being made by press leaks! It was an outrage—a personal insult!

They put on full battle dress and dug in deeper. The Pentagon budgeteers cranked out some trivial and pro forma cut options, as Meese had requested, but Weinberger had no intention of endorsing any of them. The stage was set for another showdown—right after Labor Day.

The penultimate duel between me and Weinberger occurred a few days later, on September 9. The President was getting tired of the issue and—I suspected—bored by it. I just wouldn't go away. The White House staff had allotted Weinberger and me fifteen minutes each to make our presentations.

Weinberger went first, and had he come prepared. The Pentagon's graphics display department had obviously been working overtime. Madison Avenue ad agencies can be pretty slick, but I doubt they could match what DOD had cooked up for this meeting.

Weinberger launched gleefully into his presentation. He talked and pointed, as Carlucci changed the charts on the easel. There were so many of them Carlucci worked up a pretty good sweat by the time the show was over.

It lasted not fifteen minutes, but an hour. I have to hand it to him. Weinberger made a devastating case for a US military buildup. There was but one problem with his courtroom-thorough brief. He was pleading the wrong case.

The only issue before us was how steep an increase in defense we were going to have. The notion that we were 'cutting' the defense budget was, well, ridiculous. Both the OMB and DOD plans provided a larger increase in the defense budget than either the Korean or the Vietnam wars had brought about.

The question was whether the massive buildup would add up to $1.33 trillion or $1.46 trillion over five years: thirteen versus fifteen carrier battle groups; fifty-five versus seventy-five days of wartime ammunition stocks; 2.136 million men in uniform versus 2.286 million; 948 new Air Force fighters versus 1,192; fifteen additional billion-dollar-per-copy nuclear attack submarines versus seventeen; 198 Marine light attack aircraft versus 228.

But Weinberger addressed none of that. Instead, he gave what was known in the trade as a 'red versus blue' briefing. It had only one point: to show how awesome the Soviets were and how far behind we were. The none-too-subtle implication was that anyone proposing even to nick his budget wanted to keep us behind the Russians.

As he droned on, my temperature went above 98.6. If he wanted to question my patriotism, fine; but almost all the red versus blue comparisons on his charts involved weapons categories I wasn't even proposing to change.

One of the real eye stoppers was a chart showing an overlay of a Soviet tank factory on top of a map of Washington, DC. It covered the whole Mall, from the Capitol to the Lincoln Memorial and then some. The arsenal of Marxist-Leninism was larger than the heart of the Capitol of the free world! Great pitch—only I wasn't proposing to cut a single tank out of his budget.

Still another chart compared the Soviet's two new strategic bombers, the Backfire, which was already deployed, and a new giant bomber in development. Our side of the chart showed the aging US B-52.

'Sir, our planes are older than their pilots,' Weinberger reminded the President. The President nodded.

He did not remind the President that OMB supported full funding for the B-1 bomber program, as well as every dime of the (classified) budget for our new Stealth bomber.

Then came the chart showing the comparison of Warsaw Pact divisions with US and NATO forces. The Pentagon charts vividly displayed the fact that our adversaries had scores more divisions than our side. But what was the point? The OMB plan funded sixteen active Army divisions, just as the Pentagon's did. No one was arguing about force structure or the number of divisions.

His briefing was a masterpiece of obfuscation. Incredibly, Weinberger had also brought with him a blown-up cartoon. It showed three soldiers. One was a pygmy who carried no rifle. He represented the Carter budget. The second was a four-eyed wimp

who looked like Woody Allen, carrying a tiny rifle. That was—
me?—the OMB defense budget. Finally, there was G.I. Joe himself,
190 pounds of fighting man, all decked out in helmet and flak jacket,
and pointing an M-60 machine gun menacingly at—me again? This
imposing warrior represented, yes, the Department of Defense
budget plan.

It was so intellectually disreputable, so demeaning, that I could
hardly bring myself to believe that a Harvard-educated cabinet
officer could have brought this to the President of the United States.
Did he think the White House was on Sesame Street?

He had even more of these goodies, but someone pointed out that
he had almost quadrupled his allotted time.

'Just wanted to be thorough, sir,' Weinberger quipped in the
President's direction as he sat down.

So I began my own presentation. Just to make sure we weren't
going to get bogged down in another meaningless argument over
whether we were using 1984 dollars or 1982 dollars, I had had all the
poster boards redone in Weinberger's constant 1982 dollars. That
had cost the taxpayers several thousand dollars, but Lord knows it
was for a good cause. With any luck these new charts might save the
taxpayers nearly $100 billion.

I had also devised a special chart in case the President brought up
his point about JFK's defense budget having a larger share of the
overall budget than ours. You beat swords out of dollars, not budget
shares. So my chart showed that under the OMB plan, the Reagan
defense budget would rise to $262 billion. Using constant dollars,
JFK's 1963 budget had only been $181 billion.

Thus, the President's defense budget would be nearly fifty percent
larger than Kennedy's. True, it was a smaller share of the total
federal budget, but that was due to the rise of the welfare state, not to
short-changing defense.

Once again I tried to make them understand the error we had
made in February in calculating the seven percent real growth rate.
Due to our February 'get well' package, the still pending 1982
defense budget had skyrocketed to $222 billion. That meant that in
just two years we would have raised the defense budget by almost
$80 billion, or forty-seven percent. Now, the Pentagon was
demanding a seven percent real growth rate per year based on *that*.

The fact was that the massive buildup Ronald Reagan had

promised had already been guaranteed. What remained was to settle on a prudent rate of increase for the out-years.

It was so damn self-evident that I despaired at Weinberger's and the President's inability to see it. But as I moved along, I could tell the President wasn't listening. His pencil was out and he was doing arithmetic on his briefing book.

By now I knew what that meant—he'd arrived at his own conclusion. So I hurried through the rest of the briefing and braced myself for the verdict.

As soon as I sat down, Al Haig declared, 'I'm *appalled* by this proceeding. I'm wondering who thinks they are the Secretary of Defense around here.'

Glaring at me, he continued: 'Now, I think we've got to give Cap what he needs. We can't keep going through these theoretical lectures on defense spending. Mr President, you've got to make a decision and put a stop to this.'

This was just Haig doing what he did best, being a bully; but he, Weinberger, and the rest of the national security community did not have an inkling that the Treasury's coffers were empty.

They should have, because that fact had profound implications for defense, foreign aid, and national security policy. The State Department and DOD couldn't be granted the luxury of declaring they were immune from such considerations. They were in the fiscal sweat box along with everyone else.

The President continued to fiddle with his pencil as the war of the briefing charts raged around him in the Cabinet Room. Toward the end of the meeting, he issued his standard admonition.

'Now why don't you fellas get together and see if you can work it out in this area in between,' he said pleasantly.

Both Meese and Baker knew that was as likely as peace in the Middle East. Weinberger and I were now hardly on speaking terms.

The meeting was adjourned, but not before Meese and Baker had agreed to stay with the President and help him to pick some numbers, then inform Weinberger. Baker would then inform me.

At this point, a grotesque miscarriage of numbers began, and the confusion that ensued was astounding.

There were two sets of numbers—budget 'authority' and 'outlays'—for each of the six defense options on the table: DOD's, OMB's, Meese's three options, and one submitted by Baldridge. I kept focusing on outlays, Weinberger on budget authority.

This was natural enough. Defense 'outlays' are the cash flowing out of the Pentagon each day when bills are paid to contractors for delivery of tanks or spare parts, missiles, whatever. You can only reduce the federal deficit by cutting outlays.

Not surprisingly, Weinberger had stuck to budget authority, the Pentagon's credit card, as it were. The Pentagon uses its 'authority' when placing orders for aircraft, ships and cans of paint that in most cases aren't delivered for years. As with American Express, however, the bill eventually arrives. Sooner or later, every dime of budget authority becomes an outlay.

But when you're on a buying binge, the authority—or credit card—numbers are much higher than the outlay numbers because of the lag in the billing cycle. In this case, DOD's proposed 1984 budget authority was $288 billion, but outlays were only $252 billion. Hence, under the present circumstances there was a vast and crucial difference between defense budget authority and outlays.

Dick Darman had feared that with so many options and two sets of numbers for each, the President would get lost without a scorecard. So I had helped him prepare such a scorecard, which laid them all out neatly.

Now, the President, Meese, and Baker were huddled in the Oval Office fishing around on Darman's and my scorecard—but without either Darman or me present, it was, alas, a case of the blind leading the blind.

None of them understood the essential difference between the outlay and budget authority banks. They had no idea that, because of billing cycle lag, a cut from the budget authority bank would reduce outlays—and the deficit—by *only half* of the amount they had chosen.

Consistent with the President's inclination in this and apparently all matters, they split the difference between the OMB plan and the DOD plan right down the middle. But they split the budget authority numbers rather than outlays. Over the period 1982–84, it came out to $26 billion in savings. That sounded just right to Baker. He had been telling reporters that we were going to cut $20–30 billion over three years, and this figure was almost smack dab in the middle of that.

The President called Weinberger to tell him. Weinberger was

delighted. Why shouldn't he have been? As far as his 1984 budget was concerned, it meant he would have to live with a mere $3 billion less than what he had said he would be able to live with under 'extreme duress'.

Shortly afterwards, Baker called me. 'The President came through for you,' he said in a jaunty tone. 'We've got you $26 billion of your $30 billion.'

He proceeded to read me the solomonic numbers they had arrived at in the Oval Office.

'Oh, no!' I groaned. 'You used budget *authority*. Our $30 billion target was in *outlays*.'

I explained that their proposed cut would only reduce outlays by about $15 billion. 'And there's something worse,' I continued.

Darman's scorecard had used DOD's own internal planning numbers, so they would match those on Weinberger's charts. DOD's internal planning numbers, however, were slightly higher than the original February levels, meaning a still smaller cut than they assumed: $11 billion over three years.

'Jim,' I said, 'we need $75 billion in 1984 deficit cuts *alone*. I was counting on $15–17 billion of that from defense. But the way it's come out, the President's three-year cut gives us only $4 billion in 1984 deficit reduction. We're out of business.'

Baker instantly knew we were in trouble. 'I believe we've just stepped into some deep manure,' as he put it. He instructed me to put all of these mysteries into a memo. Still, the decision would have to be reopened.

By now Meese had left town again, and Baker felt that he had already broken his pick on defense. The President was getting angry about all this. He had made his decision and it *still* wouldn't go away. So Mike Deaver was delegated to take my memo to the President and tell him—good news!—that the issue had to be reopened yet again.

Deaver somehow managed to come through. The President agreed to meet with Weinberger and me at 10.00 am the next morning for a 'final' effort at mediation. This time the President understood the defense cuts had to be settled in terms of the outlays.

The meeting the next morning, September 11, 1981, was historically significant. Baker, Meese, and Deaver were conspicuously absent. It was the only time, to my knowledge, that the President's troika ever turned two policymakers loose in the Oval Office unchaperoned. That gave me a slight queasiness. Not that I wanted them to hold my hand, but it portended that Ronald Reagan was fed up with this thing, so much so that they didn't want even to be around.

At the appointed time, Weinberger and I joined the President at his desk. He motioned to us to take a chair on either side. Weinberger took the one on the right.

The President was busy working on correspondence that had been forwarded to him from the White House mail room. He told us about what several American citizens had written to him and his planned answers. One or two of the letters were fairly heartwarming, another was inspirational. I shifted uneasily as he read from them. It was clear that he was not very happy about plunging into Department of Defense budget numbers.

'Fellas,' he finally began, 'we've got to get this defense thing settled. It's starting to look bad to everyone out there. The other side might get the wrong idea.'

Weinberger chuckled (another bad sign). Oh, he said, he agreed entirely. 'Sir, we can get this over in two minutes. We just need to recognize how sound your original budget was. The Defense Department would be more than happy to stick with it.'

I smiled weakly. Well, I said, we had got ourselves into a heap of confusion over the numbers. I had proposed a $30 billion cut over three years. The Secretary of Defense had said that, if necessary, he could accept a reduction of $8 billion. The difference constituted the issue that had to be settled.

Baker had told me he thought the President would go for $20 billion, so I brought my request down to $25 billion, thinking we could haggle our way to $20 billion from there.

It was a mistake—a total, utter, complete mistake. Weinberger sat on his number like a Sphinx. No, no, no, he said. Even an $8 billion cut would be pushing it. DOD would have to 'give up' some 'things' which were vitally needed. He never said what 'things'.

Every time he got the floor, Weinberger talked in perfectly modulated five-minute monologues about the disgraceful condition Jimmy Carter had left the armed forces in. He answered none of the points I brought up, which was now a well-established pattern. He seemed to pretend I wasn't there, which I'm sure he wished had been the case. He pleaded the case for his client, the Pentagon, and would accept no verdict except his own.

I tried every way I could think of to get the discussion back in focus. But Weinberger refused to budge. After more than an hour of desultory sparring, I could see that the President was getting uneasy, even desperate. The White House fellas had given him a chance to settle a big problem on his own, and he wasn't getting anywhere.

We were stalemated because Weinberger had enough gall to sit there until hell froze over. In the Oval Office three feet away from the President of the United States, he was petulantly demanding to have it one hundred percent his way.

By then I realized the President didn't have it in him to overrule his Secretary of Defense, so I prepared to beat a face-saving retreat, more for the President's sake than my own. It was clear my own plan for a significant defense cut was hopeless, and the President had not laid out a single marker or suggested any compromise figure.

So I lowered my number to $23 billion and filibustered for a few minutes longer. Weinberger still wouldn't budge. He wasn't interested in bargaining.

'Mr President, we can't stay here much longer,' I said, after a short interval. 'You've got other things on your schedule. Besides, we're going to have a strong defense either way. Cap's proposal amounts to a one percent cut and my figure to two percent.

'Halfway between $8 and $23 billion is $15 billion, if you split the difference Cap's way,' I continued. 'Maybe we should try something in that range.'

The President looked relieved. He turned to Weinberger. 'Well, what about it, Cap?' he said. 'Can you live with fifteen?'

'Sir, you're the Commander-in-Chief,' Weinberger responded. 'We will do our very best with any number you give us.

'But as your Secretary of Defense,' he continued, 'I would be negligent if I didn't warn you of the consequences. We'd have to give up some things that are very important. Vital. I would feel exceedingly reluctant about going beyond $11 billion.'

Now the President turned to me. 'Would that help?' he asked.

Suddenly I felt like a beggar. Eleven billion over three years was almost a bad joke. It saved no more than $5 billion in 1984, and we needed to reduce the deficit by $75 billion.

I explained this and pleaded, 'We really have to do better.'

The President picked up his pencil and started subtracting. 'How about $2, $5, and $6 [billion over three years]?' he inquired. 'That would give us $13 billion in savings.'

'If that's your decision, sir,' Weinberger said, feigning an air of deep reluctance, as if he had just been cut out of Uncle Sam's will without a cent, 'we'll find some way to manage.'

Manage? All I could do was nod. The sum was too ludicrous to denounce. The President smiled and said he was glad the issue had finally been put to rest. As I closed the door behind me, I looked back. He was already reimmersed in his constituent mail.

I shuffled down the West Wing hallway toward Baker's office. I looked like someone who really had just been cut out of a rich uncle's will—the picture of complete dejection. The decision had just dealt a mortal blow to my entire September Offensive.

Weinberger's recalcitrance signalled double trouble. Cutting defense had never been on my real ideological agenda. My aim had always been to force down the size of the domestic welfare state to the point where it could be adequately funded with the revenues available after the tax cut.

All my efforts to cut defense had been to provide political lubricant for the other cuts. The February calculator error had been significant and real, but not as a matter of theory and ideology. It was wholly possible, even reasonable that an adequate defense of the free world could cost $1.46 trillion. When fully implemented, the DOD plan would cost 7.5 percent of GNP. That was not too much. We had spent far more of our national output on defense, eight to ten percent, in the 1950s and 1960s when the Soviets had been far weaker.

The cuts I had requested were plausible and defensible. But they were based on pragmatism, not principle. Both the President and Weinberger had decided to stick with principle.

Curiously, by sticking—literally—to their guns, they had both reminded me why I had been in the Oval Office arguing about the defense budget in the first place. I had panicked because the politicians had compromised us into near-bankruptcy on the big tax and spending cut bills. Now I was the one grubbing about for dollars wherever I could find them. The grand vision was fading, the real world intruding. And as I made my way to Jim Baker's office, I felt a great sense of ambivalence.

I was still furious with Weinberger, sure, and not entirely because he had been so stubborn on the numbers. He had refused to give me a decent, clean, competent professional debate. A sound principle deserved rigorous defense—not platitudes, postures, and blown-up cartoons.

But Jim Baker was not ambivalent by the time I had got to the end of my account.

'That sonofabitch Weinberger,' he practically shouted at me and Darman. Baker had good political antennae and he knew Weinberger had just put us in deep manure on the Hill. 'He doesn't even think he's part of the administration. He's going to bring the President down right with him before this is all over.'

After the three of us had taken turns roasting the Secretary of Defense in absentia, Baker shrugged and said, 'Do me one more favor, would you? Get these sad-ass numbers written down on a piece of paper with Weinberger's signature on it. I don't want this issue taking another flop into the ditch.'

Incredibly, that is precisely what happened next. As Weinberger and Carlucci interpreted the $13 billion three-year reduction, it was to be subtracted from the higher current numbers in DOD's pending long-term defense plan.

In other words, the way DOD saw it, they had only to make a (preposterously) small $8 billion three-year cut from the President's official budget. It came down to a reduction of . . . one percent.

The White House press office was chomping at the bit to put out an announcement on the President's decision on defense. It had been expected for weeks. But how could we do that if the DOD interpretation prevailed? And how could we expect that the DOD interpretation wouldn't prevail, given all that had happened?

What a fine statement it would have made: 'In view of the now serious deficit threat, the President has announced that he intends to slash the 1984 defense budget dramatically, from $248.6 billion to $245.7. We can only hope that the Soviet Union will not take advantage of this . . .'

Once I confirmed DOD's interpretation, I immediately phoned Baker.

He sounded weary.

'The boss has already gone out to Camp David,' he said, 'so you better draft up another memo.'

There was a pause of the pregnant variety. 'On the other hand,' he said, 'unless you know an 800-pound gorilla that can deliver the memo, it might be better just to save the paper.'

Nonetheless, my memo reached the President somewhere in the vicinity of the Camp David swimming pool the next day.

No 800-pound gorillas volunteered for the assignment, so Baker and Darman had taken the job. They came down the mountain with a signed directive, which meant it was something Weinberger and Carlucci could do nothing, but nothing, about. A presidential directive is a loud voice over the speaker saying, 'Now hear this . . .'

The President's '$2, $5, and $6' billion cut would be subtracted from his official mid-session budget after all. Now all I had to do was cut another $69 billion out of the 1984 budget.

The whole episode was a critical turning point. If I had to pinpoint the moment when I ceased to believe that the Reagan Revolution was possible, September 1981, the day Cap Weinberger sat Sphinxlike in the Oval Office, would be it. From here on, the question ceased to be what should be done, and became what *could* be done. It is the question politicians ask, not ideologues.

The decision on defense pulled the pin on a grenade that would explode two weeks later when the President went before the nation on TV. Reagan had never failed to rally the country with one of his speeches, but this time it would be different—not a clarion call, but a pathetic whimper, a tacit admission that the revolution was in retreat.

My behavior during that two-week period was so erratic that I am at a loss even now to explain it. Certainly it wasn't rational. I have only one consolation. I had a lot of equally irrational company throughout the ordeal.

There had been a lot of talk about crossing the Rubicon over the past months, but by mid-September 1981 we had emerged, dripping wet on the far shore, and found ourselves staring up at a solid cliff wall. All our theories and plans and fixes were stopped dead.

I met with my old sparring partner and ideological adversary Bill Greider for the last time on the eve of the ordeal. The season's battles had come to an end, and so had our arrangement. As I walked into the lobby of the Hay-Adams Hotel on September 12 for our last breakfast, I reflected that I would miss these sessions.

Even before the orange juice arrived, I could see that Bill was not going to let me off with one last free meal, a slap on the back, and an 'Auld Lang Syne'.

'Well,' he said, 'it certainly didn't work out as you expected.'

The jury had reached a verdict, he said. Supply-side theory was being trashed by the collapsing financial markets, rising interest rates, and now, recession.

I was surprisingly feisty, considering the handwriting—in large block capitals—on the wall.

'I wouldn't concede that for a moment,' I shot back. 'Hell, much of the goddam thing hasn't gone into effect yet.'

'I could play you back old tapes,' he said coyly, 'where you said that as you got this program moving in Congress, the financial markets would see you were serious.'

'Yeah, well, that was a misjudgment.'

I then launched into a new rendition of a familiar melody. Sure his empirical assessment of the economy was correct. I wasn't going to deny the facts of life. But—his interpretation of what this condition *implied* was utterly wrong.

The dire condition of the financial markets reflected the failure of *politics*, not of the economic theory behind the Reagan Revolution. The market was saying that the tax cut was not going to be redeemed by a commensurate reduction in spending. But that wasn't our fault, it was Congress's.

'There was a good quote I pulled out of the paper this morning from the head of Salomon Brothers or somebody,' I mentioned. 'He said, "It doesn't add up."'

'But what he's implicitly saying,' I continued, 'is that the political system has been pushed to the limits and it won't make any more spending reductions.'

Greider wondered if I had abandoned the supply-side gospel and reverted to balanced budget orthodoxy. No, no, I said, just the opposite. The supply side demanded fiscal equilibrium.

What had convinced me of this more than ever was the behavior of the politicians on returning from their August recess. They were now in open panic over the high interest rates, and with their usual perspicacity, were angrily pointing their fingers in blame in exactly the wrong direction.

During a private meeting with the LSG at the White House,

Howard Baker had thundered: 'We're going to have to put our foot on Volcker's neck!' Politics is truly the art of indicting the innocent and rewarding the guilty. Baker and most of the Republican rank and file were hotly accusing the Fed for causing the traumatic disinflation now under way.

Disinflation is never painless. But the pain of economic recovery was being exacerbated by the cowardly lions on the Hill. They'd returned from their recess posturing against more spending cuts—the very cuts they had promised to make in order to offset the revenue loss brought on by the tax cut.

All of this had scared the pants off the bond market, which foresaw a huge, permanent structural deficit.

Faced, thus, with the consequences of their own fiscal indiscipline, the politicians were now calling for easy money. It proved beyond doubt that inflationless, 'hard' money and budget deficits were inherently incompatible. Deficits were the switches that made the printing presses run at high speed, bringing in inflation.

'You can tolerate small deficits but not large,' I told Greider. 'For the obvious reason we saw last week—this mindless Fed-bashing.'

There was only one thing we could do, and it was unavoidable. Either we completed the revolution by making additional, deep spending cuts—or we could watch the ruinous unraveling of the whole plan.

Greider was sceptical. 'When you put down your cut list, Congress will choke all over again,' he predicted. I said,

> They've made a choice that's not been fully articulated. You can't have your cake and eat it, too. If you make the choice that the government's tax claim on the economy has to come down to eighteen percent of GNP in order to invigorate private enterprise, then bureaucratic enterprise has to be substantially reduced and the premises on which it was based have to be rejected.

I had no illusions that attempting such a sweeping shrinkage of existing expenditure commitments would touch off a nuclear explosion on Capitol Hill. But I had always assumed it would have to be done to complete the job. The markets were now demanding that we face facts.

'That's what's got to happen next. And throwing more baggage over the side is going to be the most traumatic political experience for this system we've seen since Vietnam.'

'The Wall Street judge is saying that you can't do any more spending reduction,' Greider said. 'Well, argue against that.'

'Pretty soon everyone's going to understand the structural deficit,' I mused,

and then you're going to have a debate about generic options. There are basically three alternatives. Mine, which is to shrink domestic government. The second will be new revenue sources, and the third will be to chop back defense to some 1970s-type level. Either of those three can solve the problem, or nearly solve it. You see, we'll have more leverage here than some of the cynics think. The revenue increase constituency is very weak now. The anti-defense constituency isn't very strong. We may come out with a little bit of everything, but we're in a good position to steer the political debate toward maximization of option one and minimization of the second and third options.

I was drastically wrong about another matter that day. All along I had assumed that my differences with the others on the supply-side central committee were a matter of emphasis and nuance, not of fundamental doctrine. I was about to find out that that too was exactly backwards. When the political and economic facts of life became irrefutable, the other supply siders would turn out to be only half-revolutionaries as well.

They had been gradually transforming the whole supply-side doctrine into a fetish about tax cuts and a crackpot claim that restoring the gold standard would magically cause the huge fiscal and financial mess we had created to—poof!—vanish. This was sheer revisionism, and it proved that George Bush had been right all along. What they were advocating was 'voodoo economics'.

I was about to become the Trotsky of the supply-side movement, and some of the original comrades—Paul Craig Roberts and Jude Wanniski—would turn out to be the intellectual hooligans of the group, to use Lenin's term. Fortunately for me, in America even revolutionaries are subject to the blessed reign of law, order, and non-violent politics. They came at me with Op-Ed pieces* instead of axes.

As I had described the supply-side doctrine to Greider one last time that morning in the quiet of the Hay-Adams, it was dramatically at variance with what the central committee had been saying for a long time, and in utter conflict with the pitch they would soon be publicly espousing.

I described the milewide chasm between my own view and that of the other supply siders. Now I see that I had been covering up for them intellectually all along. It would only take a few nasty personal encounters to get me to admit it—and those were coming.

'There are two major actions happening,' I told Greider.

One is we're disinflating the economy. The other is we're stimulating production. And unfortunately the two must happen in the same time sequence. The fiscal leg of this policy stool will determine whether the two are compatible or not.

In other words, if the permanent deficit remains, then the monetary policy will probably cancel the supply side.

That was the sum and substance of what would happen over the next fifteen months. But the other supply siders denied this straightforward, if bitter, truth with vehemence. They stuck their heads in the sand and pretended that the deficit either didn't exist or it didn't matter. They ended up creating an economic fantasy theory to replace the one that had been defeated by politics. It was both a-historical and anti-economic. It promised instant, painless economic redemption from all the cumulative damage, disorder, excesses and imbalances that were embedded in the American economy as a result of prior politics.

So as I sat there insisting that our differences were a matter of 'atmospherics', I was in fact describing profound difference of doctrine. And Bill caught this.

'I'm still trying to get a vision of your optimistic scenario for the next nine months,' he persisted.

'It's not optimistic,' I said.

I'll admit, some of the naïve supply siders just missed this

* Opinion page articles.

whole dimension. They say the whole economy is going to grow at six percent and that nothing is going to happen by way of twists and turns and pains, like International Harvester going bankrupt or S&Ls* going under. But if you're going to disinflate the economy, a lot of people that have inflated land values are going to take a bath. A lot of hot shot financial executives who spend two hours a day at the country club are going to spend quite a few hours with white knuckles on the balance sheet. That's the only way the inflation can be purged.

That all causes political pressure. *Somebody's got to bail us out on this* . . . They're all going to be down in Washington looking for help faster than you can say Jack Robinson, because that's in the American political culture now.

This prospect imposed an even more insuperable challenge to the fiscal equation of the Reagan Revolution. But these realities had to be faced. Inflation was the consequence of political excesses and indiscipline. The former couldn't be purged without facing up to the latter. The supply-side revolution was in the final analysis a political revolution.

What the Treasury supply siders were doing, I feared, was fleeing the misery of politics by turning economics into magic. I concluded my final discussion with Greider by epigrammatically anticipating precisely what would soon happen.

'So they thought they could abolish politics with the tax cut,' I lamented. 'But to get the end result they want, you're going to have more politics than you've ever seen before.'

The President's defense 'cut' went down about as well as could be expected.

'Laughable!' one irate Gypsy Moth called it. Claudine Schneider of Rhode Island was only saying aloud what many of her colleagues were thinking, or saying in less public circumstances.

Budget Chairman Pete Domenici was as alarmed as I was by now; we realized that the important thing was to do something about the threat facing us, no matter whose fault it was.

So, in a mid-September meeting with the President, he said

* Savings and Loan institution.

soberly, 'We can't hide from reality, the balanced budget is long gone. It's the whole economic recovery and Republican future that's now at stake.'

I looked at the President to see if there was a reaction. None.

Domenici then reminded everyone of the basic budget math: sixty percent of federal spending was Social Security, debt service, and defense.

'To the extent that we don't do it in military cuts,' he continued, 'we have to do it in entitlements.' Well, we *hadn't* done it in defense.

Minority Whip Trent Lott immediately pounced on Domenici. 'I sure hope the distinguished budget chairman of the other body isn't talking Social Security. There ain't a corporal's guard for even touching that on our side. But there's still a lot of fat to cut in domestic spending.'

That brought a swift salvo from the other side of the table. 'Mr President,' Sil Conte said, 'we've got these domestic appropriations bills so tight they squeak. You couldn't buy a cup of coffee with what's still in there that can be cut. I know the young slasher here doesn't agree,' he continued, with a nod in my direction, 'but you must remember. He doesn't have to live up there every day with his snout in the trough like us. He's basing it all just on numbers.'

Bob Dole filled the slightly awkward void left by Conte's remark. He had very skillfully driven almost all the low-income program reconciliation bill cuts through the Senate. His two committees—Finance and Agriculture—had been responsible for the big reforms in AFDC, food stamps, child nutrition, and others.

'We've got a few more ideas that might fly,' he said now, 'but we've about tapped out the big dollars. Somebody else is going to have to start taking a hit besides welfare recipients.'

I thought: 'I wish he hadn't said that.' The word 'welfare' always triggered a presidential anecdote about the California experience.

'Bob's getting at the same thing we found in California,' the President observed right on cue. He went on to make a point precisely the opposite of Dole's, but it did temporarily relieve the tension that had built up. Heads bobbed in courteous unison as the President recited his familiar saga of removing thousands from the California welfare rolls.

The relief, however, was temporary. Minority Leader Bob Michel had met the day before with a large group of House Republicans who had returned from the recess hustings paranoid on the subject of further domestic spending cuts. Their constituencies were now organized, mobilized—and mad. The President's decision only to nick defense hadn't helped. There was a revolution going on, all right—among the House GOP rank and file.

Now, having listened to the debate, Michel finally took the safety catch off and started firing. His shots were aimed randomly around the room.

'We got to face up to the real world,' he boomed. 'If it were up to me, I'd support every dang one of these cuts. Social Security, discretionary—the whole shooting match!

'But it's *not* up to me. I'm the leader, not the dictator. The votes just aren't there for any kind of big package—no matter how you slice it.

'Now, Mr President,' he said, turning to the man sitting next to him, 'I know you've got to have your defense numbers. I know what Cap tells you.

'But Judas priest!' he exploded, 'There's got to be more than $2 billion of fat in that thing! We've got to have some more give on defense, or we might not get *anything* at all up there in the House.'

This outburst triggered another, from John Tower, chairman of the Senate Armed Services Committee. Tower was a wicked debator and a brilliant student of defense policy. He had forgotten more about defense budgets than everyone else around the table combined knew.

'This loose talk about defense cuts is mischievous and dangerous,' he said. 'It redounds to no one's benefit except the Kremlin.

'We're not going to go the hollow Army route again,' he continued. 'We're not going to starve readiness, spare parts, and ammunition stocks. If you want to cut defense any further, we're going to take it out of force structure. We'll pull back a brigade from NATO. Mothball some ships. Deactivate a CONUS* division.

'That would be exceedingly ill-advised,' he concluded; 'foolhardy, even. But keep up this talk about defense cuts and you're going to force us to do it.'

Jake Garn of Utah held vehement, and contradictory, views on the subject.

* Continental United States.

'John Tower is right,' he asserted. 'I've been hearing this defense cut talk since February. Well, I'm sick and tired of people whining about defense.'

He shifted gears. 'I'm with Pete Domenici. Anybody who thinks we can live with these deficits is dreaming. So let's stop making excuses about all these miserable domestic programs and start cutting. That's the only answer, and everyone here knows it.'

Thus, we reached the high water mark of the September Offensive. It was unmistakably clear that the governing party was riven with deep divisions on the entire fiscal dilemma that stood before us.

The retreat began the next morning. Opening my paper, I had expected to hear mutinous murmurings from House Republicans about Social Security cuts. Not at all. I was startled by what the *New York Times* had to say.

'White House officials took pains today to say that no new cuts in Social Security would be urged on the Congress at the present time.'

I stood there in stubble, slippers, and bathrobe staring at it. It had to have come from Baker or Dave Gergen. It was a Steve Weisman story, and they tended to keep him well fed.

At the LSG meeting scheduled that day, the September Offensive was on the agenda, and the very first line of the briefing memo read: 'Defer all cost of living adjustments until October 1, 1982.' I wanted to make sure we all agreed on what we had to do.

We didn't. As soon as we were all gathered in the Oval Office, Baker started in.

'Mr President,' he said, 'if you go along with this, you're going to step into a pile of political manure. It'll stink. You'll be up to your neck. The Democrats are just waiting for you to make another move.'

I acknowledged there were political risks to taking on Social Security, but I harped on the numbers just the same.

'We've decided to leave defense pretty much untouched. I understand that. But we just can't close another door,' I insisted, 'no matter what the political risks are.

'If we duck on Social Security, then . . . bang!' I slapped my hands together, 'you've just put one-half trillion of the budget out of reach. With nothing on Social Security where are we gonna be? Nowhere!'

The President pondered a moment. 'No, we're not talking Social Security *cuts*,' he said. 'We're only delaying the increase for three months. Once we explain it, the people will understand.'

Baker and Friedersdorf persisted. They argued strenuously that we should at least take a thorough 'temperature reading' on the Hill before 'locking in' anything 'specific' involving Social Security. The President had no objections.

Over the next several days the LSG fanned out with thermometers. When they brought them back to the White House, they showed that the Hill was running a high fever on Social Security. Moreover, even the congressional Republicans were either squeamish about, or hostile to, any September Offensive at all.

As usual, the College of Cardinals was willing to take the plunge on Social Security, but on one condition. 'We're not going along if it means picking buckshot out of our hind ends fired by House Republicans,' one of them stressed. We agreed that this was a reasonable concern.

But on everything else there were deep differences. Mark Hatfield of Oregon, chairman of the Senate Appropriations Committee, was the most vocal dissenter.

'Now, the White House is going to have to recognize,' he said, 'that this budget is a three-legged stool. You've got defense, revenues, and domestic spending. You can't eliminate the deficit with just one leg. These other two are going to have to pull some of the weight.'

Hatfield's three-legged stool lecture was becoming standard fare in these sessions, but now it provoked an arctic blast from Majority Whip Ted Stevens of Alaska.

'You're all wet, Mark,' he said. 'And for that matter, so is the White House.'

'You want to get something done about these interest rates? Then get that sonofabitch Volcker in here and tell him to let up. He's killing us—just killing us.'

'But, good God,' he declaimed, 'leave the damn budget alone! Stop this panicking about the deficit. Give the tax cut a chance. If something needs to be done, we can look at it next March.'

What had infuriated Stevens was an element of our September

Offensive that the President had agreed to: a twelve percent across-the-board cut in domestic appropriations. It would save about $8 billion in 1982 alone, more in the out-years.

On the House side, meanwhile, word of the twelve percent cut already had the Gypsy Moths and others howling 'Double cross!' In the case of low-income energy aid, for example, this amounted to nearly a billion-dollar per year funding cut from our compromise agreement in Gramm–Latta II.

Later that week about two dozen of the Gypsy Moths made their rebellion public. They threatened to vote against the entire new budget package unless the size of the defense cut was more than *quadrupled*.

'You better get one thing clear,' Stu McKinney of Connecticut stormed at one meeting, 'you're not going to get away with dismantling programs for the northeast that some of us have spent years creating. This ideological crap is being carried too far.'

Another one to speak out was my former House colleague from Michigan, Carl Pursell. Fifteen months earlier, I had stepped over him in order to get the platform committee seat at the GOP convention. Now it was his turn.

He and his Gypsy Moth caucus had another, new angle: The administration was courting the Boll Weevils too much. They were getting all the gravy—a massive, giblety flow of new defense contracts to the Sun Belt districts. Well, that's where the defense contractors were.

So, as Gypsy Moths were stating the problem, it wasn't just that the defense budget was too big. It was more that the bucks were landing in the wrong geographic vicinity.

'Northern Republicans are people, too,' Congressman Larry DeNardis of Connecticut had vapidly declared at the Gypsy Moth press conference.

The House Republicans had had a bad recess. They smelled economic trouble, recession. The spending constituencies had regrouped and were orchestrating local pressure. And now the congressmen wanted a real recess—from the Reagan Revolution. The spring and summer budget-cutting exercises had been nothing more to them than a seasonal fad. They weren't inclined to any permanent anti-spending mobilization, no matter what the numbers looked like. They were tired and they were cranky.

It was my old supply-side comrade, Jack Kemp, who turned out to be the strongest proponent of the House GOP's 'do nothing' line. He had never shown any enthusiasm for the first round of budget cutting and now he was going his separate way.

I was sitting at my normal spot on the big blue couch in Michel's office. My black books were strewn on the coffee table, as on so many past occasions. I had just finished going over a short paper for them that outlined the September Offensive options still under review at the White House. The room was crowded with GOP members and staff.

'With all due respect for our brilliant and hardworking friend,' Kemp began, 'I think this whole effort is a drastic mistake.' I looked up.

'What happened to the party of growth and opportunity?' he continued. I knew we were in for a full-throated speech. 'At the first sign of trouble we're being stampeded into the slash and cut medicine that kept us in the minority for decades. This is just more root canal politics.

'I won't apologize for the deficit for a minute, but we can't be panicked by it either. Treasury has numbers that are a lot lower. Besides, the real cause of high interest rates and a weak economy is monetary policy. I know it will upset some of you, but we have to start dealing with a four-letter word—gold.'

Kemp's rhetoric was always clever, but now he was sounding like Jim Wright.

'The cutting edge is now on the monetary side,' he went on. 'Fiscal is secondary. Our model must come from the Germans and Erhardt, from the French and Jacques Rueff. The Friedmanites are demand-siders. Their cure for inflation is recession. It didn't work for Hoover. It didn't work for Eisenhower. It didn't work for Nixon. It didn't work for Ford. It won't work for Ronald Reagan . . . '

Kemp now had a good head of oratorical steam up. He would have gone on with his monetary lecture a good while longer, but people were rolling their eyes and shifting around in their chairs as if from a sudden plague of hemorrhoids. Michel finally cut him off.

'OK Jack,' he said irritably, 'you've said your piece. There's some others around here who want a chance.'

For a moment, I was thankful for Michel's intervention. Kemp's fanciful gold standard talk hadn't surprised me. I knew he was being drilled with anti-Milton Friedman harangues by his confessor, Jude Wanniski. But I had been shocked, and disappointed, that Kemp had come down so hard on the September Offensive. We had remained close friends through all the battles, despite occasional disagreements on doctrine and tactics. But this was a kind of betrayal. He hadn't even warned me in advance.

As it turned out, I would have been better off if Kemp had kept talking. What the others in the room had to say was more practical—and more discouraging.

'Social Security is dead in the water,' Trent Lott put in. 'That's like in—no way. Period. End of discussion. Not a prayer!'

Numerous others said the same thing. The Democratic campaign committee already had ten million letters ready to roll. They were preparing to unleash Claude Pepper again. *When was the White House going to learn something about the political facts of life?*

It was too much. 'OK', I exploded, 'then where in the hell are you going to get the savings? We can't cut defense. The Gypsy Moths are jumping all over my carcass and low-income programs. You've got a budget-busting farm bill coming down the pike. The Appropriations Committee is screaming to high heaven about discretionary programs taking too big a hit.

'So what does that add up to? A deficit that's out of control and an economy heading for the ditch. But nobody wants that, either.

'Talk about the facts of life. The main fact is we now have our big tax cut and we've got to earn the right to keep it. Sure, the politics are tough,' I concluded, 'but nobody ever said it was going to be a free lunch.'

The instant I finished, everyone jumped in. Bob Michel struggled to find a landing zone amidst the cross fire. The meeting had gone on for over two hours, and nerves were getting frayed.

'We're not going to sit here and ignore this deficit,' he said. 'Some of you around here have given enough speeches against the deficit to choke a horse on. Well, now's the time to put up or shut up.' He turned to me.

'But the White House doesn't have a monopoly on the answers, either,' he said. 'We'll put our heads together and come up with something doable. Shoot, I know it won't be what the President wants. But he's just not going to get his own way every time.'

All right, but I knew his do-it-yourself deficit reduction plan would collapse after about two meetings of the GOP rank and file. I didn't even have to wait for the proof.

'The White House is going to have to face up to something.' The room suddenly turned quiet. It was Dick Cheney of Wyoming who had spoken up. He did not do that often, being a taciturn westerner. But he was highly regarded by all the GOP factions.

'This isn't the right time to launch a new bloodletting,' he continued. 'People aren't convinced it's needed. They want more time to see how things are going to work out.

'We've been through seven months of political trauma around here,' he reminded me. 'You can't go back to the well over and over. People are shell-shocked and antsy. You're not going to get a consensus for anything very big or meaningful.

'So I think we have to ride it out awhile. Let's see where we are in January. The deficit isn't the worst thing that could happen.'

Dick Cheney was not like the other GOP politicians at all. On policy and ideology he was a rock, an unwavering fiscal conservative and sympathetic to the supply side—my version of it. Unlike Kemp, he had his feet firmly on the ground. He knew there were two sides to the fiscal equation; the giving had to be matched with the taking.

He had never whimpered and haggled over budget cuts as so many of the others had. In earlier years, he had been a tough ally in my campaigns against the Chrysler bailout, the synfuels boondoggle, and other fiscal claptrap. He was more than prepared to go up against the organized spending constituencies.

At the same time, he was not a right-wing snowflake. He had been Chief of Staff in the Ford White House, and he had a broad, sophisticated view of politics. Neither a parochial pol nor a sectarian ideologue, he didn't ask 'How much?' every time a squeaky wheel demanded grease. He did not tilt at windmills or indulge in the make-believe intrigues of the New Right.

With Phil Gramm, Dick Cheney was the closest there was to a competent, principled advocate of the Reagan Revolution in the political mainstream. And his speech was a bucket of cold water in my face. I had always put more stock in what he had to say than most of the rest of them combined. All along, he had been my secret litmus test of what was possible. And now he had suddenly made it explicit—clear as the skies over his home state—we had reached the end of the line.

I stewed about the 'Cheney conclusion' all evening, talking to Darman about it at length. I knew it had a profound meaning, but I had to figure out precisely what. In terms of the immediate fiscal equation, the meaning was clear. Without a sweeping September Offensive, my whole scenario would collapse. The financial markets would remain in disarray, and interest rates would not come down.

The Fed's anti-inflation policy would thus crunch the economy. The latter would quickly plunge into recession. The budget numbers and deficit would soar out of sight. The February fiscal plan would end up in shreds. Now was the last chance to rescue it — but it wasn't going to happen.

Yet the Cheney conclusion also shed even more powerful light on an even more fundamental matter. All year long I had rationalized. The enormous loose ends, the IOU's, the asterisks, the numbers that didn't add up . . . all along I had assumed that somehow tomorrow it would all work out. Time would cure all ills. Everything could eventually be fixed. All we needed was one more inning. Now, suddenly, with a little help from Dick Cheney, I realized that my grand scheme depended on a theory of perpetual revolution. There would always be a clean slate. Every event, decision, or setback could be erased. There was no history, only a wide-open future of limitless possibility. Defeats were never permanent facts, merely temporary, reversible disappointments.

The swift and conclusive demise of the September Offensive put the torch to that theory, and as I sat after midnight in my quiet office, with none of the solacing hum of day's activity, I finally understood that the war was over. We had run out of tomorrows, and now the revolutionary forces would have to stage an orderly retreat or risk a calamitous rout. Now I would have to be guided by what was politically possible, not by what was doctrinally correct.

The *coup de grâce* came a few days later when Pete Domenici called with the news.

'You can forget Social Security and the COLAs*,' he said. 'Your spineless House Republican friends have poisoned the well. Nobody over here is going to fall on their swords if they're going to cut and run in the House.'

*   *   *

* Cost of Living Ajustments.

On Friday 18 September Darman and I met in my office to try to design the retreat. The September Offensive couldn't simply be scrapped, it had become a highly visible administration initiative. We had set off the alarm bells about the swelling deficit. The Cabinet had been given its marching orders the day before, and a presidential television speech was promised for the following week.

Everywhere we looked—defense, Social Security, the twelve percent appropriations cut, Meese's pitiful 75,000 bureaucrats and two cabinet agencies—we came up with not nearly enough. We were boxed in.

Then Darman recalled our conversation in the West Wing parking lot the day of the July tax cut orgy in the Cabinet Room.

'I think the time has come to fix it,' he said.

I nodded. 'Here are the numbers.'

I had already come to the same conclusion and had prepared the calculations. The second and third installments of the twenty-five percent tax cut would have to be delayed by at least a year. That would ease the deficit surge and buy time to work on a revised plan for fiscal stability. The sheet I handed Darman showed that the 1984 deficit could be reduced by $21 billion by delaying the tax cut.

'How are we going to get this done?' I asked.

Darman said we should go to Baker first. Baker knew things were falling apart. He'd be willing to make a run at delaying the tax cut because it was the only practical option.

Then the three of us would work on Meese. You never knew where Meese would come out, but there was a chance he would go along. He hadn't always been as hard-line on the tax cut as the outside world thought. Then, the four of us would surround Don Regan and bring him on board. Finally, we'd take the tax cut delay proposal to the President, early next week. Complete secrecy and swift action were imperative. Darman would start the ball rolling by talking to Baker one-to-one.

As I thought about it over the weekend, I became more and more convinced that this was the right course. The unions, civil rights organizations, and so-called Poor People's Lobby staged their big anti-Reagan demonstration in front of the White House that Saturday. Next week's papers would be full of wild charges of unfairness and hardship due to the budget cuts. That would only scare the already timid Republican politicians, at the very moment the next round of battle was scheduled to begin.

The weekend wrap-up stories in the newspapers strengthened the impression that the GOP ranks were in open rebellion. The papers reported they were drafting their own alternative package and asking the White House to delay the President's address.

Saturday afternoon I boarded a plane for another GOP fund-raising speech, this one in Atlanta. I was dead tired from the week-long scramble, but I figured this one would be worth the extra effort.

It was for Newt Gingrich of Georgia, one of the original supply siders in the House and a peripatetic young turk. Gingrich was an interesting combination of intellectual ideologue and political street fighter. Like me, he refused to take 'no' for an answer.

Just before dinner, we had a private moment alone. He used it to give me an unexpected message, and not a pleasant one.

'You guys are making a fatal mistake,' he said. His voice had a note of defiance. 'You've taken us for granted. Just because the White House makes a decision, it doesn't mean that everyone just falls in line.'

Then he told me I'd been 'working too hard'. He said, 'Step back and get some perspective. Let some of your friends on the Hill take a shot at it. We'll find a better answer.'

Well, Gingrich was whistling through his hat. There *weren't* any better answers. Push had come to shove and now for all his conservative talk, he too was flinching.

I was furious. But I still told the dinner audience of contributors that Newt Gingrich was the greatest thing since sliced bread. By now I had given so many dozens of these testimonials on behalf of the GOP that it was just a matter of walking up to the podium, plugging a new name into the tape, turning on the mental switch, and letting the fulsome praise gush forth. The audience warmed to it, but my heart wasn't in it this time.

Early Sunday morning, Baker called. I was still trying to catch up on my sleep after a late night flight back from Atlanta.

'I've talked to Darman,' he said. 'Can you come into the office later today? We'll make a run at Meese.'

Needless to say, Ed Meese was not keen on delaying the tax cut. But at least he was willing to hear the case. I explained to him that so far all we had come up with was a mouse; we needed an elephant.

We went over the numbers and the remaining options. When Meese buried his head in a briefing paper, he could add and reason as well as anyone. His problem was that he didn't remember anything very long. He would never 'stay put' on a conclusion. But today he agreed: delaying the tax cut was essential to a meaningful deficit reduction package.

'The President needs to see this option,' he concluded. 'It's the only choice we have left.' Darman, Baker, and I were relieved.

The next morning the LSG convened for a 'pre-meeting' before taking the plan to the President. Don Regan now had to be brought into the plot.

'Dave's drawn up a briefing paper,' Baker began. 'It updates where we are on the September Offensive and outlines the remaining options. We need to all go over it carefully before we go see the President.'

The paper was entitled 'The Current Budget Facts of Life.' The first page had two headlines. 'Social Security Plan Is Dead' read the first. 'Straw That Breaks the Budget Back' was the second.

I began to summarize its major points. After a few minutes, I noticed that Regan was flipping ahead through the pages. Suddenly he tensed, turning red in the face and working his jaws so hard that the blood vessels in his neck stood out.

He had reached page eight, where it said, 'Delay effective date of second and third installment of the tax cut.' I knew the explosion was coming.

I stopped talking. Everyone looked at Regan. Then it came, with the suddenness of a summer storm.

'I'm the Secretary of the Treasury!' he roared. 'You're not going to make a fool out of me with this plot!' Baker started to say something, but the Secretary of the Treasury was not nearly finished.

'I'll fight every one of you on this to the last drop of blood!' he shouted, as he furiously shoved my briefing paper across the table. I think it was me he really wanted to shove.

'This is the last time anybody is going to make tax policy behind my back.' He was sputtering now.

'Some heads are going to roll around here—starting right now.'

He got up from his chair, implying he was going to charge down to the Oval Office right then and there.

Baker stood up and peered down at him. It was eyeball-to-eyeball.

'Cool down, old friend,' he said, while slapping Regan lightly on the back. Regan stopped shouting but remained standing.

'Why do you think we're having this frigging meeting in the first place?' Baker continued. 'If you're not on board, now's the time to discuss it.' That seemed to satisfy him. He took his chair.

The discussion remained heated, however, and at length it was agreed that my options paper would go in the ash can. Regan would 'think' some more about the revenue question. We would discuss the tax cut delay 'informally' with the President, but would not push for a decision. Also, later that same day the congressional Republican leadership was scheduled for another session with the President on the September Offensive. After we heard them out, we would take another look at the tax cut delay proposal.

But the President soon made it clear that he didn't buy the notion that delaying the tax cut had become unaffordable.

'What would the people think?' he said, when I broached the idea in the Oval Office. 'We shouldn't even be discussing that idea. If our critics ever heard about it, they'd jump for joy.'

'Mr President, we at Treasury agree with you one hundred percent,' Regan jumped in, fixing me with a quick acid glare. 'Go with your instincts—these big deficit numbers you're getting are just projections, anyway.'

'I agree,' Meese chorused. 'If we do anything in the revenue category, it should be strictly under the heading of loopholes. We don't want to end up like Carter—flip-flopping all the time.'

I groaned inwardly. Meese should have known. Once again he was proving himself an expert at it.

Baker gave me a discreet thumbs-down signal. I got the message. Another door had just slammed shut.

The meeting later on with the GOP congressional leadership brought more bad news. Bob Michel set the tone, and grim it was.

He never came right out and said it, but he outlined our plight clearly enough. We no longer had a viable coalition; no longer had the majority 218 votes. We were stuck in the mud with a half-revolution.

'Mr President,' he began, 'when we met in the Oval Office way back when, we talked about how I could best serve you as House Republican leader.

'I told you to expect that if the going got tough, I'd let it all hang out. I'd give it to you straight and uninhibited. No eyewash.'

Michel's voice rose. 'Well, it *just ain't there*.' As he said it, he slapped his hands together with a piercing crack.

'You're the boss,' he continued. 'I have to be your handmaiden the best I can. But I also have to be credible and not go beyond the art of the possible.'

He then explained that the House coalition was falling apart, and that he didn't have a majority for much of anything. Social Security and the entitlement COLA plan was gone. The Gypsy Moths wanted their reconciliation compromises adhered to. People were nervous about going after low-income programs like food stamps and Medicaid. The farm belt guys were nervous about a threatened veto of the farm bill. The Appropriations Committee was restless, and felt it was getting the short straw.

In the end it all came down to the defense decision.

'Your $2 billion cut just isn't going to wash,' he told the President. 'We can't win anything on a number like that.'

The President rose to its defense.

'We round-tabled it right here,' he told Michel, 'we are all in agreement—we can't retreat any further. On defense, we don't determine the budget. The other side does. You have no choice but to spend what you need.'

The governing party was now falling into what would become a familiar pattern: fiscal gridlock and a desultory internal debate that always went in circles. That was the outcome on September 21.

After the meeting, Darman and I huddled but were virtually at a loss as to what to do. Our quiver of options was empty.

Darman finally said, 'The President at least deserves a clear, undiluted review of the strategic choices.'

We agreed to draw up a paper that laid out the fiscal facts of life. Tomorrow, we would present the President with the true range of policy choices—whether he was eager to hear them or not.

In the meantime, I decided to try to wet Don Regan's fuse. I called him. He had calmed down.

'You heard Michel,' I told him. 'I think the President deserves at least a calm review of the options.

'There'll be three of them,' I went on, 'and the tax delay will only be in one of them. Go ahead and trash it if you feel compelled to.'

Regan promised to do just that, but he did agree to the three-option approach.

The next morning I got a call from Domenici. He said he'd been up pacing the floor all night. The previous day's leadership meeting had left him deeply depressed.

'Doesn't the President understand what's *happening*?' he asked.

'I don't know,' I confessed. 'Today, we're going to lay it out cold. I've been up all night, too, working on it. I'll let you know afterwards.'

Later that day we gathered in the Oval Office and laid out the basic facts. The paper I'd prepared was straightforward: cumulative deficits for 1982–84 threatened to total *one-quarter trillion dollars*. And that assumed no recession for three years, and a drop in the Treasury bill rate from fifteen percent to seven percent within twenty-four months.

Next, we reviewed the basic structure of the federal budget. Defense, debt service, Social Security, and the foreign aid–related programs cost $507 billion. All these items were now off the table. That left about $200 billion in non-Social Security entitlements and $150 billion in domestic discretionary programs from which to get all the needed savings.

Both of the latter two numbers were big, but they covered a field of political land mines.

Nearly $100 billion of the $212 billion in entitlements consisted of veterans' benefits, Medicare, and Supplemental Security Income for the aged, blind, and disabled. Substantial savings were possible and justifiable, but these programs raised 'the same explosive political issues as Social Security.'

Another $46 billion consisted of low-income benefits—food stamps, Medicaid, AFDC and the like. '$6 billion in savings is realistic here,' the paper said, 'but $10 billion borders on the draconian.'

Cuts in discretionary programs would yield substantial savings, *if* we were willing to go to the political mat. The $5 billion revenue-sharing program could be terminated. The Great Society education and social service programs could be cut forty to one hundred percent. Energy subsidy programs could be thrown overboard. Subsidies for mass transit, water projects, economic development, and business could be slashed. We could save $20 billion or more here; however, 'the political cost would be pervasive and severe', as the paper noted. And the prospects of legislative success were negligible.

In view of these new, unpleasant facts of budgetary life, I had outlined three 'generic' fiscal strategies. The first was entitled 'Govern First—Revolution Later'. It described a major political bargain with the Congress.

The administration would offer to delay the tax cuts and place Social Security in the hands of a bipartisan commission. In return, the administration would demand 'moderate' reductions in discretionary spending and other entitlement programs. The whole package would reduce the 1984 deficit by nearly $50 billion.

The second generic option was entitled 'Hard-line Anti-spending Strategy'. Essentially, it was the 'throw baggage overboard strategy' I had advocated to Greider ten days before. It could save nearly $50 billion 'by confrontation rather than consensus'. It had not a prayer of working.

The last option was called 'Muddle Through'. It called for moderate savings in domestic spending, and zero change in Social Security, defense, or the tax cut. Of course, it would leave the out-year numbers awash in red ink. By choosing that course, we would 'risk loss of control over the deficit, economy, and legislative process.' And that, I argued, was where we would end, by default, if we didn't do anything. I had closed the paper by saying that it would be irresponsible and dangerous to do that.

The President browsed through the paper, then took off his reading glasses. He looked up and suggested that perhaps he hadn't made himself sufficiently clear.

'On the tax, *no*,' he said. When he wanted to make an unequivocal point, he always started in mid-sentence.

'Delay would be a total retreat.' He was vehement. 'We would be admitting that we were wrong. I'm just not going to stand for any more of this talk.'

I shifted in my seat and said, tepidly, 'Mr President, I never dreamed I would be recommending this. But we're down to the short straws. The other two options won't work. This will at least preserve the full tax cut, even if it takes longer to get there. It will give us time to get back on top of this deficit before it explodes in our face.'

It wasn't the deficit that exploded, but the President.

'Well, damn it, Dave, we came here to attack *deficit spending*, not put more taxes on the people,' he said sharply.

'We better go back to the drawing boards,' Baker interposed. 'We'll come back with something tomorrow.'

It was pretty late to be going back to the drawing boards. The TV speech was scheduled for Thursday evening. We were still on square one and had only forty-eight hours left. Six different drafts of the speech were now circulating inside the White House. But as of Tuesday evening, no one knew what the contents or the thrust of the message would be. Now the White House began leaking like a sieve. The two words that were most in use in the West Wing that afternoon were 'disarray' and 'chaos'.

The next morning's paper quoted an anonymous (naturally) White House source saying, 'Things are changing around here so fast you can't tell the players without a scorecard.' Had to be Gergen, I mused. He was getting truly desperate. Speeches were his department. What was he supposed to have typed up onto the teleprompter—a string of magic asterisks?

Later in the afternoon the mood was harried. Darman, Baker, Regan and I put our heads together in Baker's office. Regan had testified in the morning before the House Budget Committee and was now happy, having burned our bridges behind him. He triumphantly passed around the ashes, in the form of a wire service story:

REGAN BARS ANY DELAY IN TAX CUT

But that was not all he had brought. Never let it be said Don Regan was not magnanimous in victory. He told us he was prepared to recommend to the President a small list of tax loophole closings. They consisted of eliminating energy tax credits, industrial development bond subsidies, a speed-up in corporate tax collections, 'and the like', he said. They would reduce the deficit by $22 billion—over three years.

It didn't amount to shucks, but by then we were down to the bottom of the barrel. We were desperate. The loopholes were at least a basis for some deficit reduction package that might be minimally respectable. I was relegated to work on the numbers overnight.

Before I set off, Baker gave me another unhelpful present to assist me in my work. Up to then, the September Offensive had included a phaseout of general revenue sharing by 1984. Once the phaseout was complete, it would save $5 billion per year. Cutting that one off was the least we could do. In the face of potential triple-digit deficits, the program simply amounted to 'deficit sharing'.

But no—local Republican officials had got wind of my plan to kill the program. Rich Williamson, Baker's aide in charge of holding the hands of State and local officials, had leaked it to them. Within hours, he had managed to stir up such a phone campaign that the White House switchboard circuits were overloaded.

'The President wants revenue sharing out of the package,' Baker insisted. By that time, I was too numb to argue.

'You got it,' I said.

That afternoon, Darman and I took another walk around the parking lot. Soon we had come up with a new idea. Darman called it Ping-Pong.

As far as substance went, the September Offensive was now a September Nothing, but perhaps we could use the idea of an offensive to start a game of back-and-forth with Congress.

We at least had some numbers, however pitiful, that we could place under four major deficit reduction headings: defense, revenues (Regan's loopholes), non-Social Security entitlement reforms, and domestic appropriations cuts. We would dress up what little we had under these headings with another magic asterisk. This time the asterisk would denote additional unspecified savings that we would submit as part of the FY 1983 budget in January.

The whole thing could be gussied up to look like $100 billion or more in three-year savings. That number, along with the four categories, would provide the 'framework' for a major assault on the deficit. Once we lobbed it at Congress, we would see what legislative opportunities might arise. We would count on the solid Senate leadership—Domenici, Dole, Baker, and Paul Laxalt—to force the next step. They would then come back to the White House with a more meaningful and viable plan. We would then respond. And the ball would keep moving back and forth until we could reach a solution.

When I got back to my office, I had an urgent call from Jack Kemp.

'Tell me it isn't so!' he exclaimed, as I picked up the phone. 'You *didn't* recommend delay of the tax cut!'

Kemp didn't even wait for me to fess up. He already knew from the supply siders at Treasury. He probably had my briefing paper on his desk.

But he wasn't mad. Kemp was incapable of anger. On these occasions he just machine-gunned you with a full bandolier of exclamation points.

'Hooverism . . . green eyeshades . . . static thinking! It's terrible. Flat earth economics! Herb Stein! Arthur Burns!'

Kemp hit me with every expletive in the supply-side lexicon. Then he caught his breath.

'Are you still coming to dinner?'

I assured him I was and told him not to get indigestion before I'd even arrived. The President was totally opposed to any delay in the tax cut. Kemp knew that, too.

The dinner at his house that evening turned out to be an untimely meeting of the central committee. Art Laffer, Jude Wanniski, Paul Craig Roberts, Norm Ture, Irving Kristol—they were all there. The guest of honor was the Israeli Finance Minister, who was interested in supply-side economics. 'What a time for him to find out about it,' I thought to myself.

The other members of the central committee weren't nearly as good-natured about my apostasy as Jack had been. My fiancée Jennifer had the pleasure of sitting next to Jude Wanniski, who hectored her nonstop all evening, interrupting his denunciations of me only to ask her to pass the salt.

Why was I going over to the other side? Who was I talking to? They couldn't get through to me any more. What was Jennifer's home and office number in case Wanniski had to get an urgent message through to me? Why wasn't I returning his phone calls?

The next day I checked my phone logs. The reason I hadn't returned any calls must have been due to the fact Wanniski hadn't called me for four months.

Come to think of it, the last time I had heard from him was in that morning's *New York Times*.

He was quoted making the pronouncement, 'The deficit is not a problem. In 1945 we had a deficit of 22 percent of GNP. Today it is only 1.9 percent.' I wondered if I had been expected to call him to find out about such useful information as that.

After dinner Roberts and Ture cornered me, and boy were they mad.

'When are you going to straighten up and fly right?' Roberts raged. 'You're undercutting the President. You better get back on the team or get out.'

He began to shout. 'You're panicking everyone on the deficit! You've objectively joined the enemy camp.'

I have reasonably thick skin and a high threshold for abuse, but that last one was a bit much. How, pray, did Paul Craig Roberts suppose the tax cut had been enacted in the first place? By telekinesis? Objectively, he had had nothing to do with it.

Over the prior nine months, Regan had permitted him to show his face in the White House exactly once. He had never attended a real working meeting with the President or congressional leadership. Mostly what he had done was to sit over at the Treasury and keep ideological tabs on people. He had been a commissar—and a fountain of press leaks and gossip.

There are occasions when sweet reason is called for, and there are occasions when people need to be told to go to hell. This was one of the latter.

'Craig,' I said, 'go to hell.' It felt remarkably good.

The following day, September 23, our new September Offensive package finally began to shape up. It had to. The President was going to be describing it on TV within twenty-four hours, sounding the call to battle against the rising deficit.

In the final White House flail, however, still more spending-cut proposals were swept off the table. With Social Security and entitlement COLAs now completely untouchable, I proposed to increase the pro rata cut in a number of Great Society–type programs from twelve percent to twenty-five percent. These included subsidized housing, urban development programs, education grants, student aid, Head Start, the Job Corps, health and social services grants, and job training.

'Given where we are on taxes, defense, and Social Security, these programs are going to have to be eliminated entirely in next year's budget,' I'd insisted. 'We might as well get started now and let the Congress know what's on the agenda.'

Baker and Gergen were horrified. They protested that some of these new cuts would open holes in the administration's social 'safety net'. Since the clock was ticking, there was no time fully to explain that the safety net was no longer compatible with the administration's fiscal policy. It had to be shredded in order to close the budget gap.

Meese argued that everyone would understand even-handed, across-the-board cuts, but no deep selective reductions. Again, it was too late to show him that the fiscal gap couldn't be closed with token, across-the-board cuts. If he didn't understand by now, I doubted he ever would. Paying for the President's tax cut meant we had to throw whole programs overboard. And so, with one or two exceptions, my 'deep cut' proposals were rejected.

As the final paper described it, the September Offensive now consisted of laying out 'a *policy road map* for holding down the FY 1982 deficit and closing the out-year gap.'

If it was a road map, the highway led into very uncertain terrain. The plan the President would outline on Thursday evening called for reducing the 1982 deficit by $16 billion and for additional deficit reductions of $115 billion over three years. Sounded good, but $84 billion of those savings consisted largely of a new magic asterisk.

Regan's loophole closing measures comprised $22 billion of the total savings. But he wouldn't even allow the details of the package to be released with the President's message. Treasury didn't yet know what they were. We essentially had another plug number. Congress would get a detailed plan 'sometime later' in the fall.

Another $28 billion of the savings was accounted for by entitlement reforms excluding Social Security. These savings were vaguely described as pertaining to additional cuts in Medicare, Medicaid, AFDC, food stamps, student loans, and federal retirement. We had no details on these, either.

To be sure, I had plenty of ideas. My staff had been working on a 'second round' of entitlement reforms all summer. But when we ran out of time on Wednesday, I told them to give me a high-side and low-side estimate of potential savings from the proposals under development. I split the difference and plugged in $28 billion in the budget table for the September Offensive. We would send the details on specific measures to Congress later in the fall, too.

Another $35 billion in savings had a familiar ring. The White

House fact sheet described it as 'remaining savings to be proposed in FY 83–84 budgets.' That was nothing but the magic asterisk again.

We still had not come up with any way to deliver the 'future savings' so integral to the original February budget plan. Now the IOU was being extended, until next year's budget was delivered in January 1982.

That's what my 'bold' and 'decisive' fall offensive had come to—$84 billion in promises. Mañana. The only real, tangible measure in it was the $13 billion defense cut. There was also the twelve percent across-the-board cut in domestic appropriations, but that had been declared dead-on-arrival, pre-arrival.

Getting this fuzzball launched caused a final moment of sweaty madness. Dave Gergen looked harried on calm days; now he looked like the wreck of the *Hesperus*. All day Thursday he scrambled furiously to make the speech draft consistent with what was now known as the 'Fall Budget Program'. Even we did not have the gall to call it an 'Offensive' any more.

By late afternoon the President's speech was still being chopped, scissored, and pasted together in the Roosevelt Room. This was unusual, to say the least. Ordinarily, nationwide presidential addresses are wrapped up days ahead of time. Gergen, Deaver, the speech writers, and I were all shouting and throwing papers around, trying to make it come together.

'Where's the graphs on Social Security?'

'Page two.'

'Two? Damn it, we're not leading with that—bury it in the back. I've said this six fucking times.'

'All right, all right.'

'We don't have anything on the loophole closing measures.'

'Regan hasn't *given* us anything on loopholes yet.'

'The section on entitlement needs beefing up. It says here—'

'We have to make it clear those exclude Social Security. It sounds like we're zapping the widows again. It's not clear enough here—'

In the midst of this someone raced into the room and said the typewriter had broken down. A new round of groans, gasps, and sweat beads broke out around the table. The wounded device was not just any old IBM Selectric. It was the machine that produced the text for the teleprompter. Even the White House had only one of these. Gergen picked up a phone and began screaming some obscenities into it. Apparently this managerial technique worked. The phone rang not long after with news that the machine had been repaired.

Shortly before 7.00 pm, with just over an hour to go before air-time, Gergen and I raced across the West Wing parking lot toward the Old Executive Office Building where the teleprompter typing machine was. In his hands Gergen clutched the tattered remains of the September Offensive. One of the pages blew out of his file folder. Gergen's six-foot four-inch frame lunged after it as the wind sent it flying.

'Let it go!' I yelled. 'Nobody will notice another missing page, anyway.'

At eight o'clock, the President spoke to the nation. He explained that we now needed 'a second round of budget savings to keep us on the road to a balanced budget.'

The speech contained a memorable allusion. At one of the White House meetings, Pete Domenici had recalled the words of heavyweight champion Joe Louis just before he stepped into the ring against Billy Conn. The speculation was that the fleet-footed Conn might escape Louis's lethal right hand. Informed of this, Louis said, 'He can run, but he can't hide.'

'That's just what we're facing on runaway federal spending,' the President told the American people. 'We can try to run from it, but we can't hide. We have to face up to it.'

These were strong words, but they were a caricature of the truth, and they marked a profound turning point. On 24 September 1981, the Reagan Administration went into hiding from the massive fiscal disorder it had unleashed only months before—and it would never again come out, despite the wisdom of Joe Louis.

I was so distraught and embarrassed by what we had produced that I went into temporary hiding, too. I couldn't even bear to hang around the White House and listen to the President deliver the speech.

So I went up to Capitol Hill to attend a previously scheduled private dinner with the Moynihans. There was a good bit of irony when my hosts turned on the TV screen. The President was sitting calmly at his Oval Office desk, ready to begin the next phase of the Reagan Revolution.

THE MORNING AFTER: THE FINAL LESSONS

I was standing in Liz Moynihan's kitchen. She had the wooden spoon in her hand and she was making spaghetti sauce—just as she had been the day I rocketed off to Washington eleven years before.

Just as she had that day, she picked up the phone.

'Maybe Pat has some ideas,' she said. 'I'll tell him you're here and to hurry home.'

This time Pat Moynihan wasn't in the White House—I was. Now he was among the politicians in the Senate. But I still needed his help.

Over dinner I told him, 'You guys on the Hill are going to have to rescue this. We went too far with the tax cut and now I can't get them to turn back.'

He scolded me a little, muttering about the danger of young men in a hurry to remake the world.

'We've got a fiscal disaster brewing. You know that,' said my old rabbi. 'But I'm not sure whether anything can be done about it or not.'

We moved into the living room. He stoked up the fireplace and got out the brandy. We talked long into the night. It felt like the good old days, but it wasn't. Now I was as responsible as anyone for the terrible thing that had happened to the nation, and even a brandy, nostalgia, intellectual talk and the company of an old friend could not dissipate that hard realization.

PART THREE

11
Days Before *The Atlantic*

By October 1981, political reality had nearly overtaken the Reagan Revolution. Now economic reality would come crashing in too, in the form of recession and the massive invalidation of Rosy Scenario. But the true magnitude of the deficit should not have remained hidden so long. We hadn't been the victims of a sudden and unexpected economic earthquake. Instead, we had deceived ourselves nearly from the beginning and had subsequently covered up the forecast debate when it urgently needed airing.

In June, we had been required to publish the official mid-session update of the President's budget. Even then Rosy Scenario was being nullified by the adverse conditions of the financial markets. The administration's two most competent and honest economists— Larry Kudlow and Jerry Jordan of the Council of Economic Advisors—had begged the high command to face up to the numbers.

Yet, we ended up doing the opposite. If the SEC* had jurisdiction over the White House, we might have all had time for a course in remedial economics at Allenwood Penitentiary.

The fateful decision to cover up what we knew to be the true budget numbers was made in Jim Baker's office on the afternoon of June 5. All the heavyweights were there: Baker, Meese, Don Regan, Dave Gergen, Marty Anderson and Dick Darman. I was in Canton, Ohio, cheerleading for the Reagan Revolution. Kudlow went to the meeting in my place, but his faithful report of what transpired amounts to the proverbial smoking gun.

Not having been there does not exonerate me. The next day, I read

* Securities and Exchange Commission.

Kudlow's report, grumbled, and shoved it into my drawer. I had every opportunity to do something about it. Back in June, the White House people sometimes listened when I spoke, including the President. But I was too preoccupied with the reconciliation bill campaign, too busy proving the politicians wrong to take the time to fix the far more consequential economic forecasting mistake upon which we were basing our entire radical transformation of the American economy.

'As you expected,' Kudlow had written, 'the political advice overwhelmed the economic analysis. Baker, Meese, Gergen, Regan . . . Harper all argued that *any significant change in the economic forecast would jeopardize the tax bill*.'

That particular day, Paul Craig Roberts was allowed to attend, as I recollect, the only serious White House meeting of his career. Unfortunately, what he had to contribute was both nonsensical and expedient. It confused the others sufficiently to enable them to sweep the issue of the forecast under the carpet with a minimum of bad conscience.

The forecast issue itself was clear. By early June, two of its lynchpins were seriously in doubt. Both short-term interest rates and long-term corporate bond yields were higher than they had been in January. With no sign of a financial market turnaround in sight, the push-pull hypothesis had become at best a dubious bet. But without push-pull and its four to five percent real growth beginning in the fall quarter, the budget numbers would have plunged deep into the red.

Immediately prior to the June 5 meeting, Kudlow and Jordan had submitted a memo to the senior staff warning that our money GNP estimates were wildly excessive in light of our actual monetary policy. Revenue estimates in the February forecast had therefore also been grossly overestimated: 'Revenue overestimates will cause the Administration considerable political embarrassment during the 1982–84 period.' Jordan had also highlighted the heroic real growth and investment assumptions in the February forecast. 'Real investment spending was projected to increase more rapidly over the five-year period than any historical experience,' he noted. 'Business fixed investment was projected to rise to 15 percent of GNP, compared with a historic range of 9.7 to 11 percent.'

Kudlow's and Jordan's attempt to revise the economic forecast, however, generated an equal and opposite reaction from Paul Craig

Roberts and the other supply siders at Treasury. They got Don Regan cranked up to defend all the inconsistencies and errors that had been there since the beginning. This was about the time Regan reclaimed his primacy as the administration's leading economic spokesman.

A few days before the June 5 meeting, he had circulated a memo to Weidenbaum, Anderson and me, defining where Treasury stood on the matter.

'It is Treasury's view,' Regan proclaimed, 'that it is not *propitious* at this time to make substantial changes in the pattern or level of economic projections reflecting the President's economic program.'

The memo, written by Roberts, went on to reveal that the Treasury supply siders were smoking something you didn't get from a cigarette machine.

They wanted to revise the economic forecast all right—*upward*. In February, we had forecast a growth in cumulative real GNP between 1980 and 1982 of 6.7 percent. The recession was about to knock that down to zero. Nevertheless, Regan and Roberts went into the June 5 forecast meeting advocating that the two-year growth total be raised to nine percent.

Actually, they wanted to raise the real growth forecast even more, but demurred for reasons that were labyrinthian. The memo said that 'Any substantial adjustments to the scenario could be interpreted by the Administration's opponents as *politically motivated to win passage* of the President's economic policy package.' In other words, to admit that our forecast was in error would be a political boon. Well, that was logical—if you believed that the real-world scenario was actually even rosier than we had said it was. Never mind that almost no one believed that in June 1981 because there wasn't a shred of evidence around on which to base it.

The fog that afternoon couldn't have been cleared with a giant fan. Kudlow's report noted that toward the end of the meeting, Meese mentioned that 'a friend of his had an interesting theory' that 'large government deficits were absorbing available savings. And this was pushing up interest rates.'

This theory, about as novel as the theory of evolution, was the stark reality that every financial market from Tokyo to London had been complaining about daily. There were probably five human beings alive who disagreed with Meese's friend. Unfortunately, two of them—the Treasury Secretary and his principal assistant—were in Jim Baker's office.

'Interest rate increases were strictly a monetary problem,' Roberts now assured everyone in the room, 'and had nothing to do with deficits and government borrowing.'

Kudlow tried to make them all understand the bottom line. The net result of these inconsistencies in the forecast was that we were presently underestimating the out-year deficits by substantial amounts. Did we really want consciously to mislead the Congress and the public?

Here Kudlow's report depicted an almost Nixonian *But-that-would-be-wrong* reaction:

'In response to this came a chorus of oh no we don'ts led by Gergen and Meese and jointed by Harper, Roberts and Regan.' The self-deception was consummated. Everyone protesting against exactly that which they were doing. Once again, the truth had been buried, and this time the White House had done it deliberately, in order to win the tax battle.

Kudlow's report closed on a wistful note. 'Don Regan didn't say much, except to support the political case. All in all, it was a particularly long seventy-five minutes.'

And a particularly disastrous mistake. Now, five months later, all the subsequent mistakes had been ratified. Regan was guarding the tax cut like a junkyard dog. Weinberger had surrounded his defense 'topline' with tanks. Jim Baker had fobbed off Social Security to a bipartisan study commission whose instructions were to take a year to think about it. The College of Cardinals had gutted most of the twelve percent appropriations cut and were preparing to give last rites to the rest. The House Republicans were sitting on their hands, bellyaching about being asked to close $3 billion worth of tax loopholes.

That was about as close to gridlock as you could get. We had painted ourselves into a corner. The score was $150 billion deficit, zero savings.

In the days after the President's September Offensive speech, the political and economic facts of life pounded away at what remained of the Reagan Revolution. Congress and the White House became stalemated. 'With his speech last night,' wrote David Broder, 'President Reagan came down from the stratosphere of last spring's euphoric first round of budget cutting and into the trench warfare most of his predecessors have faced when they challenged deeply embedded Congressional attitudes and interest-group pressures.'

The GOP congressional politicians were almost gleefully insolent. They had forced an extremely popular President to back off from making tough budget cuts that inconvenienced them. And now they had no intention of delivering on even the tepid measures the President had proposed the night before.

'Compared to last summer,' declared Mark Hatfield of the Senate Appropriations Committee, 'there are no rubber stamps in this Congress.'

It wasn't just the GOP liberals and moderates who were pronouncing the death of the revolution. Newt Gingrich, the self-proclaimed conservative gadfly from Georgia, had made the astounding assertion that Ronald Reagan was not significantly different from Jimmy Carter.

Jack Kemp put on his golden parachute and bailed out. He started giving goofy lectures about the gold standard. At the time I was furious. Now I realize he was completely in the thrall of Wanniski and Laffer.

Those two had now gone completely around the bend, telling fairy tales to anyone who would listen that all the nation's fiscal and political problems would vanish overnight if the gold standard were restored. They were beyond convincing, but perhaps Kemp wasn't. He was still a friend, and it was sad to see him succumbing so easily to such transparent sophistry.

I still believed in the gold standard, myself, but it was not a magic cure for our problems, and was certainly no substitute for political discipline and fiscal solvency. The financial markets would be no more impressed with the government's will to enforce a gold standard than they had been with its will and capacity to balance the budget. It was not a way of avoiding hard choices and political pain.

'You've been in the bowels of OMB too long,' Kemp teased. 'You're hooked on root canal. Does it really feel that good?'

The truth was, nothing felt that good any more. I was sorry for my friend's obtuseness, but there was nothing I could do to budge him. I was sorry, too, because of what it meant to our friendship; it was unlikely that it would survive, except as a cordial formality, given this parting of the ways.

I will say this on his behalf, though: at least Jack Kemp had an alternate theory, even if it was all haywire. The bulk of the House GOP pols didn't even bother to justify their counter-revolution. They were quite content with mindless sabotage. As Broder explained, they were 'rebelling against the "Simon says" series of rapid-fire commands from Reagan and Budget Chief David A. Stockman.'

Some rebellion. They had all voted for the giant tax cut. Now they wanted the luxury of standing back and watching the fight. It reminded me of those congressmen who ventured out to watch the Battle of Bull Run and were shocked to find the other side firing real bullets.

The Honorable and consistently vapid Larry DeNardis of Connecticut came up with another rhetorical gem on behalf of the Gypsy Moths. 'We'll hold together fairly well,' he said, 'but this time it will be the Bob Michel Show, not the Ronald Reagan or Dave Stockman Show.'

'Bob Michel Show' was code for GOP consensus—but there was no longer consensus for anything by then.

For a time I responded to all this pusillanimity by making militant pronouncements. On October 1, I told the House Budget Committee members that they were doomed to spend the rest of their careers cutting spending.

'There's no final vote,' I told Congress then. 'Twenty years of history aren't going to be corrected in twenty weeks. We're going to have to go at it again and again and again until we establish fiscal sanity.'

Jim Jones, the Committee's chairman, said that if we were so concerned about the deficit, when would Congress get the details of the administration's 'fall budget program'?

The President had promised $28 billion in new entitlement reform savings alone, he reminded me, but the Congress had thus far not received a single proposal. I dutifully promised a detailed plan by October 20.

The autumn leaves were long gone, however, by the time it reached Congress. And even then it wasn't remotely close to what we had promised. The attitude inside the administration by now simply mirrored that on the Hill.

The days of the Cutting Room were over. To come up with the

new cuts, we had to form a multi-agency task force. It was composed of dozens of departmental officials among whose passions dismantling the welfare state was not numbered. They spun their wheels for a month and finally produced anemic recommendations amounting to $12 billion per year in cuts—out of a spending base of $200 billion, excluding Social Security. Radical these recommendations were not. We were down to the bottom of the barrel. The Agriculture Department resisted further deep cuts in food stamps and child nutrition. HHS got squeamish about major reductions in Medicare and Medicaid. The Pentagon wouldn't support any reforms in the bloated military retirement system—save for rounding down pension checks to the next lower dollar. That saved the grand sum of $7 million per year from a $17 billion program. The story was the same on guaranteed student loans, civilian retirement, subsidized housing, and welfare. We were down to the bottom of the barrel even on our side.

Darman's Ping-Pong game didn't go very far, either. The President's fall budget program was supposed to have provided the framework and aggregate deficit reduction targets —$16 billion in 1982 and $115 billion over three years. The Senate Republican leadership would then come back to the White House with the same totals but a revised mix.

A larger share of the savings would mysteriously 'migrate' over to the revenue and defense column in the Senate response. That was the scenario. Then Howard Baker and his team would meet with the President and his team in the Cabinet Room. The President would reluctantly go for the Senate plan because everybody else in the room would be for it—the Senate team and, alas, his team, too.

Howard Baker started the script in motion by appointing a budget task force consisting of his major fiscal committee chairmen. They worked for several weeks to develop the 'Pong'. At an October 16 meeting in Howard Baker's office, several Senate committee chairmen told Baker, Darman and me that they were willing to play Ping-Pong, but—Catch-22—since we were now sixteen days into the new fiscal year, the administration should forget about trying to get the $16 billion in cuts for 1982. Instead, we should concentrate on trying to get the cuts we wanted for 1983 and beyond.

I let out a loud screech when I heard that. I argued that 1982 was the first full budget year of the Reagan Administration. If we threw in the towel on 1982 and the deficit soared over the original target of $42 billion, then Wall Street's apprehensions about uncontrolled deficits would be confirmed. Our credibility would be nil, after our first go around the track.

But the meeting left no doubt as to why the College of Cardinals was demanding surrender on the 1982 cuts. Half of the $16 billion in 1982 savings was attributable to the twelve percent cut in domestic appropriations. The latter constituted barely one seventh of the total federal budget. But it was where the bacon was.

The prospect of these cuts gave them the heebie-jeebies. Water projects would run dry. Amtrak would run out of diesel fuel. The Bureau of Land Management would have to increase cattle-grazing fees. Postal subsidies for rural newspapers would have to be cut. Local voters would have to pay for their own sewer treatment plants. Social workers would get laid off. Small businessmen would have to go to the bank rather than the SBA* to get a loan—and pay the market rate. Some of the eighty percent of US counties declared 'depressed areas' by EDA** wouldn't get the money they needed to lure factories away from other depressed counties. People would have to pay a nickel more to ride local mass transit systems. These were but a smattering of the unspeakable horrors that would result from a twelve percent across-the-board appropriations cut.

Mark Hatfield insisted that $1 billion, not $8 billion, was all that could be 'legitimately, honestly and politically' cut from the more than $150 billion in non-defense appropriations. But reducing the administration's proposal to that kind of a ludicrous pittance was not my idea of Ping-Pong.

It was now obvious that the appropriations committees were stalling. If they resisted the new cuts long enough, the continuing resolution we had agreed to would expire. We would have to extend it into February or March of 1982. But by then, half the fiscal year would be over and it would be impractical to make the twelve percent cut.

Realizing what they were up to, I had prepared a counter move that called their bluff. By invoking the so-called deferral mechanism, I had impounded twelve percent of the funds in each appropriations account for the duration of the continuing resolution, until

* Small Business Administration.
** Economic Development Administration.

November 20. What's more, we announced we would keep on deferring the funds until they started cutting.

Predictably, Hatfield had gone into a rage on learning about it. 'The White House is threatening to tear up the Constitution,' he exploded.

'We'll knock them down,' Sil Conte huffed. 'Our committee did a heck of a job. We've gone through enough. First they [the White House] come through the front door and then they come in through the back door.'

Actually, the impoundment wasn't a new cut, and it had nothing to do with any back door. It was only a temporary way of implementing what the President had proposed on September 24, a perfectly legal device to prevent the twelve percent cut from being invalidated by the calendar.

But never mind. By calling Congress's bluff, we were guilty of nothing less than 'trampling upon the right of the legislative branch.' I assumed the 'right' they were talking about was the right to keep on spending, for I could think of no other.

No one was more upset than the Gypsy Moths, according to Michigan's Carl Pursell. They were going 'on strike' until other things got cut first.

'We're not prepared to support further cuts in social programs,' Bill Green declared, 'until we see the same kind of scrutiny given to cuts in defense, water projects, tobacco subsidies, and other areas.' The fact of the matter was Green considered any federal dollar that landed in the vicinity of Manhattan Island a 'social program'. The National Endowment for the Arts' subventions to local museums and symphony orchestras apparently were now part of the safety net, too.

Thus, in the week of October 19, the Ping-Pong ball turned into lead. It never bounced again, it just rolled off the table and landed on the floor with a thud.

Howard Baker urgently requested a Sunday morning meeting with the LSG at the White House.

'This dog ain't gonna hunt,' he flatly told us, referring to the twelve percent appropriations cut. The only antidote was for the administration publicly to indicate that it would accept a half loaf and withdraw its veto threat, except in the case of out-and-out 'budget busters'.

That was too much. I couldn't sit still.

'You're just giving Hatfield and the rest of the appropriators a free ride,' I protested. 'If we take the impoundment off and drop the veto threat, it's Katie-bar-the-door. We won't get a dime of the twelve percent cut. And that's the only fig leaf of deficit reduction we've got left. I think the President should go to the mat with the Senate Appropriations Committee—if that's what they want.'

My outburst provoked something unheard of in Washington. At long last the unflappable Howard Baker exploded in red-hot anger. Before I had even finished the last sentence of my diatribe, he whirled around in his chair and glared directly at me.

'Don't you ever, *ever* lecture me again on how to run the United States Senate,' he seethed. 'I know what my job is and I'll do it by my best lights. But don't even *try* to get in my way once I've made a final judgment on what can or can't be done!'

Jim Baker tried to break the tension by telling an off-color joke. As he did, I sheepishly put my head down, lit a cigarette, and tried to smoke it. My hand was shaking.

The Senate Majority Leader's indignant words had ripped right through my self-confidence. They stung as much as my father's leather strap.

Suddenly I felt like the unwelcome interloper I actually was. It was time to grow up and stop posturing fecklessly like a clay-footed tough guy, or a make-believe revolutionary.

Coming from Howard Baker, the warning was all the more devastating. By then I had come nearly to idolize him. At my last session with Greider I'd said that he would outclass Lyndon Johnson hands-down as the greatest Senate Majority Leader of modern times. 'He's good,' I'd remarked, 'one of the greatest legislators in decades. That guy is better than anybody else who's ever been on the track.'

Until that Sunday morning I had thought Howard Baker took me seriously, considered me a force to be reckoned with. Now I realized *that* was an illusion, too. He was drawing a line that marked the boundary of political necessity's awesome force. Neither my Grand Doctrine nor my budget math had any hope of penetrating beyond it.

The LSG agreed to Howard Baker's demands. The Senate would move forward with the 1982 appropriations bill. The Majority Leader would endeavor to persuade the College of Cardinals to make a 'best efforts' attempt to realize part of the $8 billion cut in domestic appropriations. (We ended up getting only $2 billion and had to veto a continuing resolution to achieve even that much.) The White House, meanwhile, would cool down the confrontation atmosphere and find some way to back down on the impoundments. My bold September Offensive to cut $75 billion was now reduced to four billion of 'maybe' money.

To compensate us for our trouble, Baker mentioned the possibility of getting $7 or $8 billion in 1982 tax loophole savings instead of our target of $3 billion. Temporarily out of touch with his supply-side advisers, Don Regan agreed to look into it.

This led to a spate of press stories the next day, October 19, saying that the administration was backing away from its budget cuts. Instead, the White House would seek larger 'revenue enhancements'.

Since we had not yet told the President that we had caved in on the twelve percent cut, Larry Speakes was trotted out to deny everything. Nothing had been negotiated or agreed on, he said. 'The ball's in their [the Senate's] court.'

But the mere hint that another change in the budget plan was afoot again brought the House Republicans out of the woodwork. By then, the mutual distrust and suspicion between the House and Senate GOP was severe.

'You don't raise taxes during a recession,' Kemp predictably remarked. But even Kemp's old nemesis, Barber Conable, warned against the idea.

Conable hadn't forgotten for a moment that we had kicked the Ways and Means Democrats squarely in the shins during the July tax cut fight. If we were now to ask them to bring a revenue increase bill to the floor in order to rescue us, they'd be spoiling for revenge. Who could say what kind of disaster might emerge?

The rhetorical volleys between the House and Senate GOP intensified as the week wore on. They held several joint leadership meetings to try to reconcile their differences—meetings from which the White House was pointedly excluded.

It was hard to tell whether the purpose of these meetings was to dump on the White House or to bash away at each other. The heated sessions in Howard Baker's office produced both kinds of angry noises.

'We're going to have more of a congressional imprint on what we decide up here,' Michel told reporters after one session, 'rather than just swallowing what they send us from downtown.'

Since the President was in Cancun, Mexico, attending the Conference on Third World Development, the Republican leaders made the most of the opportunity to do it their way. By the end of the week, they had themselves in interlocking handcuffs.

'House and Senate leaders announced today that they had reached tentative agreement on President Reagan's new round of budget cuts,' *The New York Times* for October 23 reported.

> . . . The agreement basically consisted of allowing each chamber to go its own way.
>
> The Senate Republicans committed themselves to an *unspecified* mix of new taxes, spending cuts and reduction in [entitlement] benefit programs. But the House Republican leaders opposed raising taxes in a recession and were leery of further cuts in benefit programs, such as Medicare and food stamps.

Domenici summed up the state of affairs aptly. 'You've got two problems. First of all, you've got no agreement on a plan, and second of all, you've got no agreement on what's happening.'

The September Offensive was thus dead as a doornail. By a fluke we had half of the Reagan Revolution in place. But now it was clear that there was absolutely no capacity to cope with the consequences among the GOP politicians who had helped enact it.

On October 18 the President was boarding a helicopter on his way to Yorktown, Virginia, where he would celebrate the two hundredth anniversary of the Battle of Yorktown with his ideological opposite, President François Mitterand of France. On his way past the reporters gathered on the South Lawn, Reagan let a giant economic cat out of the bag. He confirmed what outside economists had been suggesting for weeks, that the US economy was entering a recession.

'I think there's a slight and, I hope, a short recession,' he said. 'Yes, I think everyone agrees on that.'

This off-hand remark led in a matter of days to a dramatic change of perception regarding the fiscal situation inside the White House. It symbolized the fact that the veil of the future was parting.

The failed September Offensive had been aimed at reducing the 1984 deficit by $75 billion. Now the deficit estimate had increased by an order of magnitude—to $150 billion. We were suddenly faced with the stark reality of what had been hidden from the beginning. Our sweeping fiscal plan had led straight into the jaws of triple-digit deficits.

In early November, I briefed the President and senior White House staff on this radical transformation of the budget outlook. I now projected nearly $400 billion in red ink for 1982 to 1984.

'Since July, the budget estimates have *deteriorated drastically*,' the briefing paper said. 'We are now in a totally different economic policy ball game—which will require a significant mid-course correction.'

We had to acknowledge that the push-pull hypothesis was dead. The economy would go through several quarters of contraction rather than rocket into five percent real growth beginning in the winter of 1981–82. Disinflation would take its toll in lost output and temporarily surging unemployment just as it always had. We had not discovered any shortcuts to restoring economic and financial health.

Likewise, the blatant inconsistency between our monetary policy recommendations and our bloated February money GNP forecast had come home to roost, too. We now had to lower our forecast for 1982–84 GNP by the staggering sum of *one-half trillion dollars*. The consequence was that nearly $150 billion in phantom revenues embedded in the February budget disappeared over the same period.

We also had to admit that our original interest rate assumptions were 'wildly off the mark'. The financial markets had seen through our brave insistence that the budget would be balanced in 1984. The fiscal expectations theory had been consequently tossed on the scrapheap, too. Interest rates would remain high, with more double-digit billions added to the deficit estimates.

The dilemma at the moment was awful. Now that we saw the real magnitude of the problem, we were out of political muscle to cut domestic spending and the President was unwilling to change the tax and defense programs.

*   *   *

In the wake of the President's acknowledgment that we had entered a recession, a strange calm descended on the normally clamorous precincts of Capitol Hill. For a blessed moment, the fiscal world stood still.

The politicians realized that these gargantuan deficits meant trouble for everyone, including them, and so they turned in the direction of the White House not to throw rocks but to ask, in earnest, what the game plan was now.

'We don't know *what* the Administration is proposing at this point,' complained Congressman Del Latta, co-'author' of the Reagan Revolution's legislative agenda. It was a telling remark. Among all the GOP politicians, Latta was the single most eager to support the White House.

'I don't have any intention of providing a committee alternative,' said House Budget Chairman Jim Jones. 'Basically, it's the President's program.'

'Any further deficit cuts will have to come from the President,' Speaker O'Neill commented.

'We need some real official iteration on where this budget is going and what the White House really expects us to do,' Pete Domenici chimed in.

It was Ralph Regula, Republican of Ohio, who defined the quandary in a nutshell. It was now the President's turn at bat—not the presidency, but Ronald Wilson Reagan himself.

'People are waiting to get a clear signal from the President on what he wants to do,' said Regula. 'Therein lies the problem.'

The bitter truth was that Ronald Reagan faced an excruciating test of presidential decision making. After an exhausting and prolonged political struggle, he had emerged in July triumphant. Only three months later, he had to admit that the triumph had been an illusion.

Even worse, it had not been his fault. He had been misled by a crew of overzealous—and ultimately incompetent—advisers. The original budget plan I had devised for him had been fatally flawed. It is even harder to eat crow when you haven't cooked it yourself.

The situation was now a pathetic parody of the warning he had issued to the politicians in his September Offensive speech. The President could run, but he couldn't hide. Who would help him? Not the Democrats, who were sullen and revengeful; not the Republicans, who were hunkered down in their separate camps, frantic and confused. The only real option open to him was retreat. Economic reality and democratic fact had conspired to make it so. The American welfare state had found its permanent boundaries and the politicians had drawn their defensive perimeters. The laws of sound public finance and economics ruled out a free lunch—permanent continuation of the half-revolution embodied in the giant tax cut.

He had no choice but to repeal, or substantially dilute, the tax cut. That would have gone far toward restoring the vitality of the strongest capitalist economy in the world. It would have been a great act of statesmanship to have admitted the error back then, but in the end it proved too mean a test. In November 1981, Ronald Reagan chose not to be a leader but a politician, and in so doing he showed why passion and imperfection, not reason and doctrine, rule the world. His obstinacy was destined to keep America's economy hostage to the errors of his advisers for a long, long time.

During the first week in November, the President met with his economic policy team every day. This time he got all the facts and heard all the arguments.

Nothing was buried in thick, incomprehensible black binders of line-item budget cuts. We brought the big picture right into the Oval Office.

There were no longer any magic asterisks, just the unvarnished numbers. The issue was no longer how to attain a balanced budget, but how to prevent a triple-digit deficit disaster.

Amid the almost insulting clarity of the presentations we made to him that week, there was only one complication to muddy the picture: Donald Regan. The Secretary of the Treasury was determined to prevail for the sake of prevailing in these desperately needed policy review sessions.

In preparation for our session with the President, Marty Anderson, Murray Weidenbaum, Don Regan and I assembled a revised economic forecast. Everyone had signed off on it, including Regan.

The new economic forecast finally brought our GNP forecast into harmony with our monetary policy. This reduced our revenue estimate for 1984 alone by $65 billion. It also included a 1982 recession and higher interest rates.

What came out of the OMB budget models when this new forecast was applied was horrifying. For 1982, the deficit figures *started* at $97 billion—more than double the $42 billion we had been straining for all year. The deficit for 1984, the year of our balanced budget, rose to $146 billion. After that the numbers just kept rising, until they reached $170 billion by 1986, the final year of our five-year fiscal plan.

Thus the new consensus economic forecast resulted in a budget which showed cumulative red ink over five years of more than *$700 billion*. That was nearly as much national debt as it had taken America 200 years to accumulate. It just took your breath away. No government official had ever seen such a thing.

It did not, however, take away the breath of the supply siders at Treasury. They were soon kicking up a stink about OMB's 'deficit mongering', even though their own boss had agreed to the forecast. But they swiftly convinced Regan that the forecast was too 'pessimistic', and that it showed no faith in the tax cut.* So they marched their boss into the White House with a revised, 'optimistic' forecast.** But even with the so-called optimistic Treasury forecast we got triple-digit deficits—$111 billion in budget red ink by 1984.

So we should have been all on the same side. Only eleven months earlier we had confidently laid out a fiscal plan that was explicitly and dramatically targeted to a balanced budget in 1984. We had said over and over that it all added up—we would get there despite the sceptics.

Now even the most outlandishly optimistic forecast available gave us triple-digit deficits—not just in 1984 but as far as the eye could see into the future. Under the best of circumstances the outcome was going to be radically different from the promise. We were way off course—even by Treasury's own numbers.

On November 2, the economic team and the LSG assembled to

---

* The fact was that even our new consensus forecast proved to be too optimistic. Rather than growing at 1.3 percent in 1982, the US economy in fact contracted by 2.1 percent. The actual 1982 unemployment rate averaged nearly 10 percent rather than just under 8 percent, as our consensus forecast assumed.

** The Treasury's optimistic forecast assumed cumulative real GNP growth of 8.2 percent for 1982 and 1983. Due to the depth of the recession which actually ensued, the two-year real growth amounted to only 1.4 percent.

give the President the bad news. Dick Darman and Marty Anderson had imposed a new rule for the occasion. Any point that was important enough to make had to be simple and clear enough to fit on one page.

The first page of the briefing paper told the whole story succinctly. It showed three forecasts: the revised 'consensus' forecast; Treasury's 'optimistic' forecast; and a monetarist outlook. Then it showed the deficits that would result under each forecast. For 1984, they ranged from $111 to $185 billion—compared with zero under the original plan.

But the President did not believe in out-year budget projections and did not see the numbers; he only heard the words, and the words he found most soothing were those of his Treasury Secretary.

'Mr President,' Regan declaimed, 'your program has only been in effect thirty-three days. Let's not write it off yet. There's no reason for all this gloom and doom.

'We at Treasury think these figures are too pessimistic. They assume your tax cut isn't going to work.'

I was about to say something, but the nation's chief financial officer was not finished.

'Let me give you a homely analogy,' he continued. 'It's as though speculators in grain were to say that we're going to have a crop failure a month after the farmer has planted his seeds. How could they know that? Anything can happen. Let's give these seeds we've planted a chance to grow.'

This boorish non sequitur was as shrewd as it was erroneous. Regan had outsmarted us by speaking to the President in language the President understood: the folksy *Reader's Digest* anecdote. The fact was that the piece of paper on the table staring up at the President had nothing to do with meteorological vagaries and a three-inch-high crop of corn. To extend the analogy, Treasury's own forecast assumed absolutely perfect economic weather for years, but even then its figures showed record crop failures—deficits amounting to a half-trillion dollars over three years.

Following one of these early November sessions, Regan explained to the press what was going on inside the White House.

'The problem is that the naysayers are having their day,' he was quoted.

At the next session we took up the question of 'what have we come here to do?' as the President put it. How much more domestic spending was it realistic to believe could be cut?

To be sure, I wanted to continue the fight against all the misbegotten projects of the American welfare state. But I now realized that we had to use a discount factor. We were only going to squeeze out of the politicians a small fraction of the spending cuts we had asked them to make.

Accordingly, I prepared the kind of analysis the President should have had in February—it showed him the *political* feasibility of additional domestic spending cuts.

The message fairly leaped off the page. We weren't going to bring the deficits under control with domestic spending cuts alone. We wouldn't even come close.

'This is the conclusion of our people,' I told the President. 'It was round-tabled by the Cabinet—Dick Schweiker, Ray Donovan, Ted Bell, Jack Block and Sam Pierce.'

So there we had it. The three major domestic spending categories amounted to more than one-half trillion dollars. That was everything in the budget except defense and debt service. But no matter how you sliced it, you couldn't get politically viable savings of even $35 billion compared to a deficit problem of $100 to $185 billion.

The backup detail told why. The best outcome in Social Security would be a $4 billion savings from a COLA delay. Non-Social Security entitlements cost nearly $200 billion, but the administration's own task force had only been able to save $12 billion. The last spending category included $158 billion in domestic appropriations. But that included a lot of spending we wanted. Nearly $30 billion was earmarked for foreign aid and security assistance, nuclear weapons production, NASA, the State Department, and the Justice Department. There were billions more in the 'our spending' category. The more relevant perspective was to take a hard look at where we were on the Hill from the twelve percent cut in this category. We had proposed to save $8 billion from our March funding request. But the pending appropriations bills in the Senate *added* a billion, and the White House version added $4 billion.

There was only one minor additional prospect for savings. We could hold down federal pay raises and keep trying to trim the bureaucracy. But the outside savings limit was an additional $5 billion.

By now I knew this nickel and dime issue would get us off the beaten track, yet I had to include it or Meese would squawk. He'd say I hadn't presented all the options, the President would start talking about Sacramento again, the discussion would degenerate, and nothing would be decided. Wearily, I included the bureaucracy cut. But I attached a strong caveat to it.

'Mr President, we need to go after padded payrolls,' I agreed. 'But it's going to be *tough*. Even the Cabinet isn't coming through. Their budget requests for next year realize only 15,000 of the 75,000 employee reduction target we set in September. The cabinet proposals will save less than one-half billion dollars.'

The President nodded. 'That's just what's going to happen when the management efforts of our people take hold,' he replied.

Somehow, he had drawn the exact opposite conclusion from what I had just told him about how little the Cabinet was willing to cut from the payroll.

'It's the same thing we found in California,' he continued. 'Every agency was layered with more people than they needed.'

He was off and running. There was nothing to do but sit back and listen.

'We found in one case, it was the vehicle registration department,' the President recalled. 'In that department they kept the records in thousands of metal filing cabinets. Except the records were twice as wide as the file drawers.

'So they had people standing there all day doing like this.' He folded a piece of paper double and held it up.

'One of our people found out you didn't have to do this. We just ordered new metal cabinets which were twice as wide, so the records would fit without folding. It saved thousands of work-hours. This,' the President concluded, 'is the kind of thing that management can accomplish.'

I would hear the filing cabinet story many times over the next four years. It was the single lens through which the President viewed the federal budget. I would try many times to dissuade him from that point of view, never with success.

What was too big wasn't the number of filing cabinets but the number of entitlement checks and subsidy payments going out to the American public. You couldn't solve that problem with wider drawers. You had to line up 218 votes in the House and 51 in the

Senate behind a bill to change the automatic spending laws. But the votes weren't there. The deficit was a function of politics, not inadequate management.

Eventually, we got to the crux, the issue of how to get more revenue. On the one hand, we faced a $150 billion deficit. On the other, we could only get $40 billion in domestic spending cuts under the rosiest legislative scenario. That left $90 billion and an inescapable conclusion: we would have to go for a major tax increase.

I argued for $40–50 billion per year by 1984. I was insistent that if we wanted to preserve the full individual tax rate cut, then we would have to go for excise and consumption taxes. Alcohol, tobacco, gasoline, imported oil. These were (a) economically benign, and (b) not inconsistent with the supply-side idea of restoring *income* tax incentives for production, savings, investment and entrepreneurial activity.

Now, at the time we were debating the tax issue in the White House, Senator Pete Domenici was valiantly trying to revive the 'Ping-Pong' game Darman and I had devised in September. Soon he had come up with a perfect legislative way of doing it.

Under the normal budget procedure, Congress must adopt a 'second Budget Resolution', confirming or altering what has been adopted in the first Budget Resolution in the spring. But if the spending and deficit targets are in danger of being breached, a second reconciliation bill is in order to cut more spending or raise revenue. The step is designed to bring the budget back into line with the targets.

Since we were now certain to miss the original targets by fabulous amounts, Domenici had designed a new budget plan. It cut domestic spending by $40 billion, raised taxes by $40 billion, and cut defense by $16 billion. When you added the interest savings on the existing national debt, the whole package amounted to a $100 billion deficit reduction in 1984.

Domenici's plan solved two thirds of the problem, resting as it did on Hatfield's three-legged budget stool: revenues, domestic cuts and defense. You could still haggle over the details, such as trimming defense, for instance. But the plan embodied the kind of quid pro quo essential to refashioning a legislative consensus. Indeed, given the current anarchy on the Hill, it was probably the only way to get any additional domestic spending cuts enacted at all. He had already built up a substantial amount of quiet support for it on both sides of the aisle.

But timing was crucial. Domenici's plan was the last train out of the station. If we turned it down, there wouldn't be another until the spring and summer of 1982, by which time we would be knee deep in both a recession and congressional elections. The House Democrats would be out for revenge. Fixing the deficit in that environment was not at all likely.

We couldn't wait until after the 1982 election, either, because that meant not getting to the deficit issue until the spring of 1983. By then the 1982 and 1983 budgets would be locked in. We wouldn't even have much leverage on the 1984 budget, due to the time lag in realizing tax increases or spending cuts. So it was either move aggressively now, or—wait until we actually had triple-digit deficits.

Pete Domenici had genuinely figured a way out of the mess. But Don Regan and his supply-side cohort promptly figured out a way to keep us firmly mired in it. With a single, deliberate stroke that first week of November 1981, he tore up the down payment on Domenici's plan to rescue us. As a result, we were deprived of a chance to reduce the 1984 deficit by $100 billion in 1984; and, more fundamentally, to increase revenues by $40 to $50 billion every year, *permanently*, so as to help the nation cope with a structural, triple-digit deficit.

Regan's new battle cry was now, 'You can't raise taxes in a recession.' It was a non sequitur, and it was wilfully ignorant twaddle.

All three forecasts said the recession would be over by the end of 1982. Treasury was predicting 5.1 percent growth in 1983 and 5.4 percent in 1984. That was when Domenici's $40 billion tax increase proposal would take effect—*after* the economy had started to roar back. By then, we would have to get rid of the triple-digit deficits if we wanted to keep the recovery going.

The Domenici plan was prospective—it was designed to take effect after the recession was over. But we had to get it in place before we got there. The $5 billion revenue down payment for 1982 in his plan was strictly a token, a legislative expedient. The President's own final September budget package had included $3 billion in loophole-closing measures for 1982, so the fact of near-term recession was hardly relevant to the long run.

But Regan was determined to go for the capillaries. On Wednesday 4 November, without telling anyone, he announced at a press conference that the administration would abandon its request for $3 billion in new 1982 revenues from closing loopholes.

'With the economy in recession,' he declared, 'this is not the time to raise taxes.'

That, finally, was what the debate had come to. Revenues for 1982 were estimated at $630 billion. GNP was projected at *$3,242 billion*. And now Regan was posturing, Horatio at the bridge, against the lousy $3 billion in loophole measures we had come up with only forty days earlier.

Under ordinary circumstances this would have been ludicrous. These were not ordinary circumstances, however. All the briefing papers contained at least three columns of numbers—for 1982, 1983 and 1984. But the President would only look at 1982. So the debate became: 'Taxes or no taxes in 1982.' The Domenici plan thus fell off the table.

By the final meeting with the President on November 5, I did not have much hope left. My heart was just not in tax raising as it had been in making a fiscal revolution. Still, the evidence was in, and we had to face the facts and do what was necessary. I was buoyed by the knowledge that the revolution had not been a total failure. We had tightened the money supply, sharply reduced inflation, and were making some progress on deregulation. For the first time in modern American politics, we had actually put the spending constituencies on the defensive. That was no mean feat. Nine months into the administration was the time to salvage as much of the Reagan Revolution as we could.

And so, for the fourth day in a row, I summoned all my remaining enthusiasm and pleaded the case for a big tax increase. I was about the only one left. Baker, Meese, Weidenbaum and Anderson had all seen the handwriting on the wall, and Regan was playing to every one of the President's blind spots.

I told him that even with the $40 billion in spending cuts, we would still be left with a permanent, post-recession deficit of over $100 billion.

'Mr President,' I pleaded, 'we can't live with that. It violates the basic laws of sound public finance.

'If we give up on the deficit, what will the politicans on the Hill do? They'll jump for joy. If Ronald Reagan says deficits are now OK—they'll run up the national debt like there's no tomorrow.

'But there is a tomorrow. Future generations will be paying off the interest forever. And sooner or later the financial pressures from huge deficits will start the drumbeat for easy money—for the printing press solution. Inflation will soar back up. It always has. So we have to bite the bullet and go with taxes. In return, maybe we can get another pound of flesh on spending.'

As soon as I was finished, Don Regan jumped in. He didn't want to talk about the future. He was stuck on the recession.

'The last thing you want to do is *take money out of consumers' pockets*,' he insisted. 'That will only reduce demand, cause more layoffs, and make the recession worse.'

He was making a flat-out Keynesian argument. It was perverse! But then he switched gears. 'We at Treasury,' Regan said, 'take a *monetarist* view. We should keep fighting the deficit with spending cuts—but a balanced budget has to be our third priority. We have to get inflation and interest rates down first. That's the Fed's job.'

Having thoroughly confused the issue, he now moved in for the kill.

'Mr President,' he concluded, 'you've got to keep your promise. We should reject the idea of trying to balance the budget on the back of the taxpayers.'

To this the President responded, 'No, Don is right. I never said anything but that it was a goal. A balanced budget, yes. That's where we have to be aiming to come out. Whether it comes then or is delayed or not—well, you're still heading to the point where the lines cross.'

The war was over. Regan had convinced the President he was keeping his promise to the American people by *not* balancing the budget. The President had reconciled the contradiction in a single sentence whose logic was as tortured as his grammar. There was nothing left to do but close my briefing book and finish writing down what he had said.

The wisdom of the next day's *New York Times* clarified the President's syntax and the new US fiscal policy: 'Reagan Abandons Aim of Balancing the Budget by 1984.'

On Friday 6 November, the Republican leadership was summoned to the White House. In case anyone had any lingering doubts, the President wanted to make absolutely clear that he was opposed to raising taxes. The internecine warfare over taxes and the budget had become so severe that the House and Senate Republicans were invited to separate meetings.

The House Republicans were, of course, overjoyed. They congratulated the President for not 'flip-flopping'. They praised the 'no U-turn' sign he had put up at the White House. Oh yes, they said, spending cuts were the 'only' answer. The sad thing was that the President was the only one in the room who didn't understand they were making a joke at his expense.

The meeting with the Senate Republican leaders was a different matter. During the post-Labor Day Thermidor they had not buried their heads in the sand as their counterparts in the House had. They did not come to the White House that day to make disingenuous noises about the importance of cutting federal spending.

Howard Baker, Domenici, Dole, Laxalt, Hatfield, Jake Garn—all were prepared to work something out on the budget, a mixture of defense savings, spending cuts and revenue increases. They were not happy about what had to be done, but they knew what it would take in an atmosphere in which there was no majority for any clear solution. And they knew that to put off the day of reckoning on triple-digit deficits was unthinkable. The problem wouldn't go away; it would only get worse.

To be sure, many among them were ravenous pork barrelers, and their concern for deficits could have been called hypocritical. But even these understood that you have to plant your feet on the ground in order to get your snout in the trough.

Pete Domenici spoke for the senators. He made what would be the last serious plea for confronting the problem before it was too late and went out of control.

'Mr President,' he began, 'I don't like to be the guy with the bad news. I want you to understand I'm for you. We're all behind you. You're shaking up the country just in the nick of time. We couldn't have gone on with the old ways much longer. But I've got to talk numbers with you.' He slid a single piece of paper across the table to the President.

'This budget is a monster,' he continued. 'It's got things in it none of us have heard of. But sooner or later you've got to get it down to the basic numbers and make some decisions for the American future.'

Domenici then pointed to the deficit line at the bottom. It showed triple digits every year across the page.

'This isn't old Gloom-and-Doom Domenici talking,' he said. 'These deficit numbers are what you get with Rosy Scenario—skirts, ruffles and all. They're based on Treasury's optimistic view of the world.

'Now look at your line for defense, Social Security, and interest. It starts at sixty percent of the whole blooming budget, and gets up nearly to seventy percent by the out-years.

'You're not going to save much there, Mr President. You know the reasons why.

'You can't get $100 billion in savings out of this little bitty piece that's left—the thirty percent part. You got money in there for feeding babies, for building roads, for cancer research, for the national parks, the FBI. We'll help you squeeze 'em, but we can't bleed 'em. You're just going to have to have some more revenue to make up the difference, to pay for all these things that we want or don't have a prayer of getting rid of.'

Domenici's five-minute summary of the problem was the best statement of the issue that had been made, before or since. But all it did was to make the President mad. As Domenici was talking, my eyes strayed to the President. He was getting tense, agitated. Instead of following Domenici's one-page presentation of the budget numbers, he made notes on it. He was jotting down rebuttal points.

'Damn it, Pete,' he exclaimed, 'I'm just not going to accept this. This is just more of the same kind of talk we've heard for forty years.

'I don't question your concern with the deficit and all. But there was once an economist, maybe you haven't heard of him. He said when government starts taking more than twenty-five percent of the economy [GNP], that's when the trouble starts. Well, we zoomed above that a long time ago. That's how we got this economic mess. We can't solve it with more of tax and spend.'

The room fell silent. The President never mentioned who the

anonymous economist was. Now the nation would begin an experiment to find out if he was right.

By the end of the week, Regan was hinting openly that I should resign. *The New York Times* reported that 'A Treasury official said that Mr Regan and other opponents of a tax increase had grown openly impatient with Mr Stockman, and that it was time that the budget director recognized the futility of his point of view and should consider resigning.'

It was pretty malicious stuff, but I had to be philosophical about it. I had a lot to atone for. I was prepared to take the blame and go out properly chastened.

Tuesday 10 November was my thirty-fifth birthday. Jennifer was taking me out to a restaurant later to celebrate. I hadn't been very cheerful company the last few weeks. Tonight I was resolved to do better about that, to relax with the woman I loved, to drink champagne, toast the future—whatever the hell it had in store—and forget about everything for a few hours.

Late that afternoon my phone rang. It was Dick Darman. 'Have you heard about tonight's news?' His tone was alarmed.

'No,' I said, 'I was just going over some stuff.'

Lesley Stahl of CBS will inform the nation that in the upcoming issue of *The Atlantic Monthly*, William Greider, national news editor of *The Washington Post*, had quoted me as saying that the tax cut had been a trojan horse to disguise a giveaway to the rich.

I slumped back in my chair, took off my glasses and rubbed my forehead—the gestures of a defeated man.

Within hours the White House press corps had managed to transform Greider's article from a thoughtful (only slightly erroneous) analysis of the honest failure of a radical attempt to transform US economic and fiscal policy into a tale about a budget director who had never believed in his own revolution from the beginning.

It was wrong—and it was devastating. The more intelligent and level-headed journalists, such as George Will and William Buckey, would, within a week, write their own analyses of the *Atlantic* article, pointing to the real political and economic issues it raised. But the White House press room is not a place of calm and orderly reflection. Soon I was the Judas of the Cabinet Room, the man who wilfully deceived the President and who had now shed his disguise so as to complete the betrayal.

I had been prepared to leave, and to confess my sins. But of this gross crime I was innocent, and I was damned if I would be driven out as a man disloyal to the very ideas he had fought for.

In the days following my attempted lynching at the hands of the White House mob, I resolved to clear my name of the false charge by doing everything I could to help correct the enormous fiscal error that I had done so much to bring about. That was the main reason I stayed on. I did not want to go down in history as the father of the triple-digit deficits.

It would not have been loyal to the President to remain silent about the unfolding catastrophe. That he did not yet understand what was happening was unfortunate, but not reason enough to abandon him. So I joined with the politicians. There was no longer any revolution to betray, only a shambles to repair.

In the years ahead, I continued to think that one day the President would realize the consequences of what had been done. The day never came, however.

About two months later we had another bruising internal battle on the President's 1983 budget. Baker, Darman and I almost convinced him to support a major tax increase. But at the last minute, the supply siders misled him again and our excise tax plan was dropped.

Yet since no one in the White House wanted to propose the first triple digit budget deficit in history, I finally did what the *Atlantic* story seemed to acuse me of. I out-and-out cooked the books, inventing $15 billion per year of utterly phony cuts in order to get Ronald Reagan's first full budget below the $100 billion deficit level. As on prior occasions, I rationalized this as a holding action. When the President finally came around, we would substitute new revenues for the smoke and mirrors.

By the spring of 1982 the recession was getting worse and the deficit projection was still rising. Jim Baker finally convinced the President to authorize the LSG to negotiate with the bipartisan congressional leadership on a deficit reduction plan which would include defense cuts and tax increases.

The negotiation group became known as 'the gang of 17', and it met day after day for weeks. I got a pretty good hosing in those private sessions—as the Democrat leaders especially unloaded their resentments about my previous high-handed tactics. Still, they were willing to fashion a compromise plan if the President would back off part way on his twenty-five percent tax cut.

At the final meeting we brought in the President and the Speaker to close the small remaining difference on spending cuts, a defense stretch-out and tax increases. But the two of them soon got into a philosophical debate about the New Deal; sparks flew.

Finally, the President said, 'Tip, I feel like I'm about to pass a pineapple. But OK, I'll agree to a temporary delay of the tax cut in return for these spending cuts.'

I then got a glimpse of what Democratic governance ultimately comes down to. Someone has to be a leader and take the heat. But the President again abdicated, reflecting once more the views of his political advisers.

'Mr President, are you putting Social Security on the table or not?' Tip O'Neill asked in referring to the COLA cut which was an essential ingredient of the compromise plan.

'You're not going to trap me on that,' the President shot back. The summit meeting soon collapsed, and a permanent fiscal gridlock set in that would last for years.

The President had tried but he never really understood why this and dozens of subsequent attempts to tackle the deficit monster failed. His stout opposition to a major tax increase obligated him to lead the fight to shrink the American welfare state's giant entitlement programs like Social Security, not just castigate 'spending' in the abstract while ducking the real bullets. You couldn't have it both ways, but ultimately that's how he usually came down.

When I finally left, in August of 1985, the President read a tribute to my budget cutting abilities from a set of three-by-five index cards. It seemed fitting. He had accepted, but never grasped the political consequences of the revolution I had brought to him on the eve of his election. And now he had no idea of the fiscal failure I was leaving behind.

12

The President and the Pony

It was January 1983, and Jim Baker and I were in the third-floor residence of the White House, briefing the President.

'You're telling me this trigger tax is actually going to happen, aren't you?' The President sounded crushed.

'Yes,' I answered, 'I don't see how it can be avoided.'

'Oh darn, oh darn. It just can't be. I never thought it would come to this.' Slowly he took out his pen and scratched 'RR' on the paper I had brought to him. His 1984 budget was thus approved, calling for a tax increase of $50 billion per year, on top of the large tax increase he had approved just a few months earlier. I had never seen him look so utterly dejected.

Ordinarily, Ronald Reagan was an incorrigible optimist. One of his favorite stories was the one about the two boys getting their Christmas presents. The first boy was a pessimist, the second an optimist. The pessimist gets a roomful of toys. He's miserable, because he's sure there's some catch involved. The optimist gets a roomful of horse manure. He's delighted. He digs around in the room for hours on end. With all that horse manure, he figured there just *had* to be a pony in there somewhere!

Well, I had just unloaded several tons of horse manure into the Cabinet Room, and it appeared that Ronald Reagan had finally given up looking for the pony. God knows he had tried. But now even he understood that major tax increases were needed to restore the Treasury's depleted coffers. Over the previous two months I had given him evidence upon evidence that if we didn't impose this trigger tax, the already frightening deficit would soar to $277 billion by 1986. As it stood now, we would accumulate *$1.4 trillion* in red ink over five years.

Yet up to now he had stoutly resisted any further tax increase, no matter what the evidence. In his mind, the three-year $100 billion tax increase (TEFRA) that Bob Dole and the College of Cardinals had insisted upon the summer before would be the absolute limit of his retreat. He had accepted that only with great reluctance, as a *quid pro quo* for additional congressional spending cuts. In fact, he had managed to convince himself that it wasn't really a tax increase at all.

'This bill only collects taxes we are owed already,' he told the group of dubious House Republicans in the Cabinet Room. 'It won't raise taxes on the legitimate taxpayer at all.'

That was true only if you considered people who bought cigarettes and owned a telephone 'illegitimate' taxpayers; they and millions of others were the ones who would now be paying more taxes. In order to get him to go along with it, we had gussied up* Bob Dole's tax increase bill so that it seemed like some bench warrant issued at midnight to permit a raid on America's criminal underground.

But even that had not been enough. Over 1982, as the economy plunged deeper into recession and inflation continued to collapse, Rosy Scenario looked less and less rosy. The structural deficit turned out not to be $150 billion, as we had thought during the November 1981 debate, but nearly double that. By the end of 1982, the fiscal situation was an utter, mind-numbing catastrophe.

To convince the President it really was as bad as I was saying, I invented a multiple-choice budget quiz. The regular budget briefings weren't doing the job. I thought this might be the way.

The quiz divided the entire budget up into about fifty spending components and gave him three spending-cut choices on each, ranging from a nick to a heavy whack. Next to each choice was a description of what the impact of the cut would be (how many people would be thrown out into the snow), and of its political prospects (i.e., 'previously defeated 27–2 in committee').

One typical example of a heavy whack showed that he could save $1.3 billion by eliminating the tourism bureau, dropping 2.5 million households from the heating assistance aid program, cutting child welfare grants by thirty-five percent, and eliminating the senior employment program and the minority business program entirely.

* Prettied up.

By contrast if he merely nicked this set of programs, he would save only $47 million.

The President took the quiz in November 1982. During several long sessions in the Cabinet Room we had gone through all fifty budget components. The quiz allowed him systematically to look at the whole $900 billion budget, to see it brick-by-brick. It also allowed him to get his hands dirty, maybe even bloody, with the practical chore of nitty-gritty cutting. Once the President went through it, he would understand that the budget was not a matter of too many bureaucrats and filing cabinets, but a politically explosive, vast, complex network of subsidies, grants and entitlements. He would see that to cut COLAs by $14 billion meant taking $1,263 dollars a year out of the pockets of 36 million Social Security recipients and several million more military and civilian retirees.

The President enjoyed the quiz immensely. He sat there day after day with his pencil. He listened to his senior staff and the economic team discuss the relevant policy and political ramifications, then announced his choice and marked the appropriate box.

And rarely chose to make a whack. They were mostly nicks. 'Yes,' he would say, 'we can't go that far.' Or, 'No, we better go for the moderate option or there will be a drumbeat from the opposition.'

The last session was on a Friday afternoon. I could tell the President was delighted about having endured the ordeal. It had occasioned a number of anecdotes about the federal monster and he had happily dispensed them to the group assembled at the cabinet table.

When we told him what his grade was early the next week, he was not so pleased. He had flunked the exam. After making all his cuts, the five-year deficit remained at a staggering $800 billion.

I went into the meeting in which I would present the President with his grade, thinking, 'Well, the moment of truth has finally come.' But not yet. I still did not understand how determined the President was to find his pony.

I made sure that his report card highlighted all the positive aspects of the cuts he had made, but it also showed the negative ones, too. Such as the fact that the remaining deficits meant the government would need to borrow *over half* of the nation's net private savings over the next four years. Such as the fact that under his budget, the total national debt would reach *two trillion dollars* by 1988.

When the discussion turned to taxes, his fist came down squarely on the table.

'I don't want to hear any more talk about taxes,' he insisted. 'The problem is *deficit spending!*'

It is difficult politely to correct the President of the United States when he has blatantly contradicted himself. The $800 billion worth of deficits were the result of the spending he didn't want to cut.

But now came two new ideas. 'It's time we got something out to the people,' said the President, 'and that is to show them we didn't cause deficits. Now, what would they have been under the policies before we got here?

'And we should also show them where the deficits would be if Congress had given us all the cuts we asked for.'

I cautioned that neither approach would make the huge deficit numbers in front of us go away. Moreover, that what the President was suggesting might not prove as exculpatory as he thought.

But now Meese began chanting the California mantra. 'That's just the point,' he echoed. 'We *inherited* this mess. Bad as it is, we need to get out how much worse it would be under the old tax-and-spend approach of Carter.'

Soon a Saturday radio speech was being cooked up along the lines of, If 'we' flunked the test, 'they' would have flunked it worse. I was instructed to make the numbers prove all this.

Well, you couldn't. No known method of accounting could. The numbers simply would not prove either point. A few days later I sent the President a memo saying, 'I would recommend you not pursue these points in the Saturday speech.'

My memo pointed out that by 1986 the deficit would still be $150 billion, even if Congress had enacted *every* cut in our original budget. It would have actually been $200 billion save for the magic asterisk. And, in truth, we had never 'actually proposed this due to the deadlock over Social Security.'

As for the mess we'd inherited from Jimmy Carter, well, oops! Under his policies, the deficit by 1986 would only have been $80 billion. 'A weak argument for our case,' I noted.

I succeeded in aborting the radio speech pinning the blame on the donkey. Now it was time to take another look at the problem. But what could be done?

One day Dick Darman and I were sitting on his office couch

wringing our hands, when he suddenly got up and darted for a pad of paper lying on his desk.

'Don't get offended now,' he began, 'but you might as well know it. When you sit there going over the deficit projections, the man's eyes glaze over. He tunes out completely because he doesn't fully appreciate that the pony is already built into the numbers.'

Darman meant that the President did not think in terms of more than one year at a time. He looked only at the current year's deficit numbers and wrote them off as attributable to the recession. He just didn't believe in the over $250 billion figure for the out-years, because he thought the coming economic recovery would drastically shrink the deficit numbers by 1987 or 1988. Never mind that the briefing book already showed a booming recovery beginning in 1983 and lasting through the end of the decade.

'The economic assumptions are all right there,' I protested to Darman.

'But they're on a *different page* than the budget numbers,' said Darman. 'He doesn't make the connection.' He sketched furiously on his pad. When he finished, I saw what he was up to, and was chagrined I hadn't thought of it myself.

His sketch showed a chart done in the exaggerated manner of the political cartoonist. At the center were big red bars showing the deficits rising year after year. Off to the side were black bars showing unemployment declining year after year. The President would see his pony (economic recovery and optimism) *and* the deficits on the same page. It would be impossible to miss the point.

Back to the OMS graphics department. Soon I had the finished chart. It was a thing of beauty.

'I've got the pony galloping one way on the same page with the deficit soaring the other,' I bubbled over, showing it to Darman. 'This has got to do the trick!'

By any kind of reasoning I can think of, it should have worked. Right there on the page you saw the economy getting better and the triple-digit deficit getting worse. The deficit bars rose from $200 billion the current year, to $219 billion, $241 billion, and on up; right square against them was the figurative pony, the US economy racing forward in flat-out recovery. The unemployment bars dropped from 10.1 percent, to 8.2 percent, to 7.5 percent, to eventually 6.0 percent in the last budget year. So, after five years of roaring recovery (averaging 4 percent real growth) and after reaching practical full employment you would have a quarter trillion per year deficit, unless spending was cut where possible and new tax revenues were put into the coffers.

I took it in to the next meeting in the Cabinet Room. The President just stared at the first page and turned it. But the next page showed the same point: the spending bar was at 24.5 percent of GNP and the revenue bar with existing taxes was at 18.9 percent of GNP. He turned the page again, and saw the same point again. The deficit bar for 1986 absorbed 72 percent of net private savings, 'crowding out investment and economic growth.'

And when he turned the page again, there it was again: a bar for the CETA boondoggle under Carter at $9 billion; but the bar for the 1983 enacted budget was only $3.7 billion, meaning we didn't have much left to cut. By contrast, a few pages further the bar for Social Security and retirement programs was $212 billion, or *fifty times* as high; and basically we had no hope for savings except for the minor trimmings that Jim Baker's bipartisan Social Security Commission was still heatedly debating.

After going through all the pages, the President sat at the cabinet table, staring at the paper, looking concussed. No one in the room seemed to have the nerve to bring up the tax increase issue yet again, and I was weary of being the only person who would. I'd been sure Darman's graphs would finally cause the President to say, 'Yes, we do need more revenue.' But now there was an awkward silence.

Meese finally spoke up with the usual solution. 'We'll have to go back to the drawing boards over Thanksgiving,' he said, 'and then we'll see where we are in December after the Cabinet comes in with their ideas for new budget savings.'

Back to the drawing board! We had all—the President included— just spent a full week chained to the drawing board and we still had come out $800 billion in the red.

New cuts from the Cabinet! The Cabinet had not volunteered so much as a single cut on its own since Inauguration Day.

But that's the way it was to be. The President kept hoping, Meese kept deferring, the clock kept running—and the problem kept growing.

In December, we had another so-called budget bloodbath with

the Cabinet over spending cuts, except by now the blood had become so thin that you needed to add red food dye in order to see it. All the easy cuts had already been made, and all the major spending components, such as Social Security and defense, had been taken off the table. Still, faced with deficits of $250 billion, there was nothing left to do but go at the Cabinet hammer and tongs over what scraps there were still left on it.

I no longer bothered with any more dramatic showdowns in the Cabinet Room in front of the President. None of the significant cuts stood a prayer of being accepted on Capitol Hill. Trying to force any on the Cabinet would have been sadistic, and sending them up the Hill to defend them put me in mind of the ending of a compelling movie showing at the time: *Gallipoli*.

And besides, the President wasn't even doing much split-the-difference pencilwork any more. Now he took all appeals back to the Oval Office, where Baker, Meese, Darman and Fuller would sit around with him trying to figure out who in the Cabinet needed a 'win' and which of the contested cuts they could afford to throw my way.

The successor to the Budget Working Group became the Budget Review Board, BRB, consisting of me, Baker and Meese. I played my customary role of hairshirt and Baker his of political pragmatist. Meese's self-chosen role was that of the Capillary Cutter.

By now we were reduced to such as reviewing the Export–Import Bank's appeal on two cuts I had requested. It wanted an increase of $5 billion for a 'war chest' of subsidies with which to counter alleged foreign subsidies, and it was refusing to fire the ten employees we had asked it to.

Meese spent all his time on the ten hapless employees, and I argued endlessly with Mac Baldridge, Bill Brock and Ray Donovan over the $5 billion 'war chest'. Finally, we had to take it to the President. He couldn't decide. The senior White House staff couldn't decide, so since nobody could decide, we added another magic asterisk to the budget—saying we were prepared to spend the $5 billion but wouldn't count it just yet.

Thus went the battle against deficit spending in December 1982. In due course the ridiculous was added to the picayune. Dick Schweiker submitted a forty-five-page appeal for restoration of 'devastating' OMB budget cuts, such as $1.5 million for his anti-smoking campaign, $5 million for FDA* research labs, money for seventy Indian nursing scholarships, $3 million for a Hispanic Health and Nutrition Survey, $5 million for Native Americans' social and economic development strategies, and $1.5 million for a national medical ambulatory care survey.

There we sat, pulling out each other's hair over this trivia as we waited for the President to decide there was no pony after all.

When all the 'blood' had been spilled, I sat down over the Christmas break to see where we stood.

After a month of cutting, we had come up with a grand total of $25 billion in savings. And now we were about to propose a 1984 budget containing $1.1 trillion in deficit spending over five years.

Now our old companions, Confusion and Incomprehension, made their reappearance.

Over the holidays the President played golf with George Schultz, who by now had replaced the General** as Secretary of State. I do not know at exactly which point in their game Schultz mentioned the notion of a flat tax to the President, but the sand trap suggests itself as the perfect setting.

A flat tax would turn the revenue code upside down, slashing rates and eliminating every single deduction, credit, loophole and shelter. But the way Schultz presented it, it sounded like a born-again Laffer curve. The former University of Chicago economics professor told the President that a low-rate tax that treated all income the same way would eliminate the waste and inefficiency caused by tax loopholes. That, in turn, would cause the economy to grow faster and the revenues to increase.

By the eighteenth hole the President was convinced this was a way to reduce the deficit without increasing taxes. He passed on Schultz's idea to Meese and Regan, and soon everyone around the White House was talking flat tax. As an economic policy matter the flat tax is the closest thing to perfection I'd ever seen. But there was one rather major problem with Schultz's brainchild: it would do nothing to reduce the deficit. The economic forecast already contained all the money GNP the Fed could produce through the end of the decade without reigniting inflation. This meant that even if the flat tax

* Food and Drug Administration.
** Al Haig.

caused a miraculous growth in real GNP, it still wouldn't generate a single dime of new revenue; and it wasn't likely to beat the four percent growth assumption we already had.

Yet to the President, the proposal seemed to indicate that his beloved pony might be lurking down there beneath the manure after all.

'No,' he said, 'the flat tax is something we could go for. It wouldn't be a *new* tax, it would be a *lower* tax.'

The usual heads started nodding, and I saw what was coming: another back-to-the-drawing-board session. It was now only a matter of days before the budget had to go to the printer, and somehow this fuzzball of a flat tax was supposed to sop up $1.1 trillion of red ink.

Martin Feldstein, the Harvard economist, had by now replaced Murray Weidenbaum as chairman of the Council of Economic Advisors. When he caught up with me after the meeting, he looked a little shocked. Poor Marty was new to this sort of 'thinking'.

'They don't actually believe this mumbo-jumbo, do they?' he asked, in the hope I might reassure him that he had not signed on for duty in a lunatic ward.

I told him, yes, they probably did. But, I said, when you reached the point of true desperation, there was only one thing to do. 'It's too late to think logically. The time has come to start thinking hard.'

After a lot of hard thinking, Darman and I came up with a perfectly disingenuous plan.

The fact was, it would take at least until 1990 to design, legislate and implement the kind of radical flat tax that Schultz was talking about. We weren't just suddenly going to up and cancel everyone's mortgage deduction tomorrow. (Actually, we were never going to do that.) So there was going to be a long transition period to the flat tax. But, why wait for the alleged revenue bonanza? Darman's and my calculations showed that this revenue bonanza would 'surely' amount to one percent of GNP or $50 billion per year. Right? So if that's what the flat tax would someday bring in in higher revenue, why not just impose a plain old regular tax now to start collecting it in advance? Oh, call it a 'placeholder'. Once the flat tax finally took effect, way down the road, it could take over the job of collecting the $50 billion a year from the placeholder tax.

We unveiled our plan to the economic advisers and senior staff in early January.

Regan was still opposed to the idea of 'raising a tax in a recession'. On the other hand, by now he had finally begun to lose faith in his supply-side advisers. A year ago they had convinced him to go out and predict that the economy would 'come roaring back by spring'. Before the first cherry blossoms had burst out around the Jefferson Memorial, it had contracted another five percent.

So now he would go along with the placeholder tax, as long as it didn't take effect until 1986—presumably when we were safely out of recession. Our current economic forecast, of course, assumed we would be out of recession by January 1983, which come to think of it, was right now.

To wait another two years would add $400 billion to the deficit; but we had to do something, so we went along with Regan's preposterous idea of waiting until 1986.

Then the Secretary of the Treasury was seized with another brilliant thought. The budget cuts we had just come up with amounted to about ten percent of the projected 1984 deficit. If the Congress doesn't approve and enact them, said Regan, then the placeholder tax should be cancelled. I suppose his theory was: if they want to make the deficit bigger, we'll see them, raise them, and make it even bigger. All this was discussed in a big Cabinet Room meeting with the President, with everyone presenting his own version of how it would work, or, more to the point, what it actually was we were talking about.

It was mostly described as the 'thing'—a rather apt term. It became, alternately, a 'flat tax', a 'reformed tax', a 'simplified tax', the 'second installment of Kemp-Roth', a 'down payment on future tax reform', a 'temporary tax', a 'trigger tax', a 'maybe tax'. I have forgotten its other titles, but there were more to describe this tax that dared not speak its name. I didn't really care *what* they called it. By hook or by crook I was going to put $50 billion in new revenue into the budget.

But then Darman and Baker started to get worried that 'flat tax' had a politically dangerous implication to it. They were right, it did. It meant we were fixing to cancel the mortgage deduction and tax the welfare checks of blind people. So Schultz's original flat tax idea was packed off to Siberia, in this case a 'deep study mode' at Treasury with a view to 'broadening, simplifying and reforming the income tax.'

My $50 billion 'thing' was officially rechristened a 'contingency tax', which would be put in the budget as a 'modified magic asterisk'. As with its ancestor asterisk, it would reduce the deficit—on paper, that is. Meanwhile the White House would propose no legislation to enact it until Congress had first approved the entire pathetic sum of additional spending cut we were sending it. In that improbable event, we would then recommend a combination of income surtax and a tax on crude oil so as to raise the $50 billion in revenue.

It remained only for the absurdity to play itself out. Jack Kemp and the supply siders had now launched a boisterous campaign charging that OMB had cooked up the big deficit numbers in order to pressure the President into a tax increase. The $250 billion, it was said, had popped out of some mysterious—indeed, insidious— 'black box' that I kept stowed away in my office safe.

If it had not been so ludicrous, I might have been upset, but by now I had become quite resigned to this kind of mumbo-jumbo. Logic was, well, irrelevant. Never mind that the $250 billion deficit estimate had been produced by the one thousand green eyeshades throughout the executive branch. Never mind that, in turn, the eyeshades had based their estimates on our new economic forecast, which projected twenty *straight quarters* of four percent real growth. Never mind that the forecast had been approved by the President, Meese, Regan, and everyone else. Nope, somebody was displaying inadequate faith in economic growth. This tax wasn't needed. *We demand to look inside Stockman's safe!*

Well, the canard made the President and Meese nervous all over again, so the 'thing' was diluted even further.

It was agreed that we would raise taxes three years hence to cope with the trillion-dollar deficit, if (a) Congress made all the spending cuts, (b) the economy was not still in recession, and (c) the economy had not grown sufficiently so as to lower the deficit to 2.5 percent of GNP or less. Given conditions (a) and (b), (c) was about as likely as an invasion of Martians. By 1986 our recommended deficit was going to be $213 billion, about five percent of GNP. So to avoid triggering the tax, the deficit would have to drop to $100 billion, solely as a result of economic growth above and beyond the already optimistic assumptions factored into the $213 billion figure.

As Jim Baker and I sat in the residence, I explained to the President that the conditions which would forestall the tax increase just weren't going to happen. When he reluctantly scratched his initials at the bottom of the budget, I was sure that he had at least given up his search for the pony.

Once again, I was wrong. It took a magnificent episode of sheer bungling by the California Reaganaut trio of Ed Meese, Cap Weinberger and Bill Clark to do it, but soon we were back digging in the manure looking for that pony again.

When the President's 1984 budget was released on 31 January 1983, I thought we had finally succeeded. The White House was now sending Congress the unmistakable signal that we were trying everything we could to fight the deficit. We had proposed about $95 billion in 1986 deficit reduction, consisting of $50 billion in contingency tax revenues, $35 billion in domestic cuts, and $10 billion in defense savings.

That was a powerful inducement to get the politicians to play a serious game of budget Ping-Pong with us. After a lot of negotiations, mixing and matching, we would end up with a deficit reduction package of $100 billion, including a major tax increase that was sure to be triggered.

So far, so good. But I had not taken into account Cap Weinberger's intractability, and he was now about to give the term a resonance it had not enjoyed since the stonewall days of Watergate. I should have seen it coming. In putting the final touches on the budget, we had had another showdown on defense in the Oval Office.

I had come to the meeting with a perfectly straightforward — and modest — point. When Weinberger and I had made our calculations on my pocket calculator many moons ago, we had come up with a 1986 defense budget of $367 billion. That figure, of course, had assumed an average inflation rate of seven to eight percent annually. But inflation was now running at under four percent, so I was simply going to ask Cap to give the difference back, lest the Pentagon reap a windfall budget increase from the miscalculation. It would not affect defense's 'real' growth at all, obviously.

Informed of this, Weinberger turned to the President and launched into a speech I had heard before. A feeling of heaviness came over me.

'Sir,' he said, 'you're the Commander-in-Chief and we will manage with any figure you give us. But you should be aware there would be a serious risk in making any cuts.'

I couldn't believe I was hearing this. How was an unneeded inflation allowance supposed to stop Soviet tanks? But the President did not grasp the difference between constant dollars and current (inflated) dollars. Weinberger and I engaged in our usual pushing and shoving and by the end of it I managed to get back $11 billion. That brought the 1986 defense figure down to a mere $356 billion.

It also brought down the roof on Capitol Hill. With inflation so dramatically down, the Pentagon only needed $340 billion to buy what we had earlier assumed would cost $367 billion. Thus facing unprecedent deficits, we had actually managed to *increase* the defense budget in constant dollars. Now we were turning out to be The Gang That Couldn't Deflate Straight.

By March, Pete Domenici and the Senate Budget Committee were prepared to play Ping-Pong. They had agreed informally on a $100 billion deficit reduction package for 1986, modeled after the President's own budget. This time we wouldn't be derailed by an argument about raising taxes in a recession. Domenici's revenue increase didn't take effect until 1986; and at about $60 billion, it wasn't much bigger than the President's own contingency tax.

But there was one thing the Senate Budget Committee would not put up with: since we hadn't even taken all of the original inflation allowance out of the defense budget, the administration's budget now called for eleven percent real defense growth two years in a row.

They had given the Pentagon a twelve percent real increase in both 1981 and 1982, and one of eight percent in 1983. For 1984–86, Domenici's Committee was drawing the line at five percent. It was perfectly reasonable. After adjusting for inflation, the Pentagon would still be receiving ninety-five percent of its original 1986 defense budget. This could hardly be called 'gutting defense'.

Enter the President's new director of the National Security Council, William 'Judge' Clark. Clark was in many ways a sympathetic man. He was a shy and quiet person, who by virtue of years of loyalty to Ronald Reagan now suddenly found himself in a job for which his qualification was a desire to serve his country as best he could.

Among his many lacunae was his inability to tell a deflator from an incompletely filled hot-air balloon. But that was not going to get in the way of his standing up to this Senator Domenici, whoever he was, and his plans to undermine the security of the free world.

He proceeded to get the President stirred up about Weinberger's no-longer-needed inflation allowance, and then, without bothering to inform those to whom the budget was more than a passing concern, Clark had the President call Domenici and insist that he not do anything about his budget plan for several weeks. A nationwide TV address was then scheduled—so the President could take his case for a strong defense to the American people.

'The boss is going to lay it on the line,' Clark began telling everyone around the White House. 'Those Republican senators will be back on the team by Easter.' He also hinted that there would be a 'little surprise' in the speech that would leave all those defense cutters on the Hill swooning and gasping with admiration.

On the night of March 23, amid great speculation, the President gave his big speech on defense. Now, the big fight brewing on the Hill was all about the inflation allowance and the rate at which we would build up our conventional forces over the next few years. Conventional forces account for about eighty-five percent of the defense budget, and except for the MX missiles, which even we could not figure out how to deploy, the Congress had not cut a dime from our strategic nuclear program.

But the President's speech had not been scheduled to discuss that, principally. The big surprise Judge Clark had been telling everyone about came in the last few minutes, when the President unveiled his Strategic Defense Initiative, the space-based anti-missile defense system that shortly became known as 'Star Wars'.

Whatever its merits, 'Star Wars' was rather dramatically beside the immediate point. We were about to take the 1984–88 defense budget to Capitol Hill, and now the President had, in a fairly spectacular way, taken the debate over Congress's head—all the way to outer space.

Domenici was livid. The entire Senate Budget Committee was livid. They had accommodated the White House so as to give the President time to rally the nation behind a larger defense budget figure, which Domenici was perfectly willing to entertain as long as someone would rustle up the necessary votes on his Committee. Instead, Clark's surprise had opened up an instant, raging debate over strategic weapons doctrine in such a way as to rupture a twenty-year-long consensus on deterrence policy.

After Easter, there were no more votes for the administration's defense budget among the Senate Budget Committee Republicans than there had been before. Howard Baker now smelled a good-sized collision coming between the Budget Committee and the White House, so we began to promote what became known as the 'Howard Baker compromise'.

On the surface, it seemed plausible enough; what it brought about was near-insanity. It called for real defense growth of 7.5 percent in 1984 and a slightly lower rate of increase in the out-years. Being approximately halfway between our requested eleven percent and the Senate Budget Committee's five percent, it was the natural point of compromise.

But by sheer coincidence, the Baker compromise would have meant giving the Pentagon within $1 billion of what the White House and the Congress had agreed on the previous summer. That agreement was part of Bob Dole's tax increase package, in which the President was promised three dollars in spending cuts for every one dollar of revenue increase he proposed.

Those promised spending cuts had included nearly $50 billion in defense savings over three years. After we agreed to it, Weinberger later persuaded the President to rule that out. Thus it appeared that Howard Baker was now proposing to cut the *same* defense dollars that had already been cut the summer before.

Pete Domenici was not about to get excited over a used cut, and Weinberger was not about to stand for a cut that he had succeeded in welching on the first time it came around, so—stalemate.

Howard Baker scrambled about trying to find takers for his used cut. Meanwhile, the White House started putting out the line that you couldn't make a budget deal with Congress because they wouldn't keep their word!

That came about because a misguided scribbler by the name of Jack Kemp gave Don Regan and Ed Meese some numbers showing that the Congress had not delivered on its three dollars in spending cuts in return for our one dollar of tax. The President believed it, and was now convinced he had been hornswoggled.*

* Bamboozled.

As soon as I realized what was going on, I jumped in and said, Whoa.

Of the spending cuts Congress allegedly owed, $100 billion consisted of savings in debt service that Congress couldn't do anything about; $40 billion was management savings that we had promised to come up with, and hadn't; another $30 billion had actually been delivered in Medicare reimbursement reforms and other measures. Most of the remainder was the $50 billion in three-year defense cuts Howard Baker was proposing to cut again—and which Weinberger was refusing to accept again.

So as of April 1983 we were sitting in the mud and denouncing the Congress for all the wrong reasons. Finally, Howard Baker met with the President privately and warned him, flat out, that his 7.5 percent compromise was going to be looking pretty good a few months from now, compared with what a hopping mad Senate might do on its own. Reluctantly, the President told Jim Baker and Clark that he would go along with the Baker compromise if Cap Weinberger would agree to it.

That same morning, I got a message from Domenici saying that his Committee had run out of patience. They were going to vote against his $100 billion per year deficit reduction plan—including the five percent defense growth—by the end of the day unless they heard the President had publicly endorsed Howard Baker's compromise.

I immediately alerted Jim Baker and Judge Clark that we had to get Weinberger to sign off on the compromise right away. Around noon I went over to Clark's office in the basement of West Wing.

Now that the President was amenable to compromise, Clark no longer felt that the Senate was a threat to the security of the free world. All he had to do was find Weinberger.

This shouldn't have been too difficult for two reasons. First, Weinberger had by now modified his own position considerably. He was willing to accept as a 'last resort' real growth rates of 7.9 percent, 7.5 percent, and 6.4 percent over 1984 to 1986, the three years covered by the Senate Budget Resolution. Howard Baker's numbers were 7.5 percent, 7.0 percent, and 6.0 percent. The difference between the two sets of figures was so small a magnifying glass was needed to see it.

The office of the director of the National Security Council has almost as Secure telephone lines as the Secretary of Defense's office, so ringing up Weinberger should not have been all that hard. But Clark tried several different lines and still could not raise the Secretary of Defense. Finally he left an 'urgent' message at the Pentagon requesting an 'immediate' return call.

Had he explained just how urgent it was, I demanded? Yes, he'd explained. If his message had been any more urgent, Cap might have thought he was calling about a surprise nuclear attack.

The clock kept ticking . . . 2.00 pm, 3.00 pm, 4.00 pm . . . and still no return call from the Secretary of Defense to the National Security Adviser. Incredible, I thought. What if it *were* a surprise attack?

Out of desperation, I had moved down the hall to Darman's office, figuring I could just as well keep up the phone vigil there. Soon a phone call did come in, but not from Weinberger. It was a withering blast from Domenici, suggesting that we all perform anatomical impossibilities on ourselves. And while we thus engaged ourselves, his Committee would be preparing to vote out his plan within the hour.

Desperate messages were sent out from Clark's office to the Secretary of Defense, but incredibly he still could not be found. Indeed, so incredible was his non-availability that it was hard not to conclude that it was deliberate.

Darman and I were upstairs in Jim Baker's office when we finally got word that Weinberger had been found—not by the multi-billion-dollar ultra-Secure defense communications system. No, a White House secretary had spotted him sitting serenely in the Oval Office anteroom waiting for a scheduled photo session with a group of military academy cadets, right next to the jelly bean jar. Clark was brought up to talk to Weinberger, who then agreed to step into the Oval Office and tell the President that the Howard Baker compromise was OK. But it was too late. When the President finally reached Domenici, it was too late. The Committee had already voted out the five percent defense plan and adjourned.

In the following days and weeks, the White House put out a new line, fulminating against the 'Domenici double-cross'. Another game of Ping-Pong was over; the contingency tax was dead; the nation was guaranteed $200 billion per year of deficits for the foreseeable future. Weinberger's unreturned phone call may have been the costliest in history.

At a cabinet meeting on the budget outlook, I made another plea to revive a compromise budget plan in the full Senate. Without the contingency tax and some modest entitlement reforms, the budget would just roll forward on automatic pilot. 'There will be $200 billion deficits as far as the eye can see,' I warned.

At last I had predicted something accurately. But what a thing to be right about. In any event, my warning was drowned out by a new line from the Gang of Three (Weinberger, Clark, Meese). There wouldn't be any compromise budget deal with Congress. No, it was time (again) to take off the brass knuckles on domestic spending. We should adopt a tough 'veto strategy', chopping down every 1984 congressional appropriations bill that was a dime over the President's budget.

'Use your veto, Mr President,' Weinberger urged. 'The Senate Budget Resolution is just an effort to manoeuvre you into another tax increase. You didn't come here to raise taxes, and you shouldn't let them get away with it again.'

I had heard a lot in the Cabinet Room over two years, including some outright lies. But when I heard that, I actually slapped a hand over my mouth to prevent myself from committing an indiscretion. It wouldn't have been right to shout '*Bullshit*' in front of the President of the United States.

And that's exactly what it was. The President's own budget had $200 billion in tax increases over three years, which was the only thing keeping it below the $1 trillion in deficit spending that the Cabinet had come up with. Now Weinberger was telling the President not to let 'them' enact the tax increase we had requested.

The audacity of it was staggering. Weinberger had doggedly pushed up defense outlays from $133 billion in 1980 to $377 billion by 1988—a one-quarter trillion dollar budget increase in just eight years. And now he was throwing stones at the people who were trying to raise the taxes to pay for it. Never, before or since, did I hear anything so outrageous and irresponsible uttered in the Cabinet Room.

'I can't wait to get my pen out,' the President said, grinning enthusiastically. And so began the era of the hard-line veto strategy.

Over the next eight months, the President's pen remained in his pocket. He did not veto one single appropriations bill, all of which combined came in $10 billion over the line. Come to think of it, he did use his pen—to sign them.

One of the more giant appropriations was the Labor, Education and Health bill, and to protect it the politicians quietly but emphatically told the White House that if we vetoed it, the defense appropriations bill would suddenly find itself in even more trouble than it already faced.

I nickeled and dimed away until I got it down to a mere $4.4 billion over budget, an overrun of seventeen percent. The Legislative Strategy Group decided that since our chances of sustaining a veto were slim, the President should sign the bill.

'Fine,' I said, 'but let's have him sign it in the middle of the night so no one gets the impression we're happy about this budget-buster.'

The communications team had a different idea. Here was a big fat social programs bill, and we had been taking a lot of heat on the so-called fairness issue. Besides, there was an election coming up in only twelve months.

So invitations were sent out to the champion pork barrelers to attend a signing ceremony in the Oval Office. The members of the Labor, Education and Health appropriations subcommittees attended, among them Senator Lowell Weicker of Connecticut, one of the biggest spenders to bother calling himself a Republican this century. I was invited too, but I did not trust myself to attend.

I heard it was quite a scene, though. After the signing, the President handed a pen to all the people he had been denouncing over the years as the ones who had 'not given us all the cuts we've asked for.' What, I wondered, would the President's speeches say now?

Pretty much the same thing, as it turned out. But at this point it didn't really matter what the President said.

Nevertheless, the occasion provided me with a little ironic satisfaction a few weeks later. Education Secretary Ted Bell had submitted the largest education budget in history, which must have been the Dubious Achievement of the Year, given that the President had vowed to dismantle the department a little while back. Naturally, I hacked it up good and sent it back to him.

When Bell arrived at the White House to appeal his case, he expressed shock at my butchery.

'I have just one question,' he simmered. 'Why is my 1985 budget deemed so out of line when it is not a dime above the enacted 1984 funding bill?' Whereupon he passed around a sheet of paper containing his major justification for the budget he had requested. It was a picture of the President in the Oval Office handing out pens to all the porkers.

'Bravo!' I thought. How were we supposed to argue with that?

There were other epiphanies during the period of the tough veto strategy.

The Interior appropriations bill was twenty-five percent over the line, to the tune of nearly $2 billion. I recommended that the President veto it. The $2 billion was earmarked for such urgent national priorities as buying more local park land, raising the budget of the National Endowment for the Arts, and funding a half-billion dollars worth of energy boondoggles.

We had a showdown of sorts in the Oval Office when the Senate Committee chairman, Jim McClure of Idaho, came to plead for its approval. He made his customary speech about facing up to runaway entitlements rather than nitpicking the Bureau of Land Management, the National Park Service and the Forest Service.

'These things are important to your friends in the west,' McClure urged the President.

In response I pointed out the obvious, that a bill twenty-five percent over the line was a budget-buster under any definition. Could we really afford to raise subsidies to private forests by 140 percent? Did we truly need to layer the Bureau of Mines and Geological Survey with more bureaucratic fat? Did we need $170 million worth of additional employees at the Indian Health Service, the free world's most spectacularly inefficient organization?

'You want to talk about deficit spending,' I concluded. 'This bill defines it.'

I sat back and waited for Meese and the other veto strategy advocates to support that. Instead, there was total silence.

'On this, yes, I agree,' the President finally said. 'This is not the kind of thing we had in mind to veto.'

On the way out of the Oval Office, McClure said something that made me realize I should have saved my breath.

'You're sending an excellent man over to the Interior Department,' he told the President. 'We look forward to working with him.'

Of course. Judge Clark, the President's faithful retainer, was the new Secretary of the Interior. The President wasn't about to inaugurate his stewardship by vetoing the department's funding bill. It was a fiting demise of the veto strategy, since Clark had been one of its staunchest advocates.

The 1983 deficit had now already come in at $208 billion. The case for a major tax increase was overwhelming, unassailable, inescapable and self-evident. Not to raise taxes when all other avenues were closed was a wilful act of ignorance and grotesque irresponsibility. In the entire twentieth-century fiscal history of the nation there has been nothing to rival it.

Yet nothing was done. Nothing has *yet* been done. Why? Because after the dark days of January 1983, the President renewed his search for the pony. Once the recovery started booming in the spring of 1983, there was not a thing you could tell him to shake his absolute faith that these massive deficits were simply going to vanish. Ronald Reagan is a terminal optimist.

When real GNP expanded at better than seven percent during the last three quarters of 1983, he began to hear the whinnying. The tax cut was working—the Laffer curve was happening. The budget deficits were fading. A new era in economic history had started!

A few weeks later Marty Feldstein and I made one last run at reviving the contingency tax in the next (1985) budget.

This time the President did not say, 'Oh darn, oh darn.' He came down on us like a ton of bricks with a twenty-minute lecture on economic history and theory.

'There has not been one tax *increase* in history that actually raised revenue,' he proclaimed. 'And every tax *cut*, from the 1920s to Kennedy's to ours, has produced more.

'We have always warned that the problem is *deficit spending*,' he continued. But 'they' had this theory that it didn't matter because we just owed it to ourselves. So this deficit isn't our fault. It was here before we got here. Now they're all just waiting for us to admit we were wrong so they can go back to tax and spend.

'There is another thing about this that people overlook,' the President continued, 'the idea that the budget has to keep going up every year, no. When Eisenhower left office, his budget was smaller than when he started. The spending line actually went down.

'It was after that that people forgot what happened. Spending went up 400 percent but the deficit zoomed up seventeen hundred percent. That point never gets mentioned.

'We never believed in this,' he went on. 'We always said deficit spending couldn't go on. I still dream of the day when we actually have a surplus, when we can start retiring the national debt. That's what we have to be thinking about; not just cutting the deficit but eliminating it.

'There was a time when government took less than ten percent from the people. But that has gone up and up and up. And that's where all the trouble started. I remember some economists warned about it at the time.

'Some of our people discovered this in California. The state automatically shared part of its revenue with the local governments. And since it wasn't their money, they would spend it on things you never dreamed of. They would hire people for the parks just to stand around and watch other people work.

'So that never has worked. Carter tried it. He came up with the largest tax increase in history for Social Security and it was already bankrupt when we got here.

'No,' the President concluded, 'we have to keep faith with the people. Everywhere I go they say, Keep it up! Stick to your guns! Well, isn't that what we came here to do?'

What do you do when your President ignores all the palpable, relevant facts and wanders in circles. I could not bear to watch this good and decent man go on in this embarrassing way. I buried my head in my plate, and as I looked down, there it was again—the perfect scoop of tuna salad with an olive on top.

This time he was doing all the talking, but his pony made no more sense than my revolution. It was hard to say which was the greater delusion.

The next day I told Jim Baker that I was going to resign. I couldn't defend a planned trillion-dollar deficit; I couldn't defend no taxes; I couldn't defend a policy of fiscal know-nothingism.

'I can't make a fool of myself any longer, Jim,' I told him. 'This budget is so bad, it's beyond the pale.'

Baker came back at me with a voice I hadn't heard since 11 November 1981. It was ice-cold.

'You do that and you'll stab the President right in the back,' he said. 'The Democrats will have a field day in the 1984 campaign.

'Let me remind you of something, my friend. He stuck by you. Now you stick by him. You've made as many mistakes as the rest of us around here. So stick that unwarranted pride of yours right up your ass, and get back in the trenches with the rest of us.'

So I did, because I knew Jim was right. As I shuffled back to my office on that brisk January day in 1984, it seemed ironic that in only four years my Grand Doctrine for remaking the world had turned, finally, into a dutiful loyalty to nonsense. That was the worst lesson of all.

Epilogue: The Triumph of Politics

'You ain't seen nothing yet.' The White House made that its official campaign slogan for 1984. When it did, I knew that my own days were numbered, and that even the reluctant loyalty I had maintained during the long battle to reverse the President's tax policy was no longer defensible. Now I had to resort to out-and-out subversion—scheming with the congressional leaders during the first half of 1985 to force a tax hike. But that failed too, leaving me with no choice but to resign in the knowledge that my original ideological excesses had given rise to a fiscal and political disorder that was probably beyond correction.

Politics had triumphed: first by blocking spending cuts and then by stopping revenue increases. There was nothing left to do but follow former Governor Hugh Carey's example and head out of town, whupped.

That the politics of American democracy made a shambles of my anti-welfare statte theory I can now understand. Whatever its substantive merit, it rested on the illusion that the will of the people was at drastic variance with the actions of the politicians.

But the political history of the past five years mostly invalidates that proposition. We have had a tumultuous national referendum on everything in our half-trillion-dollar welfare state budget. By virtue of experiencing the battle day after day in the legislative and bureaucratic trenches, I am as qualified as anyone to discern the verdict. Lavish Social Security benefits, wasteful dairy subsidies, futile UDAG grants, and all the remainder of the federal subventions do not persist solely due to weak-kneed politicians or the nefarious graspings of special-interest groups.

Despite their often fuzzy rhetoric and twisted rationalizations,

EPILOGUE: THE TRIUMPH OF POLITICS

congressmen and senators ultimately deliver what their constituencies demand. The notion that Washington amounts to a puzzle palace on the Potomac, divorced from the genuine desires of the voters, thus constitutes more myth than truth. So does the related proposition eloquently expressed in the editorial pages of *The Wall Street Journal*. Somehow it manages to divine a great unwashed mass of the citizenry demanding the opposite of the spending agendas presented by the Claude Peppers, the homebuilders' lobby, and the other hired guns of K Street.

But those who suggest the existence of an anti-statist electorate are in fact demanding that national policy be harnessed to their own particular doctrine of the public good. The actual electorate, however, is not interested in this doctrine; when it is interested at all, it is interested in getting help from the government to compensate for a perceived disadvantage. Consequently, the spending politics of Washington do reflect the heterogeneous and parochial demands that arise from the diverse, activated fragments of the electorate scattered across the land. What you see done in the halls of the politicians may not be wise, but it is the only real and viable definition of what the electorate wants.

I cannot be so patient with the White House. By 1984 it had become a dreamland. It was holding the American economy hostage to a reckless, unstable fiscal policy based on the politics of high spending and the doctrine of low taxes. Yet rather than acknowledge that the resulting massive buildup of public debt would eventually generate serious economic troubles, the White House proclaimed a roaring economic success. It bragged that its policies had worked as never before when, in fact, they had produced fiscal excesses that had never before been imagined.

The brash phrasemakers of the White House had given George Orwell a new resonance—and right on schedule. In 1984 we were plainly drifting into unprecedented economic peril. But they had the audacity to proclaim a golden age of prosperity.

What economic success there was had almost nothing to do with our original supply-side doctrine. Instead, Paul Volcker and the business cycle had brought inflation down and economic activity surging back. But there was nothing new, revolutionary, or sustainable about this favorable turn of events. The cycle of economic boom and bust had been going on for decades, and by election day its oscillations had reached the high end of the charts. That was all.

To be sure, credit is due where it is deserved. Paul Volcker will surely go down as the greatest Federal Reserve Chairman in history for the masterful and courageous manner in which he purged the American and world economy of runaway inflation. This success turned out to require the traditional, painful, costly cure of a deep recession, but it took all that Volcker brought to the task—a strong will, an incisive mind, and a towering personal credibility—to see it through.

There is also little doubt that Volcker's feat would not have been possible without Ronald Reagan's unwavering support during the dark days of 1982. The President stands almost alone among Washington's current politicians in his instinctive comprehension that inflation is a profoundly destructive phenomenon. He has often been misled by the mumbo-jumbo of his advisers. But when it counted, the President gave Volcker the political latitude to do what had to be done. It was a genuine achievement.

Unfortunately, Volcker's hard-won victory was not what the White House media men had in mind when they proclaimed that 'America is back'. They were boasting of something far more grand: that the business cycle itself had been vanquished and that the nation had entered an era of unprecedented economic growth and wealth creation. As they had it, profound new possibilities for economic performance and social progress over the long haul had now been guaranteed by the policies in place. It sounded too good to be true and it was.

'You ain't seen nothing yet' was to have unintended, ironic meaning. It pointed to a frightful day of reckoning, a day that will reveal just how arrogant, superficial, and willfully ignorant the White House phrasemakers really were.

By the end of 1985 the economic expansion was three years old and the numbers demonstrated no miracle. Real GNP growth had averaged 4.1 percent—an utterly unexceptional, prosaic business cycle recovery by historical standards, and especially so in light of the extraordinary depth of the 1981–82 recession. The glowing pre-election GNP and employment numbers, therefore, had manifested only the truism that when the business cycle turns down, it will inevitably bounce back for a while.

Still, the White House breastbeating had to do with the future, and that depends upon the fundamental health of the economy and the soundness of policy. Yet how can economic growth remain high and inflation low for the long run when the administration's de facto policy is to consume two thirds of the nation's net private savings to fund the federal deficit?

The fundamental reality of 1984 was not the advent of a new day, but a lapse into fiscal indiscipline on a scale never before experienced in peacetime. There is no basis in economic history or theory for believing that from this wobbly foundation a lasting era of prosperity can actually emerge.

Indeed, just beneath the surface the American economy was already being twisted and weakened by Washington's free lunch joy ride. Thanks to the half-revolution adopted in July 1981, more than a trillion dollars has already been needlessly added to our national debt—a burden that will plague us indefinitely. Our national savings has been squandered to pay for a tax cut we could not afford. We have consequently borrowed enormous amounts of foreign capital to make up for the shortfall between our national production and our national spending. Now, the US economy will almost surely grow much more slowly than its potential in the decade ahead. By turning ourselves into a debtor nation for the first time since World War I, we have sacrificed future living standards in order to service the debts we have already incurred.

Borrowing these hundreds of billions of dollars has also distorted the whole warp and woof of the US economy. The high dollar exchange rate that has been required to attract so much foreign capital has devastated our industries of agriculture, mining, and manufacturing. Jobs, capital, and production have been permanently lost.

All of this was evident in 1984, and so was its implication for the future. We had prosperity of a sort—but it rested on easy money and borrowed time. To lift the economy out of recession against the weight of massive deficits and unprecedented real interest rates, the Fed has had to throw open the money spigots as never before. This in turn has stimulated an orgy of debt creation on the balance sheets of American consumers and corporations that is still gathering momentum today. Its magnitude is numbing. When the government sector's own massive debt is included, the nation will shortly owe $10 trillion—three times more than just a dozen years ago.

One thing is certain. At some point global investors will lose confidence in our easy dollars and debt-financed prosperity, and then the chickens will come home to roost. In the short run, we will be absolutely dependent upon a $100 billion per year inflow of foreign capital to finance our twin deficits—trade and the federal budget. Faced with a sinking dollar, the Fed will have no choice but to suddenly and dramatically tighten monetary policy, forcing up interest rates to attract the foreign savings needed to underwrite our lavish current spending.

This action will cause a recession, but this time neither Paul Volcker nor Ronald Reagan will have the wherewithal to stay the course. American politics will resound with the pleas of debtors demanding relief in the form of out-and-out reflation. Since our balance sheets already reflect the highest ratios of debt in peacetime history, there will be no margin at all to weather an interruption of cash flow: not at the federal level, where we are borrowing three times more relative to GNP than at the comparable stage of any previous cycle; nor at the corporate and household level, where debt service relative to income has soared off the charts.

The clock is thus ticking away inexorably toward another bout of inflationary excess. If we stay the course we are now on, the decade will end with a worse hyperinflation than the one with which it began. Indeed, the increased fragility and instability of the global economy, along with still fresh memories of the debauched financial assets of the 1970s, will make this inflationary cycle even more violent and destructive.

One reason I plotted to raise taxes in 1985, then, was to help correct an economic policy course that was leading to long-run disaster.

But there was also another, more compelling reason. As the original architect of the fiscal policy error now threatening so much grief, I was appalled by the false promises of the 1984 campaign. Ronald Reagan had been induced by his advisers and his own illusions to embrace one of the more irresponsible platforms of modern times. He had promised, as it were, to alter the laws of arithmetic. No program that had a name or line in the budget would be cut; no taxes would be raised. Yet the deficit was pronounced intolerable and it was pledged to be eliminated.

This was the essence of the unreality. The President and his retainers promised to eliminate the monster deficit with spending cuts when for all practical purposes they had already embraced or endorsed ninety-five percent of all the spending there was to cut.

The White House itself had surrendered to the political necessities of the welfare state early on. By 1985, only the White House speechwriters carried on a lonely war of words, hurling a stream of presidential rhetoric at a ghostly abstraction called Big Government.

The White House's claim to be serious about cutting the budget had, in fact, become an institutionalized fantasy. I had tried diplomatically and delicately to convey the facts that made this so, but the only response I got was a new whispering campaign led by Ed Meese: Stockman is too pessimistic; he's been on the Hill too long; he's one of *them*!

Maybe so. Ever since September 1981 I'd been reduced to making one-sided spending deals. The politicians mosly got what their constituents wanted, but here and there we trimmed the edges. But my relentless dealmaking inherently yielded savings that amounted to rounding errors in a trillion-dollar budget because it was based on bluff and searching out for obscure tidbits of spending that could be excised without arousing massive political resistance. Thus, for example, we did get the second-tier COLA in the railroad retirement program capped below the inflation rate. This reduced overall spending by 0.0001 percent!

But nothing meaningful could be done about federal spending because even the President no longer had a plausible program to do anything about it. The White House had thrown in the towel on all the big spending components that could make a difference on the deficit. And it had abandoned nearly every policy principle that could have been the basis for organizing a renewed anti-spending coalition.

The domestic budget is huge, but nearly ninety percent of it is accounted for by a handful of big programs: Social Security and other social insurance; Medicare; the safety net, veterans, agriculture, and transportation.*

By 1984, the White House had explicitly decided not to challenge these big components of the welfare state budget in any significant

---

* See Appendix for details.

way. Jim Baker had been proven correct about the political consequences of attacking the basic entitlement and COLA of the 36 million citizens receiving Social Security and Medicare. I had eventually been reduced to trying to get the Congress to modestly trim the Medicare entitlement. But in the election/budget year of 1984 even the President rejected proposals for increased patient cost sharing, and then went on to plant his feet in concrete against any cuts in Social Security at all.

These two programs accounted for half of the welfare state budget, yet by 1985 the only option we had left was to squeeze a few percent of their massive $270 billion cost from the doctors and hospitals that delivered the services the old folks were now guaranteed to receive. Right then and there the fiscal arithmetic of coping with a $200 billion deficit through spending cuts alone had become prohibitive.

The President had also inadvertently safeguarded the smaller civil service retirement system from cuts, too. The administration budget carried a proposal to cap civil service COLAs and penalize early retirement (before age sixty-two), but its legislative prospects depended crucially on applying the same concept to the even more generous military retirement program. Both proposals were put in the President's budget, but the Joint Chiefs of Staff soon complained loudly. The President then cancelled the military reforms, buttressing the $25 billion civil service retirement program as he did so.

Likewise, the $27 billion complex of veterans' programs was also given immunity in a curious way. The White House appointed a VA administrator, by the name of Harry Walters, who spent a large part of his time denouncing the President's budget director at American Legion conventions. Whatever tiny veterans' cuts I managed to stuff into the budget were made instantly non-operative by Mr Walters's ability to claim with impunity that he spoke for the President. No one at the White House ever said he didn't.

After the first round of cuts in the $75 billion complex of welfare, food stamp, and safety net programs, the White House raised the white flag there, too. The President promised the governors not to tamper seriously with Medicaid—the largest program—and appointed a task force which recommended that we repeal some of the nutrition program reforms we had already made. While we continued to send up to the Hill small, technical proposals to nick a billion or two, the clear White House message was that the safety net was now inviolate.

That position reflected the overwhelming sentiment of the public, and in that sense was justifiable. But it also constituted another big block of evidence that the President's anti-spending rhetoric amounted to an illusion.

By the mid-1980s the Reagan transportation budget in constant dollars topped Jimmy Carter's best year by fifteen percent, Johnson's by about forty percent, and Kennedy's by about fifty percent. Big Government? That was something for the speechwriters to fight as long as they didn't mention any names. The problem with all these local roads and buses was that other politicians had an equally strong case for aiding local projects—classrooms, public libraries, day care centers, alcoholism clinics and jailhouses. Spending continued largely unabated in all cases.

Indeed, the White House record was nearly bereft of any consistent anti-spending policy principles by 1984, and that fact had not escaped the notice of all the other politicians on Capitol Hill. Early on we had demonstrated that even in the politically easiest cases there was no consistent standard for what constituted appropriate federal spending.

That's why we ended up giving several billion dollars to Exxon, Union Oil and some gas pipelines to build synthetic fuel plants. When Meese chimed in with the point that these corporations had already invested a small fraction of one percent of their own equity in these projects, the President had an answer.

'We can't cause an honest business to lose money,' he said. All these projects turned out to be total white elephants, but the lesson was clear. If Exxon couldn't be permitted to drill a dry hole right in the Roosevelt Room where the decision was made, what other business subsidy had a chance of being eliminated?

Nor was this an aberration. Right before the 1984 election, the giant timber companies sought an economic bailout that would cost $1.5 billion over several years. We had fought this proposal since 1982, but now it was alleged to make the crucial difference that would put Oregon in the President's electoral column, possibly along with the other forty-nine states. I protested that the bill would hand over $15 to $30 million each to seven Fortune 500 companies, including poverty cases like Boise Cascade. 'No,' replied the

President, 'we can't veto. The companies wouldn't really pay us that money anyway. They would just pass it on to consumers.'

If there was any thin sliver of the welfare state where the Reagan Administration might have raised the free enterprise and anti-spending banner, it was against the socialistic enterprises of US Agriculture. But by 1984 we had accommodated to the political facts of life here, too. As I contemplated the task of formulating a strategy to deal with the nation's massive deficit after the election, two White House episodes regarding agriculture stood out in my mind vividly. They were the smoking gun which proved that the White House couldn't even tackle the fabulous excesses of the farm pork barrel, and that was the very bottom of the whole spending barrel.*

The first episode had occurred in the summer of 1982. The issue was agriculture marketing orders, an out-and-out socialist relic from the New Deal that tells every California orange and lemon grower how many of these little fruits can be marketed each week.

The established growers like this kind of lemon socialism because it keeps prices up, supplies down, and new competition out of the market.

By then I knew better than to argue on behalf of 'marketplace efficiency', 'consumer welfare', and the supposed right of free Americans to produce and sell whatever kind of fruits, nuts, and widgets they want.

So I'd located some photographs of this lemon socialism at work. They showed gargantuan mountains—bigger than the White House—of California oranges rotting in the field. The reason for all this deliberate garbage creation was that the USDA orange commissar had cut back the weekly marketing quota, fearing that a bumper crop would drop the price and give consumers too good a deal on oranges.

Since we'd also just talked about a free food program for the homeless, my pictures did seem to suggest something rather ludicrous, and everyone around the cabinet table began to laugh. But then the California politicians swung into action.

Dick Lyng, an old California Reaganaut and Under Secretary of

---

* This was verified in December 1985 when the President signed the most expensive farm bill in history. It will cost $50–75 billion over three years, exceeding even the bill he signed in 1981 that had established the previous record.

Agriculture, said I was fibbing. 'The USDA had nothing to do with this. The growers elect their own committees to stabilize the market.

'You remember, Mr President,' he added, 'that a lot of our friends out there depend on these marketing orders.'

Well, OK. Some of our friends are members of the Navel Orange Growers Soviet. It wasn't a compelling argument.

Meese then glanced at his Adam Smith tie and took his turn. 'We need to study the possibility of long-range reform,' he said, 'but remember these are businessmen. It would be wrong for the government to suddenly disrupt their market.'

Disruption thus had a new definition. Every week the growers rig the market in what would be a violation of the anti-trust law, and now, if the Agriculture Department didn't use its power to exempt them from federal prosecution, well, that was 'disruption'. But never mind. Meese's deputy, Jim Jenkins, who was the White House welcome mat for special interest groups, had a better idea.

'Without marketing orders you would never get the multi-million-dollar investments in refrigeration equipment and storage facilities necessary for a year-round supply. A competitive market would be too risky.'

I asked him how about year-round Florida oranges that come right off the free market, with no supply control by a Florida Orange Grower Soviet at all. He said my point wasn't valid because I was mixing oranges and oranges.

Jim Lake, the Reagan campaign press secretary and paid lobbyist in the off season, had another point. He just went up to the Hill and got a law passed making it illegal for the director of OMB even to read the marketing orders before they were stamped out by USDA. That was that for free enterprise in California. Needless to say, there remained equally compelling cases for other variations of Big Government in the other forty-nine states.

It was the handful of dairy states which in fact brought the second episode to a head. In late 1983 Ed Meese had called me to his office to deliver some truly stunning news.

'I thought you would want to know,' he said crisply, 'the President just signed the dairy bill.'

'Ed, I'm so shocked, I don't know what to say,' I muttered in response, 'except that you're turning this whole thing into a bad joke.' I then huffed out of his office.

It was shocking. Ronald Reagan had just signed a bill paying dairy farmers $1,300 per head *not to milk their cows*! It also contained a hidden tax on consumers which would be used to pay farmers to slaughter their whole herd for the equivalent of *$5 per pound of hamburger.*

I'd been fighting this $2 billion per year rip-off for fifteen months. Time after time I had brought the dairy bill up at LSG meetings. Everybody's on board for a veto, right? Nobody's going to pull the rug on me, right?

Each and every time Meese had earnestly bobbed his head in the affirmative, so I had spread the word high and low on Capitol Hill that the bill was a goner.

Now I was the fool, and the reasons revealed the final answer as to why the Reagan White House's anti-spending rhetoric could not be taken seriously. The Reaganites were, in the final analysis, just plain welfare state politicians like everybody else.

In this case the three culprits were Ed Meese, Dick Lyng, and Jesse Helms. You hardly needed to know any more.

Meese always came to the lick log with his Adam Smith tie on and usually left without his shirt. The political consequences of the Reagan Revolution's free market and anti-spending principles were just too unsettling for him to tolerate.

Dick Lyng believed in free markets but had also learned all about farm pork politics in Sacramento. While Jack Block, a decent and well-intended hog farmer from Illinois, was the nominal Department Secretary, there was never any doubt that Lyng was the political engineer who ran up the USDA budget.

Jesse Helms was, well, tobacco, and he couldn't get reelected at all without bringing home the socialist bacon from Washington.

And the bacon of politics didn't come one slice at a time. It was always maddeningly interlinked. That's what this dairy bill fiasco exemplified perfectly.

I had anticipated the dairy bill because I had originally thought it was an exception to the rule. Rather than being protected in an omnibus farm bill with all the wheat, corn, cotton, sugar, peanuts, rice, and mohair constituencies locked together arm in arm, the 1983 dairy bill was going to have to roll down Pennsylvania Avenue all by its lonesome. Then: *zap!*

But at the eleventh hour Jesse Helms got desperate about tobacco.

An earlier so-called allotment reform bill had decreed that by December 1983 certain absentee allotment holders had to sell their state-granted licenses. This turned out to include churches, YMCAs, 4-H Clubs, and Boy Scout chapters. What all these presumably God-fearing adults and children were doing owning tobacco allotments, I never did find out. But I quickly learned that Jesse Helms was determined to postpone the statutory deadline.

So he did what every politician does when he wants something bad enough. Helms added his tiny little amendment to rescue the Boy Scouts' tobacco allotment to the dairy bill. He then put his shoulder down to the log and started rolling it toward the White House.

By the time the dairy bill reached the President's desk bedecked with the tobacco rider, it had a new informal title: 'The Jesse Helms Re-election Act of 1984.' That transformed the whole character of the bill, causing a strange chorus to arise from the anti-socialist New Right: *this bill's for Jesse, no other bill will do.*

That's where Meese suddenly entered the picture. Helms and the New Right pulled his political chain and in a flash he was in the Oval Office pushing the President's official pen toward the signature line.

In the same flash something else happened: the single cleanest, easiest, and most justified shot at budget cutting during the entire Reagan presidency was kicked in the ditch. If this one couldn't be done, then nothing, but nothing, could be done about federal spending.

Needless to say, news that the President had signed the bill after several months of heated veto threats from his budget director brought an instantaneous response on the Hill: unadulterated guffaws, hilarity, and belly laughs. The politicians now knew without a doubt what had been true since June 1981. The only thing the Reagan Administration could do about federal spending was: fake.

As I prepared to make one last run at the deficit monster in late 1984, I soon found myself impaled upon an awful dilemma. Given the fiscal facts of life, I somehow believed that the White House would be prepared to wriggle out of its militant no-tax-increase campaign pledges. With everyone for the welfare state and no one against it, the only thing left to do was to pay for it. But I was mistaken once again. Ed Meese made that crystal clear at the first post-election meeting of the cabinet.

'We have three great goals for the second term,' he said, 'but the first and highest is to keep our pledge not to raise taxes.'

So now our goal was '*Dont pay for a red cent of Big Government, just blame "them" for all the red ink of it.*' After four years in office the Reaganites had no more sense that governance involved making unpalatable choices than they had in the Wexford garage way back at the beginning.

So I attempted to stimulate one more round of Ping-Pong. The final play *had* to yield a tax increase. It was vital.

The first step was easy and involved the establishment of a $50 billion target for deficit reduction in the President's 1986 budget—the minimum credible goal under the circumstances.

I next got out my supply-side catechism book and scrounged for spending cuts that would not poison the political environment or violate iron-clad presidential commitments. This eliminated most of the budget—Social Security, the safety net, veterans' benefits—but there was still one small corner to work in.

Dozens of small economic subsidies and state and local grants could be attacked on principle, even if there was little hope of prevailing on Capitol Hill. I thus targeted Amtrak, EDA, the Ex-Im Bank, federally owned power marketing authorities, student aid, the Small Business Administration, mass transit subsidies, REA, and many more. These savings barely added up to $35 billion, but with a small defense trim, the usual quota of smoke and mirrors, and debt service savings, the President's 1986 spending-cut total was gussied up to match the $50 billion target.

But not without a struggle, because the relevant cabinet officers fought to the last drop of blood against even these minor cuts. Jim Sanders, the SBA administrator, was soon even visibly campaigning on the Hill to defeat my proposal to eliminate subsidized loans for used-car dealers.

The next step was to get the Senate GOP leadership on board. The College of Cardinals was more than willing to get the disagreeable business of raising taxes over with. Dole, Domenici, Hatfield, Laxalt, Packwood, Simpson, Danforth, Heinz, Chafee, Boschwitz, Gorton, even Armstrong and McClure, were ready. To a man, they knew you weren't going to meaningfully reduce the deficit without additional revenue.

But the responsible leaders of the Senate were now in a quandary.

If they came right out for higher taxes, they would soon be on a collision course with the White House, inviting renewed stalemate.

Finally we came up with a long shot: We would try to cobble together the largest spending-cut package possible in the Senate. All those who knew we also needed to raise taxes agreed to bite their tongues for a while. The Senate spending-cut-only package would be the final housecleaning of the welfare state. Anything we could persuade fifty-one senators to cut or throw overboard would be included in it.

Then we would bounce it over to the House side. Since the Democratic majority wanted to cut no spending at all, they would bounce back a budget package with taxes in it. The politicians of Capitol Hill would next compromise between the two and then bounce a decent-sized deficit reduction package which included both tax increases and spending cuts down Pennsylvania Avenue. Then we would find out if it was Clint Eastwood—'make my day'—or a modicum of reason that would determine the nation's economic and fiscal future.

Dole and Domenici worked the strategy all spring. Day after day we round-tabled in Dole's office, and this time it was the real thing. We marched through one program at a time, one Republican faction at a time, until we had got through the whole trillion-dollar budget. Never before had the game of fiscal governance been played so seriously, so completely, or so broadly as it was in Bob Dole's office in the spring of 1985. Rarely before have two political leaders displayed such patience, determination, and ability as did Bob Dole and Pete Domenici.

By May it was time for the Senate to start voting on its package designed to reduce the deficit by $55 billion in 1986, and by rising amounts in the out-years. One by one the Republican politicians came with their final demands as to what *couldn't* be cut if we were to have their vote. And we needed nearly every single vote among the fifty-three Republicans because no Democrats would play this lousy game of having to tiptoe around the President in public.

As the long, final day of the Republican budget round-tabling passed into the middle of the night in Bob Dole's office, I finally saw, as the politicians circled the budget one last time, the awesome staying power of the Second Republic.

We had killed impact aid in February 1981 in the Cutting Room, but it had been resurrected repeatedly in the interim until the Dole–Domenici budget abolished it again. Now along came Senator Jim Abdnor of South Dakota, who stood to lose $300,000 at a single Air Force base school district out yonder in the badlands. In the end his vote went in the yes column and $100 million in impact aid went back into the budget.

The Johnson War on Poverty was long dead, and what remained was only a $300 million echo in the federal budget. The Dole–Domenici budget silenced this echo, but only until ultra-conservative Senator Charles Grassley of Iowa came along and traded his vote for LBJ's tattered legacy.

Senator Bob Kasten was a Kempite anti-taxer, so he visited Dole's Cutting Room too. He wanted to make sure that we were not planning to raise a tax in a recovery year. He also wanted to make sure that we were not planning to cut any spending for farm subsidies and UDAG in an election year. He left satisfied on all counts, for, like all the others, his was the last vote that added up to fifty.

Bill Cohen from Maine was justifiably mad because the northwestern senators had prevailed in overriding my plan to make the Bonneville Power Administration pay back its debt to Uncle Sam. I had pleaded until I was blue in the face with Senators Gorton, Evans, and Hatfield for even a token $100 million per year in repayment on its $8 billion debt. But they had three votes, I had none, and so we had saved no money.

Bill Cohen said rural housing was just as important to his state, but unlike them he would compromise rather than insist on rule or ruin. After $4 billion in spending had been haggled back into the budget, he pronounced the remaining cut reasonable.

We had come up with a $5,000 annual cap on college student aid that saved billions, but Bob Stafford, chairman of the Higher Education Subcommittee, regretted that he couldn't go along. Someone might need $8,000 or $10,000 from Uncle Sam to go to Harvard or Middlebury College in Vermont. We gratefully took his vote and a token cut in lieu of real reform and moved on.

We ended up adding money back for the Ex-Im Bank, soil conservation, Medicare, mass transit, Amtrak, child nutrition, education for the handicapped, National Institutes of Health, vocational rehabilitation, and the Small Business Administration, too.

The latter four programs had got about $1 billion in added funding when Senator Lowell Weicker had glared my way and bellowed, 'How long are we going to allow this little pissant to dictate around here? He's had his head up his ass from day one.'

If it hadn't been for the difficulty of speaking from that position, I might have called him a name too. But I had some quick figuring to do because the vote was coming shortly.

We had cut about $54 billion from the 1986 budget. That consisted of $24 billion in defense and about $10 billion in debt service and smoke and mirrors. So after all the round-tabling in Bob Dole's Cutting Room, we had picked through the half-trillion-dollar welfare state budget and come up with $20 billion that Republican senators were willing to cut.

Ninety-six percent stays, four percent goes. That's what we had come to in Bob Dole's Cutting Room after the most thorough, inspired, and detailed attempt ever made by the collectivity of the nation's Republican politicians to decide what it was they wanted from Big Government and what they could do without.

Just the same, the Senate Republicans were heroes that night when they walked the plank and passed the Dole–Domenici budget. They had put a cap on the COLAs of 40 million voters. They had cut, nicked, and squeezed wherever their collective politics permitted. It was utterly the best that could be done.

But it was all for naught. In rapid order the remainder of the Republican politicians weighed in, blowing the Dole budget and the Ping-Pong game to smithereens.

Jack Kemp joined Claude Pepper in leading the charge to save the COLAs of the old folks. The Merrill Lynch bull charged in again and agreed with Kemp and the House Republicans. Nobody was going to walk the plank on Social Security.

Dole and Domenici then came up with an oil tax to fill up the hole left by the COLAs' demise. The President said absolutely not. He would wait for the pony.

There was not a rational possibility left to deal with the irrationality that had descended upon the nation.

I gathered up my black books, knowing that what I started four years before had come to a dismal end.

I could not help recalling what my father had said about that mess out in the tomato field twenty-seven years before.

'*What counts around here is what you do, not what you intend.*'

What I had done was helped make another mess.

'*One of these days you will learn,*' he had said.

Maybe at last I had.

Some will be tempted to read into the failure of the Reagan Revolution more than is warranted. It represents the triumph of politics over a particular doctrine of economic governance and that is all. It does not mean American democracy is fatally flawed: special interest groups do wield great power, but their influence is deeply rooted in local popular support. Certainly, it does not mechanically guarantee the inevitability of permanent massive budget deficits or economic doom.

Its implications are deeply pessimistic only for the small and politically insignificant set of anti-statist conservatives who inhabit niches in the world of government, academia, business, and journalism. For us, there is no room for equivocation. The Reagan Revolution amounted to the clearest test of doctrine ever likely to occur in a heterogeneous democracy like our own. And the anti-statist position was utterly repudiated by the combined forces of the politicians—Republican and Democrat, those in the executive branch as well as the legislative.

This verdict has implications, however, which go well beyond the invalidation of anti-statist doctrine. The triumphant welfare state principle means that economic governance must consist of a fundamental trade-off between capitalist prosperity and social security. As a nation we have chosen to have less of the former in order to have more of the latter.

Social Security, trade protectionism, safety net programs, UDAG, and farm price supports all have one thing in common. They seek to bolster the lot of less productive industries, regions, and citizens by taxing the wealth and income of everyone else.

The case for all this redistributionism is lodged in the modern tradition of social democracy. In America we have seldom explicitly acknowledged this principle of governance, but it is in fact what we have. And to some degree it works. On the basis of private cash income alone, more than 55 million Americans would end up below the so-called poverty line. But after all the welfare state's cash and in-kind benefits are paid and taxes are collected, the number of the statistically poor drops by nearly two thirds. So although it is riddled with inefficiency and injustice, the American welfare state does fulfill at least some of its promises.

But it does so at the expense of a less dynamic and productive capitalism. The kind of high growth and constant economic change envisioned by the supply-side doctrine is not possible if government taxes away economic rewards, blocks capital and labor reallocations, and funds a high safety net.

Social democracy also encourages the electorate to fragment into narrow interest groups designed to thwart and override market outcomes. That these pressure groups prevail most of the time should not be surprising. The essential welfare state principle of modern American governance sanctions both their role and their claims.

Viewed in this light, our political system performs its intended function fairly well. Its search to balance and calibrate the requisites of capitalism with social democracy's quest for stability and security has produced a surprising result. By any comparative standard, American politicians have created a more favorable balance between the two than in any other advanced industrial democracy.

Local, state, and federal spending in the United States now amounts to slightly over thirty-three percent of GNP. Ten percentage points of that are consumed in servicing our governmental debts and paying for our national security. So under the broadest measure possible, the American welfare state costs about twenty-two to twenty-three percent of GNP. By contrast, while the Japanese are frugal, they still spend nearly thirty percent of their GNP for domestic welfare. The cradle of social democracy—Great Britain—still spends nearly forty percent of GNP on its welfare state, the valiant efforts of Prime Minister Thatcher notwithstanding.

The Germans spend nearly as much as Great Britain, and the fading socialists of France spend even more. Sweden is in a class by itself, spending over half of its GNP on its vast, debilitating welfare state, or more than double what we do.

So we can afford to be the arsenal of the free world and have our modest welfare state, too. The only thing we cannot afford is to continue pretending we do not have to finance it out of current taxation.

This observation brings us to the true crossroads of the future. Our budget is now drastically out of balance not because this condition is endemic to our politics. Rather, it is the consequence of an accident of governance which occurred in 1981. That it persists is due to the untenable anti-tax position of the White House. After five years of presidential intransigence, all of the normal mechanisms of economic governance have become ensnared in a web of folly. But this condition can be remedied whenever the White House decides to face the facts of life.

Meanwhile, the economic danger mounts and the fiscal folly of the Reagan Revolution's aftermath reaches new heights. The recently enacted Gramm–Rudman deficit reduction law stands as testimony to that proposition. It is truly difficult to conceive of a more mischievous, unworkable blunderbuss than this alleged automatic budget-cutting device.

Gramm–Rudman will never reduce the nation's giant and dangerous budget deficit by any significant amount. After one or two years, its mechanical formula for across-the-board expenditure reductions in the fifty percent of the budget not exempted or protected would produce havoc. The defense cuts would be so draconian as to amount to unilateral disarmament; a large portion of the IRS staff would be fired and we would collect no revenue at all; life-saving new drug applications would pile up at the Food and Drug Administration unreviewed; our airports would become a parking lot for cars, people, and planes because the FAA would be too short-handed to manage even a fraction of the normal traffic.

All of this chaos and much, much more is inherent in the arithmetic of Gramm–Rudman, and is the reason it will be eventually repealed or drastically amended. Hopefully, the Supreme Court will spare us much trouble by ruling it unconstitutional.

Still, extricating ourselves from the fiscal folly now upon the nation by means of an alternative legislative solution will test our institutions of governance and our political leaders as rarely before. Folly has begotten folly, and the web has become hopelessly entangled in a five-year history of action and reaction. But the politicians of both parties still have a sound and valid reason for disengaging from the Reagan Revolution's destructive aftermath. A radical change in national economic policy was not their idea; economic utopia was not their conception of what was possible in 1981, when the policies of the past collapsed. Republican and Democratic politicians together can tell the American people that a few ideologues made a giant mistake, and that the government the public wants will require greater sacrifices in the future in the form of the new taxes which must be levied.

The politicians can tell the American people that a dangerous experiment has been tried and an old lesson has been demonstrated once again. Economic governance of the world's greatest democracy has been shown to be a deadly serious business. There is no room in its equation for scribblers, dreamers, ideologues, and passionate young men bent upon remaking the world according to their own grand prescriptions. The truth to be remembered is that history in a democracy does not live to be rewritten and rerouted; it just lives for another day, finding its way into the future along the trajectory of its well-worn and palpable past.

Since repudiating the debt through inflation will soon be revealed as the inevitable consequence of the course we are now set on, there remains a slim hope that we will turn back before it is too late. Despite all his illusions, Ronald Reagan is still our President, and he instinctively understands and abhors the evils of inflation. When the choice between raising taxes and debauching our money finally comes to him, I somehow believe that he will yet do the right thing to save his presidency and the nation's economy. It is still not too late for the nation's most imposing politician to join with the other politicians and do what together they must: Trim a little more spending where the democratic consensus will permit it, and raise a lot of new taxes to pay for the government the nation has decided it wants.

This solution will not bring about economic perfection by a long shot. Taxes will end up too high and government will end up too big. But catastrophe will have been avoided, and that is the main thing now.

These prescriptions do not add up to a shining City on the Hill. But what is attainable—a return to a modicum of national fiscal solvency and economic stability—is far preferable to the dangerous course we are now on.

In a way, the big tax increase we need will confirm the triumph of politics. But in a democracy the politicians must have the last word once it is clear that their course is consistent with the preferences of the electorate. The abortive Reagan Revolution proved that the American electorate wants a moderate social democracy to shield it from capitalism's rougher edges. Recognition of this in the Oval Office is all that stands between a tolerable economic future and one fraught with unprecedented perils.

Appendix: The Fiscal Facts

Looking back, the only thing that can be said to have been innocent about the Reagan Revolution was its objective of improving upon what we inherited. The inflation-battered American economy of 1980 was no more sustainable or viable than is the deficit-burdened economy of 1986. Likewise, the bloated American welfare state budget of 1980 was not very defensible; it merited at least a strong and principled challenge.

But the Reagan Revolution's abortive effort to rectify these inherited conditions cannot be simply exonerated as a good try that failed. The magnitude of the fiscal wreckage and the severity of the economic dangers that resulted are too great to permit such an easy verdict. In the larger scheme of democratic fact and economic reality there lies a harsher judgment. In fact, it was the basic assumptions and fiscal architecture of the Reagan Revolution itself which first introduced the folly that now envelops our economic governance.

The Reagan Revolution was radical, imprudent, and arrogant. It defied the settled consensus of professional politicians and economists on its two central assumptions. It mistakenly presumed that a handful of ideologues were right and all the politicians were wrong about what the American people wanted from government. And it erroneously assumed that the damaged, disabled, inflation-swollen US economy inherited from the Carter Administration could be instantly healed when history and most of the professional economists said it couldn't be.

By the time of the White House debate of early November 1981, it had become overwhelmingly clear that the Reagan Revolution's original political and economic assumptions were wrong by a country mile. By then the veil of the future had already parted and we were viewing reality from the other side. What we saw invalidated the whole plan—right there and then.

The ensuing years only amplified what we had already learned by the eleventh month. The final reckoning—seen in Table 1 below—of the original fiscal plan of the Reagan Revolution shows where we were headed as we debated optimism versus pessimism in November 1981.

We were not headed toward a brave new world, as I had thought in February. We were not headed toward a vindication of the President's half-revolution, as Don Regan and the supply siders fatuously insisted in November. Where we were headed was toward a fiscal catastrophe.

The budget numbers printed in February 1981 said you could have a big tax cut and a big defense buildup, and still have a balanced budget by 1984. That would be followed by a $28 billion surplus by 1986. But it all depended upon Rosy Scenario.

Looking at the table, line two shows the same tax cut, the same defense buildup, the same sweeping domestic cuts including the $44 billion magic asterisk that the President proposed to Congress on February 18, 1981. It assumes that everything was enacted 100 percent as originally proposed; that Congress turned itself into a rubber stamp for five years just as I had implicitly assumed it must.

The only difference between the first two lines is that Rosy Scenario didn't happen. Line two is based on the actual path of the economy that unfolded over the five-year period. What was at the

TABLE 1
The Trillion-Dollar Error in the Original Reagan Budget
(Deficit or Surplus in Billions of $)

	1982	1983	1984	1985	1986	Total
The Reagan February 1981						
Budget with Deficit:						
(1) Rosy Scenario	−45	−23	0	+6	+28	−34
(2) Actual Economics	−113	−197	−183	−223	−226	−942
November 1981 Budget						
Outlook Deficit:						
(3) Reagan Plan with No Magic						
Asterisk and Tax Bill	−100	−232	−244	−296	−320	−1,193

APPENDIX: THE FISCAL FACTS

end of the line on the day the Reagan Revolution was launched was *one trillion dollars* more in national debt, and a permanent, structural deficit in excess of *$225 billion* per year, or five percent of GNP.

In early November 1981, the political and economic facts of life said that the Reagan Revolution was plunging into the drink. But it was still not too late to have changed the course. We were only one month into the plan then, not sixty months and countless irreversible decisions later, as we are today.

Line three shows the final reckoning of what we faced during that heated week of debate. The decision that ensued was to stay the course. But by November we knew two more things than we did in February, knowledge which made the November decision to do nothing even more irresponsible than had been the original February plan.

We knew by November that the $44 billion per year magic asterisk had already been invalidated. Those cuts were not going to come because the President had reaffirmed the original defense budget and Jim Baker had shipped Social Security off to a bipartisan commission. The only places the $44 billion cut could have come from were thus off limits.

We also knew what the bidding war on the tax bill had cost. The extra cost was all in the out-years, but everybody had the score sheets which toted it up. Most certainly the Secretary of the Treasury did. Morover, it was now the law of the land: either the policy had to be changed, or the revenue hemorrhage was guaranteed to occur.

Line three then represents the original Reagan budget plan, with the extra cost of the tax bill bidding war and magic asterisk added to the deficit. It shows where the fiscal policy in place and reaffirmed in November 1981 would have led. At the end of the line was a *$320 billion per year deficit*, a red ink total as large as Mexico's and Brazil's relative to GNP.

We hadn't seen this final reckoning yet in November 1981, but we'd seen more than enough. The deficit number for 1986 then on our briefing papers was between $150 and $200 billion. But did we really have to know any more when only eleven months earlier we had confidently proclaimed the 1986 destination was a $28 billion surplus?

So there we sat looking at a fiscal shambles, heading for a

monstrous deficit in excess of $300 billion by the middle of the decade. And in marched Donald T. Regan, Paul Craig Roberts, Jack Kemp, Jude Wanniski, Art Laffer, and Irving Kristol, saying, *We're still not wrong. Stand firm. It will go away.*

Fortunately, there came along an irony: the politicians who had warned and feared that the Reagan Revolution would end up a fiscal fiasco forced the administration to raise taxes four times between 1982 and 1984 and to dramatically scale back the planned defense increases.

The four tax bills alone raised 1986 revenues by $80 billion per year and brought taxes up to nineteen percent of GNP. The defense cutback amounted to more than $60 billion per year by 1986. These actions brought the deficit down to $200 billion. That's where it festers now, threatening one day to shatter the financial integrity of the American economy.

Table 2 shows why the supply siders merit the epithet of the Folly Brigade. They fought, resisted, and denounced every one of the tax increase bills enacted after 1981. But consider the proposition they were implicitly defending with all their anti-tax talk.

The smoking gun is on line six. It shows that had taxes not been raised after the 1981 tax cut, this year (1986) we would be collecting only *16.9 percent* of GNP in taxes. Built-in spending (not shown) amounts to about twenty-four percent of GNP. What kind of crackpot theory says the federal government can issue new bonds in the amount of seven percent of GNP each and every year and not ruin the economy?

The answer is: the one advocated by Jack Kemp and his supply

TABLE 2

The Fiscal Impact of Rosy Scenario and the Tax-Bidding War

Tax Policy Target under Rosy Scenario and February 1981 Budget	1986 Revenue Share of GNP
(1) Pre-Reagan Tax Law	24.1%
(2) Kemp–Roth/10-5-3	−4.5%
(3) Planned Tax Share of GNP	19.6%
Tax Policy under Actual Economics and 1981 Tax Act	
(4) Pre-Reagan Tax Law	22.0%
(5) 1981 Tax Act	−5.1%
(6) Actual Tax Share of GNP	16.9%

APPENDIX: THE FISCAL FACTS

siders month in and month out from November 1981 until the present.

They never stopped insisting that growth and gold would make these appalling and indisputable fiscal facts of life go away. But the table proves that that was nonsense, too. Gold would have made the budget numbers worse and more real growth would have helped only a smidgen.

Line one shows that under Rosy Scenario, we projected that inflation and bracket creep would have raised the federal tax share of GNP under pre-Reagan tax law to over twenty-four percent by 1986. The original Kemp–Roth and 10-5-3 tax plans presented in February 1981 would have cut this inherited tax base by 4.5 percent of GNP (line two), bringing federal revenue down to just under twenty percent (line three).

That was not an implausible target at the time, had the politicians been willing substantially to scale back welfare state expenditures. But it was also a false target resulting from the inconsistency between Rosy Scenario and our anti-inflationary monetary policy.

Line four shows the true picture. It displays the inherited tax base with the low inflation, low nominal GNP economy that actually materialized over the five-year period. Due to far less bracket creep, the inherited tax policy would have generated only twenty-two percent of GNP in revenues by 1986. Two percent of GNP doesn't seem like a large number until you remember that in a $4 trillion economy, it amounts to $80 billion.

Then the bidding war raised the cost of the tax bill to 5.1 percent of GNP by 1986, as shown in line five. In short, we started with a much smaller tax base than we projected and cut taxes significantly more than we had first intended. With both errors going in the wrong direction, the nation's revenue base fell into the basement. Instead of ending up with a tax system generating nearly twenty percent of GNP in revenues, we actually enacted in the 1981 tax cut a revenue policy that would have generated less than seventeen percent.

The error in the 1981 fiscal plan was thus staggering. Table 3 highlights Rosy Scenario's contribution to the mistake. It shows that money GNP in 1986 ended up *$660 billion* lower than what Murray Weidenbaum slapped out of his computer. The money GNP number turned out so much lower after five years because both of its two component parts, real GNP and inflation, increased far less than we

TABLE 3

Rosy Scenario and Money GNP: The $2 Trillion Error

(Money GNP in Billions)

Year	Rosy Scenario	Actual Economy	Error
1982	$ 3,192	$ 3,054	$ 138
1983	3,598	3,229	369
1984	4,000	3,581	419
1985	4,398	3,839	559
1986	4,812	4,152	660
Total 1982–86	$20,000	$17,855	$2,145

Actual GNP based on 1985 mid-session review.

had projected. Since the revenue share of GNP is driven up by both real growth and inflation (prior to tax indexing), we began our revolution with almst no margin to cut taxes at all.

This money GNP outcome proves why the supply siders, including me, were wrong from the very beginning. We wanted an inflationless gold standard economy as embodied in the Second Napkin Kemp drew up at the Republican Convention in July 1980.

But in a perfect world with a perfect gold standard monetary regime, money GNP can only grow at five percent per year at the very best, consisting of five percent real growth and zero inflation. Even in the low, four percent inflation Volcker standard economy, however, money GNP grew by much more than the gold standard's five percent limit. The average money GNP growth rate for 1982 to 1986 was actually about eight percent.

This means that had we actually got our gold standard economy, money GNP would have been dramatically lower than shown in Table 3, and bracket creep would have been almost nonexistent. Consequently, the tax share of GNP would have been lower after the big 1981 tax cut than even the 16.9 percent which actually resulted.

All the palaver about more growth and gold solving the deficit problem was just that. Neither could make the money GNP numbers higher; neither could lift revenues out of the basement at 16–17 percent of GNP.

The supply siders keep pretending that the fiscal truth is escapable, an illusion that makes them more dangerous than ever.

APPENDIX: THE FISCAL FACTS

To save Laffer's discredited Tax Cut Napkin, they are proposing to tear up the Second Napkin—the gold standard statement against inflation. They are now trying to rescue their free lunch economics with easy money and inflation. They are demanding that Volcker pump money into the economy at an even more rapid and inflationary rate than he is being forced to do already owing to our huge fiscal deficits.

The supply siders' new inflationist policy might temporarily lift revenues out of the basement, but it would end up putting the whole economy in the drink. That is the irony of what has now come to pass for Jack Kemp and his faithful band.

The original supply-side idea back in the days of the Kemp seminar was inflationless, capitalist prosperity. In the crucible of national economic governance over the last seven years, the Kempites have reduced it to a free lunch message and a mindless political addiction to tax cutting without regard to the fiscal consequences.

The supply siders are not the first revolutionaries who have perverted an twisted their original idea beyond recognition. But like all the others before them, they continue in a way that suggests that they would rather bring on calamity than admit that they were wrong.

The final reckoning makes another important reality clear, too. The Republican quarrel with the American welfare state is over. The half-trillion-dollar budget which remains in 1986 after five years of sustained ideological challenge is there because the rank and file of GOP politicians want it for their constituents no less than their Democratic counterparts do.

Table 4 compares the cost of the welfare state we inherited with the actual budget for 1986. Some progress has been made. But a nine percent, or $52 billion, shrinkage of the half-trillion welfare state that was already in place by 1980 does not amount to a policy revolution by any definition of the word.

In fact, after five years of the most anti-spending administration in history, nearly the opposite conclusion can be drawn. During that period nearly every welfare state premise embodied in this half-trillion budget was questioned or attacked—usually by me.

This year-after-year challenge amounted to an ongoing democra-

TABLE 4

Impact of the Reagan Revolution on the American Welfare State
(Spending in Billions)

Budget Component	1986 Pre-Reagan Policy	1986 Actual	Spending Reduction Amount	%
(1) Social Security, Medicare, Unemployment, & Other Social Insurance	$308	$288	−20	−7%
(2) Agriculture & Veterans	64	63	−1	−2%
(3) Means-Tested Safety Net	82	74	−8	−10%
(4) Great Society Grants & Services	45	33	−12	−25%
(5) Transportation, Public Works, Economic Subsidies	69	58	−11	−16%
(6) Total	$568	$516	$−52	−9%

Note: Pre-Reagan policy priced out under 1985 economic assumptions.

tic referendum on what should remain in the budget and what should be excised. A few things were taken out, such as the $5 billion per year make-work jobs boondoggle. But almost everything that was in the budget when we went to work in the Cutting Room in late January 1981 still remains.

To be sure, many programs have been trimmed and squeezed, accounting for the bulk of the savings. But what causes us to spend $500 billion in 1986 and save only $50 billion is that no significant welfare state premise has changed. The giant Social Security entitlement is unchanged; UDAG still builds its hotels; the cattle ranchers still get cheap federal grass on which to graze their cattle. From top to bottom, the welfare state budget rolls along much as before.

That is another irony of the Reagan Revolution. In the crucible of political challenge and under the gun of massive budget deficits, the GOP politicians were forced to reexamine its programs and the premises time after time.

In the end, it was up to them to decide; it was they who had been elected by the American people to struggle with such choices. In the process, they heard from the squeaky wheels and interest groups; they heard from the local voters and grass roots constituencies.

They decided when all was said and done to ratify the American welfare state as it had evolved by 1980. They decided not to roll back the tide of history.

Social Security, Medicare, and other social insurance programs account for fifty-six percent of the spending that is left after the Reagan Revolution made its challenge. These are the megabucks of the budget, and it is now evident they will not move. No one need incite Claude Pepper again in order to prove that the GOP politicians of the Congress will not take on the 36 million who get the social insurance checks.

There are only two ways to reduce the cost of Social Security. The easiest way is to cap the COLA below the inflation rate, thereby eroding the real cost and purchasing power of the benefits. We did that once, as part of the 1983 bipartisan Social Security rescue plan. It clipped the purchasing power of everyone's check by the grand sum of two percent. To date, that's all that the Democratic politicians have been willing to tolerate; and the rank and file of Republicans have had no stomach whatever to challenge them.

The other way is to cancel or modify entitlements; that is to say, take current or future checks out of the mail.

My Grand Doctrine contemplated major surgery of this sort, but facts are facts. Neither the politicians nor the people will tolerate it for a minute. A couple of tiny entitlements were eventually cut: the student benefit was eliminated, the minimum benefit was phased out prospectively, the death benefit was curtailed and disability benefits were modestly tightened.

But that was it. All of Social Security's other unearned benefits and its core mechanism of wage indexing—induced real benefit growth still remain in place. Someday we will get to a new, higher retirement age of sixty-eight also put in by the 1983 bipartisan solvency plan. But that will not occur until about 2030, if you want to think that far ahead.

The story with Medicare is the same—it has already been cut close to the politically feasible rock bottom. We have saved billions by clamping down tightly on reimbursements to hospitals and doctors. But you can only squeeze so much out of the medical providers unless you want to risk jeopardizing the quality and availability of medical care.

To be sure, we could create a competitive health care market and give the old folks money instead of Medicare, letting them shop around for their medical services. Over time, this would save a bundle of money because competition would put some incentives for economizing back into the health care system. But that solution won't happen, either. The doctors' lobby, the hospital lobby, and the old folks' lobby would combine to kill it in a nano-second.

So the only way to seriously reduce the $75 billion Medicare budget any further is to cut the entitlement. Most of the old folks could afford to pay more and the ones who couldn't would be automatically subsidized by Medicaid. But in five years, we made almost no progress in cutting the basic Medicare entitlement.

The insurance premium for physicians' coverage was raised from twenty to twenty-five percent of the cost; it amounted to a few extra dollars per month for each Medicare recipient. But there the GOP politicians joined the Democrats in drawing the line on raising costs to beneficiaries, a line that is not likely to recede in the near future.

All in all, the big social insurance programs are here to stay pretty much as they are. They are the legacy of the New Deal's social democratic impulse. All of them consequently are not means-tested, meaning that equal goodies go to David Rockefeller and the impoverished widow. The idea defies rationality, but it is embedded beyond reach in our democratic politics.

This fact of democratic life shattered the Reagan Revolution's fiscal equation from day one. But the fiscal implications of maintaining the status quo in the nation's giant social insurance system were not understood in the slightest by the supply siders in 1980, by the Reagan Revolution's architect in 1981, or by the President and the rank and file of the Republican Party even today in 1986.

Owing to the myth of social insurance, we have imposed *payroll taxes* sufficient to fund most of Social Security, Medicare, unemployment insurance, and the smaller social insurance programs. In 1986 these programs will cost seven percent of GNP, and their dedicated payroll taxes will collect seven percent of GNP. For better or ill, then, social insurance is the one part of the budget that is in balance.

What does that mean for the remainder of the budget? In 1986, defense, debt service, and the entire remainder of the budget excluding social insurance will cost about seventeen percent of GNP. We now take in nineteen percent of GNP in taxes, but when you set aside the seven percent accounted for by payroll taxes dedicated to social insurance, only twelve percent is left. That's all we have to cover spending amounting to seventeen percent. For every dollar of non-social insurance spending in 1986, we will raise 70 cents in taxes and borrow 30 cents.

There is not one case in history where a government has borrowed 30 cents on each dollar of spending for a sustained period of time and not caused an economic upheaval. Yet that is the policy which is in practice in the free world's greatest economy today.

Even less progress was made in the second category of the welfare state budget: agriculture subsidies and veterans' programs. In 1986 we will spend only $1 billion, or two percent, less than under the inherited policy of the Carter Administration.

The reason is self-evident. From March 1981 forward, the GOP–Boll Weevil coalition made it clear that the whole $60 plus billion was a *sacred cow*. Never mind that the $10 billion per year veterans' hospital system is a giant boondoggle of inefficiency, waste, and duplication. Never mind that we will pay out $20 billion to wheat, corn, rice, cotton, and dairy farmers in order to keep several hundred thousand unneeded and bankrupt farms in business. The message of the conservative politicians was to keep on spending, and so we did.

This brings the godfather of the neo-conservative movement to the roasting pole. In 1980, before any of this fiscal disaster had happened, Irving Kristol was a guest speaker before the House Republican Caucus.

Even then, as he sat there dispensing 'political realism,' he was making me exceedingly nervous. 'Don't be foolish!' he told the Republican politicians. 'Your constituents are the elderly, the farmers, and the veterans. Don't alienate them, don't cut their programs.'

They obviously took his advice. There was but one problem with what the godfather had to say that day. These three constituencies account for *two thirds* of the entire cost of the welfare state. How you were supposed to have the giant tax cut he also endorsed that day and still exempt two thirds of the welfare state from spending cuts he didn't explain.

Kristol has always been a trend setter, and that day he outdid even himself. Standing before the nation's conservative party, he invented the most fabulous free lunch fiscal theory ever proposed. At the time,

I thought this wasn't to be taken literally, that it was some kind of godfatherly caution about not going off the deep end politically. But for five years Kristol has not altered his message: *Don't cut spending, it's bad politics. Don't raise taxes, it's bad politics. Don't worry, $200 billion deficits are nothing to fear because they'll go away on their own.*

It's enough to make a true neo-conservative turn in his membership card. Kristol's free lunch economics is the worst kind of intellectual sophistry there is. The politicians inherently go for free lunches anyway. For one of the nation's leading conservative intellectuals to rationalize such destructive policies and urge the conservative political party to adhere to them is unpardonable.

Every several months now Kristol appears right on schedule on *The Wall Street Journal* Op-Ed page, with another tiresome rendition of It's all going to be OK, Jack. Volcker just needs to print some more money and things will go from good to perfect.

Never mind that since mid-1982 the money supply has already grown at a record rate of ten percent. A new surge of inflation is thus already baked into the cake, an inflation surge that only a punishingly high dollar exchange rate can continue to suppress.

So Moynihan was right, after all. Kristol has led the supply side into the free coinage of silver. There, presumably, he will take his place along with William Jennings Bryan, Wright Patman, and other great financial thinkers of days gone by.

In the other categories of welfare state spending, it would appear that we did a little better. But the ten percent decline in safety net spending is largely attributable to a single policy breakthrough. In the 1981 reconciliation bill we did succeed in removing the working poor from the food stamp and welfare programs. It was a solid and justified reform, but the liberal politicians have never accepted it.

Each year they chip away, adding partial benefit restorations to whatever hostage legislation comes along. Such provisions were added to the deficit reduction bill in 1984 and the farm bill in 1985. Over time, much of what remains of the 1981 social safety net cut will also be reversed.

In the meantime, one thing is clear. There isn't a corporal's guard of Republicans in Congress doing anything more about the safety net programs. They cost $75 billion per year, and they are part of the permanent budget cost of the welfare state.

That is a serious tragedy. The existing welfare programs are family-destroyers. They subsidize a culture of poverty, dependency, and social irresponsibility. But no one has any ideas on what to do about the systematic harm wrought by these programs because any feasible alternative would initially cost more than $75 billion, not less. So the dependent poor suffer too, additional victims of our bankrupt fiscal policy.

Under any consistent theory of conservative fiscal policy, the cost of the Great Society programs should be zero compared to the $33 billion still in the budget. Every dime of these funds goes for purely local education, health, welfare, and employment services. If federalism has any meaning at all, it is that these kinds of endeavors are properly the responsibility of state and local government.

To be sure, the twenty-five percent cut in the Great Society category as a whole looks impressive. But nearly two thirds of the $12 billion reduction is attributable to sacking the makework public jobs program and other job-training-related excesses. Small successes should not be dismissed lightly, but an $8 billion cut from a now *half-trillion-dollar* budget does not a revolution make.

The $33 billion which remains for health, education, and social service programs is deeply embedded in the political consensus. It tells the more revealing story about why the Reagan Revolution failed.

Under the last full Carter budget in 1980, federal education spending hit a record level of $17 billion in constant (1986) dollars, compared to $3 billion in the last pre-Great Society year of 1964. In 1986, Ronald Reagan will spend $17 billion in education, the same as Carter.

There has thus been no change in the education budget total, and every Great Society premise has been ratified. We are still putting money into local classrooms for the handicapped, the disadvantaged, the gifted, and almost everyone in between. We still have an open-ended spigot to six or seven million mostly middle-class college students, a scheme so lavish that a $100,000 per year family can get thousands of dollars in subsidies to send its children to Harvard.

This outcome is due to mutual back-scratching between the two parties. The Democrats insist on aiding tens of thousands of the nation's elementary school classrooms, and they get Republican help. The Republicans insist on shoveling out big middle-class college student subsidies, and they get Democratic help. The $17 billion cost of both together won't change, not by a nickel.

Federal constant dollar spending for local health, welfare, and social service amounted to $2 billion per year prior to the Great Society, but had exploded to $15 billion by 1980. By virtue of hacking and slashing in the Gramm–Latta budget in 1981, we got the figure back to about $12 billion. It has stayed there ever since, with hardly a dime being cut in the last four budgets. So eighty percent of that element of the Great Society also remains in place, and shows no sign of going away.

The final category in the table boils down to the good old-fashioned pork barrel. Since 1981 it has been put on a diet, and has lost sixteen percent of its weight. But that is all.

Every big program and every piddling program that marched out of the Cutting Room dead or bleeding in February 1981 lived to tell about it another day. Table 5 provides a few examples of the post-Cutting Room recoveries that occurred on Capitol Hill. In these cases, Republicans were on the first aid team, as the earlier narrative made clear.

TABLE 5
Pork Barrel Spending: Cutting Room
Target vs. Actual Funding
(1986 Spending Level in Millions)

Program	Cutting Room Target	Actual 1986 Spending
(1) Non-Nuclear Energy Subsidies	$ 800	$ 2,000
(2) UDAG	0	550
(3) Economic Development Administration	0	230
(4) Appalachian Program	0	200
(5) Amtrak	300	900
(6) Postal Subsidy	500	1,000
(7) Small Business Administration	250	1,300
(8) Water Projects	3,700	4,300
(9) Highways	8,500	14,000
(10) Mass Transit	2,800	4,100
(11) Airport Subsidies	500	800
(12) Total	$17,350	$29,380

Note: Includes off-budget outlays.

APPENDIX: THE FISCAL FACTS

The overall bottom line is this: the 1981 tax bill cut the revenue base by $210 billion by 1986. Since then, the inherited welfare state has been shrunk by about $50 billion. The tax revenue giveaway implemented by the Reagan Administration has amounted to *four times more* than the spending takeaway. On that equation, a responsible fiscal policy could never be constructed.

Why did the conservative, anti-spending party (GOP) end up ratifying a half-trillion-dollar per year welfare state? In the answer lies the modern dirty little secret of the Republican Party: the conservative opposition helped build the American welfare state brick by brick during the three decades prior to 1980.

The Reagan Revolution failed because the Republican Party decided to stick with its own historic handiwork. It could not and would not disown after November 1980 the 'me-too' statism that had guided it for all those years in the political wilderness.

To be sure, the 1980 Republican platform sounded anti-statist at the time it was drafted in John Tower's office. What I failed to appreciate then and rue today is that the ideas never did leave his office. There was no political home for them in the Republican Party. They should not have been forced into the platform. A Reagan Revolution fiscal policy should never have been constructed around them.

In the waning days of the Carter Administration, there was not a Republican orator around, old guard or supply side, who did not joyfully bash the 'runaway federal budget'. There were few Republicans who did not denounce Big Government.

But the 'runaway' Carter budget of 1980 was running away for two reasons only. One was the massive growth of the social insurance system over the previous thirty years. The other was the explosion of Great Society and safety net entitlement programs over the previous fifteen years. The GOP helped accomplish both.

Since the days of John F. Kennedy's New Frontier, nothing else in the budget had grown in real terms or as a percentage of GNP: not defense, foreign aid, space, agriculture, highways, the national parks, veterans, or law enforcement. In fact, by 1980 these cost far less than they had in 1960.

Not so with Social Security and the other social insurance programs. In 1954, they cost about $25 billion (1986 $), or 1.5

percent of GNP. By 1980, they cost *$230 billion*, or 6.5 percent of GNP. Those numbers tell the story of the modern welfare state in a nutshell; they were the megabucks that made Big Government appear so big in 1980. In after-inflation dollars their cost went up *ninefold* and as a share of GNP more than *four times*.

There are two other numbers which tell the remainder of the story. Between 1956 and 1977, Congress passed thirteen major acts expanding or liberalizing the social insurance programs. These included creation of the disability program in 1956, Medicare in 1965, big benefit increases in the early 1970s, and automatic indexing of Social Security in 1972. Over two decades an average of *eighty percent* of House Republicans and *ninety percent* of Senate Republicans voted for these expansions.

Republicans were thus part of the social insurance consensus from beginning to end. It's not surprising that they didn't turn against it during the Reagan Revolution of the 1980s. But social insurance was the overwhelming reason why Jimmy Carter's budget was bigger than Eisenhower's (relative to GNP). Since Republicans had helped create this giant system, they had no reason in 1980 to be talking smaller government and lower taxes on account of social insurance.

The other part of the budget that skyrocketed prior to 1980 was the poverty programs, consisting of the means-tested safety net and Great Society service programs. They cost $15 billion in after-inflation dollars in 1962 and $112 billion by 1980. Table 6 makes clear that the preponderant share of the growth occurred during the Nixon–Ford era.

TABLE 6
Growth of Poverty Programs
(Constant 1986 $ in Billions)

	Cost
Pre-Great Society (1962)	$ 15
Growth During:	
Kennedy–Johnson	+27
Nixon–Ford	+54
Carter	+16
Reagan	−5
1986 Funding Level	$ 107

APPENDIX: THE FISCAL FACTS

It was under a Republican regime that SSI was made nationally uniform and subsidized low-income rental housing was massively expanded. Food stamps and the other nutrition programs were also greatly liberalized, rising in cost from $1.5 billion in 1969 to $14 billion in 1977. The education, social and health service, and job-training budget also grew mightily during the Nixon–Ford era, more than doubling Johnson's last budget in real terms.

The two Republican administrations of the 1970s certainly had more than enough help from a Democratic Congress in this massive spree of budget growth. But the fact remains that all the new and expanded programs were signed into law by Nixon or Ford. Nearly all the major Nixon–Ford era poverty program legislation was approved with large Republican majorities on Capitol Hill.

That in turn is the major reason that the Reagan Revolution made so little difference to the poverty programs. The Senate committee chairmen and ranking House Republicans during the 1980s had nearly all been in on the ground floor during the Nixon–Ford era. Bob Dole was there along with George McGovern when the nutrition programs were created; Bob Stafford and Bill Goodling were there when the education programs were expanded; Dick Schweiker had been a champion of health and mental health programs; and the senior Appropriations Committee Republicans like Hatfield and Conte were there from beginning to end.

The poverty programs too were part of the bipartisan consensus to expand the welfare state prior to 1980. Aside from some modest reforms and trims forced through in 1981, the bipartisan consensus has been to maintain about the same amount of poverty program Big Government that had existed before the Reagan Revolution started.

The final table brings these considerations down to the budget's bottom line. What made Big Government big in 1980 was social insurance and the poverty programs. They accounted for all of the increase in the spending share of GNP between Kennedy and Carter, and then some. The same is true today after the Reagan Revolution.

Republicans were part of the consensus for this expansion. In 1986, these two welfare state components will still cost *9.5 percent of GNP just as they did in 1980*, because Republicans have been part of the consensus to protect and preserve them.

What about the rest of government—the 14.5 percent which is

TABLE 7

The Budget Consequence of GOP Support for the Social
Insurance/Poverty Program Consensus
(% of GNP)

Budget Sector	1962	1980	1986
Social Insurance and Poverty Programs	4.1%	9.6%	9.5%
Defense and All Other	15.4%	13.3%	14.5%
Total Federal Budget	19.5%	22.9%	24.0%

smaller than it was under Kennedy? Nearly 10.5 per cent of that is for defense, debt service, and international affairs programs. That figure reflects the cuts Congress has already made in the 1986 budget for these activities. It is now at the rock bottom level necessary for national security.

As a consequence, there is only four percent of GNP left for everything else. Into that small envelope Republicans must stuff their farm and veterans boondoggles, the highway funds and UDAG grants, law enforcement, federal pensions, water projects, energy projects, and the Washington Monument. It will all just barely fit on a day when good behavior and restraint is being practiced by all.

Those are the reasons why we're spending *twenty-four percent* of GNP, compared to raising only *nineteen percent* of GNP in taxes. They are also the reasons why the White House and the Republican Party should not have told the American electorate in 1984 that we don't have to raise taxes. It wasn't true.